APOCALYPSE

A Spiritual Guide To The Second Coming

DR. JIM RICHARDS

Apocalypse: A Spiritual Guide to the Second Coming
Dr. Jim Richards

ISBN: 978-1-943852-00-0 (Hardcover)
ISBN: 978-1-948794-97-8 (paperback)
ISBN: 978-1-943852-01-7 (ebook)

For additional content and resources please visit this book's companion website: http://www.secondcomingguide.com

True Potential, Inc
PO Box 904
Travelers Rest, SC 29690
www.truepotentialmedia.com

Printed in the United States of America.

I dedicate this book to my children and my children's children.

They are inheriting a world filled with Luciferian corruption: an economic system designed to enslave, an education system engineered for unbelief, governments addicted to power and a worldwide media that calls good evil and evil good.

Know this, *where sin abounds grace does much more abound! Christ in you makes all things possible!* You hold in your hands the truth that will keep you and your children walking in the light in a world of darkness.

Tonya, Angela, Christy, Amy, Summer and Julie, teach these truths to your children so they can guard their hearts against the coming deception. Prepare them to be overcomers when the rest of the world is being enslaved.

Contents

How to Study this Book ix

Introduction xi

SECTION ONE

1. Introduction to Section One 3
2. The Father of All Lies 7
3. The Birth of the Occult 13
4. Mystery Babylon: The Beginning 20
5. Nimrod: The First Antichrist 31
6. The Mother of Heaven 43
7. The Birth of a Nation 55
8. Conclusion to Section One 63

SECTION TWO

9. Introduction to Section Two 71
10. The World Divided 75
11. The Antichrist Nations 85
12. The Rise of the Gods 95
13. Giant Killers 104
14. The Eternal Reminder 111
15. Conclusion to Section Two 119

SECTION THREE

16. Introduction to Section Three 125
17. The Rise of Atheism: The Root of Reason 131
18. Satanism: The Root of All Lawlessness 143
19. Secret Societies: The Child of the Great Harlot 153
20. America and the New World 163
21. The Universalism Church 171
22. Elitist Utopianism: The Goal of the Enlightened 183
23. Conclusion to Section Three 195

SECTION FOUR

24. Introduction to Section Four 201
25. The World's System 211
26. Control through Fear 221
27. Elite Utopianism: The New World Order 227
28. The Illusion of Freedom 239
29. Education: The Path to Enlightenment 251
30. Science: The New Religion 263
31. Medicine: The Ultimate Control 277
32. Control the Money and Control the World 293
33. Conclusion to Section Four 305

SECTION FIVE

34. Introduction to Section Five....315
35. The Primary Message of the End....323
36. The Last Great Deception....329
37. The Beginning of the End....337
38. The Antidote to Deception....347
39. What No One Saw Coming!....357
40. What Happens Next?....367
41. Reading the Signs....375
42. War with the Lamb....385
43. A Thief or a Lightning Bolt?....393
44. Winning Over Evil....405
45. The Final Vindication....419
46. Jesus: The Bridegroom....427
47. Conclusion....435

Glossary....453
About the Author....463

HOW TO STUDY THIS BOOK

This book is written to provide a clear spiritual history of the world from the fall of Lucifer to the present time. Based on a biblical understanding of the history of the world we will have a framework from which to understand the future. Unless we use what God has said about Himself, the World's System*[i], and the work of the devil we will interpret futuristic prophecies from our personal opinions or current events. This means we will face the most challenging time in human history without the facts we need in order to understand and respond in faith!

This book is divided into what I believe to be crucial periods of history that serve as demarcation points for understanding the way Satan's tactics have shifted and been refined. Understanding each of these historical periods gives unique insight into the strategy of our archenemy and his plans for our destruction. But more importantly, knowing these strategies combined with the specific instruction of our Lord equips us to be overcomers in any situation.

The historical sections are divided into these time periods:

- Section 1 From Lucifer's Rebellion to Abraham
- Section 2 From the Tower of Babel to the Church
- Section 3 From the Middle Ages to the 20th Century
- Section 4 From the 20th Century to the Present
- Section 5 From the Beginning of Sorrows to the Millennium

---

i See glossary at the end of this book for this term's definition.

It is important to work your way through each section in order to have a full understanding of every word Jesus spoke concerning our preparation for overcoming. If you jump straight to the last section you will not understand the significance of the simple instructions Jesus provided for us to face the end times as well as any period of persecution.

It is not the goal of this book to explain all the possibilities of eschatology.*[ii] Hundreds of books that attempt to do so already exist. The goal of this book is to do what I have found in no other book on the end times. I want us to pay close attention to what Jesus taught us to do to prepare for the end times or any other period of persecution or hardship. It doesn't matter what we know if we don't know what Jesus told us to do!

The end of each chapter will include a "Spiritual Guide" section. I encourage you to ponder, consider and meditate on the points raised in this section of each chapter. You may even want to make a list of these points to review regularly as you develop your spiritual life around these priorities. There will also be links to a companion website that will provide expanded information on specific topics.

Some of the terminology in this book may not be familiar to you. Some terms are theological and some are terms I created to avoid the confusion that comes through misused terminology and religious definitions. **When you see an ASTERISK * following a specific term, its definition will be included in the glossary at the back of this book.** The digital editions of this book include live hyperlinks to the companion website which will provide definitions and/or expanded information.

The Introductions and Conclusions to each section will help you maintain perspective. In those sections that include so many negative historical events it is essential that you are able to bring your thoughts back to the ways in which God consistently gave provision and protection through Holy Spirit leadership for all who were willing to listen! If you feel unsettled after reading any section of this book go back and read the introduction and conclusion again. Focus on God's faithfulness and settle your heart back to a place of peace. When you trade peace for fear, you lose focus on God, our Deliverer, and over-focus on the work of the evil one! The goal of this book is to equip you, to provide a spiritual guide for the return of the Lord Jesus.

---

ii See glossary at the end of this book for this term's definition.

INTRODUCTION
Ears to Hear

A hearing ear has no preference other than hearing!

If you were to ask any Christian - in fact, almost any person on Planet Earth, if they want to always know the truth, the answer would be an emphatic "yes!" But if that were really true the world would not be the chaotic mess it is today! Truth, while becoming harder and harder to discern, can always be known by those who truly seek it above all else. Truth is not simply accurate information; truth is accurate information and all it implies. Unless we understand the implications, accurate information can be used to deceive. Jesus came to bring us truth: all that was implied and intended by every word God had spoken.

As the most catastrophic events ever experienced on Planet Earth unfold it is essential that we know the truth.

This book is not written from the perspective that the insights presented here are the only way to interpret the material, but it is written in a way that will increase your capacity for the truth. As the most catastrophic events ever experienced on Planet Earth unfold it is essential that we know the truth. In this case the truth about the end has little to do with our interpretations of the events but has everything to do with the warnings and preparations taught by our Lord Jesus.

Too often we hear a message about the return of Jesus that plunges us into fear, overwhelms us with information, or in some manner paralyzes us. The emphasis seems to always be more on end time tragedy than Jesus' personal return, or the horrors of the devil instead of the protection of the Lord. God's Word, even His revelations about the most horrific events, are always designed to warn, equip and comfort those who know Him and are fully committed to following Him. It is His intention that all His children be overcomers* or at the very least capable of enduring*. But in our quest for end time knowledge we have ignored the most important single capacity for absolute victory: *ears to hear what the Spirit is saying to the Church.* *

There can be a variety of reasons someone does not want to hear the truth. As Jesus said, we sometimes close our ears lest we hear! The need to be right drives us to only want the portion of truth that confirms the notion that our opinion is correct. When we have something to lose we tend to long for a version of the "truth" that appears to protect us from loss. If a particular truth presents the possibility of danger or hardship it is human nature to deny, discredit, or otherwise convince ourselves of an "account of truth" less threatening. All of these factors can cause us to twist what we read and what we hear in our heart to something more palatable. In Revelation 2:7 Jesus repeats an admonition given while preaching the essential aspects of the Gospel of the Kingdom. In this case He added this phrase: *"... what the spirit says to the church."* When He originally said these words there was no Church! But in Revelation He had a message to the churches of Asia. *"He who has an ear, let him hear what the Spirit says to the churches."* The Book of Revelation is one of the most challenging and difficult books of the Bible to understand. Yet, within it is the key to overcoming during the world's most difficult period of history. It is a message to the Church, the body and bride of Christ, His most valued love, those for whom He sacrificed His life and fought the most significant spiritual battle in all of history! Even though these words were originally spoken to a particular group, like all His words, they are life for the Church of all ages. This is something He wants us to hear and understand.

There can be a variety of reasons someone does not want to hear the truth. As Jesus said, we sometimes close our ears lest we hear!

The other books of the Bible, with the exception of some futuristic prophecies they may contain, relate to past history. It is easy to look back and understand what they meant because we have the historical record for comparison. But the Book of Revelation is the future; we have nothing with which to compare these events… or maybe we do!

If instead of attempting to interpret these future events based solely on current events we used past history and other events documented in the Bible as the main key to interpretation, we could demystify that which seems so complex. One of the most important keys to biblical interpretation is this: let the Bible interpret the Bible. Failure to utilize recorded biblical past events may be a major contributor to confusing and often erroneous doctrinal, as well as prophetic, interpretation. We must compare these futuristic prophecies to what God has said and done in the past to best understand them.

As you will discover, a major aspect of the world-wide conspiracy of the father of all lies is to twist our understanding of both biblical and secular history. Of course, the phrase "biblical" and "secular" history is to some degree a misnomer. It is impossible to properly interpret any account of history without an accurate knowledge of biblical history. Biblical history is the light whereby we judge all accounts of history. Failure to do so not only leads to a perversion of the truth of God's Word, but will also lead to an antichrist*, Luciferian* opposition to the truth. If we understood history from a biblical perspective we would not be vulnerable to so many false theological doctrines about God. In fact, armed with the historical, spiritual facts our understanding of the future would be almost crystal clear.

Perhaps there is another factor that makes end time teaching so difficult to understand. There are so many people teaching various versions of the coming events. We not only have information overload, we also have contradictory information overload! Obviously, there are doctrinal positions that are so theologically murky they cloud the pool of biblical knowledge. We feel compelled to choose one teaching over another. Sometimes a particular interpretation may have very accurate information mixed with a very inaccurate situation. Maybe we have put our attention and efforts in the wrong place. Maybe we should start with what we do know, and there is nothing more clear than what Jesus said we must do to prepare.

The days that are coming will affect the entire world unlike anything that has ever happened. As you will soon discover, there will be many paths of destruction working in various ways. We will look at many of these demonic factors and show the reader how they are all different dimensions of one spirit working toward the collapse of the entire world.

We know in the end there will be a *great falling away.* I believe part of that falling away will occur because believers will think God failed them. Those who set their entire hope on a particular unfolding of events will be rendered hopeless if they are wrong. It is possible to be so committed to a predetermined position we will not recognize when or if the Spirit of the Lord is leading in a direction we did not expect. This book is written to move you to put your trust in God, to be able to hear His voice and be willing to follow - no matter how things unfold.

John 9 recounts the story of Jesus healing a blind man. In verse 39, while explaining that He came so the blind could see, the Pharisees ask, *"Are you saying we are blind?"* He then points out in verse 41 the reason they were blind was from their insistence they could see! A key to hearing God with pinpoint accuracy is realizing we may not really see as clearly as we think. The one who has *ears to hear* will have a working knowledge of the Bible, will be aware of the different possibilities of how the events unfold, and will be open to hear the voice of God in their heart. As much as anything, it requires the surrender of all egotistical attachment to our opinions.

In the final analysis, having *ears to hear* is not necessarily going to depend on how much Bible we know, although that can be an incredible antidote to deception. It will be about our ability to hear and know the voice of God in our hearts. After all, the Spirit of God is not nearly as interested in proving us right in our eschatology as He is in leading us into the realm of the Kingdom where God's power, provision and protection abound!

Have you ever trusted the wrong person, invested in a bad business deal, married the wrong person, or taken the wrong job? We all have! These are all times we did not have *"ears to hear."* God always attempts to lead us but for various reasons we either fail to hear or refuse to follow. We have never made a bad decision from which God was not trying to protect us. Owning this truth is the starting place to opening the ears of our hearts to hear. I am not as interested in changing your theology as I am in helping you develop a *"hearing ear."*

Spiritual Guide

Learning to walk with God from your heart today is the only solution for facing the future with any real hope of overcoming. And remember, the promises in the Book of Revelation are to those who overcome. Begin today to develop a life of meditation, reflection and prayer. Make all of your decisions with a deliberate intention to yield to the Holy Spirit no matter how He may lead. If you need tools for developing an awareness of Christ visit www.heartphysics.com and get *Essential Heart Physics*®. This is a 30-day life-renewal program designed to help you create an abiding awareness of Christ in you, which is the first step toward hearing the voice of God in your heart.

In the final analysis having *"ears to hear"* what the Spirit is saying exceeds the boundaries of an open mind, an understanding of eschatology or anything else that depends on an intellectual understanding of the end times. There are so many factors that we do not and will not recognize until they happen. In the end what really matters is, "Will I hear the voice of God as He is leading me and my family into protection, safety and provision when my logical mind is telling me all is failing?"

I want you to know, hear, trust and follow the voice of God in your own heart ... not just in the end, but now, in life. In fact, I do not want you to live like we are living in the end times. I want you to discover this incredible paradox - live like everything Jesus said about the end is true and happening soon, but at the same time enjoy a life alive to the Spirit of God. Live with a certain awareness of eternity for yourself and others; yet, be able to experience abundant life here and now. Above all, follow the Holy Spirit every day as if your life depends on it. If we do this we will be as prepared as possible.

I want you to know, hear, trust and follow the voice of God in your own heart ... not just in the end, but now, in life.

Unlike any end times book I have ever read, at the end of most chapters I provide you with some practical or spiritual steps you can take to prepare yourself for what you learned. This section is termed "Spiritual Guide."

I will present you with concepts that may be different than anything you have heard concerning the end and how to prepare for it. I am not trying to get you to reject your current views as much as I want you to open your mind to the possibility of different scenarios and how they could unfold. This willingness to see other possibilities will open you to the voice of the Spirit as He leads you *"through the valley of the shadow of death, unto green pastures, still waters,"* strong protection and supernatural provision! The most important thing you should know is this: while the world is plunging into total darkness the Bible provides an account of the individuals who stood against all the powers of darkness and won. This cloud of witnesses provides a model for how to win against all odds. The common denominator in all of these people of faith is that they trusted God and then followed the leading of His Spirit!

The common denominator in all of these people of faith is that they trusted God and then followed the leading of His Spirit!

As you read the introductions and conclusions to each section, your perspective will be brought back to one reality: *greater is He that is in you than he that is in the world!* You and God are a majority! We have this cloud of witnesses who stood and overcame. You are more than a conqueror because the true Conqueror lives in you and you in Him!

SECTION ONE

APOCALYPSE

CHAPTER 1

INTRODUCTION TO SECTION ONE
From Lucifer's Rebellion to the Flood

To understand the end we must understand the beginning!

JESUS SAID THE TIME OF THE END WOULD BE JUST AS IT WAS IN THE DAYS OF NOAH.[i] The problem is, few believers have a true biblical picture of what really happened in the years preceding the Flood. Yet, in order to recognize what will occur in the world just prior to the physical return of the Lord Jesus, we must decipher world events. Even more important is the fact that those who served God were delivered from darkness prior to the Flood and their deliverance occurred in many different ways. The one common denominator was they heard and followed the voice of God as He led. In other words, they had *"ears to hear."*

One of the most important rules of biblical interpretation is the law of first reference. The law of first reference says we must go to the first time something is mentioned in Scripture to get the clearest, most concise understanding of a

i Matthew 24:37, But as the days of Noah were, so also will the coming of the Son of Man be.

truth. Although other factors could compound or augment our understanding of that truth, they can never change that truth.

One of the darkest eras in history occurred when Christian Era Religionists* departed from the teaching of the Old Testament as a basis for understanding many of the most fundamental aspects of God's plan and His nature. The Old Testament is full of types that were fulfilled in Jesus. To fulfil something means to "bring it to its fullest expression and intention." For example, all the feasts, holy days, sacrifices, rituals and ceremonies were types that had their true and full expression in the life, death, resurrection and inheritance of the Lord Jesus Christ.

One of the darkest eras in history occurred when Christian Era Religionists* departed from the teaching of the Old Testament as a basis for understanding many of the most fundamental aspects of God's plan and His nature.

The rejection of those types meant the Religionists would create their own definitions and explanations of the cross independently of what God had revealed. The confusion comes when they use biblical terminology with secular definitions and explanations. The hearer thinks they are talking about the Bible when, in fact, they may be talking about an occult[ii] Luciferian doctrine but disguising it in biblical terminology!

This has happened in every area of biblical doctrine, but for our purposes we must consider how this has occurred in eschatology[iii]. Religionists have hijacked the truth of God's Word and made it impotent and powerless, devising bizarre interpretations of Revelation and other end time prophecies that contradict things God has made clear in the Old Testament. The Bible foretold with uncanny accuracy the years the Messiah would be born and then crucified. This is why Herod's astrologers were so intently looking for the sign of the Messiah at that particular time.

---

ii Occult means "hidden." It covers practices that are not approved of by God. (https://carm.org/dictionary-occult)

iii Eschatology is the study of the teachings in the Bible concerning the end-times or of the period of time dealing with the return of Christ and the events that follow. (https://carm.org/dictionary-eschatology)

While we obviously do not know the exact time of His second coming, we can know all the signs with absolute clarity. In fact, Jesus and Paul comforted us with the fact that while those days would come *as a thief in the night* to the world, we are not of the world that those days should take us unaware! There is no reason for us to be shocked, surprised or unprepared for anything that occurs in our lifetime whether it is the end of the age or just a time of persecution.

Without understanding the beginning of biblical history we are like someone who wandered into a mystery movie an hour late. We are trying to figure out the plot and killer based only on what is being revealed before our eyes. We are attempting to relate the storyline to other movies we have seen, but we get it all wrong because we missed the first half of the movie. The average Christian has very little knowledge or understanding of what happened in the beginning. We have no real clue how the world got where it is and without that understanding it is impossible to understand how Scripture says this present age will end up. In the absence of God's spiritual account of history we rely on a secular, atheistic, false science to explain what can only be understood from God's Word.

Reading this section you may experience a dramatic shift in your current understanding and perspective of biblical history, and with each subsequent section you will get a clearer picture of world events from God's perspective, all of which will make understanding end time events far more simple and clear.

The early sections of this book may seem very negative, but remember, these are events that have already happened and they speak for themselves. There is no way to make a war on earth by fallen angels and a world-wide flood happy news. But we will find the positive nuggets in some incredibly dark times in history. Most importantly, we will discover how to find and connect with God and experience His power, protection and provision no matter what comes. We will learn these lessons from those who have fought and won!

SPIRITUAL GUIDE

If you struggle with these concepts, please feel free to visit http://www.secondcomingguide.com which will give you expanded information and other resource material. If you want *"ears to hear"* it starts now with prayer and the intention to hear what you may have never heard, see what you may have never seen and embrace ideas you may have never considered!

APOCALYPSE

CHAPTER 2

THE FATHER OF ALL LIES

Very little we believe about the devil is based on God's account of the facts!

IT IS IMPOSSIBLE TO FULLY COMPREHEND WHAT WILL HAPPEN AT THE END IF WE DO NOT UNDERSTAND WHAT HAPPENED IN THE BEGINNING. Unless we clearly understand Satan, his rebellion, how he works, and his precise goals we cannot understand his strategies. In fact we can actually support his strategies thinking we are doing God a service. The tragedy is that very little of what we believe about the devil is based on God's account of the facts. Most of it is based on occult concepts, which means it originated with the devil. Ironically, it is through religion that Satan introduced a deception about himself. We then teach these "religious" concepts as the basis to create our strategy for victory over him. No wonder we are always fighting what, up until now, has been a losing battle!

Everyone knows the devil is a problem, but much of what we believe about the devil and how he operates on this planet is, in fact, based on the lies he told about himself. Much of what we believe about the devil came through Greek paganism. These ideas, as you will soon discover, were the foundation of an elaborate, world-wide deception which would be the basis of all false religions. All Luciferian doctrine and logic is based on erroneous concepts of both God and the devil.

Once these demonic doctrines were absorbed into the Church they altered the way we read, understood and believed the Bible. Starting from a false concept of the evil one, the believer can over-exaggerate the devil's power and authority making him a near rival for God. This concept of Dualism completely distorts the biblical account of who Satan is and just what has been accomplished through the death, burial and resurrection of Jesus. This false concept of the evil one creates a battle the Apostle Paul called *"shadow boxing"* - fighting an imaginary opponent. While the devil is very real, our approach to spiritual warfare has been predominately delusional.

Then there are those who do not believe in a personal devil. They see him merely as a metaphor or idea. Of course, those same people do not take much (if any) of Jesus' teaching literally. Either of these extremes accomplishes the goal of the wicked one. This book is not the place to explore all of our unscriptural concepts of Satan. If you desire to research that path read my book, *Satan Unmasked.*[i] It will open your eyes to what Jesus accomplished through His resurrection in relation to the devil.

We do know, based on his name, title and description "the devil" or "Satan" is a [ii]liar, slanderous, false accuser, an adversary, destroyer and murderer. In John 8:44, while addressing the religious leaders Jesus said:

> *You are of your father the devil, and the desires of your father you want to do. He was a murderer from the beginning, and does not stand in the truth, because there is no truth in him. When he speaks a lie, he speaks from his own resources, for he is a liar and the father of it.*

Satan has no purpose on Planet Earth but to *steal, kill and destroy* (John 10:10). While "Christians" often agree with this on an intellectual, conscious level, at a deeper level they may believe just the opposite.

In the Garden of Eden we see Satan accusing God to Adam and Eve. By implying that they were not already like God, that God was withholding

---

i http://www.impactministries.com/product/satan-unmasked-book/

ii Thayer's Greek Lexicon, Electronic Database. Copyright © 2000, 2003, 2006 by Biblesoft, Inc. All rights reserved.

something from them, he was making many subtle but consequential accusations against God. First, he was posing the idea that God cannot be trusted. The Bible says *"without faith* (trust) *it is impossible to please God."* From the beginning God wanted to be our Source. He would provide all we needed if we would trust and follow Him. Second, if God cannot be fully trusted He is not completely good. From these two accusations all religious lies are birthed. Religionists are those who believe and preach these concepts that undermine the truth about God.

A third subtle, but powerful lie was birthed into the thoughts of man in the Garden that if God could not be trusted then Satan could be trusted. After all, he is the one who brought enlightenment to man. He gave man the knowledge that God did not want them to have. With this knowledge he implies that it is possible for man to have a quality of life much better than is offered by God. He can free man from the tyranny of an oppressive, controlling God.

In the Garden a new religion was born - Humanism. Humanism is the birth of philosophy, a concept that places man at the center of all equations. Man, through his own logic and reasoning, can decide good and evil for himself. Man becomes his own savior; philosophy and "science" become his bible. His own logic becomes the "voice of the spirit," which leads him in the path of life. The doctrine, logic and spirit of this and all the world's religions is iniquity. "Iniquity" means "lawlessness, no law, or anti-law." All that would destroy man would occur by creating philosophies, religious concepts, sciences and social structures contrary to God's truth. The state church of this new religion that began with the Tower of Babel (a pyramid of sorts) will, in the end times, culminate in an educational system whose dogma, no matter how incorrect, unscientific, illogical or perverted would be guarded with a demonic viciousness ready to destroy all who disagree!

In the Garden a new religion was born - Humanism. Humanism is the birth of philosophy, a concept that places man at the center of all equations.

In the beginning God gave authority on this planet to man. The idea that when man fell he gave his authority to the devil is a religious lie, found nowhere in God's Word. God gave man His authority so only God can take it back and give it to another. But the twisting of this simple truth begins much of our ignorance about the devil, how he works and how we can easily resist him. It is also the basis for so many perverted doctrines of God.

Since we are the ones with the authority on this planet, Satan can only do what he does on this planet through humans. We have the authority and the right to declare what occurs in this realm. Nothing happens in Planet Earth without man's participation. Why would demons bother to possess a human* if they could destroy him from their own realm of existence? If Satan had authority on this planet he would have freely and quickly destroyed us all. Instead, he has to deceive us into cooperation. It is our authority that destroys us, not his.

Through the false doctrine of Dualism* we think God and Satan are warring over Planet Earth, but the truth is Satan and man are warring over this planet. Jesus has already won the absolute victory. In Him we are more than conquerors. In other words, He won the victory and we can enjoy the spoils. Our issue is one of faith. Do we believe Jesus won the victory over the devil and do we believe we share in that victory? Since we have authority in Planet Earth it is up to us to believe what we have in Christ and function accordingly!

Through the false doctrine of Dualism* we think God and Satan are warring over Planet Earth, but the truth is Satan and man are warring over this planet.

The fact that Satan has no authority explains why he needs false religion and why it is so important to convince man to believe lies that alienate us from God's power, protection and provision. He cannot do it forcibly, so he must do it by deceit and seduction. He must present himself as an angel of light,* the one who brings illumination through science, secret societies, new religions and personal enlightenment. The one thing all these have in common is iniquity - the rejection of God's Word as the absolute truth. The moment we begin to consider there is another way to have what God has promised, we are embracing a logic that is just a single thought away from believing there is another way of salvation.

When people struggle with the devil it is only because they give him their authority. Some do it through fear and unbelief and others do it as a means to get what they want independently of God. In the end the antichrist will rise to power. The Bible says he has authority to oppress and kill God's people.

We ignorantly think it is because God has given him that authority, but the truth is that authority is given to him by men. Men will give the antichrist authority to rule over them the same way men give crooked politicians a seat of authority whereby they fill the earth with corruption, war and violence. Christians who think more like Humanists than believers buy into the politically correct social order of anti-God politicians because they have been seduced by a corrupt educational system, false science, a corrupt media and humanistic values.

To capsulize Lucifer's history to date: Lucifer fell because of his pride. He looked at himself, dismissing the fact that he was a created being and became engrossed in his own grandeur. He determined he should be the one to sit upon God's throne. This resulted in him and his followers (one-third of the angels) being cast out of Heaven. It seems that prior to the resurrection of Jesus he was still able to access the presence of God and bring accusations against mankind. At the resurrection he was stripped of all authority and power. He was cast out of Heaven and never allowed to return. He then came to Earth with great fury because he knows that his time is short.

Contrary to the foolishness taught by Religionists about the devil, Satan knows that, for him, all is lost. He knows he will be cast into Hell.

Now, contrary to the foolishness taught by Religionists about the devil, Satan knows that, for him, all is lost. He knows he will be cast into Hell. He knows there is no redemption for him. He knows there is no way to win, yet through seduction and lies he works to bring about the destruction of those whom God loves and those for whom Jesus died. His only goal: to steal, kill and destroy.

SPIRITUAL GUIDE

Sadly, men are destroyed by their own authority. Through ignorance, unbelief, or greed they participate in self-destruction. Then, because they believe the lies of the devil, they blame God for their suffering and still will not repent. If you choose to believe that which is contradictory to God's Word you become powerless against Satan's wiles.

There are some absolute decisions you must reach to understand the end of this age: how it will come and how to avoid destruction. You may have to begin by praying: "God, I haven't read anything like this before. I don't know if I even actually believe what is written here, but I am willing to trust You. If this is Your truth bring me to this understanding!"

1. God is good and only good. Every good and perfect gift is from Him.
2. All pain and suffering is directly or indirectly the work of the devil.
3. The devil is beaten. He knows he is beaten and he knows he cannot win.
4. If the destruction of the devil comes into my life it is because I have, on some level, allowed it by believing a lie. He has no authority over me; I can resist him by believing the truth.
5. God will never give the devil or his followers authority over me.

Two great resources to help you establish your heart in the goodness of God and the absolute victory over the devil are *The Gospel of Peace*[iii] and *Satan Unmasked.*[iv] If you struggle with the consistent, reliable goodness and faithfulness of God, you may want to read *The Gospel of Peace* before finishing this book!

To learn more about the resources mentioned and for additional support material for this chapter please visit www.secondcomingguide.com.

---

iii http://www.impactministries.com/product/the-gospel-of-peace-book/
iv http://www.impactministries.com/product/satan-unmasked-book/

CHAPTER 3

THE BIRTH OF THE OCCULT

The occult initiates and brainwashes. It leads its followers into degrees of deception until they totally reject God's revelation of Himself given to all the world through His eternal Word!

IT WOULD SEEM AT FIRST GLANCE THAT SATAN FELL, SHOWED UP IN THE GARDEN OF EDEN, AND DID LITTLE ELSE TO DESTROY MAN IN THE BEGINNING. But a closer look at Scripture exposes a rebellion that included one-third of the angels.[i] Genesis 6 shows Lucifer's and his fallen angels' next strategic move to destroy mankind.

> *There were giants* on the earth in those days, and also afterward, when the sons of God came in to the daughters of men and they bore children to them. Those were the mighty men who were of old, men of renown.* (Genesis 6:4)

Genesis and other books of the Bible, the writings of Josephus, the historical record and scientific documents record the fact that giants have lived on

---

i Revelation 12:4

nearly every continent in the world at some point in history. We have somehow failed to link this fact to what the Bible explains about the origin and activities of giants.

While there are many references to giants in the original language, the Bible doesn't provide a lot of detail about this demonic endeavor to destroy mankind. Fortunately, we have other sources that provide detailed insight into what may have been the strategic efforts of this group of fallen angels. Genesis 6:4 and the following verses provide some important information. The first and most obvious factor which led to the Flood of Noah's day was the corruption of man's bloodline. It had been prophesied in the Garden that the seed of man would be the one to destroy the works of the devil.[ii] If the bloodline of all mankind had been corrupted Jesus could not have been born. The corruption of the human bloodline was a direct attack on God's plan of salvation.

The word "occult," contrary to popular thought, does not mean "demonic" or "evil." According to *Encarta Dictionary* the word comes from Latin and simply means "secret," or "hidden."

This verse also tells us there were giants at this particular time in history as well as some other times (after the Flood). It tells us the offspring of these ungodly cohabitations at some time became the mighty men of renown who were destroyers. They ruled over man and brought all manner of iniquity into the world. We will plunge into all of that in a future chapter, but for now we want to explore the birth of the occult which seems to have occurred as a result of this demonic infestation.

The word "occult," contrary to popular thought, does not mean "demonic" or "evil." According to *Encarta Dictionary* the word comes from Latin and simply means "secret," or "hidden." What are referred to as occult are witches' covens, satanic groups or secret societies that attempt to use hidden knowledge to manipulate and control the destiny of individuals as well as the world. Secret formulas, incantations and curses are just a few examples of the use of occult knowledge as a means to manipulate, hurt or bring about good fortune. The question is, "Where did this secret knowledge come from? Is it legitimate? Can it actually affect others? Can it affect the world? Why is it evil?"

---

ii Genesis 3:15 And I will put enmity Between you and the woman, And between your seed and her Seed; He shall bruise your head, And you shall bruise His heel."

A quick glance at ancient history uncovers the fact that in ancient times man built structures on earth that would rival any modern engineering know-how. In fact, many of the ancient structures which were built without the use of computers or heavy equipment cannot be recreated by modern man because we do not have the technology. These structures were built with exact engineering precision and are in perfect alignment with astronomical markers and astrological symbols. Equally amazing is that many are in perfect alignment with other structures around the world. Some scientists believe they formed a type of world-wide energy or information grid.

Evidenced by these structures, ancient man had technology that, according to our "scientific" knowledge, should not have been possible. Most continents contain pyramids, mounds, drawings in the earth, and other technological accomplishments that prove nearly everything we have been taught about history and anthropology is not only wrong but is part of a global cover up. How is it possible that ancient man (who should have been nothing more than hunters/gatherers) could have used technology that does not exist today? How is it possible that all across the Americas, Europe, China, and the Middle East there are thousands of burial mounds filled with the bones of giants that range in height from seven feet to over thirty feet? Much of the scientific community knows this, yet our textbooks tell a completely different story and do not provide a single reference to giants and their amazing accomplishments. These questions will never be answered by the World's System, but the Bible gives us insight into all this and more.

We know where the giants came from; the Word of God is crystal clear. They came from the cohabiting of angels and women. Some are quick to protest, "Angels cannot have sex with women; they don't have an earthly body." But there are many types of angels. The Old Testament records that angels appeared to men in human bodies. In ancient times these beings were called "watchers." These angelic beings, here to serve and protect mankind, were the ones who gave birth to the giants. So we know where they came from, but the question that begs to be answered is "Where did they get their knowledge and how could that affect us today and at the end of the age?" It would seem logical that as angelic beings they brought knowledge to Planet Earth that was (and still is) beyond the intellectual grasp of man. They had much of the secret knowledge of creation. But we should remember, there was a time in world history that man became so proficient with this knowledge that God Himself said: *"Indeed the people are one and they all have one language, and this is what they begin to do; now nothing that they propose to do will be withheld from them"* (Genesis 11:6). This superior and forbidden knowledge* once again brought the earth to the brink of destruction and mankind to the brink of spiritual annihilation.

Fortunately, we do have an extra-biblical source that expands upon what the Word of God says and gives us additional details to what common sense has revealed. The Book of Enoch is directly quoted in the Bible and seems to be referred to more than once. It has long been considered to be a reliable source to understand things that occurred in the pre-flood world. Enoch tells us that these angels taught men secrets that up until that time had only been known in Heaven.

The Book of Enoch also tells us the fallen angels taught men how to make weapons of war and how to kill with them. They taught mankind geometry, astronomy, astrology, and how to read the signs of Heaven. They taught them how to make charms and employ the mystical arts. They taught enchantments and root cuttings. They taught them all manner of sexual perversion. In other words, having been privy to many secrets of creation,[iii] they understood the laws of creation and how to use them to bring about what we would call supernatural events. This knowledge became the core of all ancient religions and secret societies that exist up to this day.

It is important that we realize the world and the physical universe were created by absolute laws of physics.

It is important that we realize the world and the physical universe were created by absolute laws of physics. In other words, God is the Supreme Mathematician and these absolute, orderly laws are the foundation which gives rise to the material creation. These laws are benign, neither good nor evil, but they can be used for good or evil based on the heart and intent of the one applying the knowledge. Fallen angels of the old world and secret societies of the new world seek to use these laws to create a world "after their own image" and liking. They seek, as Lucifer did in his original intent, to be god of their own world. Only by understanding this ancient phenomenon will the Book of Revelation and end time events ever be understood. What we call "mystical laws" are, in fact, laws of physics that were used in ancient times and are being used in the world today. They have been preserved and

---

iii The Book of Enoch Chapters 6-8

handed down through ancient religions and secret societies and will be used in the end times to overthrow and oppress the entire earth.

This knowledge is what the Luciferian religions of Egypt, Babylon, and the ancient Sumerians used to oppress the world while attempting to destroy the children of God. This knowledge has been kept hidden because it is the hope of those who would create a utopian, one-world government, a society in which there is no middle class, just the very poor and the very wealthy, where all knowledge of God is destroyed. In this godless society the enlightened* rule over the poor who only exist for the pleasure of the enlightened. The enlightened serve their god who brought man knowledge and freed him from the oppression of a wrathful, unloving, tyrannical creator.

> What we call "mystical laws" are, in fact, laws of physics that were used in ancient times and are being used in the world today.

These secret societies and ancient religions have always thrived on bloodshed, sexual perversion, violence, oppression, greed and deceit. But at the core of all their driving philosophies is **iniquity***. They seek to build an anti-God world - not just a world that is against God, but one where every rule is contradictory and totally opposite to that which God has established as truth. This is why the Book of Daniel tells us that this man of wickedness will seek to change the laws.[iv] Paul describes the antichrist as a man of lawlessness (iniquity).[v] Social justice, political correctness, the new fairness doctrines and social order are all components of a New World Order that opposes all that God declares to be truth and life. The governments of the world are almost completely godless. Global governmental agencies exist for the sole purpose of ushering in the New World Order, a world that consciously and deliberately rejects all that is godly and seeks to force all of mankind to reject all knowledge of God. But the wicked will not rule the world. Their leader is a murderer who destroys those who follow him. After he moves them all to turn on one another he will lead them into a battle he knows he cannot win.

---

iv Daniel 7:25, And he shall speak great words against the most High, and shall wear out the saints of the most High, and think to change times and laws:

v 2 Thessalonians 2:9-10, The coming of the lawless one is according to the working of Satan, with all power, signs, and lying wonders, 10 and with all unrighteous deception among those who perish, because they did not receive the love of the truth, that they might be saved.

The Book of Revelation reveals a time when the man of lawlessness (iniquity) finally has enough of the population in agreement with him that he emerges to achieve by violence that which has, up until now, been achieved primarily through deception and seduction. At the end of this struggle all of the talk about fairness, equality, peace and hope is nothing more than a ruse to fulfil the only intention Satan ever had for mankind: destroy all that God loves and values. In the end Satan and his truest followers know that an eternity in Hell awaits them and their only joy is knowing the millions they take into damnation with them.

At the end of this struggle all of the talk about fairness, equality, peace and hope is nothing more than a ruse to fulfil the only intention Satan ever had for mankind: destroy all that God loves and values.

SPIRITUAL GUIDE

The only protection against the seduction that has come upon the whole earth is to trust in a loving God who is good and only good! Every word, every commandment uttered by God, and all that was intended and implied has been for man's good. Religion, so skewed by Luciferian thought, makes it nearly impossible to see God as He is and trust His every word for what He intended. But this is light in the darkness, the wisdom when all else fails, the path we walk, and the hope to which we cling. If you are unsure of the consistent goodness of God and His Word, ask for His help. Ask Him to open your eyes and then cast down every negative thought that comes to your mind concerning God. Do not be afraid or ashamed. To the degree that religion has influenced your concept of God you will struggle with these essential truths. If you admit your struggle you can then open your heart for a life-changing experience of His unfailing love.

When we know His truth and are empowered by His Spirit we have no need for the secret knowledge of the occult. We have the life and power of God. When we feel His love we are never alone and never fearful. When Jesus is our Lord we love His Word and recognize His voice. In Him, by Him and through Him we are more than conquerors! We overcome the world and the wicked one because *greater is He that is in us than he that is in the world!*

To learn more about the resources mentioned and for additional support material for this chapter please visit www.secondcomingguide.com.

APOCALYPSE

CHAPTER 4

MYSTERY BABYLON: THE BEGINNING

ALMOST EVERY THINKING PERSON HAS AT SOME TIME SUSPECTED A WORLDWIDE CONSPIRACY OF POWER, BUT THE THOUGHT OF SUCH AN INTRICATE GLOBAL ENTITY REACHES BEYOND THE SCOPE OF OUR COMPREHENSION. We can easily recognize conspiracy in government, especially within the parties. As long as the idea of a conspiracy is seen only as related to governments and world organizations it is limited to the scope, influence and intellect of natural man. Very few people recognized that the world-wide conspiracy discussed in this book is clearly laid out in the Bible. Even those who have seen it lack any reasonable way to respond to it that would make a difference in our lives.

There has been an invisible force corrupting the world since Lucifer's rebellion. Before the Flood the strategy was different; it was more individualized. Infect the human race with the demon seed and eventually destroy all of mankind. As man began to spread across the earth after the Flood the strategy changed. It became more political and began to play on man's need for safety, fueled by his perverted concept of God's true identity and nature. From this strategy we see the emergence of the first political-religious* system aimed at creating a one-world government for the purpose of alienating man from God.

This strategy has been the basis for all world-wide conspiracies, tyrannical governments and corrupt religions. It is the root of all deception and seduction. It is the strategic hope and effort of the ungodly who seek an elitist, utopian world* independent of God. Like so many essential truths for abundant living this anti-God philosophy is clearly described in Scripture, yet ignored by the Church. Sadly, for centuries the cult-church became the primary force through which this demonic strategy fulfilled its objectives.

Paul warns of an influence that has always been around and will consummate in the coming of the man of lawlessness (iniquity) who opposes all that is godly. This power that has always been here is called the *mystery of iniquity.*[i] In the Book of Revelation we see a world-wide spiritual influence called *Mystery Babylon* that has existed since the formation of the first human government. As we examine this spiritual entity we see the real goal behind the function of this spirit is world-wide iniquity - the rejection of God's Word, laws and commandments as the standard of love, morality, ethics and absolute truth.

This spirit works in present day governments. Communists call it "demoralization." The political left calls it "social justice". Satanists*, Communists*, Socialists* and Progressives* know they can overthrow a country only if they first "demoralize" the people. This is accomplished through perverting the laws, courts, politics, educational system and media. Demoralization consummates in a society rejecting God's Word as the absolute moral standard and ultimately in rejecting God. After the people are demoralized the next step is to collapse the economy and create massive social chaos. The citizens cry out to the corrupt government for protection and are seduced into giving up their freedom in exchange for security. This strategy has succeeded in societies around the globe.

Demoralization consummates in a society rejecting God's Word as the absolute moral standard and ultimately in rejecting God.

---

i 2 Thessalonians 2:7-11, For the mystery of lawlessness is already at work; only He who now restrains will do so until He is taken out of the way. 8 And then the lawless one will be revealed, whom the Lord will consume with the breath of His mouth and destroy with the brightness of His coming. 9 The coming of the lawless one is according to the working of Satan, with all power, signs, and lying wonders, 10 and with all unrighteous deception among those who perish, because they did not receive the love of the truth, that they might be saved.

The United States government is following this same process through social justice, the fairness doctrine and political correctness, which create class warfare. This process forces American public policy into a corrupt set of values, thereby rejecting God's commands. Creating a welfare state gives rise to a pool of codependent, needy people who support a corrupt government as a means of meeting their physical needs. Through social programs the country is overloaded with unmanageable debt. Government fiscal practices that make no sense are easily recognized by anyone with business experience as destructive choices. They are the fruit of the devil's goal to steal, kill and destroy played out on a national level. There are many different strategies and political names for it, but it all leads back to Lucifer and lawlessness!

A saying used by the secret societies that seek world domination is *"out of chaos comes order."* This is akin to the statement *"Never let a crisis go to waste."*

A saying used by the secret societies that seek world domination is *"out of chaos comes order."* This is akin to the statement *"Never let a crisis go to waste."* In other words, exploit crisis. Use it to incite anger and chaos, especially among the races. The order they seek is not peace and prosperity, it is the New World Order.* So the powers that be create social and economic chaos and financial collapse. Out of ignorance and distress the unwitting public turns to the very source of the chaos to ask for help. They relinquish their rights and give the government their authority. When the people are helpless they become the pawns of the "enlightened elitists." The enlightened are those who know and adhere to the secret knowledge. This is the World's System and it functions through Luciferian principles. It dresses wickedness in politically correct terms, hides behind the rhetoric of peace and acceptance and it lulls the world into a false security so it can destroy everything God loves.

In the Book of Revelation 17:1-2, the Apostle John has a vision of a woman sitting on a scarlet beast drinking from a cup. An angel says:

> *Come, I will show you the judgment of the great harlot who sits on many waters, with whom the kings of the earth committed fornication, and the inhabitants of the earth were made drunk with the wine of her fornication.* (NKJV)

It is explained to him that the waters represent the people of the world. These people were influenced by kings (governments) and thereby made drunk from the cup of the wine of her fornications. Her fornications are the seductive promises and lies she made to the kings (governments) in exchange for their loyalty. In other words, the kings (governments) abandon the wisdom of God and embrace the lies of the wicked one in order to obtain the power they crave, the fame that feeds their ego, and the wealth with which they corrupt themselves. They violate all principles of godly leadership and use the populations to fulfill their personal lusts. The entire earth is led by spiritual fornicators, including the USA.

Revelation 17:14 goes on to explain: *"And the woman whom you saw is that great city which reigns over the kings of the earth."* This verse points out that this harlot, in fact, rules over the kings of the earth and that she is a harlot symbolizes her manner of dominance. She exerts her rule through seduction. Like all whores she gains dominance by simply offering men (in this case leaders of nations) what they already want!

Revelation 17:5 gives us another piece of the picture, helping us understand her true identity. *"On her forehead a name was written: MYSTERY, BABYLON THE GREAT, THE MOTHER OF HARLOTS AND OF THE ABOMINATIONS OF THE EARTH."* Now we see that she is a mystical city. Strong's[ii] definition of the Greek word for "mystery" gives us our first real clue to the world-wide conspiracy that does exist and is an influence on all governments of the world. The Greek word "musterion" is from a derivative of "muo" (to shut the mouth); a secret or "mystery" (through the idea of silence imposed by initiation into religious rites). This is not a natural city with a geographic location; it is a secret city or society into which one must be initiated.

This secret society, entered into by initiation, is said to be the mother of all harlots and abominations. The harlotry which is spoken of here is all unfaithfulness to God. This harlotry is the mother of iniquity (lawlessness). Lawlessness (iniquity) is the rejection of God's laws as the standard of truth, love, morality and ethics. Iniquity, however, doesn't stop with the rejection of God's Word; it **always** morphs into Humanism, the fulfillment of the original sin. Man rejects what God says and replaces it with his philosophies of

---

ii James 1:14-15, But each one is tempted when he is drawn away by his own desires and enticed. 15 Then, when desire has conceived, it gives birth to sin; and sin, when it is full-grown, brings forth death.

right and wrong, thereby making man a god unto himself. But, as we will discuss, being a god unto oneself is actually a form of passive Satanism. To reject God's truth is to align with the wicked one. As Jesus said, *"He who is not with us is against us."* As James pointed out, all we have to do to cause the devil to flee is resist him. The word "resist“ means "to set over against." We do that by submitting or aligning ourselves with God and His truth. We don't have to fight, scream, rebuke, pray or "do warfare"; Satan flees when we align ourselves with God and His truth.

The Religionists and many misguided believers have promoted the illusion that temptation starts with the devil. He whispers in our ear and causes us to want that which is wicked.

The process of iniquity is nothing more than a religious, philosophical means to justify and fulfill our lusts. Kings of the earth want power. They want their version of justice. They want, as much as anything, to build a legacy that glorifies them and their heirs. The harlot simply offers a means to fulfill those selfish, egotistical goals.

The Religionists and many misguided believers have promoted the illusion that temptation starts with the devil. He whispers in our ear and causes us to want that which is wicked. This has never been the case. Temptation doesn't originate with the devil, it originates with us. We are tempted when we are drawn away by our own lusts. Then like any harlot, he simply gives us an ungodly way to fulfill our desire.

The fact that we turn to a source other than God to fulfill our desires is rooted in our acceptance of the Luciferian doctrine: "God is not good and He cannot be trusted. He doesn't want you to be happy. You grow through suffering." Since we do not believe that God is good and only good we do not believe He will give us life-producing ways to fulfill our desires; so we seek an alternative route. Then when our sinful act is finished we say in our hearts, "The devil made me do that which I really didn't want to do." Or, we justify what we did by its end result. But the truth is, the devil's philosophies showed us a way to have something for which we were not willing to trust God.

James 1:15 points out that the end of this process is always death. In other words, we may fulfill our desire, but there is always "the devil's due." It is essential to understand this process. Not only is this the way of sin with individuals, it is the way of sin with the kings (governments) of the earth. They offer mankind that which he wants, which is usually some type of security or entitlement. But in the end we (the people, the waters on which the harlot and the beast trampled) are the ones who pay the price. Of course, the most effective way for a government to avoid the scrutiny of the righteous is to eliminate God's truth as the standard. Once we become drunk on her fornications we will not condemn the government who does the same.

The Great Harlot is a master of seduction and manipulator of power. Keep in mind that man has authority over Planet Earth and the harlot can forcibly do nothing. She exploits the natural and corrupt desires of human beings who, by fulfilling their desires, fulfill her desire: the destruction of all that God loves. Like all prostitutes she has no real power. She cannot forcibly enslave her lovers. Her powers of seduction are the only cords that bind her lovers who become *"drunk on her fornications."*

The Great Harlot is a master of seduction and manipulator of power. Keep in mind that man has authority over Planet Earth and the harlot can forcibly do nothing.

Revelation 17:4 gives us even more insight into this harlot.

> *The woman was arrayed in purple and scarlet, and adorned with gold and precious stones and pearls, having in her hand a golden cup full of abominations and the filthiness of her fornication.*

We begin to see an association between the harlot and wealth. Revelation 18:3 makes it even clearer *"...the merchants of the earth have become rich through the abundance of her luxury."* We see a connection between the harlot and the merchants - the market. When the harlot is destroyed there is rejoicing in Heaven, but on earth it is the merchants, those who are made rich by her, that mourn her destruction.

We now have a clear link between the harlot, governments, the market and all spiritual fornication and abominations. It doesn't take a genius to understand that the greed which drives the marketplace determines the laws that are passed by the governments. After all, what does every nation crave? A strong market! Financial wealth and stability has become the justification for every corrupt and unreasonable law. Morality, God's laws against charging interest, controlling private property, concentrating power, honesty in contracts, (equal weights) and a regular period of time to reset the economy would make it impossible for the ruling class to seize power. All those "bad, unfair, controlling, antiquated" laws stand in the way of a robust market and a strong economy that we all know eventually lines the pockets of.... So who exactly is getting their pockets lined?

At first glance the answer would seem to be all those greedy millionaires who play the market. The socialistic, progressive, social justice message deceives the simple-minded. The bankers and the governments create laws that make it possible for people to become wealthy by corruption. Then they point to those whom they have made wealthy and convince you they are taking bread off your table. You could have more money if it weren't for them. All of your wrath and attention is focused on the "wicked wealthy." They are the cause of your lack.

The socialistic, progressive, social justice message deceives the simple-minded.

You then vote and petition lawmakers to make more laws to restrict the wealthy, but the new laws always end up only restricting the middle class working population. This is the chaos necessary to eventually bring about the "enlightened ones'" version of order. Ironically, the wealth of those we have been taught to hate is nothing compared to the wealth controlled by the few families that actually control the world's banking system.

All banks of the world are owned by just a few banks, which are owned by just a few families. The central banks like our Federal Reserve, to the surprise of most, are not a part of our federal government. They are owned by a small group of people who use their financial influence to shape world policies and control world markets. The banks form what many have called the "unseen hand" that silently influences everything. They will work through influence until they have amassed enough power to control by force. Then, and only then, will they reveal what once was only known by those who had been initiated into their societies.

Modern banking was started by a secret society. Secret societies are religious in nature but they seek to hide their religious nature as a means of seduction. The mother of all secret societies (secret religions) began at Babel. Through the millennia it has morphed, changed names, masked and adapted to the diverse cultures of the world through various religious or political entities. In Babel it was the worship of Nimrod and in Egypt it was the worship of Osiris and Isis. In Rome it was a polytheistic blend that exalted Jupiter as the ultimate god. In Greece it was Zeus. In Europe it was the Templars and Free Masons. In America it is the Illuminati and at least a dozen other religious-political entities. They have existed under many names to hide their true identity and purpose. Today in our country and in Europe they have many fronts - religious orders, corporations, political and financial organizations, as well as fraternities and multiple splinter groups.

Modern banking was started by a secret society. Secret societies are religious in nature but they seek to hide their religious nature as a means of seduction.

Initiation rituals are key to their power, seduction and secrecy. Many of these societies only expose their initiates by incremental degrees to their true purpose, desensitizing them little-by-little to their anti-God, Luciferian agenda. Their ultimate intentions remain secret (even to most of their initiates) until they are deemed worthy. Many initiates spend their entire life serving and financially supporting secret societies and never actually understanding their demonic purpose. Communism is the perfect example of this strategy. They have all manner of layered propaganda. To the inductee it seems to be a humanitarian form of government that only has the intention of serving the working class to create equality for its citizens.

Lenin found what he called *useful idiots* to be most valuable in the initial stages of destabilizing a free nation. Useful idiots were naive idealists, usually college students, who had no idea concerning the true agenda. They freely gave their time, resources and youthful enthusiasm. What few people know is that Communism has its roots in Satanism. Karl Marx and many other of the world's most influential Communist leaders were actually Satanists. They hated the game they had to play to seduce people. They hated Socialism, but saw it as the best possible means to enslave the entire world. Very few of Karl Marx's writings have ever been released to the world. They are kept hidden because they reveal his true commitment to Satan and his godless passion to destroy the world. One would think the hundreds of millions who have been murdered in the name of Socialism could grasp Jesus' teaching: *"You can know the tree by its roots!"* But they seek a life not under the dominion of God's truth and they become too drunk on their own lawlessness to discern reality.

Lenin found what he called *useful idiots* to be most valuable in the initial stages of destabilizing a free nation..

Governments, like the secret societies that control them, seldom reveal their true intentions to the population. Governments stay true to genuine Luciferian strategy; they operate through deception and seduction. And it appears, based on how so many politicians change when they go to Washington, they too are initiated by degrees into how the system really works. Then, like most useful idiots, the voter and the politician seldom realize the voice "behind the curtain" belongs to Satan. The "small compromises" they make for the good of the people are really the means of destroying those whom God loves and those for whom Jesus died!

If we follow the trail of power and deception it looks like this: people are seduced by governments into giving away their authority and freedom in exchange for false security. Governments are controlled by financial institutions with which they exchange the freedom of their population for the means to fulfill their lust for power and expansion. Financial institutions are controlled by secret societies that have the agenda of creating an elite utopian world ruled by "the enlightened" who reject all knowledge of God. They, like the fallen angels who sought to make the world a habitation for their wicked offspring, seek to create a utopian world whereby they and their offspring rule the world, control all of its resources and live as gods. Therefore, they knowingly give the authority to the wicked one in exchange for the secrets whereby they intend to dominate the world!

For years I wondered why government leaders succumbed to the control of bankers. After all, governments control weapons of war. They could default on loans, point a missile at the homes of the bankers and take over. But banks offer more than money. They hold secret formulas and incantations shared with heads of governments that give them power. And as spooky as it sounds, they claim to hold the keys to immortality, independently of trusting and following God.

If you've read "the end of the book" you know this evil world system is emerging and will ultimately express itself in a man who is openly **the antichrist**! Not just an antichrist, but the personification of all that is evil. He will oppress the world for 3 1/2 years. Ultimately Jesus will return, destroy him and his followers, and establish His earthly Kingdom.

Governments seldom reveal their true intentions to the population. Governments stay true to genuine Luciferian strategy; they operate through deception and seduction.

SPIRITUAL GUIDE

There may be a remote possibility that we can postpone how soon this will happen. But, as you will discover, if those in power have their way this will happen very soon. Fortunately, the steps we need to take to live during any challenging time are the same steps we need to take to live and overcome through the dark days of wickedness. All victory starts by discovering and experiencing what Jesus accomplished through His death, burial and resurrection. You may consider my series, *Three Days that Changed the World* [iii] in order to come to a more biblical understanding and value for the cross. After all, our faith is not based on what Jesus accomplished in His life; it is based on what He accomplished through the cross.

The Bible tells us we need to believe on the resurrection of Jesus in our heart. It has to be experienced. It must become our reality. When that happens we will have shifted in our sense of self. Our identity will become one with His identity. Any truth that is believed in the heart changes our sense of identity and gives us the capacity for effortless, victorious living.

As a result of believing what Jesus did for us through His death, burial and resurrection we must decide if we will surrender to Him as Lord. The decision for Lordship is the primary way we protect ourselves from iniquity. If He is my Lord I choose to believe His Word. His truth is my absolute standard of integrity, love, morality and for all my understanding of God. When I submit myself to God, by aligning with His truth, I have put myself in opposition to Satan and his deception. He will flee from me. *"Therefore submit to God. Resist the devil and he will flee from you. Draw near to God and He will draw near to you"* (James 4:7-8).

Being unwavering about what you believe Jesus accomplished through His death, burial and resurrection and the absoluteness of your commitment to Him as Lord is your foundation determining the degree to which you will experience the life and power of God. This is the foundation upon which all your other beliefs about God must stand.

To learn more about the resources mentioned and for additional support material for this chapter please visit www.secondcomingguide.com.

---

iii http://www.impactministries.com/product/three-days-that-changed-the-world/

APOCALYPSE

CHAPTER 5

NIMROD: THE FIRST ANTICHRIST

GENESIS 6:4 TELLS US TWO IMPORTANT THINGS ABOUT THE GIANTS (OR NEPHILIM AS THEY ARE CALLED IN HEBREW:) *THERE WERE NOT ONLY NEPHILIM THEN (BEFORE THE FLOOD), BUT LATER AND THEY BECAME MIGHTY MEN OF RENOWN.* This prepares us for the fact that there were Nephilim after the Flood, i.e. *later.* There is much debate about how this could have happened, but how it happened doesn't concern me. The fact that it happened and how that relates to past and future history is the concern of this book.

When making reference I prefer to call them Nephilim instead of giants. The term "giant" focuses solely on their size. I use "Nephilim" in order to focus on them as beings who were not only gigantic but also had what would have appeared to the ancient world as having knowledge of how creation worked which would have made them appear to be superhuman or god-like.

Enoch* tells us these Nephilim consumed the resources of mankind and eventually turned against man. He also tells us they became involved in bestiality and every kind of sexual perversion. This word for "evil" is not just "badness," but also "misery" and "distress."[i] It says the imagination of their heart was

i Theological Wordbook of the Old Testament. Copyright © 1980 by The Moody Bible Institute of Chicago.

evil; thus, they created unending misery and distress for mankind. This word for "imagination" is a compound word which includes the concept of meditation*. Meditation is neither good nor evil; the intent of the person determines whether something is good or evil. Isaiah 26:3 uses this same word when it says, *"I will keep him in perfect peace whose mind (imagination) is stayed on me!"* Meditating on God and His Word is key to having a heart of faith and peace.

Meditation[ii] is a tool God gave man to use for good. My purpose in pointing this out is to show that this capacity we have to imagine or meditate is so powerful the Nephilim used it in their attempt to overthrow the world. Satan, the great imposter, uses for evil that which God created for good. Regrettably, through the influence of Luciferian doctrine, some believers consider all meditation as evil and are thereby defrauded of one the incredible resources God has provided for man.

Meditation is neither good nor evil; the intent of the person determines whether something is good or evil.

This word "imagine," as previously stated, is related to the concept of meditation which means "to give shape" to something or "frame it up." They were using their ability to imagine or meditate to invent or create evil, misery and despair. The King James Version of the Bible says God "repented" of making man. That word means "to sigh or be sorrowful." Actually, it doesn't stop there; it says He was grieved that He had made man on the earth. This could very well get into the fact that He put man on earth and gave him authority. Had he not placed man on earth all of this misery could not have come upon Him.

Whatever the case, earth was polluted and the human race was being destroyed. There is an interesting point here that history bears out. Satan has no love or loyalty to his own followers. His own destroy one another. History records that the Nephilim turned against one another. They did it then and even now wicked men loyal to Satan kill one another while fighting and struggling for territory, possessions, land and glory. In the end the two primary forces that he used to overthrow the world will actually be at war against

---

ii "At this point you must let go of any preconceived ideas or narrow religious judgments about meditation and allow yourself to consider biblical meditation as God's means of connecting with mankind in the heart." (from *Moving Your Invisible Boundaries*)

each other. Daniel's vision of the last days' kings reveal that they cannot cleave together in as much as they are a mixture of iron and clay (Daniel 2:33). Evil has no loyalties.

God was moved with sorrow by the reality that He had no alternative but to destroy nearly all of mankind. All except Noah. The Bible tells us *"all flesh"* was corrupted (Genesis 6:12). The English translates it as "corrupted his way." It wasn't just the ways of man that were corrupted, it was the fact that his genealogy had been corrupted. These Nephilim had the spirit of the devil and the flesh of man. They had so filled the earth that the human race was very near extinction.

Even now wicked men loyal to Satan kill one another while fighting and struggling for territory, possessions, land and glory. In the end the two primary forces that he used to overthrow the world will actually be at war against each other.

Genesis says of Noah: *"This is the genealogy of Noah. Noah was a just man, perfect in his generations. Noah walked with God. And Noah begot three sons: Shem, Ham, and Japheth"* (Genesis 6:9-10). Not only was Noah a just man, his genealogy was perfect or uncorrupted. This was the last pure human bloodline on earth capable of bringing forth the Savior, the Son of Man. The Luciferian "angry God doctrine" planted in the earth at the Garden was reinforced by the Flood and abides until this day: "God is an angry, vengeful God who, in His wrath, destroyed nearly the entire human race," or so the Religionist propaganda says. But the fact is, God was saddened by the state of man. In His mercy He destroyed the demonic beings that would have annihilated mankind. He preserved the bloodline of Jesus so man could eventually inhabit Heaven with his Creator and Father for all eternity.

Once Satan's second attempt (first in the Garden, then through the Nephilim) to destroy mankind failed he wasted no time devising and giving birth to a new strategy that would last until the end of time - a false savior, the first antichrist. Contrary to popular thought, Satan is not omniscient; he can't see into the future, and while he does have knowledge beyond that of man, he is not wise.

Satan and his followers had knowledge unparalleled by mankind in the areas of mathematics, metallurgy, astrology, astronomy and what we would call "the sciences." After all, they were in eternity when God was in the process of creation. They thought they knew all of God's secrets, but I see Satan like a disciple in an old martial arts movie that studies under his master for years. Then at some point, filled with pride he sets out to defeat his master only to discover that the master had not taught him all his secrets. Satan was and is no match for the Creator! He is only a shadow of God's reality. He is all "smoke and mirrors," yet, while being devoid of wisdom, he did have knowledge… secret knowledge.

Contrary to popular thought, Satan is not omniscient; he can't see into the future, and while he does have knowledge beyond that of man, he is not wise.

In the Garden the first prophecy concerning a Savior is given by God. *"And I will put enmity Between you and the woman, And between your seed and her Seed; He shall bruise your head, And you shall bruise His heel"* (Genesis 3:15). Even though these words were not committed to writing for centuries, they were orally passed down from generation to generation. But once it was spoken Satan heard this prophesy and set out to create an imposter. Keep in mind, Satan had warred against the other angels and lost. He knows he has no hope of winning over God; his only hope, his only goal is to destroy what God loves - the human race!

After the Flood God told mankind to go into **all** the earth, to be fruitful and multiply. I have heard Jewish rabbis say that each man was meant to find his own unique place to dwell in the earth. He should go out and find the place where he could prosper according to what was in his own heart. Man was never created to be copies or duplicates of one another. We are all unique, and God's desire was to fuel that uniqueness. Man was not told to create cities, governments or centralized power. But we soon see another Nephilim arise who, out of his pride, ego, crooked (iniquitous) heart and deep hatred for God, sets out to gather men unto one place for the purpose of control through fear and oppression. He built a city unto his ego and a tower in opposition to God. His name was Nimrod and his city was Babel.

According to Jewish tradition Nimrod instilled the anti-God doctrines of Lucifer into man. He convinced man they should come together under his protection as a way to guard themselves from the judgment of God. In the same way that we ignore God's Covenant of Peace* made in Jesus that promises us freedom from wrath, generations after the Flood disbelieved God's covenant to never destroy the world by water and to never curse the ground because of man. Nimrod played on the fears of man that had, no doubt, been doctrines of demons propagated through centuries since the Flood.

We are all unique, and God's desire was to fuel that uniqueness. Man was not told to create cities, governments or centralized power.

Nimrod was a grandson of Ham, the son of Cush. Nimrod was a Nephilim, one of the mighty men of renown. His very name means "rebellion" or "we will rebel." He was a leader of rebellion against God. Genesis says he was a hunter before the Lord. This does not refer to Nimrod as a hunter of animals as much as it does a hunter of men. The phrase *"before the Lord"* means "in front of for the purpose of opposing, implying hostility."[iii] History tells us he was a hunter of men for the purpose of creating a rebellion against God. Nimrod subdued and conquered men and forced them to comply with his rule in opposition to God. According to Josephus, Nimrod taught men that to trust God was cowardice. They didn't need God. He convinced them their prosperity was not because of God's promise but by his leadership and their own doing.

Nimrod's rule was the beginning of Socialism. As in all socialistic governments he would turn a message of hope and prosperity to a rule of tyranny and oppression. His need to provoke mankind to hold contempt for God was a prerequisite to seducing them into following him. This is the same as

---

iii *The Gospel of Peace*, James B. Richards

demoralization used by Communists, Socialists, Progressives and Satanists today. Josephus says, "He *gradually* changed the government into tyranny, seeing no other way of turning men from the fear of God, but to bring them into constant dependence upon his power."

Codependency is an essential tool of oppressive governments. This can be accomplished by entitlements, empty promises of prosperity, social order and the illusion of protection from a menacing enemy. It is the strategy of governments to always make their citizens feel there exists an enemy so powerful they cannot survive without the help and protection of the government. In modern times there has been the threat of nuclear war, a coming ice age, global famine and global warming. Even facilitating the rise of ISIS and other terror groups all play into man's dependency on government instead of God.

Codependency is an essential tool of oppressive governments. This can be accomplished by entitlements, empty promises of prosperity, social order, and the illusion of protection from a menacing enemy.

Josephus also said that Nimrod, like his father, Lucifer, would be revenge on God.... Satan's wrath for expulsion from Heaven, his failed attempt at revolution, the destruction of the Nephilim and the certainty of his ultimate and eternal doom is fuel for his rage. This is probably the seed of the Socialist concept - everything is someone else's fault. All of Lucifer's consequences were the result of his own doing, yet his wrath is focused on God and those who love Him. He is like a mafia boss who seeks retaliation against an enemy by killing him, his family and all of his business associates.

Nimrod and his followers began to build a tower. Interestingly, this tower was made of bricks, not stones. The Bible calls us *living stones,* not living bricks. Stones represent individuality; each one is different. It has never been God's plan for all men to be the same. All men were given the same internal capacity for success. As we know from Proverbs 4:23, all of our true life boundaries are a product of the beliefs of our heart.[iv] We are all equal in creation, but we are not all the same in outcome. God promises if we apply His truth we can all have success, prosperity and happiness. But Socialism (iniquity) has a better

---

iv http://www.truepotentialmedia.com/product/a-conspiracy-of-angels/

plan, "more righteous" than God's! Socialism says we should all be guaranteed the same outcome. Socialism presents the idea that men are limited because of other men. Those who commit crime or fail at life are never personally responsible. This gives the government the right (in the name of fairness) to control every man's opportunities.

The bricks in the tower have two significant implications. First, it signifies all men being the same. Second, all men were called upon to build the tower instead of pursuing their own dreams. More than anything this, like all iniquity, is the intent to establish laws, values and morals that are opposite of God's Word and are based on an unrealistic fear and dread of God. Instead of spreading out over the earth, the inhabitants, fueled by Luciferian doctrine of a wrathful God, came together in one community. They surrendered their life's goals and dreams to follow the rule and protection of an anti-God leader. They took credit for the prosperity enjoyed in the earth God created. And as time went by the promises of prosperity and equality turned into tyranny. Babylon, Samaria, Nineveh, Sodom, Gomorrah, Tyre and Sidon became centers of sin in the ancient world.

God promises if we apply His truth we can all have success, prosperity and happiness.

The Tower of Babel has much historical and spiritual significance. History also tells us the signs of the zodiac were studied at the tower much like they were at the pyramids of Egyptians, Mayans and other ancient religions. It is important to once again point out God said the stars would give us signs and understanding of the times but we were not to use them to guide our affairs or replace God's wisdom. Once again Satan used something God created for good as evil. It is one thing to understand the times by what happens in the heavens, it is altogether another thing to attempt to foretell and control the future by the knowledge gained through these observations. Looking for the sign of the Son of Man was the method both Nimrod and Herod used to predict and prevent the Messiah from coming. Based on their use of these signs they murdered male babies in an attempt to destroy the seed of the Son of Man.

Babel is a compound word that means "gate of God." It is doubtful that the tower was meant to be tall enough to survive another flood. Likewise, it would not have been large enough for all the citizens to take refuge. So, there must have been another diabolical strategy employed through the tower in their rebellion against God. We know the people gathered together in place and built the tower as a means of survival should God attempt to once again destroy man (this was not God's intention in the Flood but it was the Luciferian doctrine the people believed). If it were to be a way of surviving a flood by natural means, they would not have built it in a valley and they would have built it large enough to house thousands. Remember, the word "Babel" means "gate of God." A gate signifies an entry or transition from one place to another. As many scientists surmise, the tower, like the pyramids, may have been a portal - a gateway to other planes of existence.

Occult history tells us of specific locations where spirit beings crossed over from the spirit world to Planet Earth. These places became infestations of idolatry and iniquity.

Occult history tells us of specific locations where spirit beings crossed over from the spirit world to Planet Earth. These places became infestations of idolatry and iniquity whose spiritual corruption continues unto this day. In fact, the longitudinal and latitudinal numbers of the "spirit gates" have significant mystical meaning to the secret societies. They constantly pop up in speeches given by politicians and religious leaders as secret code to those who understand their significance, but are totally overlooked by an uninitiated public.

The Tower of Babel, like the early pyramids and other structures uniquely positioned along specific planetary lines, could be portals of some kind, allowing these beings to transport across the globe or from one realm to another. We must not think of these structures, beings or events in mere human terms. These were demonic attempts to use the knowledge of creation as a seductive counterfeit for mystical power. The Tower of Babel is the birth of the Mystery Religion that has corrupted all governments of the world right down to the end times and the Great Tribulation.

History tells us that Nimrod married his mother, Semiramis, who evidently was a true follower of Satan as well. When Nimrod was killed by a descendant of Noah, Semiramis cut his body into pieces and sent them throughout the realm to prove his death. She declared him to be raised up as the sun god. She built an obelisk which represented the penis of Nimrod that people would worship and beseech to provide an heir. She then declared that the rays of the sun god shining on her impregnated her, resulting in the birth of her son, Tammuz. Tammuz was declared to be the reincarnated (resurrected) Nimrod, declaring Nimrod to be a resurrected god, a counterfeit fulfillment of the prophesy in the Garden. Thus, we have the beginning of all false religions, all abominations and the seduction of the kings of the earth.

If you watch the History Channel or listen to the corruption taught by Atheists in schools around the world you would be led to believe that the story of Jesus being born of a virgin, dying and rising again was simply a Christian version plagiarized from Sumerian history as well as Egyptian and other occult religions. The truth, no matter how obvious, does not fit their agenda (2 Peter 3:5). Ancient Sumerian literature, as well as all other accounts of a resurrected savior, were attempts to create a false fulfilment of the prophecy given in the Garden of a Savior who would bruise the head of the wicked one who would, in turn, bruise the heal of the Righteous One.

> The Tower of Babel is the birth of the Mystery Religion that has corrupted all governments of the world right down to the end times and the Great Tribulation.

The whole world was looking for a savior who would die and come back. With God portrayed as the wicked one and Nimrod portrayed as the one who delivered them from the angry God and gave them prosperity, it was an easy sell. Additionally, there is no way of knowing the entire supernatural phenomena that occurred around these events or how persuasively Nimrod presented himself as a god-man before his death.

In true Luciferian fashion, the birth of a false religion and the promise of protection, prosperity and freedom from a controlling tyrannical God became the means whereby they promoted and preserved their kingdom and power. The giants lived in defiance of God. They, like Nimrod, oppressed and tormented man. The secret arts were used to present the illusion of god-like powers. But more than anything else, the ruthless means whereby they were able to fulfill the lusts (ego and greed) of wicked men hungry for power provided the basis for seducing the kings of the earth. Nimrod and Semiramis gave birth to what became Mystery Babylon: the secret societies that embrace their dark knowledge. This was actually the birth of the New World Order, a world free from God's rule. This mystery religious-government occult, the secret knowledge and the religious rituals would provide the blueprint that has been followed until this very day to usher in a kingdom opposed to God and His rule. Through the centuries it has had many names and many disguises, but today it is called the New World Order.

Nimrod and Semiramis gave birth to what became Mystery Babylon: the secret societies that embrace their dark knowledge. This was actually the birth of the New World Order, a world free from God's rule.

SPIRITUAL GUIDE

Being patriotic is not the same as trusting in government or belonging to a "party." The Bible warns of rivalry, i.e. a "party spirit" as a work of the flesh.[v] When one follows or trusts a party they follow the group and its opinions rather than following what is godly. Our Constitution was written around the idea that governments cannot be trusted and should have very limited power. Patriotism is more about our connection to the people and the Constitution than our connection to the government or any party.

Do not misunderstand; I am in no way encouraging anarchy. Until they conflict with our biblical beliefs and convictions we should obey the laws of the land. In America we currently have the opportunity to approve our politicians. We can evaluate their voting record as well as their words and actions. Based on those factors, we should decide if we will vote for them. We can only know a tree by its fruit – or in the case of politicians, their track record. To base our decision on anything else is judgment. To give them the benefit of the doubt for a bad voting record is judgment. If they vote for laws contrary to God's definition of righteousness, morality, ethics and justice we are, in fact, conspirators in their iniquity.

Based on God's Word, **ALL** the kings of the earth drink from the cup of fornication of the Great Harlot, whether unintentionally or by devotion. Laws and morals are driven and defined by the economy which gives the government the power to bring about trust and devotion. We, on the other hand, are citizens of the household of God. Jesus is our King and Lord. We should support nothing that stands in opposition to Him and His truth!

Many conservative Christians believe that being Republican is synonymous with being a Christian. The two-party system gives the illusion of freedom, but it may be closer to what Judge Napolitano said, "The two parties are two legs on the same body." In other words, the two-party system only provides the illusion of having an actual choice. We should never vote party, we should vote values.

As the darkness emerges it becomes clear that both parties are committed to a big government, national debt, no borders and thousands of other absurd and often anti-biblical policies. But even the best government can only

---

v Galatians 5:19, Now the works of the flesh are manifest, which are these; 21 Envyings (rivalries or party spirit)

do so much. Righteousness can never be established through government. Government can, at best, give us a peaceful environment wherein we can reach our nation and the world with the gospel of the Lord Jesus Christ. The love of God in the hearts of men is the only solution for the problems of our nation and our world. Put your trust and hope in God. Live a life of peace and spread His love to all mankind.

Additionally, guard your heart against the flood of lies filling educational systems, pulpits, television and false science. If you do not know these things as the Bible presents them it will be hard to intellectually withstand the onslaught of the enemy. Knowing these facts guards your mind. Believing the truth about who you are in Jesus guards your heart. Those whose hearts are not established will be overwhelmed with the deluge that is already upon us. Just as in the times of Nimrod, the one who trusts God will be ridiculed and viewed as weak. But you, *"Be strong in the Lord and the power of His might"* and you too will stand and overcome!

To learn more about the resources mentioned and for additional support material for this chapter please visit www.secondcomingguide.com.

APOCALYPSE

CHAPTER 6

THE MOTHER OF HEAVEN

The mother of Heaven* is the great whore who calls all men to serve her son!

THE BOOK OF JEREMIAH MAKES FIVE REFERENCES TO *THE QUEEN OF HEAVEN.* Ezekiel mentions the women of Israel giving worship for Tammuz, the false Christ supposedly born by the supernatural conception of Nimrod's "sun rays" warming Semiramis. Dozens of mentions by as many terminologies are used to reference Babylon and its anti-God beliefs. By the time Israel and Judah went into captivity Mystery Babylon had infiltrated Jehovah worship. By the time the children of Israel went into captivity, idolatrous images had been painted on the walls of the temple, many of which directly deified Nimrod, Tammuz, and Semiramis. The Israelites literally participated in idolatry in the temple of God! They rejected the warnings of the prophets and every attempt on God's part to rescue them. They would not listen. Sadly, it was only after suffering the consequences of their rebellious idolatry that they turned back to God.

Likewise, the Church, after the death of the apostles, began to be infiltrated by Religionists which included the very paganism in its doctrine and form of worship that had brought about the destruction of Israel. From Constantine until the Reformation almost every component of worship had its root in the Nimrod-sun-god cult. Sadly, many "shadows" of those idolatrous components linger in modern worship. Today it is more about tradition and culture than it is about the desire to worship false gods, but these traditions do stand in the way of free scriptural worship. It is hard to consider the blatant historical facts of spiritual corruption in the Church without becoming utterly disillusioned.

The accounts of Nimrod's death and Semiramis' following deceptions vary, but the subsequent idolatrous doctrines are evident in every religion of the world, even modern Christianity! They have been the undermining of the household of God through the ages.

It is hard to consider the blatant historical facts of spiritual corruption in the Church without becoming utterly disillusioned.

One of the versions of Nimrod's body being cut up presents an interesting variation. In this version his assassin cut up his body. The one part Nimrod's body Semiramis did not find was his penis. She claimed to be impregnated through the rays of Nimrod, now resurrected as a sun god. She then ordered that obelisks be built across the region to represent Nimrod's lost penis.

Presenting herself as supernaturally impregnated by the sun god, she became a substitute for the immaculate conception and a false "virgin mother" giving birth to Tammuz, "the Christ child," and reincarnation of Nimrod. This story is repeated in nearly all of the world's false religions with different names for Nimrod, Semiramis and Tammuz. In Egypt it is Ra, Isis, Osiris and Horus. It seems the Luciferian strategy was to imitate the virgin birth so many times that the genuine event would be rejected, which is exactly what is done by Atheist historians.

Semeramis became exalted as "the mother of God," or "the mother of Heaven." As the mother of God she was to be worshipped. The exaltation of Mary is based on the model of Semiramis as the mother of God. This clearly pagan idolatry, like other heresies, was incorporated into Catholicism (Universalism) as a way of placating the worshippers of the sun god. The statues and paintings of Mary holding Jesus are actually replicas of Semiramis holding and nursing Tammuz. This was all part of the early Catholic (Universal) Church's incorporation of the worship of the sun god and the unholy trinity. Very few Catholics have any idea where this tradition came from. They have no intention of worshipping a false god. Through tradition their faith in the Lord Jesus has been undermined, rendering them spiritually impotent. We must be careful to separate the intentions of the many corrupt organizations from the intentions of its sincere followers. But we must be crystal clear on Lucifer's tactics to "water down" the gospel, render the Word of God ineffective and lead people astray. The worship of Lucifer as the sun god is alive and well in modern religion, even though most of those who do so consider themselves to be Christian.

The statues and paintings of Mary holding Jesus are actually replicas of Semiramis holding and nursing Tammuz. This was all part of the early Catholic (Universal) Church's incorporation of the worship of the sun god and the unholy trinity.

In ancient times the greatest seduction into idolatry was to worship the sun, moon and stars. Because these celestial bodies dominated the sky it was an easy sell for a cult leader. The Nephilim (called the Anunnaki in Mesopotamia) said they were from the stars. These early deceptions paved the way for today's ancient astronaut theorists who believe man was created by aliens. There is a growing cult that is looking for a New Age savior to come as an alien, which is why there was a fascination with Orion's belt by early occultists.

Moses warned the children of Israel not to worship the sun, moon and stars (Deuteronomy 4:19). But Nimrod was elevated to the sun god, Semiramis declared herself to be the moon goddess and Tammuz was god with us. We now have the "unholy trinity"! It is essential the reader realize Satan is the great imposter. He creates counterfeits. Those counterfeits do not negate the originals but Satan has a phony for every original. Today legalists condemn many valid spiritual practices like meditation and operating in faith because they think these practices originated with the devil. The devil, however, created nothing. He only imitates the genuine as a way to discredit what is ours as children of God. Sadly, the plan has been pretty effective.

When Nimrod "ascended to Heaven" to become the sun god Semiramis told worshippers to call him Baal. She began being called Ishtar. The Baal worshipping nations became primary enemies of Israel. They constantly had the annihilation of God's people as a prime goal. Baal worship was the beginning of the crescent moon as a cult symbol. Baal was linked to the bull. In time the curved, almost semicircular shape of the two horns were considered to be similar to a woman's reproductive organs. The bull or the bull's horns were common symbols of Baal. Eventually, the bull's horns became the symbol for the moon goddess, thus the crescent moon.

The devil, however, created nothing. He only imitates the genuine as a way to discredit what is ours as children of God.

In ancient Egyptian art it is common to see a figure wearing a headdress that appears to be two long horns holding a disk. This figure is a combination of the moon goddess, Isis (Ishtar, Semiramis) with the sun god, Rah, Osiris (Baal, Nimrod). In Rome we see statues that have the face of Apollo (Osiris, Baal, Nimrod) and the body of Isis. On her head is a crown with sun rays projecting from it. This false god is actually the true identity of the statue we call Lady Liberty and the statue atop the US Capitol Building.

As mentioned earlier, sun, moon or star worship shows up in nearly every religion of the world. But most significant for our understanding of the end times is the fact that Baal is the pre-Muslim name for Allah and the crescent moon as their religious symbol is for the worship of Ishtar. Muslims vehemently protest this fact, but a quick overview of the history of Baal worship reveals it. The black meteorite that "fell from Heaven" was used in the worship of the moon goddess before it was declared to be a holy Islamic relic. Here we are 6,000 years from the Garden and we see the same enemy and same religion under different names working to rid the world of all knowledge of God and thereby destroying those whom God loves.

Failure to recognize Nimrod/Osiris/Baal/Allah worship as a continuum of evil has blinded the eyes of the Church to so much of what will unfold in the last days as we rush toward the revealing of the man of sin, the antichrist, the man of iniquity. Likewise, not recognizing the tactics, goals and aims of this false religion has made the Christian Church an ignorant conspirator in the continued expansion of the Great Harlot and her power.

The Church did not remain pure very long after the death of the apostles. It is essential to remember Christ is the Chief Cornerstone upon which the apostles' doctrines are built; yet, the early Gentile Church began to replace the apostles' doctrines with all manner of cult doctrine. In fact, while the apostles were alive there was a constant struggle with the Judaizers and Gnostics, both of which have roots in Luciferian doctrine. As the Church became more of an organization with a centralized power the doctrine of the participants became more controlled by its leaders than by the Bible. An entire book could be dedicated to the extreme amount of sun god worship that has been incorporated into the Church, but I will only identify a few of the more obvious.

The idea of one figure who serves as a substitute for Christ is itself born out of Paganism and is allowed nowhere in Scripture. While this is easily identified in Catholicism it is still embraced in many Christian movements under extreme concepts of submission to authority and special anointings. Doctrine that portrays the idea that any one person can bring some aspect of God to the believer that he or she does not already possess is rooted in the Luciferian spirit. No leader can give us what we already have in Christ! Any attempt to do so is to usurp the Lordship of Jesus in the life of the believer and establish a mediator between God and man, other than Jesus.

The idea of one figure who serves as a substitute for Christ is itself born out of Paganism and is allowed nowhere in Scripture.

Very early on, the Church at Rome, as a means to entice the world to become Catholic, began to adjust its time and style of worship to fit the pagan world. Keep in mind, the word "Catholic" means "universal." It seems that at its root the Church of Rome wanted to be universal with all religions. When Rome became the Holy Roman Empire there was a mixture of government and religion the likes of which had not been seen since Babylon. As Rome conquered the world in the name of the Church, the masses were incorporated into the Church along with their pagan deities, symbols, holy days and practices. Jesus was promoted in a likeness of the sun god. Local religions and beliefs were Christianized and sanctified by the pope who claims to speak on behalf of God and serves as the substitute for Christ.

A pope or pontiff (which is a pagan title,) cathedrals, worship on Sunday, the day of the sun god, Christmas on December 25th, the birth of Tammuz, the reincarnation of Nimrod, the Eucharist and a copy of the sun god disk are just the very small tips of the religious iceberg. Ishtar was morphed into Easter and all Christian celebrations were eventually paganized so those who had been inducted in the Church by sprinkling, replacing faith-based salvation followed by public water baptism, would feel comfortable. After all, they kept all their pagan beliefs, now they simply called themselves Christian.

As Rome conquered the world in the name of the Church, the masses were incorporated into the Church along with their pagan deities, symbols holy days, and practices.

The monstrance carried by the pope and displayed widely is a disk with rays of the sun emerging. The skull cap (zucchetto) worn by the pope is a copy of the fish god worn by pagan priests. The worship of Mary as the mother of God right down to the rings drawn around her head are all based on Semiramis/Isis/Ishtar holding Tammuz. All gods of the pagan world were incorporated into Catholic (Universal) worship as saints. The use of the rosary, the symbols of Baal and Ishtar on the stole worn by the pope, and the idea of salvation by sacrificial works and donations has no place in the worship of God either in the Old or New Covenants.

The Vatican obelisk and St. Peter's Basilica are actually replicas of pagan temples in Egypt that represent the penis of Osiris and the womb of Isis. When a pharaoh died he was lain in a dome-shaped building (the womb of Isis) with an obelisk facing it which represents his passing into the other world to become the sun god. The obelisk in St. Peter's Square was actually moved from Egypt to Rome. While the pope "exorcised demons" from it, it is still no less a pagan abomination. Our Capitol Building and Washington's Monument were commissioned to be identical with the goal of our presidents becoming embodied by Osiris and thereby empowered to rule our country as one nation under god… not God, the Father of our Lord Jesus Christ, god Lucifer/Nimrod/Osiris/Baal/Allah.

The greatest destruction of the Church through the ages, however, has not been the outward trapping of temples, symbols and ceremonies. Most of the early Catholic leaders were never born again although they converted to Christianity. They never surrendered to Jesus, the Son of Jehovah, as Lord.

The Bible never became their absolute basis of truth about God. These men were participants in pagan worship. Their beliefs about god were based on pagan deities and doctrines. They began to interpret the Bible based on cult philosophies, making the Word of God of little effect in those who heard. Ceremonies and rituals copied from sun god worship replaced true worship. Instead of encouraging believers to know God personally they were told to follow the substitute for Christ.

> The Vatican obelisk and St. Peter's Basilica are actually replicas of pagan temples in Egypt that represent the penis of Osiris and the womb of Isis.

As a result of the Protestant Movement, the Church world separated from Rome geographically and politically. But Protestant, Evangelical, Charismatic, Word of Faith and now the Grace Movement are sprinkled to some degree with pagan doctrine that has been part of the Church paradigm for so long it is accepted as truth. People will cling to their religious ideas in opposition to what Scripture clearly states, fulfilling Jesus' words: *"For laying aside the commandment of God, you hold the tradition of men"* (Mark 7:8). These groups do not intentionally cling to paganism. They have no allegiance to the devil or anything evil; they simply have handed down traditions that undermine the true gospel and faith of the believer.

The list of cults, secret societies, governments and religious groups that trace their roots and beliefs back to Nimrod, Semiramis, Tammuz, Osiris, Isis, Horus, sun, moon and star worship is staggering. But to dive into those areas would take us from our point. We need to understand how this affects us as we approach the end. There are thousands of pages of research on this subject available but it can be so overwhelming that we lose sight of the most essential fact: **in the end we win!**

In summary: All nations that oppressed Israel were worshippers of Nimrod in some form, regardless of the names by which they identified him. Since the time of Nimrod, government has been the primary means that Satan used to oppress the truth. The ultimate goal of the wicked one is to once again have a government-religion which, like Nimrod, begins by offering protection, peace and prosperity apart from the tyranny of the angry God of Jews and Christians, but will, in the end, oppress and destroy.

The only way Lucifer can establish his kingdom and achieve utter destruction of the world is to eliminate faith. Moses tells us of the vast superiority of God's power working in us as opposed to that which works in the enemy. *"Five of you shall chase a hundred, and a hundred of you shall put ten thousand to flight"* (Leviticus 26:8). The New Testament version of that says: *"Greater is he that is in you, than he that is in the world"* (1 John 4:4). Satan's goal in religion is to so undermine the power we really have in Jesus that we become powerless.

The only way Lucifer can establish his kingdom and achieve utter destruction of the world is to eliminate faith.

The Church soon lost sight of the fact that our faith and the power that works in us is based in what we believe about the death, burial, resurrection and inheritance of Jesus, and the fact that we are **in Him** sharing in all He has. Over-emphasis on faith in what Jesus did in His life added to a watered-down version of the cross makes us have just enough faith to hope for the truth but not have the power to see it come to pass.

The Catholic Church, which boasts most of the Christian population of the world, has long been overrun by the worship of the sun god. Over the years its hierarchy, as is rumored, has become dominated by the Illuminati. There were prophesies given by a Catholic priest that the last pope would align the Church of Rome with the antichrist. Everything we know about the direction of the Catholic Church today says that prophecy was speaking of the current pope. This is not to say all Catholics are pagans. Millions of Catholics are born again despite what many Protestant churches teach. Born again Catholics, like born again Protestants, have no allegiance to evil. Most Catholics do not understand the inner workings of the Church or its dark history. They are seeking to live for God but experience very little power because of their limited and unscriptural beliefs. They are simply following tradition. Their cultural roots are so deep in Catholicism they are unable to break away.

The governments of the world are controlled by the Great Whore. Whether they know it or not, this is tantamount to the worship of Satan around the goal of establishing a New World Order, an elitist utopian society with no middle class which will use the "unenlightened as their slaves." Communism and Socialism first came to power through violence. In time they saw that it was more profitable for them to overthrow nations by deception leaving all the wealth and natural resources intact for their use. The "enlightened ones" seek to take the world and its resources for their own families and followers. They use Communist, Socialist, Progressive and any other anti-God, anti-Scripture philosophy to take over the world.

The secret societies finance both Communist regimes and America. They profit from war in many ways. War always makes it possible to take ownership of the losing country's resources for pennies on the dollar. There is always a shift of power following a war. Countries can not only be overthrown from within but the disruption of government prepares them for the ultimate one-world alignment of nations. Someone has likened the secret societies to the NFL: they don't care which team wins; they make as much profit regardless.

> There were prophesies given by a Catholic priest that the last pope would align the Church of Rome with the antichrist. Everything we know about the direction of the Catholic Church today says that prophecy was speaking of the current pope.

History reveals the Muslim world actually worships Nimrod. Allah is Baal, Osiris and Nimrod. What few people know, because of the politically correct rhetoric of politicians and news media, is that Islam is not nor has it ever been a peaceful religion. Its own writings point out that it was a nation inspired for one purpose: the murderous elimination of all who will not pledge their loyalty to Allah and take up arms against all who believe in Jesus and Jehovah. They have an apocalyptic vision and their ultimate goal is to bring about the end of the world. They are trying to bring about the end of the world and the return of Jesus… just not the Jesus we believe in. Their Jesus is who the Bible describes as the antichrist!

The Catholic Church deceives and disempowers it members by the worship of Mary (the mother of Heaven) and Jesus (portrayed with the light around His head, is symbolic of the sun god), the saints and the host of other gods incorporated into Catholicism.

Likewise, the Protestant Church is all but powerless through its own incorporation of traditions. Many Protestants no longer believe in the Bible as the inspired Word of God. Many do not believe in sin or a literal Hell, or a personal devil. Many of the "spirit-filled" groups have morphed into a selfish "use my faith to get more stuff" cult. The Grace Movement has been hijacked by iniquity, inclusion, Universalism and ultimate reconciliation (lawlessness). And it seems many of today's leaders are more concerned with controlling their followers than empowering them. I am so thankful for the many wonderful leaders who see themselves as servants equipping their people with the truth.

So, we the faithful are surrounded on every side, such as has never been any time in history. And as we shall soon see, established denominations and "movements" in modern Christianity are overrun with doctrines within that are based in part on iniquity. While there are local churches that stand apart from the crowd who have held to the Great Commission, the authority of the Word of God, and the Lordship of Jesus, much of modern Christianity is blind, crippled and impotent, like the Laodicean church. *"Because you say, 'I am rich, have become wealthy, and have need of nothing' — and do not know that you are wretched, miserable, poor, blind, and naked"* (Revelation 3:17).

We can arm ourselves with truth and the power of God. We can turn our hearts back to Him who gave His life for us and surrender to Him as Lord.

Should we just throw up our hands and fall onto despair? No! We know how this story ends. We can arm ourselves with truth and the power of God. We can turn our hearts back to Him who gave His life for us and surrender to Him as Lord.

Sadly, history reveals that mankind as a whole will always tend toward abandoning God in times of peace and prosperity. The theme of the Book of Judges is *"every man did that which was right in his own eyes."* It records the cycle of oppression by other nations, repentance and crying out to God. God responds by sending a deliverer, the nation lives for God until that generation dies off and the people once again resort to that which will lead them into bondage. They soon fall into oppression and the cycle begins again. When man does that which is right in his own eyes the process is always the same. He is fulfilling the original sin - iniquity. He is being a god to himself and choosing good and evil based on his own humanistic philosophies.

The Church hasn't been much different than the nation of Israel. That's why God says all of those things serve as examples to us. In countries like the former Soviet Union and China where Christians are imprisoned, tortured and murdered, as it was in the pagan world of Rome, the Church actually flourishes underground. Why? It flourishes because it is an environment that does not exist for convenience or social connections. There is no pope, no buildings and not much room for ridiculous religious agendas. These people have finally given up the delusion that government will ever save them. They actually see "behind the curtain" where the real intention of the world powers can no longer be hidden. These churches are not full of compromisers. All they have is their faith and a personal relationship with Jesus; this is sufficient for them to overcome even unto death.

Many Christians believe there will be one last great world revival that will unfold in the midst of the greatest evil perpetrated on mankind since creation. I believe that as well. But I don't think it will be what most people expect. It will not be a revival that produces more buildings or religious organizations. It will be a revival of individuals who begin to experience the power of the Holy Spirit in their own heart. They will be more like Jesus than any previous generation. But it will never be publicized. There will be no head count and no one group will be able to take the credit. There will be no public superstars!

There will be no head count and no one group will be able to take the credit. There will be no public superstars!

SPIRITUAL GUIDE

I don't think buildings and organizations are evil. God is able and willing to work through whatever culture there is as long as that culture doesn't oppose the truth. This is not a call to turn against organized religion; it is a call to know God for yourself. Develop a life of godliness through your own personal faith. Have a discussion with your family and decide now how you will live or die as you walk with God. Make the life decisions now that you should have made when you came to Jesus. The number one decision is about your relationship with Jesus as Lord. Will you trust the Word of God and Jesus' death, burial and resurrection as your absolute truth?

Jesus warned there would be lying signs and wonders, and others would come declaring themselves to be the Christ. Is your heart established in a relationship with God to such a degree that you will be unmoved by signs and wonders, great revelations and prophecies, new scientific discoveries, the appearance of aliens that challenge everything you have believed about the human race? But more than anything else, are you willing, with God's help, to face death before compromise? These are the challenges that faced the early Church, this was the decision of every convert in Communist countries, and it is the decision believers in Muslim-dominated countries are facing today. Outside of North America, true believers around the world have faced persecution for decades. We never thought it could happen here, but according to God's Word… it most surely will! In our ease we have lost touch with the eternal struggle for our soul!

First and foremost, develop you own private, intimate relationship with God through the Lord Jesus. If you are a new believer or your faith has been unstable and unrewarding you may want to take our free online course, *Living Under Lordship.*[i] Begin studying the Word of God. Don't seek theological answers; seek wisdom for living a godly, powerful life. Become a witness. Share your faith with people who are interested. Develop a serious, effective prayer life. Spend time meditating on the promises of God. Find a healthy church that believes the Bible and preaches salvation by faith. Develop healthy relationships with godly people who are seeking after God. Commit to being a disciple who is actively building your life on the Word of God. And above all, follow Jesus as your Lord!

To learn more about the resources mentioned and for additional support material for this chapter please visit www.secondcomingguide.com.

---

i http://www.impactministries.com/self-development/living-under-lordship-2/

CHAPTER 7

THE BIRTH OF A NATION

No Matter how it appears God always has a plan and His plan always prevails!

IN THE MIDST OF A WORLD OF DARKNESS IT WOULD APPEAR THAT ALL HOPE FOR HUMANITY IS LOST; BUT NO MATTER HOW GREAT THE DARKNESS, GOD'S PEOPLE ALWAYS PREVAIL. God never abandons the righteous for the sins of the unrighteous. To the religious thinker, God's deliverance seems to always come late but nothing is farther from the truth. When you truly seek God, He is always found. While there are many factors we can understand about God and His faithfulness there are some things we cannot. The confusion is usually based on judging God because of the circumstances rather than accepting Him according to His Word. The character of God is always consistent, always congruent and always motivated by love, even when we cannot perceive the love. As James said, *"Every good gift and every perfect gift is from above, and comes down from the Father of lights, with whom there is no variation or shadow of turning"* (James 1:17-18). In the darkness God is the light to those who trust Him.

Those James was addressing had fallen into the Luciferian doctrine of blaming God for their tests, trials and stressful situations. They, no doubt, had bought into the lie that God uses hardship to train and develop. But James explained that God is the One who brings only good gifts. And He is so consistently good, in perfect all-encompassing light, He would never move from His consistent character enough to cast a shadow.

God's goodness and willingness to fulfil His promises and uphold His covenant are absolutely predictable. But many of the wonders of creation are not so clear. There are laws around which God's righteousness and mercy work that are beyond our current understanding. For example, why do some world events happen around what seems to be mystery-timing? Why did God not cast Satan into the bottomless pit immediately? These kinds of questions may have unclear answers, but if we believe in the character, nature, and name of God we know the reason is always rooted in love. In the end, when we finally understand God's righteousness and fairness, we will see He did everything in the manner that assuredly led the most people to life everlasting.

What most people are confused about concerning history is the fact that God never violates His Word. He gave the authority in Planet Earth to man.

What most people are confused about concerning history is the fact that God never violates His Word. He gave the authority in Planet Earth to man; therefore, those things that occur in Planet Earth or affect mankind do so around the beliefs and choices of mankind. God is sovereign in the sense that He makes all the rules. His truth is absolute. But religion has perverted the definition and concept of sovereignty to mean that God is inconsistent, unpredictable, fickle and unfaithful. God's faithfulness, however, dictates that He cannot even violate His own Word. He is bound by what He said. If God violated His Word He would be a liar.

The type of sovereignty embraced by most believers says God is in control of everything. Everything happens for a reason and God works in mysterious (unknowable) ways. This thinking is actually Fatalism, which came from the worship of false gods that required sacrifices. The greater the request the larger the sacrifice must be. If unsatisfied the gods would bring about havoc on mankind in all manner of unpredictable ways. These false gods supposedly used hardship and punishment as the way to keep mankind in line and loyal.

It is from this demonic heresy that we have deduced this deceitful doctrine of sovereignty.

The world had fallen into the chaos of darkness. Man, in his fallen nature, was prone to fear and unbelief. Because God gave man authority on Planet Earth, He was looking for a man who would believe Him, with whom He could make a covenant, who would use the authority bestowed upon him to turn the tide of wickedness. In all that God has accomplished in Planet Earth, it required a human who would trust God and use his own authority in God's behalf.

> Those things that occur in Planet Earth or affect mankind do so around the beliefs and choices of mankind.

According to Jewish history Abraham's father, Terah, was a general in service to Nimrod. He was a worshipper of the first self-declared god-king. Nimrod, like many wicked rulers who followed, lived in fear of the fulfillment of the prophecy of a deliverer that would break the power of Lucifer and bring salvation to the human race.

At a certain time his soothsayers and astrologers came to him and warned that a deliverer was about to be born. Nimrod gathered all the pregnant women in his kingdom. If they gave birth to a boy child it was immediately murdered. If they delivered a female it was allowed to live. This may have been the very model followed by King Herod who killed all the male babies when Jesus was born (Matthew 2:16-18). Abraham's father was in charge of slaughtering the babies.

Terah was elderly and never had children. During this time his wife became pregnant. Fearing he would never have another child he hid the child from Nimrod. But Nimrod's astrologers informed him that the child deliverer lived and was born of his own servants. Terah hid Abram in a cave. As Nimrod came to confront him one of Terah's servants gave birth. He took the servant's baby and went out to meet Nimrod. He then presented him with the child as if it were his own.

Tradition says that Abram spent years living in the cave to protect his life. When he came out of the cave he saw the sun and assumed it was god. This may have come from the influence of his father. These idolatrous roots would explain why years later God commanded Abram to separate himself from his family before going into the Promised Land. In the evening the moon appeared and Abram assumed it had overthrown the sun. He would, therefore, worship the moon as god. When the sun again emerged he determined that he would worship the Creator of the sun and the moon as God. It was this simple faith in the heart of a child surrounded and influenced by idol worshippers that God used to bring about the next most important transition in world history: the birth of a nation! Terah then took Abram and fled.

It was this simple faith in the heart of a child surrounded and influenced by idol worshippers that God used to bring about the next most important transition in world history: the birth of a nation!

God saw something in Abram's heart so He revealed himself to Abram. What began was a progression of events that continued for years. Over that period of time Abram (whose name is eventually changed to Abraham) sees God's faithfulness and by degrees reaches a place where he believes God so completely that he is willing to sacrifice his son. It could be that God needed a man who would believe God to raise his own son from the dead before God could send Jesus to die and be raised from the dead. The implications of the faith of Abraham are so far-reaching it will only be fully understood in eternity. But after the Flood we see Abraham emerge as the "Father of Faith."

It is no wonder it took God so long to find the right man. After all, Abraham's life became the model and basis for how the New Covenant believer, thousands of years later, would live in faith righteousness. It would be the covenant that God made with Abraham that preceded and superseded the first covenant, providing the legal basis for those of us who believe on Jesus to live in the promise to Abraham instead of in the limitations of the first covenant. In fact, it was to Abraham and his seed (as in one, Jesus) not his seeds (as in the nation of Israel) was the covenant made (Galatians 3:16).

What is often explained as God's timing is actually man's timing. It is God waiting on mankind. God's salvation is always today; *"today is the day of salvation."* God is never late, He is never slow, and He never leaves us alone until we are about to break.

> *The Lord is not slack concerning His promise, as some count slackness, but is longsuffering toward us, not willing that any should perish but that all should come to repentance.* (2 Peter 3:9)

If God is late in Planet Earth it is because of man's reluctance to believe. If He is late in our circumstances it is because we did not, as our first option, believe the truth in our heart.

It took God centuries to find Abram. Just imagine what it would take in a man to stand up to a god-king. He was a ferocious, evil dictator. But God delivered Abram from the first antichrist just as He can deliver us from the last antichrist. No doubt, Shadrach, Meshach and Abed-nego had Abraham as a model and inspiration when they alone stood up to Nebuchadnezzar in the fiery furnace, as did Daniel when he stood up to Darius in the lions' den. These Bible stories are not mythology; they are written for our encouragement. We too can stand in absolute trust of God against all oppression.

If God is late in Planet Earth it is because of man's reluctance to believe. If He is late in our circumstances it is because we did not, as our first option, believe the truth in our heart.

How many hearts did God touch when the children of Israel faced Goliath before David responded? How many people did He call who could have gone down in eternal history as the giant killers before Joshua and Caleb said, "Here am I, send me"? I think of Mary and wonder how long it took God to find a woman who would follow Him even at the risk of public humiliation or even death by stoning. Likewise, I wonder how long it will be until humans give their authority to God to save the world as fully and fervently as the wicked give their authority to the antichrist (Revelation 17:12-13) to fulfill their lusts. We are never waiting on God! He is always waiting on us. His time for salvation is always today (2 Corinthians 6:2), and His answer to our cry for a promise is always "Yes" (2 Corinthians 1:20)!

Each time God speaks concerning His plan to redeem man the enemy narrows his focus of attack. At first it was all of mankind. The Nephilim were an assault on the human bloodline. Then the focus narrowed to Abraham and the nation of Israel which is born of his loins. Later it narrowed even more to the tribe of Judah and ultimately to the bloodline of David. It is important to realize that Satan is not omniscient. He knows many of the generalities of the future. However, for the protection of mankind, there are many things God does not reveal until their time. If He did the enemy would know to focus his attack on specific individuals. As we get closer to the end our knowledge of God's plan will increase.

We are never waiting on God! He is always waiting on us. His time for salvation is always today (2 Corinthians 6:2), and His answer to our cry for a promise is always "Yes" (2 Corinthians 1:20)!

SPIRITUAL GUIDE

It is important that we forever rid ourselves of the religious myth that Satan can read or speak into our minds. He knows what is in our mind when we reveal it by our words and actions. He puts something into our hearts because we lust for it, speak of it, and embrace his evil strategies to fulfill that lust. The Old Testament relates two different times when Satan could not read the minds of men. Pharaoh had a dream and only Joseph could know and interpret it, and Nebuchadnezzar had a dream that only Daniel could know and interpret.

Luciferian doctrines do everything from blame God for Lucifer's actions to exalt Lucifer's power to that equal to the power of God. Lucifer's only power is deception. His lies were spoken into Planet Earth by fallen angels, Nephilim, Satan worshippers, and corrupt men who espoused philosophical concepts to justify their own lusts. These false philosophical concepts are taught in schools as scientific fact and have become the world's basis of logic. Satan does not put false ideas in our minds, we choose them when we do not know or are not willing to believe the truth. We default to our secular education because we were not given a true Bible education. Give your children the Bible education you may have missed. Teach them yourself or plug them into a program that you know to be solid biblical teaching. You can also utilize the free online resources at www.impactministries.com. Before you send them away to a pagan university to learn antichrist dogma, allow them to attend Impact International School of Ministry[i] online. Don't send them out to be brainwashed in one of the most vulnerable scenarios they will ever face and expect them to come home living for God.

A corrupt concept of God makes us afraid to trust Him and an exaggerated paradigm of the devil makes us afraid of him. If we cannot trust God and are afraid of the devil where do we go for comfort? You can be an Abraham, Joseph, David, Paul or Peter. Hebrews 11 is full of men and women who trusted God and did great exploits. Know the truth about God! Get to know God! Trust God! Follow God!

There is a final principle to take away from section one of this book. **Righteousness always prevails over evil.** Remember the law of righteous power: *"five will chase a hundred, and one hundred shall put ten thousand to*

---

i http://www.impactministries.com/self-development/iisom/

flight." (Leviticus 26:8) A grain of righteousness will prevail over a bushel of evil. One man in the ancient world produced a nation that killed the giants, drove out the ungodly and has held the world at attention for centuries. ***Christ in you*** is more powerful than you ever imagined!

To learn more about the resources mentioned and for additional support material for this chapter please visit www.secondcomingguide.com.

APOCALYPSE

CHAPTER 8

CONCLUSION TO SECTION ONE

If you think wrath is what motivates God you will never be prepared to usher in the return of Jesus!

IT WOULD BE SO EASY FOR KNOWLEDGEABLE BELIEVERS TO BECOME OVERWHELMED WITH THE CONDITION OF THE WORLD, AND EVEN MORE SO WITH THE CONDITION OF THE CHURCH. Because much of the research revealing occult involvement in government is done by unbelievers it only serves to paint a picture of hopelessness. Fear and desperation is never God's goal. Those who have bought into the Luciferian doctrine of an angry, judgmental God have no refuge in such an overwhelming scenario.

The purpose of biblical end time warnings is to provide hope and confidence for the believer who is looking for and hastening the Lord's return. God reveals the end (outcome) of all things for many reasons. As it comes to pass we will know we can trust every word He has spoken. Since these events will unfold exactly as God foretells we will not be consumed by mass panic or hysteria. We, the disciples of the Lord Jesus, will be light and salt in a dark, corrupt world (Matthew 5:13-16). Much of the world will finally give up the false hope of government or any other institution saving them. We who have not succumbed to sensationalized mystical eschatology will have not only the answers, but the solutions. The hope we bring will not be through having all the right answers concerning the sequence of events; we will bring hope and comfort by introducing seekers to the Lord of Lords, the King of Kings.

One of the important lessons we can learn is that God can turn into good what the devil has done for evil. Don't misunderstand. It was never God's intention for us to suffer from what lies ahead. He warned, prophesied and provided a written record of the facts, yet they have fallen on deaf ears. But as the world becomes desperate they will finally cry out for real solutions and as the "birth pangs" intensify much of the Church will finally awaken and turn whole heartedly to God!

Luciferian doctrine says God is punishing the world. The truth is God will eventually eliminate the wicked who seek to destroy all men so the righteous can have peace.

Luciferian doctrine says God is punishing the world. The truth is God will eventually eliminate the wicked who seek to destroy all men so the righteous can have peace. Knowing what God has said prevents us from blaming God for that which is clearly a work of the devil. We must remember the tribulation is the work of the antichrist, that is the first 3 1/2 years of tribulation. The last 3 1/2 years is the wrath of God poured out on the antichrist and his armies. It is protection from the unending, merciless destruction of Lucifer manifested through those who give him their authority.

The last days are marked by the *"Beginning of Sorrows."* This is not something God brings on the earth; this is the outcome of wicked men. Wars and rumors of war are acts of corrupt, power-hungry humans who ignore God's teaching about righteousness. They are driven by greed and the lust for power, all of which embody "mammon." Mammon, contrary to pop theology, is not money; it is anything one trusts in - money, poverty, sacrifice or possessions. When we trust in anything for security, peace, safety or to be accepted by God it is mammon to us. *"You can't serve God and mammon."* No matter how religious they seem, those who crave after security from any source other than what is offered by God are trusting in mammon and will hate God.

The famines expected in the Beginning of Sorrows have occurred since the 70's when the former Soviet Union fought in African countries. They created famines to starve what they call "worthless eaters." Today Progressives in the US government are doing the same. They are creating the illusion of a global food shortage in order to accomplish the goal of population control on a small degree, but mostly to create a reliance on government for survival. There is plenty of free land in this country where people could grow crops and live very well if it were not controlled by FEMA, the EPA, the Department of Agriculture and other bureaucratic regulatory programs. Men will blame God for what are actually man-made famines. The prophets of doom will say it is because of our sin that God has abandoned us, playing into the hands of the Luciferian agenda.

The last seven years of history as we know it are divided into the tribulation of the antichrist and the wrath of God against the antichrist. Contrary to the typical wrath of God preaching the horrors of the end are the Luciferian powers working through corrupt government that bring all the hardships upon man. The first 3 1/2 years of the tribulation is the brutality of those who seek to eliminate all mention of God from the planet; it is not an angry God lashing out at all the inhabitants of Planet Earth.

The last 3 1/2 years will be the wrath of God on the antichrist and his followers. This is not God punishing the inhabitants of earth; it is God saving the inhabitants of earth. This will save the inhabitants of earth from facing the choice of converting to the antichrist or being beheaded; it will be their eternal salvation.

The lies that Lucifer imagined in his own heart are the ones he used to undermine the faith of Adam and Eve. The lies of the Nephilim who taught man to embrace the idea of a better life with the secret knowledge smuggled out of Heaven are the same ones fueling the Great Whore and seducing the governments of the earth. The same spirit that drove the original queen of Heaven is the religious lie that has undermined millions of ignorant Christians. And the same Babylonian government that forcibly oppressed the inhabitants of the world under Nimrod is the same power and force that will rise in the end to rule through corrupt governments of the world.

SPIRITUAL GUIDE

When Daniel saw his horrific vision of the triumphant Kingdom of God he said *"those who know their God shall be strong and carry out great exploits."* (Daniel 11:32) The key to surviving what lies ahead and ushering in the return of Jesus as Lord of the entire earth rests with the personal knowledge and experience of knowing God in your heart. Times will be so hard that we all could be tempted to surrender our faith. On the other hand, these same hard times will galvanize the faith of millions. Casual Christianity will be a thing of the past. There will be false signs and wonders designed to deceive the elect, but there will be genuine miracles, signs and wonders done by true disciples of the Lord Jesus. The compromised state church that promotes humanistic, Luciferian doctrine will pour out a flood of lies making those ignorant of Scripture question their own beliefs. But true believers will proclaim the message of the Kingdom of God in truth and in power to the ends of the earth. The threats of a government set on alienating all true faith will be inescapable without the leadership of the Lord. Yet, we will have such a clear, intense awareness of the Kingdom within and the coming earthly Kingdom of the Lord Jesus that we will be immovable in our resolve. And those who cannot hear and do not trust God's voice will be powerless in the face of an onslaught of evil, while those who choose to trust God's promises will experience grace to face and overcome every obstacle.

The Prophet Daniel had a vision of one horrible nation after another rising to dominate Israel and eventually oppress the Church until the triumphant Kingdom of God manifests on earth conquering all the kingdoms of this world. No matter how horrific, Daniel did not stop looking. He kept his eyes fixed on the Lord until he saw the stone cut out without hands destroy the ten-nation kingdom of the antichrist. Today we are discouraged because we look to the weak state of much of the Church and feel we could never overcome the kingdom of darkness. We have looked to our own strength more than God's.

It is not going to be America or any other nation that delivers us; it will be the personal return of the Lord Jesus Christ! We will be transformed and we will be the army He leads into absolute victory by His power and His might. Those who know their God will have the power to see beyond events that cause unbelieving hearts to melt with fear and experience the life and power of God in absolute victory. It will not be the Church led by man that ushers in the victory; it will be a transformed Church under the personal leadership of our Lord and King.

To learn more about the resources mentioned and for additional support material for this chapter please visit www.secondcomingguide.com.

SECTION TWO

APOCALYPSE

CHAPTER 9

INTRODUCTION TO SECTION TWO
From the Tower of Babel to the Church

No matter how bad things look, the believer who knows and trusts God's nature is always expectantly awaiting God's plan!

BEFORE LOOKING AT THE GROSS DARKNESS THAT COMES UPON THE EARTH DURING THIS NEXT PERIOD OF HISTORY, IT IS ESSENTIAL TO LOOK BACK TO THE WORD OF GOD AND BRING EVERYTHING INTO PERSPECTIVE. During this dark period of idolatry and Luciferian dominance, murderous cannibalistic beasts, sexual immorality and living sacrifices of both adults and children perverted the inhabitants of the earth. In light of what history reveals it seems impossible that God could have raised up a nation from one man that would so effectively prevail against the powers of darkness, but that is exactly what happened.

As the world plunged into Luciferian deception and gross darkness God was in the process of raising up a nation that will be the key to man's salvation. This book is revealing what happens when a flood of demons in the form of Nephilim spread out across the entire earth to dominate and destroy human life. Like before the Flood, this is a period of history wherein we can see the enemy's true intentions and God's ability to sustain and prosper His own people. God found one man in a family of idolaters and under the nose of Nimrod, the first antichrist, and despite Nimrod's occult powers and vicious brutality, this man would walk by faith. Out of his loins would come the Messiah. This man was Abram!

God found one man in a family of idolaters and under the nose of Nimrod, the first antichrist, and despite his occult powers and vicious brutality, this man would walk by faith.

Abraham, as his name became, showed how one man trusting and yielding to the Spirit of God could not only survive in a world dominated by the worst evil, but would, in fact, overcome. He modeled what we will experience as we usher in the return of the Lord: Holy Spirit direction, unprecedented victories and protection against the forces of darkness.

The children of Israel which grew from Abraham's immediate family to a great nation found favor in Egypt under the rule of a godless pharaoh. Then when their oppression became so great they could not bear it, they cried out to God who sent them Moses as a deliverer. Moses led the rebellious, double-minded Israelites through the wilderness to the land of Canaan. They could have made the journey in just a few days, but their unbelief turned the journey of a few days into one that took forty years. Had they arrived in the Promised Land before the old generations who lived in Egypt died, corruption and idolatry would have destroyed Israel before they could have ever become a nation. Joshua and Caleb were 80 year old men who chose to fight against the Nephilim once they arrived in the land. History indicates the Nephilim were so afraid of the Israelites they migrated to other parts of the world including America. Even the giants were no match for those who knew and trusted their God!

Throughout the period of the judges every time the people truly desired it God would raise up a deliverer who would free them from the oppression of the Luciferian nations that sought to dominate them. Consider the power of those nations and the fact that God usually used common men to break their evil grip. These common men who trusted God provide us with a perfect example of God's ability and willingness to empower every man to great exploits in His name. Samson, Gideon, David and Elijah, just to name a few, not only conjure images of divine intervention, but the fact that God will qualify and equip those He calls. These and nearly every Old Testament example of those whom God used were what James called *"men of like passions."* In other words, they were just like us, with the same fears and personal struggles, but they chose to trust God and He empowered them to do mighty conquests!

Samson killed lions with his bare hands and defeated thousands of Lucifer's best warriors (Philistines) with the jawbone of an ass. Although he was deeply flawed and often disobedient (for which he often suffered) he never lost his faith. The children of Israel routed their enemies by sending worshippers out ahead of the army. God sent hornets before them to fight their battles. David killed a lion, bear and giant with a slingshot. The walls of a fortified city collapsed before these worshippers of God. And in one instance they even made the sun stand still in order to give them an absolute victory over the enemy. And as I previously mentioned, my personal favorite, an eighty-year old man that said, "I'll take that mountain from those giants."

> These common men who trusted God provide us with a perfect example of God's ability and willingness to empower every man to great exploits in His name—Samson, Gideon, David and Elijah, just to name a few.

We forget those who did these incredible conquests were the ones who had not bought in to the "angry God" doctrine. Hebrews chapter 11 tells us the superstars of the Old Testament were men and women of faith. They trusted and relied on God's mercy, His words of promise, and the power of His Spirit - not their righteous deeds. These were flawed servants who knew God was faithful to His promises even when they were not.[i] These champions of faith lived under the law of the Spirit that says: *"one can put a thousand to flight and two can put ten thousand."* They were not limited by their mere human capacity; they experienced the limitless power of the Almighty God!

As you read every account of the world plunging deeper into sin and darkness you must remember that God always has a remnant.* He is always working a plan of deliverance and those who have *ears to hear* follow the leading of the

---

i 2 Timothy 2:13, If we are faithless, He remains faithful; He cannot deny Himself.

Spirit with all their heart! These champions of faith were not born again. The Holy Spirit would occasionally come upon them. But we are born of the Spirit; we have the gifts of the Spirit, the grace of God and the working of the Holy Spirit. According to Jesus, we are the light in the darkness!

What God did for Israel will pale in comparison to what He does in you and me, the Church, in the days ahead as we usher in the return of our Lord!

"When the enemy comes in like a flood, The Spirit of the Lord will lift up a standard against him" (Is 59:19). What God did for Israel will pale in comparison to what He does in you and me, and the Church, in the days ahead as we usher in the return of our Lord!

APOCALYPSE

CHAPTER 10

THE WORLD DIVIDED

The devil has no magic; he uses God's knowledge to accomplish an evil purpose and we ignorantly think he has power!

THE DEVIL HAS ALWAYS BEEN MASSIVELY OVERRATED. Keep in mind angels were created to be servants to the heirs of salvation.[i] As an angel Satan is a created being and has no power of his own. His ruse is to present himself as powerful and accomplished by employing laws of physics, the laws God established to sustain creation. When man witnesses what he thinks is miraculous or supernatural it is very often no more than the application of higher laws of creation, laws that man, at this moment, does not understand.

Satan has no authority to act in Planet Earth. He can only operate in and through those who invite him or allow him. He is no match for God or for man. As the Scripture says, he is not a roaring lion; he only goes about *"**as** a roaring lion"*! He is like the bully on the playground who makes himself

---

i Hebrews 1:14, Are they not all ministering spirits sent forth to minister for those who will inherit salvation?

appear to be much tougher than he actually is. Anything he had that made him outstanding was lost when he fell!

Lucifer and the host of fallen angels had been privy to many of the aspects of creation. We think of the supernatural in very mystical ways. Our entire concept of sacred and secular is unscriptural. When we see the supernatural we think we are witnessing the violation of natural laws*.[ii] What we are actually seeing are higher laws that we do not yet know and understand. It is a trick of the devil to make us believe that his use of God's laws of creation are a demonstration of his miraculous power. His goal is to alienate mankind from access to the natural resources God has already made available to us.

This world, the solar system and all the universes work from mathematical equations called "physics." According to the original language of Genesis some say that God first created the "quantum field." Some scientists believe that original light and darkness was more like polarities than light and darkness. These polarities form the field essential for the existence of matter. Then all matter was created to exist within this field based on absolute laws of physics.

Romans 1:19-20 not only supports the concept that God created the world based on what we call laws of physics, but those very laws reveal His nature and identity.

> *...what may be known of God is manifest in them, for God has shown it to them. For since the creation of the world His invisible attributes are clearly seen, being understood by the things that are made, even His eternal power and Godhead.*

How we view the beginning of all things (creation) sets us on an intellectual trajectory for how we interpret all things. As we will soon discover, the perversion of the biblical account of creation forms the basis for all Atheism. From this and other creation Scriptures we understand:

- Creation reflects all the invisible attributes of the Godhead.
- We can understand God if we properly understand creation.

---

ii Laws witnessed as universal in nature. For more about natural laws read *Anatomy of A Miracle,* James B. Richards, Milestones International Publishers, 2008.

- Any concept of creation that is different from God's explanation will always lead away from God.
- Since all created things reflect God's character nothing in creation is inherently evil.
- That which God created can be twisted to lead people away from God.

Years ago I created a program called *Heart Physics,*®* a 30-day life transformation curriculum. Using principles of biblical meditation the participant creates the abiding awareness of Christ in his or her heart. When we view all things with the awareness of God in our heart we develop a consistency and congruence in how we see and interpret all things. We can then see God in creation and God the Father and Creator becomes the center of all logic. Based on the parables of the Kingdom of God which explain life lived from the internal realm (the heart), we can know that all God does in our heart is in exact congruence with the true laws of physics.[iii] God is never inconsistent. He is never the author of confusion.

As we will soon discover, the perversion of the biblical account of creation forms the basis for all Atheism.

The current religious paradigm of the miraculous is defined as, "when God violates a law of nature." This paradigm has done incredible damage to man's faith. We must understand that if God violates a law of nature He corrupts our capacity to understand Him through nature; therefore, He violates Scripture (Romans 1:20-21).

The greater damage is done, again through this paradigm, when science figures out the law of physics whereby a "miracle" took place. At the point the miraculous can be explained away and loses credibility. This paradigm would reach the conclusion, if it can be understood or explained it isn't a miracle. Even worse, if a miracle can be explained it is often attributed to the devil!

From my understanding of science and the supernatural a miracle occurs when we operate in a higher law of physics. A miracle is just as "scientific" as any currently understood law of physics; it just doesn't fit into the current paradigm of scientific explanation. For example, the law of faith is a law of

iii For more information go to www.heartphysics.com

physics but, unfortunately, is not seen as such. By my definition, any law that explains what occurs in the natural world is a law of physics.

Satan and his minions have no knowledge or power of their own. The world, however, was created to operate based on absolute formulas and they have knowledge of many of those formulas and the ability to make what we would call "supernatural" events occur. This false perception of the supernatural is what caused ancient men (and will cause mankind in the last days) to worship them as gods. They do not, however, have supernatural power. They have knowledge of the formulas or equations of creation which were learned in Heaven before their rebellion. Then, through the authority of man (angels have no authority on earth) men repeat these equations as incantations believing them to be magic formulas, and very often an incredible phenomenon occurs. This gives the illusion that these beings are using *their* power to accomplish the supernatural and then men worship them as gods.

There is no place where this is seen any clearer than the Tower of Babel.

> *But the Lord came down to see the city and the tower which the sons of men had built. And the Lord said, "Indeed the people are one and they all have one language, and this is what they begin to do; now* ***nothing that they propose to do will be withheld from them."*** (Genesis 11:5-6)

It was at Babel under the rule of the first antichrist that we see the intention of the being, force and logic of what drives everything in the world. Satan seeks to take his limited knowledge of the secrets of creation and use it to deceive man about his power. If he can make himself look greater than he is man will slip into dualism, a lie which dominates almost all of Christianity. In dualism man sees God and Satan as near equals fighting over the fate of mankind. The godly will fear him. The carnal will ally with him in hopes of creating a world of iniquity - a world where man fulfills all his ungodly lusts. The ungodly will ally with him in the hopes of eliminating God from the planet and creating a world in their own image.

The actual purpose of the Tower of Babel is unclear. The Bible says it was for the purpose of reaching the heavens. Some researchers and scientists believe the early pyramids, ziggurats and this tower compose the equivalent of power stations that linked together to form a world-wide energy grid of some kind. It could have made it possible for the Nephilim to communicate with their kind around the world. Others think it may have been a means of creating mind control to add to their domination and deceptions of mankind. And still others believe they were portals into other realms.

Satan seeks to take his limited knowledge of the secrets of creation and use it to deceive man about his power.

While I believe all those things are possible, from a scriptural perspective we know they hoped to *reach the heavens.* We know they were not ignorant enough to think they could build a tower tall enough to escape the Flood or reach the abode of God. They had come from the heavenly realm. The tower could have been an energy portal providing a way to cross back over into the heavens. After all, the original meaning of Babel was "gate of the gods." It is not beyond realistic thought to consider that all pyramids, ziggurats and ancient structures were far more than just altars to their gods.

Occult literature, as well as the Book of Enoch, say the first fallen angels crossed over into this realm at Mount Hermon, which means "forbidden place." It became the principle temple of Baal. All other temples of Baal were positioned so when the priests offered sacrifices they would be facing the temple at Mount Hermon.

Mount Hermon is located at 33[iv] degrees east of Paris, zero meridian longitude and 33 degrees north of the equator latitude[v]. It is located in ancient Syria and was once called Phoenicia[vi]. It was where the tribe of Dan settled and went into idolatry and eventually became the lost tribe of Israel. It is this very region the Prophet Daniel identifies as the place from which the invasion of Israel will come, setting the stage for the emergence of the antichrist[vii]. It is said these coordinates are what give the number 33 such significance among occult societies and religions. But the key is, there are certain locations and/or shapes and alignments that make it possible for the spirit being to cross over into this realm.

---

iv This is why the number 33 is so significant in cult numerology

v http://www.prophecyinthenews.com/mount-hermon-gate-of-the-fallen-angels/

vi http://phoenicia.org/syria.html

vii Daniel 11:40

Nimrod built many cities during his reign. Some "scholars" question the biblical account of his accomplishments. These are the same "scholars" that reject all evidence of the Bible being true and do not believe in giants even though we have thousands of skeletal remains that prove their existence, but they do believe and attempt to protect Darwin's anti-God theories without a single piece of concrete evidence to support it. And they cannot explain the building of pyramids, ziggurats and megalithic structures that cover the earth contradicting the theories they embrace. Nimrod was a Nephilim who knew many of the secrets of Heaven. He also had advanced in occult knowledge to a point where nothing could be withheld from him and his anti-God followers. He demonstrated the biblical principle of agreement which can be used in a godly or ungodly manner.

Knowing that Nimrod built these ancient cities and understanding that Nephilim settled in Canaan is very important in understanding what motivated God to command that the children of Israel totally annihilate many of those nations. These anti-God, demon-worshipping nations were not seeking a peaceful coexistence with the children of God. Just like the Humanists, Communists, Progressives, Atheists and Islamists want the eradication of all knowledge of God.

God's intervention at Babel was not to keep man from having knowledge, as Luciferians*, Humanists and secret societies would portray. Once again God had to move on behalf of man to save the godly in the earth and prevent the hostile takeover of all mankind. Being true to His Word, God did not destroy the world by water this time.

Genesis 11:7-9 tells us what occurred.

> *"Come, let Us go down and there confuse their language, that they may not understand one another's speech." So the Lord scattered them abroad from there over the face of all the earth, and they ceased building the city. Therefore its name is called Babel, because there the Lord confused the language of all the earth; and from there the Lord scattered them abroad over the face of all the earth.*

When people speak a certain language it actually alters the way their brain functions. It is said that when a person learns a language he begins to create the capacity to think like those who speak the language. When God confused the languages it was more than simply giving each group a different language, it probably altered the way they thought, protecting the secrets of God being used for evil.

This passage also tells us God scattered the people all over the face of the earth. This is very important if we are to protect ourselves against the false science that makes Darwinism the core of atheistic propaganda under the guise of science. Nearly everything we have been taught about how the continents were settled is contrived to support Atheism. Before the people were scattered all the earth was in one place. In other words, people had access to all the continents because the continents were joined.

When God confused the languages it was more than simply giving each group a different language, it probably altered the way they thought, protecting the secrets of God being used for evil.

Genesis 10:25 gives us insight into the settling of the continents. In one of those long lists of so-and-so begat so-and-so there is always important information that tends to be overlooked. *"To Eber were born two sons: the name of one was Peleg, for in his days the earth was divided."* It has been proven by accepted scientific protocol that at one time all the earth was in one place. But according to "science" over the process of millions of years the continents drifted apart. What we are not told is there is credible science that refutes the theory of this taking millions of years.

The name "Peleg" means "earthquake"[viii]. There was a massive earthquake that caused the continents to divide. According to God's Word this is how people were spread across the face of the earth on what we now know to be the various continents. Native American oral history says when they arrived in North America there were already giants. This is supported by the discoveries of thousands of giant bones in North America. *In Search of Giants,* a popular History Channel program, includes more than 1500 newspaper articles about the discovery of giants in America. Both George Washington and Abraham Lincoln spoke of the discovery of massive graves of giant skeletal remains. Nearly every continent in the world has discovered giants' bones and

viii Biblesoft's New Exhaustive Strong's Numbers and Concordance with Expanded Greek-Hebrew Dictionary. Copyright © 1994, 2003, 2006 Biblesoft, Inc. and International Bible Translators, Inc.

pagan temples, most of which offered live human sacrifices and were accompanied by megalithic structures aligned with the stars (usually the constellation of Orion's belt). This was Lucifer's second sweeping attempt at the annihilation of mankind.

At the dividing of the continents and languages another of many significant events occurred. Now that the language and comprehension of the human race had been divided, the worship of the sun, moon, stars, Nimrod and Semiramis also became fragmented. While idolatry continued, it lacked two powerful spiritual elements. It no longer had the synergy of multitudes of worshippers and it was no longer propelled by the power of agreement.

Now that the language and comprehension of the human race had been divided, the worship of the sun, moon, stars, Nimrod and Semiramis also became fragmented.

At this division Nimrod was given as many different names as there were languages. The ancient stories of the Flood and the giants were fragmented and distilled down to the understanding and mental comprehension of each language. On one hand, the world was saved by confusing the languages and separating the people. On the other hand, hundreds of individual pagan religions were born from the now fragmented concepts, but they all have certain similarities. Besides the denial of God the Creator and His own account of Himself, they each establish their own version of creation and their own idea of the god of creation, which oddly seems to always be the image of some satanic being. The expression of this departure from the true Creator always leads to iniquity: the rejection of God's standards or morals, values and ethics.

SPIRITUAL GUIDE

This chapter provides several pivotal historical realities that must be factored in to the false science and corrupt accounts of history perpetrated by Luciferians.[ix] First is the fact that we must guard our hearts against any knowledge or revelation that is in opposition to the Word of God. The Bible warns against what the King James Version calls *"false science."* The Amplified Bible expands the definition of science to read:

> *... irreverent babble and godless chatter, with the vain and empty and worldly phrases, and the subtleties and the contradictions in what is falsely called knowledge and spiritual illumination.* (1 Timothy 6:20)

Whether it is called science, illumination or revelation those who follow it are willfully or ignorantly adhering to Luciferian doctrine. Scripture warns: *"Some people have wandered from the faith by following such foolishness"* (1 Timothy 6:21, NLT[x]).

We have been duped into the idea that everything called science is actually scientific with no agenda other than the pursuit of truth. We fail to realize that the scientific community is financed (thereby controlled) by anti-God groups with corrupt, godless agendas, not the least of which are greed and power. As believers we must reevaluate the thoughts and ideas we have accepted as facts. Historically, the Catholic Church has been notorious for attempting to control science as a means to power over mankind. But since the advent of "modern science" that role has been reversed with a vengeance. Now science seeks to control "religion" as a means to power.

Understanding the events discussed in this and other chapters will provide the basis for seeing the continual goodness and wisdom of God. It will give you the opportunity to finally, factually reject all of the Luciferian doctrines that may have crept into your understanding of God in the Old Testament. But hold on to your seat, what is to be revealed is more shocking than one could ever imagine. As we free ourselves from these faith-destroying lies, we

---

ix Luciferians hold a belief system that may or may not be theistic, that is, they may or may not worship Lucifer as a god. What they do hold in common, like their namesake, is a shared rebellion against God the Creator.

x Holy Bible, New Living Translation ®, copyright © 1996, 2004 by Tyndale Charitable Trust. Used by permission of Tyndale House Publishers. All rights reserved.

will position and equip ourselves to usher in the return of our Lord and King, Jesus, who will bring an end to all that hurts and destroys mankind!

To learn more about the resources mentioned and for additional support material for this chapter please visit www.secondcomingguide.com.

CHAPTER 11

THE ANTICHRIST NATIONS

God never leaves us in the dark. The person who will give up their personal opinions and accept God's revelation will always see clearly so as to never be taken by surprise!

AFTER THE FLOOD WE ONCE AGAIN HAVE THE APPEARANCE OF NEPHILIM.* There is no need to debate how that happened, we just know from biblical record and archeology that it did occur. Goliath is the most recognizable Nephilim after the Flood. We also know they were in Canaan opposing the children of Israel. There is also Og, the King of Bashan, and four other giants that fought against the children of Israel (2 Samuel 20:21-22). These are just a few of the many references to giants after the Flood.

The Nephilim in the lineage of the children of Ham, Noah's son, settled Canaan, the land God would give to Abram. These nations that would forever be thorns in the side of the young nation of Israel worshipped Baal, Ashtoreth and Moloch, to name a few. To Moloch they sacrificed children, specifically their first-born. They were the nations that would seek to break the Israelites down from within through compromise. It would be the very nations God told Israel to destroy that would ultimately corrupt them to the point of abandoning God.

Nimrod established his anti-God kingdoms all across the region from Egypt to modern Iraq. These would become the super-powers of the day. They would attack Israel from without and seduce them from within. In fact, these nations are the very nations that will ultimately comprise the ten last-days nations that come together under the leadership of the antichrist.

Remember, the goal of Satan and his representatives is not peaceful coexistence; it is annihilation of all that God loves. He is not offering man an alternative lifestyle, but eternal destruction.

It is paramount that we understand the ultimate goal of these nations is the removal of all knowledge of God from the face of the earth. The super-powers of the region would never have been able to overthrow Israel and take her citizens captive if the people had remained loyal to Jehovah. Like a virus that slowly cripples the health of the human body, these nations persisted in undermining the faith of the children of God.

When God sent the children of Israel into the Promised Land, He commanded that they completely annihilate these nations. The casual reader may have difficulty reconciling the love of God expressed through Jesus and what seems to be the genocidal tyrant of the Old Testament. This is where the Luciferian doctrine coupled with historical and biblical ignorance form the basis of the angry God doctrine that has turned much of the world against Jehovah while giving birth to an incredibly negative and crippling theology.

Remember, the goal of Satan and his representatives is not peaceful coexistence; it is annihilation of all that God loves. He is not offering man an alternative lifestyle, but eternal destruction. He entices mankind to discover "complete freedom" by abandoning a wrath-filled God. Satan knows he is doomed. He has no illusion of winning the battle against God or escaping eternal damnation. His goal is the genocide of the human race and the destruction of Planet Earth. But it is not enough that men die, he desires that men die an eternal death.

Allowing those nations to continue assured the breeding ground for the antichrist who would bring the worst tribulation the world has ever known. We are not talking about people who had some simple sin issues. (These heathen nations went as far as to burn their children alive in the fires of Moloch and breed excessive moral corruption through sexual worship.) God's insistence that those specific nations be eliminated was to protect the children of Israel and the world from constant war and religious compromise. Even more, He sought to protect them and the world from the antichrist nations that would arise in the last days to bring tribulation on all the earth! God was moved by love and compassion for the innocent that would suffer needlessly at the hands of the perverse anti-God religions. Nearly all global terrorism today is the result of Israel's humanistic rationale that refused to obey God's command!

He has no illusion of winning the battle against God or escaping eternal damnation. His goal is the genocide of the human race. But it is not enough that men die, he desires that men die an eternal death.

The Book of Daniel is one place where we can see the unquestionable accuracy of a true prophet. But Daniel also presents one of the clearest pictures of all the nations that will arise to oppress Israel and provide the breeding ground for the antichrist who will oppress and torment the entire earth! Daniel 2:32-35 records the dream of King Nebuchadnezzar.

> *This image's head was of fine gold, its chest and arms of silver, its belly and thighs of bronze, its legs of iron, its feet partly of iron and partly of clay. You watched while a stone was cut out without hands, which struck the image on its feet of iron and clay, and broke them in pieces. Then the iron, the clay, the bronze, the silver, and the gold were crushed together, and became like chaff from the summer threshing floors; the wind carried them away so that no trace of them was found. And the stone that struck the image became a great mountain and filled the whole earth.*

The King sought the dream's interpretation through his wise men, astrologers and soothsayers, but he refused to tell them the actual dream lest they fabricate the interpretation - just one of many examples that the devil cannot read minds. Only Daniel, who gave all the credit to God, not only tells Nebuchadnezzar his dream, but also provides the interpretation.

The King sought the dream's interpretation through his wise men, astrologers and soothsayers, but he refused to tell them the actual dream lest they fabricate the interpretation - just one of many examples that the devil cannot read minds.

Nebuchadnezzar saw a great statue-like image in his dream whose body parts revealed successive nations, each of which would dominate Israel. So, Daniel provided the interpretation of Nebuchadnezzar's dream, which along with subsequent visions not only tells us what nations shall arise, but the nature of those nations. You will notice each nation is made of a lesser quality of metal, reflecting their depreciation of greatness. The gold head represented Nebuchadnezzar and the nation of Babylon which is presented as a lion in Daniel 7. The silver chest and arms foretell of Media/Persia. In Daniel 7 he sees them as a bear with one shoulder raised, representing the superiority of one nation over the other. Again in chapter 8 it is portrayed as a ram. The brass loins represent Greece. In Daniel 7 Greece is portrayed as a leopard indicating the speed with which Greece, under Alexander, will conquer the world. The iron legs depict the Roman Empire which is divided into the eastern and western aspects of the country. In Daniel 7 Rome is seen as a vicious monster. The iron and clay feet and toes represent the ten last-days kings who will give their authority to the antichrist.

This is the beginning of just a few biblical prophecies and dreams which provide the clearest understanding of the significant nations that will play a role in the end times, prior to the return of Jesus. These are the nations that seek to destroy Israel and ultimately the Church. Regardless of any other historical factors, it is these nations we must watch if we are not to be taken unaware.

Fortunately, Nebuchadnezzar's dream and Daniel's interpretation didn't stop there. It ended with a stone being cut without hands that struck and destroyed the final and most horrible of all nations. This stone represents the Kingdom of God! The fact that it is cut without hands indicates this is God's work, not men's. This puts an end to the end times doctrine that tries to present the idea of the Church becoming more and more powerful and righteous until it overthrows the earth and sets up the Kingdom for Jesus' return. It is also the best antidote for those who are so discouraged concerning the spiritual state of the modern Church. While the world is in fear of the great tribulation, we will lift up our heads knowing that our salvation is near.

The Apostle John also brings forth an interesting aspect of his vision of the nations to watch in order to understand the end.

> *"Here is the mind which has wisdom: The seven heads are seven mountains on which the woman sits. There are also seven kings. Five have fallen, one is, and the other has not yet come. And when he comes, he must continue a short time. The beast that was, and is not, is himself also the eighth, and is of the seven, and is going to perdition. "The ten horns which you saw are ten kings who have received no kingdom as yet, but they receive authority for one hour as kings with the beast. These are of one mind, and they will give their power and authority to the beast. These will make war with the Lamb, and the Lamb will overcome them, for He is Lord of lords and King of kings; and those who are with Him are called, chosen, and faithful"* (Revelation 17:9-14).

When using the Bible to interpret the Bible, obscure passages like this become easily understood. Daniel was in the past looking ahead at history that had not yet unfolded. John was in the middle of history both looking back at what had occurred and looking ahead to what was to come. Daniel did not identify the nations that had been world powers and tormented God's children before Babylon. He only looked forward. There were, however, two world powers before Babylon that John saw as he looked back. John saw the five world powers that had already fallen: Egypt, Assyria, Babylon, Media/Persia and Greece. Rome is the nation "that is" at the time of his vision. The one that is to come is the ten league nations that will give their power and authority to the beast. They will make war with the Lamb but He and those that are with Him shall overcome these nations!

If we were to create a series of transparent maps and overlay them we would see that those ancient nations embody the territory of the Old Ottoman Empire, which was the first Islamic caliphate. A caliphate is the rule of all Islamic nations and all Muslims world-wide are under the rule of a single political-religious leader called a caliph. The caliph must be a successor of Muhammad. He will rule those nations under Sharia law*. All inhabitants must convert to Islam, be beheaded or pay a special tax. In the final caliphate no one will be allowed to pay exemption tax; everyone must convert or die.

If we were to create a series of transparent maps and overlay them we would see that those ancient nations embody the territory of the Old Ottoman Empire, which was the first Islamic caliphate.

The ten nations who follow the antichrist will be a caliphate made up of these same nations under the rule of one Islamic ruler, the Mahdi or caliph, who will usher in the Islamic Jesus. Keep in mind, these nations all worshipped Osiris/Baal/Apollo or some other name used of Nimrod. The Islamic Jesus is not the Jesus we worship as believers. He will be a false christ who will work miracles and bring peace to the Middle East. He will present himself as the true Jesus. He will announce that he was never crucified and he never said he was the son of God and he will lead many astray. In fact, he seems to fit the description of the perfect savior for which the New World Order and even the Jews are looking. He will say the message of his deity was a lie of the Christians and then he will acknowledge a false savior. He will be the false prophet on behalf of the caliph, the Mahdi.

These Middle East nations were seeded by and overrun with Nephilim and demons. Regardless of the many names they use, in the end they are worshippers of Satan and are driven by his personal goals and agendas. They have existed for the singular purpose of destroying Israel and ultimately Christianity. If we know a tree by its fruit there is no modern day group or religion as corrupt and murderous as Islam. They exist for the single purpose of bringing an end to the world!

If only Israel had been obedient these nations would not exist to persecute God's people. Once again, however, we see the authority and free will of mankind. They made humanistic choices contrary to God's command that have cost Israel, the Church and the world for millennia. Like believers today, Israel couldn't understand what God was seeking to accomplish. They, no doubt, passed judgment on God and considered His commands to be inhuman and unjust. They chose good and evil for themselves and, as is usually the case, they got it wrong!

We see the authority and free will of mankind. They made humanistic choices contrary to God's command that have cost Israel, the Church and the world for millennia.

SPIRITUAL GUIDE

God sees the end from the beginning and it is impossible for us to understand all the factors in His wisdom. Our job is to *"not lean to our own understanding"* - but to trust and obey. I'm not talking about a legalistic obedience that seeks to earn something from God. I'm talking about a trust that is based on an absolute knowledge of the love of God that leads to faith and obedience. There will be no formula for overcoming in the end times. There is no one-size-fits-all plan. God will speak to every man and those who have ears to hear will hear. Those who have a heart to trust and obey will overcome. Those who judge God's leadership based on carnal, humanistic philosophies will be overthrown.

Today the corrupt governments of the world, under the deception of the Great Harlot, are presenting Islam as a peace-loving nation. They hide the true teaching of Islam. They seek to use Islam to fulfill their own desire to stamp out all knowledge of Jehovah. The jihadists are the perfect proxy for their evil intentions. What these corrupt governments fail to understand is this is something they cannot control. In the end the beast (antichrist nations) will destroy the Harlot. Those who follow her will lose the wealth they crave and economic control of the nations.

We must not allow the Humanist, Socialist, Luciferian philosophies of the world to influence our perception. God's warning to not be unequally yoked with unbelievers is not a call to self-righteousness or rejection of everyone with whom you disagree. It is actually a warning against allowing people to influence your beliefs.

> *Do not be unequally yoked together with unbelievers. For what fellowship has righteousness with lawlessness (iniquity)? And what communion has light with darkness? And what accord has Christ with Belial? Or what part has a believer with an unbeliever?* (2 Corinthians 6:14-15)

Paul draws a comparison between believers and unbelievers, light and darkness, Christ and Belial (Satan). The key word in this passage is "communion." The word "communion" means "to share something in common." Our communion is with Christ. We share in His death, burial and resurrection, and we share God's Word - His light.

Satan was perfect until iniquity was found in him (Ezekiel 28:15). This was the birth of his rebellion. Iniquity is always about pride and rebellion. Whether it is a corrupt government passing laws that reject God's standards or a school that teaches as fact scientific information that contradicts God's Word or a believer who, in the name of love and compassion, tries to influence us with humanistic philosophy, we must withdraw and guard our heart. We are not called to attack, criticize or reject those people; however, we must not allow them to influence our beliefs, behavior or thinking. Deception doesn't begin by believing a lie; it begins in a conversation with a liar.

When Communists seek to overthrow a country they spend years and billions of dollars in a campaign of demoralization. This is done by the media, specifically the news sources. The media slants content to make those who embrace God's morals and values look corrupt or ignorant. Then they corrupt the courts and we accept a perversion of justice. The entertainment industry provides our imagination with every form of evil. But the crowning jewel of demoralization is the educational system. A nation will fall when just one generation is completely brainwashed by false science, Socialism and Humanism.

Once immorality and dishonesty is an accepted way of life those citizens will be ready to cast off what they view as the tyrannical, restrictive oppression of God's morals and ethics. As sin destroys the morals, economy, judicial system and other foundations of righteousness, new, more ungodly alternatives will be introduced, offering false hope. *"If the foundations are destroyed, What can the righteous do"* (Psalm 11:2)*?*

Morality, ethics, love and honesty are not the rules of an unreasonable dictator; they are the pathway to life. No matter who does what and no matter the cost, stay committed to the Lord Jesus, God the Father and His values (commands). When you fail, accept His forgiveness, get up, learn your life lesson and move on! We, like Israel, are surrounded on all sides by those who would force us to compromise. The Church is finally waking up to realize the wicked do not want to peacefully coexist; they want to eradicate us, our values and any mention of our God! If we compromise we will lose our confidence before God and our ability to hear and trust God will be lost!

As darkness grows the grace of God is abounding. Sometimes we get so vexed by the emerging darkness we forget the promise of Scripture: *"Where sin abounds grace does much more abound"* (Romans 5:20). We will not become a weak, impotent Church in the face of our archenemy. We will abound in the grace of God! We will reach *all who hunger and thirst for righteousness.* We will experience an inner strength that surpasses the outer threat! We will usher in the second coming of our King. No matter how great the power and influence of all those nations aligned with the conspiracy of evil, they will be overcome by the Lamb and those who are with Him! What a glorious victory we will enjoy!

To learn more about the resources mentioned and for additional support material for this chapter please visit www.secondcomingguide.com.

CHAPTER 12

THE RISE OF THE GODS

The devil has presented an imposter for every truth essential to our salvation!

THERE ARE MANY ACCOUNTS OF THE CONQUESTS OF NIMROD AND SEMIRAMIS AND THE SPREAD OF THEIR ANTI-GOD INFLUENCE. There is even credible consideration for the fact that Nimrod's kingdom may have begun in Egypt and then spread to Mesopotamia. But the details are not important. What is important is the fact most of the world was conquered and corrupted by this anti-God Christ imposter! This ancient antichrist established the first major governments of the world.

As a Nephilim, Nimrod's ultimate goal was not merely conquering the world. His real goal, which persists to this day, is the spread of iniquity - twisting of the identity of God leading to rejecting Him and His truth. We must remember, the devil and his hosts know their fate is sealed. When Christ returns their eternal doom is enforced. They need the cooperation and the de facto authority of mankind. Until one understands this Luciferian objective world events will seem vague, disconnected and meaningless. On the other hand, understanding the goal helps us understand the process. It is like having a veil removed from our eyes. Suddenly what seems like thousands of years of random events are seen as a pattern of consistent strategy.

At the beginning of Nimrod's reign the landmasses were joined. Spreading his anti-God deceptions to what would become every continent was a relatively simple task, especially for beings with advanced technology, murderous skills and near super-human capabilities. Giants have been documented as tall as 28 feet. Some had two rows of teeth. They had massive weapons. They were very often cannibalistic and historically revered for their fierceness in battle. Not only did they have the power to subdue, they could pass themselves off as gods … and that they did!

Nearly every false religion in the world has legends of gods who came from the stars, had sex with mortals and produced offspring of lesser gods.

Nearly every false religion in the world has legends of gods who came from the stars, had sex with mortals and produced offspring of lesser gods. History records that Nimrod went into Africa, Canaan, Mesopotamia, India and even Europe, establishing a global network of lies. His propaganda will be repeated by humans until Jesus' return and evidently on into the 1000 years Kingdom reign before the last and final battle. No civilization was spared from both religious and political corruption and deceit.

Possibly none has been more influential in spreading the religious deceit into the modern world than the Greeks. Mount Hermon, with its proximity to Phoenicia, was the entry point for the fallen angels and the rise of the Nephilim. Therefore, the Greek world was among the first to witness this supernatural breed of demonic offspring. Greek historians documented the many different gods and their amazing feats. But to the Western world these were considered mythological stories, or at least that is what we are led to believe. In time they were considered the classics of ancient literature and read by millions of westerners. They were even promoted through the Luciferian church: the education system.

With Nimrod's death the demonic horde lost its first hope of a world-dominating antichrist. Remember, Nimrod and Semiramis (Osiris and Isis, Baal and Ishtar, sun god and moon goddess) did everything possible to counterfeit the fulfillment of the prophecy God foretold in the Garden: *"And I will put enmity between you and the woman, and between your seed and her Seed; He shall bruise your head, And you shall bruise His heel."* (Genesis 3:15) It was crucial that they preemptively counterfeit as many aspects of the coming Christ as possible as a means of undermining the faith of the world's population.

In our schools, in what we call the "classics," our children read of the ancient giants and their glorious battles and powers. It is propaganda and indoctrination of the most subtle and deadly form. The lies of these false gods imitate the life and ministry of Jesus - going into Hell and rescuing people, dying and coming back from the dead, fighting with the evil one and a host of other supernatural feats, and are designed to accomplish at least three crucial objectives.

1. To make the life and ministry of Jesus appear copied from these stories.
2. If these stories are to be merely accepted as myth, then all stories of God, salvation and the supernatural can be relegated to the realm of myth.
3. They conceal the true account of world history that would not only validate the Word of God but would expose the anti-God propaganda currently taught as historical fact!

The ancient world was not only one of idolatry, but a world that would produce a global mindset which would corrupt the identity and worship of the true God until the return of Jesus. In polytheism there were hundreds of gods. There were gods for every day of the year and every day of the week. There were gods that oversaw every aspect of human life and emotion. In any life endeavor, whether having children, going to war, protecting against our enemies or trying to find something of value that had been lost, one would seek the counsel and attempt to appease the gods. Ultimately, the gods were in control of everything. Failure to honor or appease them brought a fate wherein one's choices were nonconsequential.

It was this Luciferian doctrine of fatalism ushered into the Church through leaders who were, in fact, lovers of iniquity, that gave birth to the false doctrine of sovereignty*. We all know God is sovereign. He made all the rules. By the laws of creation, good and bad, sin and righteousness were all defined. But through centuries of Luciferian influence in interpreting biblical doctrine we have redefined sovereignty to mean the same as Greek fatalism. God is in control. This is code for "I am not responsible; God is to blame!" This very doctrine and the way it has shaped world beliefs has possibly doomed more people to an eternity without God than any other lie.

> Through centuries of Luciferian influence in interpreting biblical doctrine we have redefined sovereignty to mean the same as Greek fatalism. God is in control. This is code for *"I am not responsible; God is to blame!"*

Fatalism, disguised as the doctrine of sovereignty, paralyzes the believer. It makes one feel that everything that occurs in his or her life is either done by or allowed by God. In our attempts to garnish God's favor we seek to appease Him so He will move on our behalf. Should we fail to satisfy Him we would surely be subject to His wrath. It gives one the sense of attempting to satisfy the payments of a mafia protection gang in order to avoid being hurt or destroyed. We've got to pray enough, give enough and sacrifice enough to appease this angry God or He will make us pay. We fail to realize these very acts of "worship" deny the propitiation of the Lord Jesus. The word "propitiation" means "satisfying of wrath." And it is, in fact, the propitiation wherein one sees and grasps the love of God[i]. The belief in an angry God neutralizes our capacity to see and benefit from the work of Jesus in His death, burial and resurrection.

The Roman polytheistic world, according to the Word of God, was the cruelest of all the world powers up until that time. Interestingly, Romans were quite religious. They prayed several times per day to the various gods they sought to appease. It magnified many of the Greek practices. But the Roman world may have been responsible for one of the most corrupt concepts woven into the fabric of early Christianity: the idea that might makes right.

In the Roman world a military victory was attributed to the gods. This means if you and I worship different gods and I kill or conquer you, that victory is proof of my god's superior power. The Romans then incorporated the gods of all of the countries they conquered into their polytheistic hoard. This accomplished two things: first was the idea that all the gods would then be on their side, giving them favor. Second, by allowing conquered people to maintain

---

i 1 John 4:10, In this is love, not that we loved God, but that He loved us and sent His Son to be the propitiation for our sins.

their own gods the Romans could maintain the loyalty of the masses. This is a practice that was continued in early Catholicism.

Constantine, the first Roman leader of Catholicism (Universalism), had a dream or vision that if he marched his armies under the banner of the cross he could not be defeated. There is no proof or indication that Constantine ever actually became a disciple, but there is monumental proof that he took a pagan thought and incorporated it into Catholicism, much of which has influenced and undermined true biblical faith for nearly 2000 years. The Church of Rome became entwined with the Roman government and existed primarily for the extension of greed and power of carnal leaders. It was simply a world government operating under the guise of Christianity. However, other than terminology there was very little similarity between the teachings of Christ and the apostles' doctrine, and the Church of Rome.

> The Roman world may have been responsible for one of the most corrupt concepts woven into the fabric of early Christianity: the idea that might makes right.

Historians falsely believe the early Church would not have survived had it not been incorporated into the Roman government. But the truth is that it has done more to corrupt the gospel, slow the true Church's spiritual development, and possibly delay the return of the Lord Jesus than any other single factor. The greatest period of growth and expansion in the Church* was before it became an institution. This fusion of government, Christianity and occult undermined nearly everything Jesus did and taught. The end of the miraculous did not end with the death of the apostles; it ended with the birth of the Church as an organization. Through this massive religious-governmental institution the Church lost its doctrine, its purpose, its power and its identity. But God always has a remnant. What looked like total annihilation from the outside did not reveal that there have always been those who have known and walked with God in their heart.

Over time the entire culture of Christianity changed. People were no longer believers and disciples; they were Christians, a meaningless terminology never used by the Lord Jesus to describe us. Being born of the Spirit was replaced with becoming a member of the Church or converting to Catholicism. The plethora of gods that were previously sought for help in daily life were called saints. The idolatrous praying to saints for help with individual problems replaced trust in Jesus and dependence on the Holy Spirit. The word of the pope replaced the Word of God. The worship of Mary, the mother of God (i.e. the queen of Heaven) overshadowed the worship of Jesus. Baptism by immersion and faith in the death, burial and resurrection was replaced with sprinkling, having no symbolism of the cross or the new birth. Repentance was substituted with penance, a corrupt way for the Church to sell the privilege to sin. Hell was deemphasized and focus was placed on Purgatory, a situation for which you could pay to have your loved ones removed. Relics, idolatrous symbols and statues were sought for power instead of relying on the gifts of the Holy Spirit. Priests replaced Jesus. The Word of God was hidden from the commoner and mass (the religious Christian service) was conducted in Latin. Church became identifiable by buildings, not beliefs. Force, torture, war and violent coercion replaced evangelism. Rome was the Church and the Church was Rome. All that was the Church was rooted in iniquity and Luciferian doctrine.

> Being born of the Spirit was replaced with becoming a member of the Church or converting to Catholicism.

Very soon after the resurrection of Jesus and death of the apostles, the Church abandoned the Old Testament. There were many factors which led to this fatal error. Rome hated Jews; therefore, it was beneficial that the Church distance itself from any connection to them. Anti-Semitic fervor was at a high pitch and became a part of the Church's official stance. But I am fully convinced it was more the crooked hearts of the early leaders that led to this philosophical shift than any other factor.

Iniquity in the heart creates a *"crooked"* or *"froward"* heart. He who has a crooked heart bends or twists the Word of God. It isn't that he doesn't understand the Word of God; it is that he doesn't desire to understand it. He has already determined the path he will take to fulfill his lusts. The Bible tells us a crooked heart cannot find good. The worker of iniquity twists the Word of God and then rejects it. They may have some lofty *spiritual* justification or a reasonable doctrinal argument, but from a biblical perspective they are working their own agenda. Their word, their doctrine, their church and their political position are their true priority. They are gods unto themselves.

Like the foolish teachers of our day, they didn't discern the difference between the Old Testament and the Old Covenant. The Old Covenant laid out the terms, the agreement whereby man would relate to God. The Old Testament is a history of God's Word and His people. We are told we should learn from that Word and their examples.

> He who has a crooked heart bends or twists the Word of God.

The Old Testament ceremonies, rituals, sacrifices and holy days are types of what Jesus accomplished through His death, burial, and resurrection. The moment we stop looking to what God's Word says we are only left with human philosophy, vain imaginations and occult lies to interpret what happened through the death, burial and resurrection of Jesus.

It is nearly impossible to wrap our minds around the global conspiracy of unbelief that operates at every level of human life. Whether the conspirators are participants by ignorance, choice, conditioning (education) or wickedness and whether it is by choice or by default, we must come to terms with the fact that there are two… only two realms: the kingdom of this world and the Kingdom of God. One shapes its beliefs by its intellect and corrupt intentions which are forged by false science, false history and false religion. The other is shaped by the Word of God in our minds and the Spirit of God in our hearts.

SPIRITUAL GUIDE

The Apostle John said all that is in the world (the World's System) is the lust of the flesh, the lust of the eyes and the pride of life. There isn't anything else. This is not a call to despair; it is a call to the only true and sure hope. Jesus will return, establish His Kingdom, rule and reign in righteousness and eventually bring New Jerusalem to earth, ushering the true new age of eternal peace and righteousness. Until then we can enter into the Kingdom realm in our hearts. We can experience righteousness, peace and joy through our intimate relationship with our Lord and Savior.

We can live by the Kingdom values revealed in God's commandments about how to treat one another. We govern our lives by the law of love. We can decipher the true principles of a happy and fulfilled life through Jesus' parables of the Kingdom. And we can experience the ultimate eternal joy of introducing others to our Savior! We don't have to wait for the outward expression of the Kingdom. We can enter this internal realm of God's Kingdom through the door of our hearts. It doesn't matter how much we change this world, we only experience the peace of God when it is found within.

In the end another false god will arise. He will come because of the sorrows that plague mankind. Eventually, the world will reach an unprecedented and unbearable level of chaos and tribulation. Through political correctness, fairness, false efforts to make all men equal (Socialism) and the eradication of all the values, morals and standards of God expressed through His commandments (iniquity), we will have a (nearly) Godless world. With the ushering in of the man of iniquity God's definitions of love will be replaced with a carnal, sensual, selfish love and men's hearts will grow cold. Brother will turn against brother, children against parents, neighbor against neighbor and race against race. Many who call themselves Christians will be so tormented and fearful they will sell their souls for the false promise of peace of an external kingdom. Like the false gods of old, the government/occult/antichrist partnership will demand sacrifice, surrender, loss of individuality and the abandoning of all allegiance to God. But we know and walk with God. We will avoid the trap of deceit, unbelief and surrender. We have an internal power *"they know not of!"*

All God has is ours now and all the benefits of His Kingdom can be enjoyed now. By learning to live in our heart, intimately connected with God, we have a peace, power and stability that few possess. But the key is to enter this realm now, in times of relative ease, so it is not foreign to you in times of great chaos. Commit to the Lordship of Jesus. Do not reject any part of His Word, even when you do not understand it. Always walk in love no matter how great of an excuse you may have to do otherwise. Always yield to the voice and leading of the Spirit of God in your heart. Hold nothing back from God. One of the important laws of the Kingdom, based on the parable of the Pearl of Great Price, is that this life, this relationship with God and His trust, must be something you want badly enough to sell all else.

To learn more about the resources mentioned and for additional support material for this chapter please visit www.secondcomingguide.com.

APOCALYPSE

CHAPTER 13

GIANT KILLERS

No matter how big the obstacle there have always been people who believed God and won!

INTIMIDATION HAS ALWAYS BEEN A CORE RESOURCE OF THE EVIL ONE. He, like most humans alive today, has consistently underestimated the fact that man was created in the likeness and image of God; therefore, mankind has an inherent compelling to overcome all obstacles. It is not in our basic DNA to give up. And the nature of God is creative and adaptive. Against all odds and in defiance of all reason, humans will find a way to overcome. This God-seed in the fabric of our being has sustained us against all evil since the beginning and it will be this inherent instinct to turn to God in times of trouble that will answer the call to the last great revival that ushers in the return of our Lord.

Satan filled the earth with violent, perverted, cannibalistic, murderous giant beings that were so impressive and supernatural they were considered by many to be gods, or at least the offspring of gods. While so many surrendered, seeking self-preservation, others died in defiance to these wicked beings. But those who knew their God didn't merely endure, they overcame.

They became giant killers. Like the Hebrew children in Nebuchadnezzar's kingdom they would rather die than be dominated by wicked.

> *"...our God whom we serve is able to deliver us from the burning fiery furnace, and He will deliver us from your hand, O king. But if not, let it be known to you, O king, that we do not serve your gods, nor will we worship the gold image which you have set up."* (Daniel 3:17-18)

In reading the horrors of the previous pages of this book, there may be a tendency to lose sight of the fact that giants are no longer here. They lost the war. They didn't die from natural causes; they were killed by mortal men. Jewish history says the grandson of Seth killed Nimrod. He beheaded the mighty, supernatural hunter of men with a sword. Joshua and Caleb, both in their 80's, chose to take Canaan, a land inhabited by giants. David, a shepherd boy, faced the mighty Philistine warrior, Goliath. He even picked up enough spare stones to kill Goliath's brothers who were also giants. Even in America, giant skeletons have been found riddled with arrowheads, killed by native people with bows and arrows.

Samson compromised his vow to God and was humiliated, blinded and put into chains. He was led into the temple of Dagon, the god of the Philistines, to be tormented in celebration of Dagon's supremacy over the God of Israel. Yet, even a backslidden Samson yielded to the Spirit of God and experienced strength beyond his own that made him able to destroy the idol of Dagon, the entire temple and the Philistines who had gathered against him. The Book of Judges is full of accounts of men and women who trusted God, overcame obstacles and subdued His enemies.

It is easy to read the Old Testament and miss these incredible life lessons. The Old Testament, which serves as an example to us, is history that reveals three simple truths:

1. Those who trust and yield to God overcome no matter what the obstacles.
2. Those who choose to do that which is right in their own eyes are always conquered and destroyed[i].

---

i Judges 21:25, In those days there was no king in Israel; everyone did what was right in his own eyes.

3. All of the examples are crystalized in the man Jesus, the Son of God who emptied Himself,[ii] yielded to the Spirit of God,[iii] experienced grace[iv] and overcame every obstacle… even the cross![v]

It is important that we realize Jesus had to overcome every demonic power in order to rise from the grave. He then stripped Satan of all principality and power before He eternally cast him out of Heaven. The One who lives in us is a greater power than anything the devil has ever imagined. "*… greater is He that is in you than he that is in the world*" (1 John 4:4)*!* Our Lord has already won! And the same Spirit that raised Christ from the dead abides in us!

Religion has robbed us of our capacity to always win and always overcome. The warning of the Apostle John seems to fall on deaf ears as Religionists swallow up antichrist doctrines, robbing us of the ability to function as our Lord modeled. Overlooking this Scripture has cost millions of believers their lives and their victories.

> *By this you know the Spirit of God: Every spirit that confesses that Jesus Christ has come in the flesh is of God, and every spirit that does not confess that Jesus Christ has come in the flesh is not of God. And this is the spirit of the Antichrist, which you have heard was coming, and is now already in the world.* (1 John 4:2-3)

Religion only accepts what fits into the finite, natural mind. The fact that Jesus, the Son of God, could somehow empty Himself and live within the limitations of man does not equate in the carnal mind. It opposes the Luciferian doctrine. As such, the example Jesus provided is of no value or hope to the average Christian. If Jesus did what He did on earth as God, then His life means nothing for us. If, however, He did empty Himself and do everything

---

ii Philippians 2:5-8, Let this mind be in you which was also in Christ Jesus, 6 who, being in the form of God, did not consider it robbery to be equal with God, 7 but made Himself of no reputation, taking the form of a bondservant, and coming in the likeness of men. 8 And being found in appearance as a man

iii Acts 10:38-39, God anointed Jesus of Nazareth with the Holy Spirit and with power, who went about doing good and healing all who were oppressed by the devil, for God was with Him.

iv John 1:14, And the Word became flesh and dwelt among us, and we beheld His glory, the glory as of the only begotten of the Father, full of grace and truth

v Hebrews 12:2, looking unto Jesus, the author and finisher of our faith, who for the joy that was set before Him endured the cross, despising the shame, and has sat down at the right hand of the throne of God.

as a man yielded to the Holy Spirit, we now have the perfect model for how we can experience life. We can fulfil the assurance of John 14:12-13 *"Most assuredly, I say to you, he who believes in Me, the works that I do he will do also; and greater works than these he will do, because I go to My Father."*

This promise can only be grasped by those who accept the fact that Jesus became a man just as we are in every way, yet without sin, and yielded to the Holy Spirit for His miraculous power. The last thing Lucifer wants you to know is you can do everything Jesus did and greater. This would be the unraveling of his plan for revenge. If you see yourself as you really are then *"... no weapon formed against you shall prosper"* (Isaiah 54:17). You would be impervious to his strategy. In fact, you would realize you are more of a threat to him than he is to you!

The last thing Lucifer wants you to know is you can do everything Jesus did and greater. This would be the unraveling of his plan for revenge.

There are many variations of antichrist doctrine. One of the religious versions is to create a false exaltation of Jesus. In most religious circles considering Jesus to have emptied Himself to become as a man is sacrilege. Yet, John makes it clear that the refusal to admit Jesus became a real human man with a real physical body is an antichrist doctrine inspired by the spirit of the antichrist for your destruction. The moment you stop seeing Jesus as a man full of the Holy Spirit you disqualify yourself from being able to do what He did.

During Jesus' days on earth Satan tried to subtly slip in this antichrist doctrine that He was not really a man. The demons in the demoniac cried out, *"Son of God have you come here to torment us before our time"* (Matthew 8:29)? This passage reveals two things. Firstly, the demons know the time of their torment is eminent and inescapable. Secondly, they were challenging His authority to act in earth. If He acted as the Son of God He was violating God's Word. God had given authority to man so only man could operate in authority on earth. Jesus repeatedly explained that He had authority in the earth because He was the *Son of Man,* not because He was the *Son of God. "For as the Father... has given Him authority to execute judgment... because He is the Son of Man"* (John 5:26-27).

Jesus clearly stated, *"He who believes in Me, the works that I do he will do also; and greater works than these he will do, because I go to My Father"* (John 14:12). The question is, do we believe on Him as the Scripture says or do we believe on Him as religion says? If you think He worked even a single miracle from His power as being God you have been seduced.

"He who believes in Me, the works that I do he will do also; and greater works than these he will do, because I go to My Father" (John 14:12).

It is such a paradox. He is God in the flesh. He is still the Son of God, but subject to **all** the limitations and temptations of man. In His life He modeled two perfect pictures. He showed exactly what God is like. Everything He did is exactly what God would have done were He here bodily, and He showed exactly what man would do if he believed the truth about who he is in relation to God and yielded to His Spirit.

SPIRITUAL GUIDE

Jesus was the ultimate giant killer. Now His disciples, those who actually believe what the Bible says about Him, His life, His death and His resurrection are potential giant killers. But Religionists have established unscriptural doctrines that provide a breeding ground of iniquity. Every denomination and every movement has woven through its doctrinal fabric some degree of Luciferian doctrine, thereby, in some manner, limiting the life of its adherents. This is why I always encourage new converts to at least read the Books of John and Acts before selecting a church. Without a biblical model of what the Church should preach and how it should influence society most people will choose a church based on where their family attends.

But you, as an individual believer, must never take on the "party spirit," that is denominationalism or loyalty to a group beyond how it empowers and facilitates your ability to more effectively serve God and our world. It is spiritually and emotionally beneficial to be a participant in a biblically-based church. However, while maintaining healthy relationships with those who lead, you must not allow any person to become an intermediary between you and Jesus as Lord. You must become a student of the Word, not in a way that merely bolsters your ego through intellectual stimulation, but as a disciple seeking to follow Jesus as Lord. Everything God ever said is valuable for life and godliness as long as it is never twisted into legalism or used as a substitute for a personal relationship with Jesus as Lord.

The concept of Lordship has been all but lost to the subtle undercurrent of iniquity that has become interwoven in fabric of most religious environments. Convenience outweighs convictions. In some circles obedience is viewed as bondage. In others obedience is considered the path to righteousness, which is simply dead works. If love, however, is our primary intention and goal, loving God, loving people and loving (valuing) ourselves, every aspect of the gospel takes on new meaning. God's commands about how we must treat one another become our standard of love. His commands about how we should live are an expression of loving ourselves; thus, none are burdensome. None are done to earn anything from God. They are observed because of our trust and reverence for God, the Father of perfect love.

As believers who believe the truth about God and the Lord Jesus, we fully commit to trust all of the Word of God. As disciples of the Lord Jesus we commit to apply it to our lives based on what He modeled in His life and teaching. The student of the Bible seeks to know what the Master knows. The disciple of the Lord seeks to live as their Lord lives.

As disciples, when we see beliefs or behavior that would not be present in the life of Jesus we put off the old man, that is any behavior, thought or idea of ourselves that is in conflict with who the Word of God says we are. We then renew our minds based on the Word of God so we think about ourselves and others as His Word proclaims. We then put on the new man. This is where we choose to believe what His Word says about our true identity. We no longer see ourselves as separate from Him. As He is so are we because we have been made one with Him. We choose to believe we can do what He did, and when the need arises, the power (grace) will manifest in us through the Holy Spirit. We know we can live as He lived.

By allowing ourselves to be absorbed in Him and His identity we realize we were in Him when He stripped the devil. He is in us when we face the devil. We too are giant killers. Like Joshua and Caleb, by His might and power we will possess our inheritance!

To learn more about the resources mentioned and for additional support material for this chapter please visit www.secondcomingguide.com.

APOCALYPSE

CHAPTER 14

THE ETERNAL REMINDER

The most brutal bully is the one who couldn't win the fight but bluffs his opponents into submission.

WHILE MAN HAS CONSTANTLY BEEN DECEIVED ABOUT THE STATUS AND STRENGTH OF THE ETERNAL PLAYERS IN THE HEAVENLY CONFLICT, NEITHER GOD THE FATHER NOR LUCIFER THE FALLEN ARCHANGEL, HAVE FOR A MOMENT LOST SIGHT OF THE ETERNAL REALITY. The moment he was incapable of overthrowing the heavenly throne Lucifer knew his fate was sealed. When he approached the human race through the body of a serpent it was obvious he could not forcefully overthrow mankind. Every time he resorts to deceit instead of power he and his demons are reminded of the massive failure of their grand scheme.

Through misinformation man has been held in darkness concerning the true status of fallen angels, which provides false hope for the Luciferians and fear for God's children. From the earliest times the Luciferian doctrine has covered the earth like a plague. Contrary to the popular religious ideas, it has not been passed on to this generation because Satan has whispered it in the ears of the unsuspecting and innocent. It has been passed on by humans from one generation to another because this is what they believed and it is what they were often taught in church.

Iniquity, which is the twisting and ultimate rejection of God's truth, is passed from generation to generation by parents, teachers and others in authority. Truth is not just what the Word of God *says;* it is also all that it implies. As man, through religious thinking, twisted the image of God to be inconsistent with His name he ignorantly destroyed the capacity of future generations to know and trust God. This was usually done through the misuse of Scripture; when that which is true is applied with the wrong motive it is no longer truth. Luciferian, New Age and cult doctrine is a compilation of Scripture and lies. By misinterpreting Scripture, moving a person through a logical sequence of extrapolation that ends in iniquity becomes easy.

The more Luciferian doctrine was woven into Bible doctrine the more the concept of dualism* dominated our beliefs about the devil. Man has suffered from three main areas of delusion that constantly force a misinterpretation of the Bible to some degree:

1. Failure to see God as He is
2. Failure to see man as he is in Christ
3. Failure to see Satan as the defeated foe he is

The Bible tells us there will come a day when we see Satan as he is. However, we need not wait until the Kingdom comes to see the truth and free ourselves from fear; we can see him as is really is now.[i] According to this Scripture, we will be amazed at the pathetic being that once destroyed kingdoms and oppressed the world.

> *How you are fallen from heaven, O Lucifer, son of the morning! How you are cut down to the ground, You who weakened the nations! For you have said in your heart: 'I will ascend into heaven, I will exalt my throne above the stars of God; I will also sit on the mount of the congregation On the farthest sides of the north; I will ascend above the heights of the clouds, I will be like the Most High.' Yet you shall be brought down to Sheol, To the lowest depths of the Pit. "Those who see you will gaze at you, And consider you, saying: 'Is this the man who made the*

i Satan Unmasked

> *earth tremble, Who shook kingdoms, Who made the world as a wilderness And destroyed its cities* (Isaiah 14:12-17).

After Lucifer's first defeat in Heaven his every experience has been a constant reminder that he will spend all of eternity in Hell. According to the Book of Enoch, Azazel and the watchers (the fallen angels who mingled their seed with the human race) prevailed upon Enoch to intercede on their behalf in pursuit of forgiveness from the Almighty. But they discovered, just as their predecessor in rebellion had discovered, forgiveness could not be granted. The Nephilim were the spirits of fallen angels with a physical body. When the bodies of the Nephilim died, according to Enoch, this left them as disembodied spirits roaming the earth looking for humans who would facilitate them, which was another reminder of their abysmal failure.

After Lucifer's first defeat in Heaven his every experience has been a constant reminder that he will spend all of eternity in Hell.

In time God established the nation of Israel with its ceremonies and sacrifices. Those sacrifices provided types and shadows of many spiritual realities yet to come. They were only shadows of the wonderful things God would do in the New Covenant, but as a shadow they provided a basis for mankind to establish vision and faith for what God would do in the future. But there were also ominous types and shadows that served as reminders of the eternal doom of the fallen angels. One of the most clearly expressed pictures of doom may have been the scapegoat.

James R. Spillman, in his masterful book, *A Conspiracy of Angels*[ii], presents the persuasive possibility that the scapegoat is not actually a type of Christ.

The sin offering involved two goats (Leviticus 16: 7-22). One was sacrificed to God on behalf of the people, but the second goat was brought to the priest who laid hands on him and imparted the sins of Israel. He was then sent away into the wilderness. In English the goat is called scapegoat and in Hebrew he is called Azazel. James Spillman describes this event and its meaning perfectly:

---

ii http://www.truepotentialmedia.com/product/a-conspiracy-of-angels/

> We see that this *"scapegoat"* is not only left alive, unlike the other goat, but is to be sent away into the wilderness with the conferred sins of Israel on its head. The first part of verse 22 sums up the purposes of the scapegoat: *"And the goat shall bear upon him all their iniquities unto a land not inhabited."* We have already spoken of the seven Hebrew words for *"goat"* in the Old Testament; the word for scapegoat was not one of them. *"Scapegoat"* is used but four times in the entire Bible and all four uses are in Leviticus 16. The Hebrew word found here translated *"scapegoat"* is *"AZAZEL"*. It is defined as *"a demon of the wilderness, a fallen angel."* The literal meaning is *"goat" (AZ) "going away" (AZEL).* Of the two goats the first was a sin offering and the scapegoat was the separation from sin. Azazel is a word that we have seen before in our study of the names of the fallen angels. In the Book of Enoch, Azazel was introduced. He was listed as one of the leaders of the fallen angels. 1 Enoch 10:8 is especially enlightening regarding Azazel: *"And the whole earth has been corrupted through the works that were taught by Azazel: to him ascribe all sin."* What a revelation! *"Scapegoat"* which is spoken of just four times in the Bible and all in one chapter, is the translation of *"Azazel"* in the Hebrew. Azazel is not just a Hebrew word for the English word *"scapegoat,"* but is the Hebrew name for a fallen angel who is blamed for all sin! How fascinating! The devil who is *"ascribed all sin"* is the very same animal namesake that carries all the *"iniquities, transgressions and sins"* of Israel on his head into the wilderness. Notice that this second goat, this scapegoat, is not a sacrifice unto God for its blood is not shed. Some have taught that this scapegoat was a type of Christ, the lamb of God, bearing the sins of man far away from him. But the scapegoat was a goat, not a lamb, and was not killed and its blood was not applied in the holy place. The blood sacrifice for Israel's atonement was made before the scapegoat was released into the wilderness.[iii]

Every time a sin offering was made every demon saw a graphic portrayal of its eternal doom. Azazel, the angel who led the rebellion, had to bear the sins of the world into Hell. While man may not have known the significance of this

---

iii A Conspiracy of Angels, James R. Spillman

metaphoric message it was trumpeted to the entire world of fallen angels. You have already lost the battle and you will spend eternity separated from God!

According to Enoch, the fallen, disembodied spirits of the Nephilim are what we know as demons. These may not be the same fallen angels that are bound in the bottomless pit that fell with Lucifer.[iv] The demons that now exist live in absolute knowledge of their eternal and soon-coming doom. No place in Scripture is this made clearer than when the demons cried out to Jesus, *"Have You come here to torment us before the time"* (Matthew 8:29)? The entire underworld abides in constant fear and dread of their day of torment.

There is, however, one event where Satan's absolute defeat was solidified more than any other time in history: the resurrection. The resurrection was more than a man simply being raised up from physical death. It was a man who had become the sins of the world, suffered all the consequences for that sin and then rose from the dead, righteous before God! There were so many "shared aspects of the cross" that forever changed everything.

When Jesus died for our sins we died with Him. When He was raised up to God we were raised up with Him. When He conquered and stripped all principalities and powers we were in Him. Jesus became all the curse of the law; thus, all the handwriting of the law that was against us was wiped out (Colossians 2:14)! Now there was no longer any legitimate means for Satan to condemn us or, more correctly, for us to condemn ourselves.

When Jesus died for our sins we died with Him. When He was raised up to God we were raised up with Him. Jesus became all the curse of the law; thus, all the handwriting of the law that was against us was wiped out (Colossians 2:14)!

Upon His resurrection Colossians 2:15 says, *"Having disarmed principalities and powers, He made a public spectacle of them, triumphing over them in it."* In the original language this does not speak of the mere winning of a battle but of winning a war and the following triumphal procession.

---

iv Jude 6-7, And the angels who did not keep their proper domain, but left their own abode, He has reserved in everlasting chains under darkness for the judgment of the great day;

When an enemy terrorized the countryside it was not just important that the king conquered the enemy, it was essential that the citizens have rest from their fear. They needed knowledge of their king's victory and subsequent protection from harm. When the triumphal king conquered his enemies any number of debilitating, humiliating things may occur. For example, they may line up the family of the failed king and slaughter them before his eyes, then they may burn or gouge out his eyes. It was believed that the last thing seen before blindness stayed burned into one's memory forever. This would strip him of any hope of ever being delivered by his heirs. All hope of a future victory was quelled. All his future days were languished by the certainty of continual doom.

It was believed that the last thing seen before blindness stayed burned into one's memory forever.

In some cases they cut off the thumbs and the big toes. This made it impossible for him to ever stand in battle or hold a weapon of war. This not only made him a non-threat in his own awareness, it proved to the citizens that he could never again rise up against them.

Then he would be caged or sometimes tied to the saddle of the conquering king to be displayed in the streets. The conquering king would lead him down the streets lined with citizens who would spit on him, throw rotten vegetation on him, kick at him or pelt him with rocks. All fear of this enemy would be eradicated. Life could once again return to normal productivity. Peace ruled in the hearts of the citizens.

In the spiritual world Jesus had a triumphal procession in the stripping of **all** principalities (rank) and powers (right) of the wicked one. It is documented in God's Word and experienced by those who believe. But some do not believe God's report; they believe the Luciferian report that says Satan is powerful. When you sin you give him your authority. But the fact is **all** authority was given to Jesus in Heaven and in earth. Despite the foolishness of religious Luciferian doctrine we can't give authority to the devil. Beyond all comprehension, after such an absolute victory some still do not believe. Some still fear the wicked one.

As long as we abide in fear of the evil one we can be manipulated, controlled and driven to double-mindedness. The tribulation of the antichrist will not be done by the power or authority of Satan; it will be the plan of Satan working through the power and authority of wicked and/or fearful human beings. Our God is the supernatural God with the supernatural power. Our Savior has authority in Heaven as God and on earth as man. At His return we will rule and reign with Him. We will be among the armies that trample the antichrist and his hordes.

Our Savior has authority in Heaven as God and on earth as man. At His return we will rule and reign with Him.

SPIRITUAL GUIDE

As the day of evil approaches let us learn to live in the authority of men created in the likeness and image of God. Let us do the works of God that all may see and believe the truth about our loving heavenly Father. Let us equip ourselves with the faith, obedience and mind of the Spirit to help deliver the weak and fearful in the day of evil. But by no means should we bow our knee in fear to the wicked one who survives only as a deceiver and liar. The more we lead others to Jesus and to a realization of their true identity in Christ, the more we hasten the day of the Lord's return.

Every time we are victorious over sin, each time we win a person to Jesus and each time we break the power of the wicked one in the life of a human being the entire underworld is reminded that Christ is in us and we are greater than any power they possess. Satan is reminded of his imminent eternal ending. To him it is as if there are millions of Jesuses walking Planet Earth. Our victorious life is a terror to the fallen ones… the Azazels.

Let us determine that we will quell every fear we have of the devil by reminding ourselves of Jesus' triumphal procession. We need not wait until the return of our Lord to see Lucifer's defeat. If we will embrace it now in the Word of God the Holy Spirit will quicken it to our heart. Armed with truth we will live in power, love and a sound mind. We will be vessels suitable for the Lord's use. We will usher in His final return!

To learn more about the resources mentioned and for additional support material for this chapter please visit www.secondcomingguide.com.

CHAPTER 15

CONCLUSION TO SECTION TWO

World history shows us the world without God; biblical history reveals the world with God. We are the ones who decide how our world will be!

THE HISTORY OF THE WORLD APART FROM GOD IS DARK AND HOPELESS. As we look at the reign of power-hungry tyrants, oppressive religions and corrupt governments we see a glimpse of the world the evil one desires. We also see an evil world that evil people desire.

We must always remember the evil that is occurring in the world is not the result of the power of the devil; it is the outcome of the evil desires of mankind. Selfish, power-hungry, greedy men are looking for a way to skirt around God's standards of morality, integrity, justice and love. Evil does not make them do the things they do. They do the things they do because they love the ways of darkness. It is a way to get what they think will make them happy.

The corrupt have taken up a godless mantra, "the survival of the fittest" and used it to justify murder and oppression since the beginning of time. In their estimation if they are able to kill you, they deserve to be here and you do not.

It is the same philosophy woven through the fabric of all elitists and through all Luciferian doctrine. The history of the world reveals it.

From the rebellion of Satan to the Flood and then from the Flood to the Church Age we see a desperate grab for world domination. This effort is successful everywhere except in a tiny nation that came to be called Israel. When they walked with God they were invincible. Solomon was admired and feared by the rulers of the world. He counseled kings and queens in the ways of justice and righteousness until he was seduced by the allure of compromise.

In our legalistic mindset we think these people who walked by faith were moral giants, but they were just like us. God worked around their personal failures and moral struggles.

The greatness of God's people was not, however, seen in a nation that walked with God. It was revealed in individuals who, regardless of the evil in the world and corruption in their own nation, walked with God. They are our examples of faith and godliness.

This period of time in the Bible reveals so much about the patience and mercy of God. In our legalistic mindset we think these people who walked by faith were moral giants, but they were just like us. God worked around their personal failures and moral struggles. The key with these people was they just kept getting up, facing their sin and reconnecting with God… **and God still used them mightily!**

We see in this period of time a very important factor we must keep in mind: **God gave authority on Planet Earth to man.** He works through man to the degree man will allow it. We see that God is never late or slack concerning His promises but men are very often late in deciding to fully trust and follow God.

Abraham, the Father of Faith, disobeyed God repeatedly. He didn't go to Canaan when he was told. He took his family along (which had deep roots in idolatry). He was about 25 years late arriving in Canaan, which resulted in hardship. He went into Egypt when he was told not to. He was even willing to give his wife to a king to save his own life. He brought a concubine back from Egypt. It took another seventeen years for him to finally believe the truth that God had promised him from the beginning.

We see that Abraham wasn't just the Father of Faith, he was the Father of Faith-Righteousness. *"He believed God and it was counted unto him as righteousness"* (Romans 4:3). Despite his personal failure he trusted God to act from His own integrity and faithfulness and be limited by Abraham's weakness. Moses, when called of God, resorted to murder trying to accomplish God's plan. As a result he spent 40 years in the wilderness delaying the deliverance of the children of Israel. In his anger he misrepresented God and was not allowed to go into the Promised Land.

The people God used were flawed. They didn't justify their flaws. They didn't turn it into some perverse doctrine. They kept getting up and following God.

The people God used were flawed. They didn't justify their flaws. They didn't turn it into some perverse doctrine. They kept getting up and following God. If God used these people surely He will use people like us… *"men of like passions."* It was these flawed, struggling human beings that became the giant killers who subdued kingdoms.

When I read the stories about the people God used I realize some very important things:

- We must never disqualify ourselves.
- No matter how many times we fail we should always get up.
- My faith is in God's faithfulness, not my righteousness.

But the most important thing about this I think we must realize is even if every person in the world were to turn against us and seek to destroy us, we will prevail if we trust God with all our heart! *"Do not fear, little flock, for it is your Father's good pleasure to give you the kingdom"* (Luke 12:32).

SECTION THREE

APOCALYPSE

CHAPTER 16

INTRODUCTION TO SECTION THREE
The Church to the 20th Century

Never count God or His people out; where sin abounds grace always abounds more abundantly. We are here to stay and we are here to win!

THE BOOK OF ACTS GIVES US THE DYNAMIC HISTORY OF THE EARLY CHURCH BEGINNING IN JERUSALEM WITH THE HOLY SPIRIT BEING POURED OUT ON BELIEVERS AND THE GOSPEL SPREADING THROUGHOUT MUCH OF THE KNOWN WORLD. Just as it was in the Old Testament, there are parallel histories occurring seemingly independent of one another, but in truth they are deeply entwined.

The early Church, under the leadership of the apostles, clearly understood Jesus' commission. While there was much about Jesus' commission which the early Church was unclear, they were crystal clear on the fact that the Church was to evangelize the world, making disciples of every man. History reveals that the most rapid growth coupled with the most pure state of existence was in those first years when the Church was more of a living organism and less of an organization.

The early Church was by no means flawless and God is more than willing to provide us with an unbiased account of their mistakes and conflicts. The early Church was like every new believer, they had a life-changing, palpable experience when they were born again. They experienced what it was to know God apart from the burden of legalism. The problem was they had no doctrinal basis from which to explain their experience. This proved to be especially problematic for both the Jewish and Gentile Church.

The early Jewish Church had an identity crisis that is played out over the upcoming centuries; they worshipped the same God as Gentile believers but they probably still considered themselves corporately to be Jews, but individually to be disciples of Christ. This conflict sets the stage for a theological battle that is raging until this day.

Jesus as a Teacher was viewed much like a rabbi. In fact, John the Baptist, who would have been in line to be the last high priest of the Old Covenant, related to Jesus much like acknowledging any new rabbi. When Jesus was baptized He had two reputable witnesses validate not only Him as a person, but as a Teacher of God's Word. By doing this, Jesus had "fulfilled all righteousness" concerning a rabbi (Matthew 3:15-17). We know Jesus had true authority because He spoke God's Word. Regardless of how persuasive an individual might be, when he or she departs from God's Word they no longer have true authority. In the eyes of the people He had authority because His ministry had been validated by John, a reputable prophet and a lineage of the priesthood. But Jesus' second witness was the voice of the heavenly Father.

The early Church did not yet have the teaching of Paul and the other apostles; they had the words of Jesus, the man whose words and life they trusted.

The early Church did not yet have the teaching of Paul and the other apostles; they had the words of Jesus, the man whose words and life they trusted. Jesus had told them to take His yoke upon them. His yoke was His interpretation and implementation of truth: God's Word. In the Hebrew world doctrine was not mere philosophy; it was a way of life. The problem with all doctrine up until Jesus came was that it relied on men with a sin nature who had never seen God for themselves to not only interpret God's words, but to explain and model what they should look like when applied in real life. This brought about a complicated legal system with hundreds of laws for daily living. There was no way they could ever fulfill all those requirements. All those laws could do was leave those who sought to follow them with an acute awareness of failure.

Jesus brought truth. Truth is not a new set of laws or rules. It is the true intention and application of all God had said. He did not come to do away with the Old Testament words of God. He came to show us what they should look like if applied the way God had always intended – with love as the motive. The stability of those early believers was not that they had all their doctrines defined; it was that they knew becoming a believer meant becoming a disciple of the Lord Jesus. They saw the truth and freedom in Jesus' teaching and the life He modeled. They took His yoke (the way He taught and implemented God's Word) upon them. They found, just as Jesus had promised, when God's Word is applied with love as the motive, the commandments, which had been made so burdensome by the rabbis, were undeniably easy and light. This clinging to Jesus and God's Word was the strength and stability of the early Church. From the birth of the Church until the 20th century the world became darker and darker to the degree that the Church and world abandoned God's Word.

The early Jewish Church was soon accosted by Judaizers. These were people who believed on Jesus but still believed obedience to the law was what made one righteous. They attempted to mix the Old and New Covenants. It was to this issue that much of the Apostle Paul's writing was focused. As he so aptly pointed out, mixing the Old and New Covenants only served to neutralize grace. Grace was the component that delivered man from functioning in his flesh, his own strength (Galatians 2:21).

In the New Covenant righteousness was received apart from works of the law as a result of being baptized into and putting on Christ. In Him we live and abide in His righteousness. Accepting His righteousness gives us access to grace, God's ability, whereby we stand (Romans 5:1-2). For centuries Jews had lived under the traditions handed down to them through these teachers. Every moment of their lives was consumed with fulfilling the law, but what the Jews taught was not God's law. In Mark 7:9 Jesus clearly differentiated between God's commands and their traditions which had come to be considered the law. God's commands were never legalistic; it was their interpretations that made the commandments legalistic. It was from this legalistic mindset Jewish believers fought to free themselves.

The Bible clearly identifies the apostles' role as maintaining a doctrinal foundation that is built squarely on the life and teachings of the Lord Jesus as the chief cornerstone (Ephesians 2:20 & 4:11-16). The apostles' doctrine, like all teaching, was at first passed down orally. In time, as the Church grew, it began to be written in letters and was always aimed at recovering believers from erroneous doctrine that was not actually built on God's Word, with Jesus' life and teaching as the focal point for interpretation.

The Gentile Church faced another threat. They didn't have a foundation in the Word of God. They did not understand the significance of the Old Testament as the basis for all truth. They had limited knowledge of the sacrifices, ceremonies and holy days and probably didn't realize without those types and shadows they would never understand the New Covenant.

Gentiles, like Jews, had the tendency to interpret the Word of God based on their personal traditions which Jesus said would make the Word of God of no effect (Mark 7:13). Jesus, not our traditions, philosophies, opinions or personal experiences, is the only basis for interpreting the Word of God.

So Lucifer, "the bringer of light," adjusted his strategy to fit the new era dawning on Planet Earth. The Word of God had reached the ends of the earth. If the Word could not be stopped it could at least be neutralized. His strategy was to establish man's own intellect as the cornerstone for interpreting God's Word. When the Word lost its effectiveness man would soon abandon it for the deceitful promise of "enlightenment." "Enlightenment" appeals to both ego and greed, but without all those pesky commandments there would be no moral or ethical boundaries. Satan's new mask was intellectualism.

Universalism or Theocrasy* became the most potent tool available. Theocracy (with a "c") and a theocrasy (with an "s") are not the same. A Theocrasy is the combining of all gods into one. The word "Catholic" means "Universal." Catholicism was the birth of Universalism as a cultural acceptable approach to Christianity. "Believing" was replaced with "conversion." The new birth was substituted by baptism. Discipleship was replaced by catechism. The Word of God was replaced with the word of the pope. The Catholic Church was a gross mixture of sun god worship, Christian terminology, Old Testament priesthood and nearly every other cult in the known world. What began as a "state church," making Christianity the official religion of Rome, ended with using force and tyranny against true Christianity and driving it underground.

The kings of Europe twisted the Word of God to justify their supreme reign; fighting against the king's tyranny was equal to fighting against the Church. The only way to break the yoke of unfair regents was to undermine their twisted, scriptural authority by disproving the existence of God. Free from belief in God, the masses could free themselves from the unjust yoke of the ruler's perverted application of His Word, thus abandoning themselves to intellectualism.

It was in this period, from the birth of the Church to the 20th century, that Lucifer would desperately work through unscrupulous men to build his church through secret societies, corrupt governments and wicked men of iniquity. Everything that happened from the birth of the Church to the 20th century set the stage for the arrival of the New World Order in 2012. Mystery Babylon would seduce governments and leaders through the allure of wealth, power and the idea of an elitist utopia* indulging the every whim of the enlightened while ridding the world of the ridiculous, antiquated idea of religion.

Everything that happened from the birth of the Church to the 20th century set the stage for the arrival of the New World Order in 2012.

Simultaneous to the Great Harlot taking control of the nations of the world there would be a resurrection of the Nimrod-antichrist kingdom. A caliphate* of nations would form their own theocrasy. All the false gods they worshipped would be incorporated into one religion: Islam. While the kings of the western world were secretly implementing their diabolical plan to take control of the world's wealth and dominate all mankind, the antichrist nations would be growing in an apocalyptic fervor to bring an end to the world. The two will grow side-by-side and will seek to use one another to facilitate their diabolical end game, that is to destroy all that God loves.

SPIRITUAL GUIDE

Right now a new Book of Acts is being written in a heavenly record. All we can see is a gross darkness emerging on the earth. With our natural eyes we cannot see that, peppered through every church in the world as well as outside of the formal Church, a new kind of believer is coming up. Men and women who, like those in the early Church, will not compromise. They will perform incredible tasks that will make the greatest miracles of the Bible seem commonplace. This new breed is sold out, committed, and ready to live or die for the Kingdom of God. Up to the 20th century the road has been paved for the greatest evil the world has ever known, but God always preserves a remnant.

The Church is like Samson. Yes, we have been corrupt, weak and carnal but there is a remnant that, like Samson's hair, is growing back. As we believe the truth in our hearts we are awakened to our true identity in Jesus. We too will destroy the enemy that has oppressed us.

The more you connect to God in your heart, the more you have an inner awareness of that which cannot be seen. Elisha prayed for the eyes of his servant to be opened, so he would not fear the great army that had come against them (2 Kings 6:16-17). When his eyes were opened, he saw the angels that surrounded them providing protection. As we see with the eyes of our hearts we too will see that there are more with us and they are more powerful than those that are against us.

If we see only with our physical eyes our hearts will sink with fear. But as we develop our ability and willingness to hear and follow the voice of the Lord we will see the world more and more from His perspective. We will not fear the darkness; we will be the light in the darkness.

To learn more about the resources mentioned and for additional support material for this chapter please visit www.secondcomingguide.com.

APOCALYPSE

CHAPTER 17

THE RISE OF ATHEISM: THE ROOT OF REASON

In the art of Luciferian deception it matters little if one believes the lies about God or denies His existence, the outcome is the same!

EXTREME ANCIENT RELIGIONS HELD MAN IN BONDAGE FOR AS LONG AS POSSIBLE BUT THEN THE INEVITABLE HAPPENED, PEOPLE BECAME TIRED OF BOWING AND SACRIFICING TO THE GODS. In what would seem to be acts of incredible courage, men began to defy the gods. If harm came to them it would be by the hands of worshippers of the gods who, because of fear of divine judgment or mere cultural addiction, would seek to avoid divine retaliation by killing the "blasphemer." However, in the absence of the action of religious zealots nothing harmful happened to the violators; Atheism was free to bloom.

The rise of Atheism didn't work against the Luciferian plan, it actually caused a quantum leap forward in the destruction of mankind. Atheism was not just a reaction against false gods and demonic tyranny of the Nephilim and their followers; it was against any concept of God. It is always the way of the evil one, whether in religion or politics, to create the problem then offer a solution that actually creates more of the same - oppression and control under another name. We have to remember, even though anyone who sought the true God would find Him, there was little accurate knowledge of God. Jehovah, to most of the world, was just one of many gods. When people stopped believing in Zeus they stopped believing in any god so Atheism gave rise to something even more deadly than the Nephilim. In the absence of the false gods man finally fulfilled the original temptation; he became a god unto himself and exalted his own intellect and reason.

The children of Abraham were the only "tribe" that knew the truth about Jehovah but nearly as soon as the tribe became a nation Judaism was corrupted by self-righteous legalism and a superiority mentality. Rather than creating a *"house of prayer for all nations"* it had become religious segregation. In the beginning other nations feared Israel because when they applied God's wisdom they triumphed and prospered. When they walked in their own wisdom the nation was weakened by political and religious corruption. They didn't want to be the nation who brought a Savior to the world, they wanted to be the nation that ruled the world under the leadership of their imagined version of the Messiah.

In the absence of the false gods man finally fulfilled the original temptation; he became a god unto himself and exalted his own intellect and reason.

They should have recognized Jesus when He came. They knew, according to the prophecies of Daniel, almost the exact year the Messiah was to be born. Scripture was very clear about Him coming the first time as a suffering Savior. He would fulfill all the types expressed in the Jewish sacrifices. But this wasn't the kind of Messiah the Jews wanted. When He came they rejected and killed Him. As was the history of the Jews they wanted a king and a savior *"like the other nations."* They didn't want an internal kingdom ruled by the Holy Spirit in their hearts, always applying truth from the perspective of love. They didn't want God's Word in their hearts and they didn't want an intimate relationship where they could grow in character, love and the fruits of the Spirit. They wanted a military leader to break the governmental oppression of the pagan nations. They didn't want to change, to become more God-like, they wanted the world to change and they wanted to rule it.

It didn't take long after the resurrection for power-hungry, carnally-minded men to highjack "Christianity." As the Church alienated itself from the Jews and took on a more Gentile influence it lost its understanding of the Old Testament as the foundation of all knowledge of God. Without the Old Testament foundation it soon lost any real sense of God's character. Without knowledge of the sacrifices and ceremonies as types and shadows fulfilled in Jesus it soon drifted into philosophical explanations of the cross. In the Western Roman Empire the Church began to drift away from the apostles' doctrines, allowing Gnosticism and other occult doctrines to become the basis of interpreting the finished work of Jesus, as well as the teaching of Paul. This laid the foundation for the rise of Catholicism (Universalism).

It didn't take long after the resurrection for power-hungry, carnally-minded men to highjack "Christianity."

The Catholic Church intentionally incorporated all manner of Paganism into its practices and dogma. Catholicism looked so much like Paganism, pagans could integrate into its membership without having to make any major changes in the way they worshipped. All of the symbols of sun god worship and other rituals of Paganism were incorporated into Catholicism. They shared the same holy days and many of the same rituals. The Catholic priests wore the same garb as their priests, and their buildings were copied after the temples. Catholicism claimed to be the only true church; therefore, to most of the world it was the Church. This political-religious institution, masquerading as the only true church, was corrupt, power-hungry and demonically driven with only the occasional casual, coincidental similarity to biblical faith.

While the Apostolic Church was committed to the teachings and lifestyle of the Lord Jesus, Catholicism was corrupted by power-hungry men seeking their share of glory, power and wealth. The way of Christ was replaced with the way of the Luciferian gods. In their bid for power and conquest, doctrines of demons, mysticism and force became the way of the Church. Love was rejected or redefined into sadistic concepts that justified torture and murder. Such torture and murder done in the name of Jesus forever crystalized this pagan concept of Christianity in the minds of the masses. For many, the Roman Church is their only concept of church. Much of what the world hates about God and the Church is based on the atrocities of a counterfeit that had nothing to do with the worship of God or the Lordship of Jesus. With the birth of the Catholic Church we have the rise of what we will henceforth call the Religionists*.

The Religionists, rather than existing to point people to the internal realm of the Kingdom of God, sought to establish a kingdom in the external realm. The Church of Rome became incredibly powerful as a political-military entity and kings sought it as a means of shoring their ability to rule over men. The tyranny of kings was facilitated by the institution called the Church. Favors were sold to the highest bidder. For a price, royalty could commit sins, murder their enemies and oppress the poor. They purchased indulgences from the Church that were supposed to absolve them of their sins.

For many, the Roman Church is their only concept of church. Much of what the world hates about God and the Church is based on the atrocities of a counterfeit that had nothing to do with the worship of God or the Lordship of Jesus.

The doctrine of the Bible was replaced with the doctrine of the Church. Twisted doctrines (iniquity) extrapolated from the Bible were used to justify flagrant corruption and abuse. Like all cults they used Bible terminology to justify their actions; they simply gave new, false definitions to those words. On nearly every level the Church became the oppressor of the people. Like pagan religions of old they coerced their worshippers' loyalty through fear and ignorance. Perceptions of Jesus and God the Father were based in part on the gods of old.

In order to rid mankind of religious brutality through the Church, the masses would overthrow the established religion and replace it with a new religion: **reason.** Carnal man likes to think he is secular, little does he realize that making himself god is still a religion.

Reason was the new religion and intellectualism, philosophy and science were its denominations. But reason had to have Atheism as its single defining purpose. The Nephilim taught man much of the knowledge that was to become the beginnings of science. Some of this information became the basis for rejecting God. Reason was the logical look at the world, but it was only considered intelligent reason if it emerged from the intellectual rejection of God. With incredibly limited knowledge and a foundation built on demonic, secret science philosophy was man's subjective attempt to explain the world, life, the purpose for our existence and all the other questions that haunt man concerning his origins.

Philosophy, seemingly independent of religious thought, actually became the gospel of the new religion. Make no mistake, philosophy was not, however, free of religion. Any process of thought that is a reaction to a previous thought is defined by the previous thought processes. Extreme religion gave rise to extreme *logic* which was, in fact, more illogical reasoning. This was merely the new expression of Humanism, which began in the Garden. No one cared what philosophy or science believed as long as God was not at the center of the equation. It must fulfil man's objective to be his own god. As his own god he could define morality, justice, love, ethics and spirituality. With the collapse of the old gods came an intellectual basis for iniquity. Now it would no longer be man giving in by force to godlessness; it would be man compelled by his own ego and greed to reject God's standards and exalt his own.

Extreme religion gave rise to extreme *logic* which was, in fact, more illogical reasoning.

Catholic dogma was the perfect vehicle to inspire violent reactions to God. The knowledge of God had been handed down orally until it was put into written form. In Job, the oldest written book of the Bible, God challenges Job concerning his subjective, philosophical reasoning. Job's beliefs about God had been colored by Paganism. He assumed God was testing him; that was, after all, the pagan idea of the gods. The poor translation of the Book of Job into English contributes even more to these theological misunderstandings. Job, like most men of the world, didn't know or trust God even though he was a man who sought to live a godly life.

God challenges Job's ideas and judgments. God asks him where he was when He set all the laws of physics in place and created all that exists. But we are quick to take Job's ignorant words and quote them as sound doctrine while completely ignoring what God said about Job's theology. When God finally begins to speak He says: *"Who is this who darkens counsel by words without knowledge"* (Job 38:2)? Until that time we had 38 chapters of Job's vain ramblings and perverted theology. Sadly, we trust his words more then God's. Job's reasoning was the subjective philosophy based on the vanity of man seeking to explain that for which he has no proof or knowledge. God challenges Job and brings Job to the reality that he didn't know what he was talking about.

Then God asks him questions he cannot answer concerning creation and the character of the Creator.

> *Now prepare yourself like a man; I will question you, and you shall answer Me. Where were you when I laid the foundations of the earth? Tell Me, if you have understanding. Who determined its measurements? Surely you know* (Job 38:3-4ff)!

After God's questioning, Job sees the light and so aptly answers the question:

> *You asked, "Who is this who hides counsel without knowledge?" Therefore I have uttered what I did not understand, things too wonderful for me, which I did not know. Listen, please, and let me speak; You said, "I will question you, and you shall answer Me." I have heard of You by the hearing of the ear, but now my eye sees You. Therefore I abhor myself, And repent in dust and ashes* (Job 42:3-6).

Job's flawed reasoning is revealed. In Job 4:17 the question is asked, *"Can a mortal man be more righteous than God?"* This is the core of iniquity. Iniquity, in the name of love, in the name of social justice, in the name of fairness and often in the name of Jesus rejects God's commands for how we should treat one another. The nature of God's standards of integrity and honesty is replaced with human reasoning (justifications). This is man saying "I am more righteous than God!" Job saw the error of his foolishness and said, *"I am righteous, But God has taken away my justice. Should I lie concerning my right"* (Job 34:5-6)? Job had blamed God for his suffering which was rooted in Luciferian doctrine that blames God as the source of pain and suffering.

But Job's justice was flawed; his concepts of God were not true and he would not lie as a means to prove himself right. Unlike occult literature that hides and twists the truth, God's Word reveals the flaws of His followers. Historical books show the error of the people so we can learn by their example. Our tendency is, however, to turn their flawed logic into our doctrine.

Even when the Church or Paganism gives man the intellectual ammunition to blame God for sufferings, at the core the real problem is that man, unless he is born of the Spirit and alive to the voice of the Spirit, is a god unto himself. As such his ego will always drive him to prove himself right. God asked Job, *"Would you condemn Me that you may be justified"* (Job 40:8)*?* The answer for Job and for the human race has historically been, "Yes, I will either deny there is a God and blame my fellow man, or I will believe in God and blame Him. But I will not take the blame or responsibility for my circumstances!"

In this new enlightenment man became too wise in his own eyes to believe in any of the gods. Lucifer's goal to destroy what God loves works best when man destroys himself and blames God. While the strategy stayed the same, the tactics changed to facilitate man's new sense of enlightenment. This gave rise to denial of the old gods but the information gained from those gods would be passed on in the form of classical literature as a means to numb the pseudo-intellectuals toward the supernatural. The limited knowledge passed on through the fallen angels would be the basis for the most lavish, egotistical appeal coupled with inaccurate information and it would be called Science. After all, it appeals to man's ego to see oneself as so intelligent to have no need for God. Worship of Lucifer, for the most part, would be hidden in corrupt governments and secret societies. These two entities seem to be the crystallizing of the two branches of Luciferian thought that would bring about his last and greatest attempt to overthrow the world. Atheism, the rejection of morals, is the perfect partner in adultery with the Great Harlot (Mystery Babylon). Although influenced

Even when the Church or Paganism gives man the intellectual ammunition to blame God for sufferings, at the core the real problem is that man, unless he is born of the Spirit and alive to the voice of the Spirit, is a god unto himself.

by the Harlot and guided by secret societies atheistic governments lead the world into iniquity and give rise to the antichrist nations.

In the Church's grab for power, blatant worship of the old gods was forbidden and punishable by death. This is ironic considering the presence of the images of the old religions in every aspect of Catholicism. There is no way to know if the true intention was some twisted commitment to Christ, the consolidation of power or simply a means of eliminating any competition for power. The hypocrisy of a murderous Church using the name of Jesus as its justification for violating so much of God's Word is beyond comprehension.

Like all things enforced by brutality, it never changes people's hearts, it simply causes them to be more secretive. All the persecution of the Church served to do was force Satanism underground which gave rise to secret societies. The secret societies flourished in the ascetic life of denial embraced by the early monks. Asceticism is, after all, a Luciferian doctrine. It is the religious abstinence from pleasure. It is the reason monks, priests and nuns are not allowed to marry. Pleasure is evil… not just evil, evil in the eyes of God. The ascetic doctrine is the basis for the vow of poverty. It, like all Luciferian doctrines, was incorporated into a corrupt Church and is now woven through the doctrines of major Christian denominations and movements. Paul calls ascetic philosophy the doctrine of demons.[i] Both inside and outside the Church secret societies flourished and gained more and more influence.

Like all things enforced by brutality, it never changes people's hearts, it simply causes them to be more secretive. All the persecution of the Church served to do was force Satanism underground.

Atheism grew from the Luciferian doctrines of the old gods being projected onto the true God. Only in the biblical view of man does God give man authority, the capacity to choose his own destiny. Only in biblical faith is man even given the choice of obeying God. In all other versions, including the

i 1 Timothy 4:1-4, Now the Spirit expressly says that in latter times some will depart from the faith, giving heed to deceiving spirits and doctrines of demons, 2 speaking lies in hypocrisy, having their own conscience seared with a hot iron, 3 forbidding to marry, and commanding to abstain from foods which God created to be received with thanksgiving by those who believe and know the truth.

corruption of the Bible, man is forced to serve the gods. Jehovah is the only God who desires a love relationship as a father loves his children.

Flawed concepts of God gave rise to reactionary atheistic logic. Epicurus, an important figure in Atheism posed:

> Is God willing to prevent evil, but not able? Then he is not omnipotent. Is he able, but not willing? Then he is malevolent. Is he both able and willing? Then whence cometh evil? Is he neither able nor willing? Then why call him God?[ii]

God was not only denounced through philosophy but, in time, He was denounced by science. But science is a religion with man as god and man's logic as its truth. Scientists, by faith, start with an unknown, unprovable opinion they intend to prove. They then establish a protocol for testing that is limited to their opinions. It is like gambling with a fixed deck. The house always wins. It is the ultimate of humanistic, willful self-deception.

God was not only denounced through philosophy but, in time, He was denounced by science. But science is a religion with man as god and man's logic as its truth.

Humanism, the worship of self, man as his own god, science as his bible and philosophy as his logic drove the godless pursuit of carnal, lust-fulfilled living justified behind a respectable mask of social order, pursuit of knowledge and the desire to make the world a better place for mankind. But the real intention has always been to throw off the controls of a righteous God.

Mystery Babylon, the initiation process into the secret worship of the old gods, never went away. It is a constant in science, philosophy and governments. To the world at large all the motives and efforts of these institutions seemed noble and even selfless; but at each level of initiation the true motives became more clear. Whether it is greed, control, ego, idolatry or Atheism at the end of the pursuit, iniquity drove the logic and the logic became the justification for more iniquity. People want what they want without their conscience bothering them, without the Church condemning them and without

---

ii Epicurus 341-271 BC

the loss of social acceptance. In iniquity-driven psychiatry the experts told people to reject their constraining beliefs in God and morality to find true freedom in self-indulgence. All mental and emotional problems will go away if only you rid your imagination of God. Thus the reality: an Atheist is so because Atheism is a necessary means to what he truly desires. God *as He has been presented* by the Religionists is an obstacle to a truly fulfilled life. Guilt is the product of false moral standards. No God… no guilt!

People want what they want without their conscience bothering them, without the Church condemning them and without the loss of social acceptance.

SPIRITUAL GUIDE

Contrary to corrupt religious doctrine, there is much accepted dogma the Bible doesn't say. It is this false doctrine that is playing a role in the great falling away. Today there are more people converting to Islam than to faith in Jesus. Many of those converting are people who grew up in nominal churches that twist God's Word. For example, the guilt you feel in response to violating God's standards is not the Holy Spirit making you feel guilty; it is your own conscience that recognizes the violation. When we identify God as our source of pain and sin as our source of pleasure it is only a matter of time until we find ourselves running from God and toward sin.

Another popular Luciferian concept is that God puts a person in pain and suffering as a way to force him to repent. God doesn't draw you to Himself through pain and suffering. The Bible says just the opposite: it is the kindness (goodness) of God that leads to repentance (Romans 2:4). Suffering is not the means whereby we learn to escape temptation. We escape the corruption in the world through the promises of God.[iii] Temptations exist because we have desires intermingled with unbelief. Every temptation begins with a natural God-given desire. We may corrupt and twist it into something defiled but no desire is evil within itself. When we do not believe there is a godly way to fulfil our desires and be happy we seek other means.

God wants us to be happy and fulfilled. He created us. He knows what will truly destroy us and what will bring us life. His commands are divine prescriptions for life at its best. Jesus delivered us from all the curses of the law. He qualified us for all the promises God ever made to anyone. Those who know the loving character of God and the faithfulness of His promises never resort to looking beyond the bounds of His Word for fulfillment.

God is good and only good. In any area where you doubt God's goodness you are vulnerable to a trap. Establish your heart and mind in the love of God expressed through the death, burial and resurrection of the Lord Jesus, and very specifically in the fact that He delivered you from the wrath of God.

It is essential that as the days become darker we do not blame God for what is coming on the world. It is the tendency of man to make a mess of life, family,

---

iii 2 Peter 1:4, by which have been given to us exceedingly great and precious promises, that through these you may be partakers of the divine nature, having escaped the corruption that is in the world through lust.

nation and the world and then blame God. *"People ruin their lives by their own foolishness and then are angry at the Lord"* (Proverbs 19:3, NLT). We must accept the world is where it is because man chose his own logic over the truth of God's Word. But even though mankind caused the problem God will never abandon anyone who calls out to Him with a true heart, trusting His Word.

To learn more about the resources mentioned and for additional support material for this chapter please visit www.secondcomingguide.com.

CHAPTER 18

SATANISM: THE ROOT OF ALL LAWLESSNESS

Satan cares not what form he takes or with whom he makes an alliance as long as the result is the destruction of that which God loves!

SATANISM IS LIKE A CORPORATE CONGLOMERATE THAT HAS ITS TENTACLES IN SO MANY ENTITIES THAT WHAT APPEARS TO BE OFFERING OPTIONS AND FREEDOM OF CHOICE IS A RUSE. True freedom does not exist when one source is controlling all the options. The illusion of options is necessary to distract and pacify us as our lives are being overthrown. The illusion of freedom is one of the greatest of all seductions!

By the Middle Ages Luciferian thought covered the earth. There were few, if any, cultures on the face of the earth untouched by its twisted religious doctrines. By and large the world believed God was angry, wrathful, hard to please, ready to execute vengeance, quick to anger, slow to mercy and basically unjust. God's laws that this twisted doctrine purported were designed to keep man from the freedom discovered through the knowledge Lucifer, the light bearer, brought to us.

Religionists reinforced the corrupt image of God. Just like the religions of the old gods, fear and ignorance were the primary means of controlling the masses. The Religionist Church did everything possible to pervert the Word of God through its instructions and forbid the people free access to the Bible. Thus, an old doctrine of demons reemerged and, as is typical in Luciferian strategy, presented itself with a new face: Lucifer is the source of light, the bringer of civilization and freedom. He is good and God, the Creator, is evil. In Gnostic doctrine, as well as in the doctrine of many modern cults, God the Father is portrayed as one of the lesser gods. According to some, Jesus and Lucifer are brothers. Proof of the Creator God is based on the fact that there is evil in creation. The perversion is magnified by the question, "If God is good why does He allow evil things to happen?" This doctrine is driven so deeply into modern thought that even believers who see the love of God in the New Covenant cannot reconcile the God of the Old Testament and Jesus in the New Testament.

This Luciferian logic goes on to say God wanted to keep man in the dark but Lucifer defied God and gave man light, that is, enlightenment. When the New Testament talks about darkness versus light it is to this very conflict that it refers. This doctrine sought to overthrow the early Gentile Church and is prevalent today. The Old Testament was an unfolding of God's character and nature. Likewise, it was an unfolding of His plan to bring a Savior into the world. His Word (commands), His name and how that was all presented through the Lord Jesus are all congruent unless twisted by religious thought. To the degree our view of God is inconsistent with His name, His Word and the life and sacrifice of Jesus, we abide in darkness. Luciferian doctrine has its strength in man's ignorance of the Word of God coupled with his egotistical need to mold an image of God that suits his intentions.

During the Church Age there was an incomprehensible irony. The worship of Nimrod, Apollo, Baal, Osiris and even Moloch was driven underground, existing primarily in the form of secret societies. Yet, these idolatrous practices and beliefs were everywhere in the Universal Religionist Church. The worship of Nimrod had morphed through many disguises, but it never ceased to exist. It simply manifested in a new name in whatever country currently dominated the world. In Babylon it was Baal, in Egypt it was Ra and Osiris and in the Church it was some perverse mixture of Christ and Nimrod plus Mary and Ishtar and the saints. Based on the culture Lucifer adapted his presentation, but the goal was always the same, to destroy what God loves. Likewise, the tool, iniquity, never changes!

There are some very polarizing dichotomies forever present in the worship of God and the worship of Lucifer. To some degree you see these strategic operations in many entities. Every organization, church, government or business reveals its doctrine in its strategies. Sadly, many organizations committed to Christ employ demonic strategies, not recognizing them for what they are. The Kingdom of God is always straightforward: this is what we believe, this is what we are asking you to do, this is what it will cost (in terms of your life), and this is the promise. You must be personally responsible for your actions and their consequences. You must make your own choices and live with your outcome because we will never use force. We will accept you and love you but we will not do for you what you can do for yourself. If you believe God raised Jesus from the dead and trust Him as your Lord you will be empowered to live in His identity and nature.

Sadly, many organizations committed to Christ employ demonic strategies, not recognizing them for what they are.

All Luciferian-driven entities are just the opposite. We do not initially reveal our true agenda; we find a humanistic, socially-acceptable mask to enlist the unsuspecting. In the beginning you are convinced it will cost nothing. You are not considered to be responsible for your actions, decisions or consequences. Society is responsible for what has happened to you. We will do for you what you should do for yourself. We create a reward for working our system, but since that reward never materializes exactly as promised we keep changing the process and blaming others. We only expose you to our true beliefs by degrees (initiations, whether formal or informal). Once you have bought into and fully committed yourself at the level of your current knowledge, we will "pull back the curtain" and show you a little more of our true beliefs and intentions. You are not responsible; let us fight your battle and save you. Lying and deceit are acceptable means of accomplishing our goal; after all, we are right and the end justifies the means. Force, coercion and intimidation are always acceptable tools. Human life is an acceptable casualty in our lofty pursuits.

One of the most utilized entities of these Luciferian organizations, political parties and religions are what Communists call *useful idiots,* people on the periphery. They are idealistic, misinformed, driven by lofty, unrealistic pursuits or sometimes they simply share a common enemy with the cause. Useful idiots have no real understanding of the true goals of the party or organization; they blindly serve and give. Some never grasp the real purpose. Communists have found college students to be most suitable for this role. They have been brainwashed in college, learning forms of government, psychology and economics that have never worked. They embrace political philosophies that have enslaved and murdered millions, yet through idealism and zeal* they are fully convinced they would work under a new name with a new leader. They have never built a business and many have never had a real job, but they are the self-proclaimed geniuses of enlightenment. These are the worker bees of Luciferian societies, governments and organizations.

One of the most utilized entities of Luciferian organizations, political parties and religions are what Communists call *useful idiots,* people on the periphery.

Despite some of higher education's benefits, by and large it has been the main indoctrination point for Luciferian thought throughout the world. It matters not how humane the stated purpose or how lofty the goals, that which rejects the truth about God as revealed by His name, His Word and His Son, is Satanism. As Jesus said, *"He who is not with Me is against Me, and he who does not gather with Me scatters abroad"* (Matthew 12:30). It does not take much leaven, even in an organization that has a godly intent, to defile the entire process and in the end do more harm than good.

As Luciferian thought spreads throughout the world it will take on many forms. It will make alliances with those it hates and intends to destroy when they share the same enemy. It is this permeation of all cultures that makes the believer, the true worshipper of Jesus, seem so out of place. Just as it has occurred many times in history, those who know their God and know the truth are treated as the enemy - the enemy of government, the enemy of social justice, the enemy of science, and yes… the enemy of the compromised Religionist Church.

To understand the unseen hand that guides the kingdoms of this world we must understand their king. Satan is the father of all lies about God and man. Since man was created in the likeness and image of God, to pervert how man sees God is to pervert how man sees himself. Satan's only purpose is to steal, kill and destroy, and he will do anything to accomplish those goals. However, there is indication that even though he will fulfil men's lusts to lead them down the path of destruction, he hates even the corrupt momentary pleasures man enjoys on this path. A true Satanist hates bringing any joy to anyone, even if it is for the purpose of their demise.

There are three key forms of Satanism. There is theistic Satanism that believes in God, the devil and the supernatural. This is a form of Dualism that believes God and Satan are pretty much equal in power. They are seen as engaging in warfare to determine the fate of the world and the winner has not yet been determined. Idolatry in any form is included in this group. This is the Luciferian doctrine embraced by most of Christianity which languishes in disbelief of Jesus' absolute victory through the death, burial and resurrection. These are the believers that will struggle in the upcoming tribulation. They don't believe the battle has been won; therefore, they take on a method of spiritual warfare. Through their good intentions mixed with ignorance they actually deny Jesus' absolute victory over Satan at the resurrection. They take it upon themselves to accomplish, through spiritual warfare, what they refuse to believe Jesus already accomplished. In this form of Satanism allegiance is given to the devil by the wicked with the hope of assisting in overthrowing God. Following Satan is the means to fulfil desires in this life. They hope to take over the world, eradicate all mention of God and gratify all their lusts in a world with no moral absolutes. This, with a few twists, is the form of Satanism embraced by many secret societies.

Atheistic Satanism is quite different. This is the type of Satanism popularized in America by Anton LaVey, writer of the satanic bible. This form denies the existence of God, the devil and the supernatural. It is more of a philosophical approach that deifies self-fulfillment. According to LaVey, self-centeredness is Satanism; thus, man lives for the sole purpose of self-gratification. Child molestation, torture, mutilation, sadism, masochism and any other forms of sexual deviancy are all acceptable if they bring the perpetrator pleasure. As LaVey presented in his teaching, self-gratification is the purest form of Satanism. According to some sources, LaVey did believe in a personal Lucifer who attempted to overthrow God; like many secret societies the more loyal were initiated into his true belief in Lucifer. Truth is not effective for recruiting and deception. It only belongs to those who have been initiated to a high level of trust and self-deceit.

Lastly, there is what I consider to be the most extreme and dangerous form of Satanism. I call it True Satanism. This is where the followers hate God and

His ways. They consider love and mercy to be foolish weaknesses. They know Lucifer attempted to overthrow God and they intend to help him complete that effort. This disciple of Satan knows he will spend eternity in Hell. Most likely he believes Satan is the prince of Hell and he will rule in Hell with him. His only hope and joy is the same as that of the devil: to destroy as much of what God loves as possible. This person destroys for the sake of destroying. This form of Satanism has brought the greatest horrors imaginable on the world and has cost the lives of millions of innocent people. It is this form of Satanism that drives Communism and its various masks of Socialism and Progressivism.

Satanism often manifests in force but quickly reverts back to deceit if confronted with equal force. If one truly seeks to understand the philosophies of Satanism there are few entities we can observe that follow the playbook more than Communism. Few people realize that Karl Marx was a True Satanist. He hated God, God's Word and God's ways and it didn't stop there. He hated the world. According to his own writings he knew he would spend eternity in Hell. Communism, Socialism and Progressivism were all birthed from True Satanism. Most of Marx's books have never been released to the world. If the world knew his true beliefs and intentions Communism and its many faces would never have survived. Marx even hated Socialism. He hated the momentary pleasure it brought mankind but saw it as the only vehicle whereby he could enslave the world. He hated the pretense of caring for the human race.

Marxist Communism sought to overthrow the world by force. Later when force failed, deception became the workable strategy. This is where we can gain wisdom. If Satan was as powerful as he presents himself he would not use deceit, he would take over by force. The ultimate expression of force will only come when, through the New World Order and antichrist nations, he finally believes he has enough of a majority oppressed, compromised or in agreement to conquer the world and eradicate all knowledge of God. Even then it will not be Satan who unleashes his mighty power; it will be the power of the people who give their allegiance to him. Keep in mind, the oppression Satan needs to conquer the world is through the means of iniquity. He must bring you to disbelieve God's Word and His commands. He must, through your own unbelief, alienate you from the grace (power), peace and leadership of God!

When Satanists (Communists, Socialists, Progressives or any other name they use) overthrow a country they have to first take that country through a phase called "demoralization." Immorality, drugs and other destructive vices are just the infancy. The news media must be controlled by those who embrace the philosophy of enlightenment and is the propaganda arm of the effort. The judicial system must be corrupt, justice needs to be difficult and the laws need to be contradictory and hard to understand. But the greatest tool of demoralization is the educational system. Through false science and rewritten history children become unbelievers, Agnostics and Atheists. Morality, ethics and godly standards are replaced with a righteousness defined by the state. All things godly are questioned, ridiculed and denied while all things corrupt are presented as fair and reasonable.

> When Satanists overthrow a country they have to first take that country through a phase called "demoralization."

Demoralization is not simply the attempt to lead people into immoral living; it is the attempt to lead people to lawlessness (iniquity). Destroy the consciousness of God. Let man determine good and evil for himself and he will oppress himself. Faith in the heart of a believer is what the devil fears more than anything else. A human being with immovable faith cannot be conquered even if he can be killed. Therefore, demoralization is the most important phase - not just the demoralization of the country, but the demoralization of the people. Communists (Satanists) have been surprised at how long it has taken to weaken America to the point of collapse. In the 70's they thought they had eradicated the knowledge of God enough to accomplish their godless goals in just a few years.

Once demoralization is accomplished they collapse the economy and blame it on conservatives or any group that embraces any degree of freedom or godly standards. When the economy collapses the real fun for the Satanist begins. A massive acceleration in riots, crime and murder occurs. Justice is perverted, man's right to protect himself is taken away, good is called evil and evil is called good. Local governments are so overburdened and underfinanced only the federal (centralized) government could possibly meet the need. The useful idiots are either from wealthy families or living on entitlements. The average working person trying to care for his family is caught in the middle and cries out to the government for protection, not realizing it is the government that has trained and is financing and organizing the chaos. The government, ever willing to help, will only require the free man to surrender the last of his freedoms to the government in exchange for protection and all will be well. But it will not be well! It is almost like the ancient legend of the vampire;

he can only come into your home and drink your blood if you invite him in. Once we are demoralized the state is our source of hope and protection.

> The useful idiots are either from wealthy families or living on entitlements. The average working person trying to care for his family is caught in the middle.

Like Nimrod, the great hunter of men who stood in defiance of God, every Luciferian government and entity has followed a similar path for thousands of years. It is his plan to overthrow any government that allows freedom, especially freedom of religion. In the book, *Rules for Radicals,* Saul D. Alinsky outlines how to overthrow nations with chaos, the way of Lucifer. One might wonder how I arrived at the conclusion that Saul Alinsky and those "community organizers" and government leaders that follow his book are Luciferian in thought. Simple! The dedication in the front of the book is as follows:

> Lest we forget at an over-the-shoulder acknowledgment to the very first radical: from all our legends, mythology, and history (and who is to know where mythology leaves off and history begins- or which is which), the first radical known to man who rebelled against the establishment and did it so effectively that he at least won his own kingdom – Lucifer.
> – Saul Alinsky[i]

i Alinsky, Saul D. (1971) *Rules for Radicals.* Vintage

SPIRITUAL GUIDE

One might decry, "You make it sound like there is evil everywhere!" My only reply is, *"all that is in the world is the lust of the flesh, the lust of the eyes, and the pride of life."* Yes, just as it was in the days of Noah, the entire world has been infected. This time it has not been with the seed of the Nephilim but with the teaching of the Nephilim, the Luciferian doctrine. Just as it was in the days of Noah, we are surrounded on every side. In the natural there is no hope for the believer. But we are not in the natural. We are in Christ! Our Savior and Lord will return and we will rule and reign with Him! The Bible warns us of these days. The signs of the times are everywhere. The Book of Revelation is unfolding before us and rather than prepare our hearts we prefer to fight against the truth. Those who fear reality make themselves victims to reality. They are like the inexperienced driver who obsessively over-focuses his attention on the oncoming car, thereby driving the car into a head-on collision.

We have to recognize these things but keep our eyes on Jesus and His promises or our hearts will fail us from fear! Wherever you focus your attention determines what grows in your experience. Forget about trying to figure it all out. Fix your eyes on Jesus, the Author and Finisher of our faith. Follow His example; keep your attention on the final end, the prize that lies before us.

> *...let us lay aside every weight, and the sin which so easily ensnares us, and let us run with endurance the race that is set before us, looking unto Jesus, the author and finisher of our faith, who for the joy that was set before Him endured the cross, despising the shame, and has sat down at the right hand of the throne of God* (Hebrews 12:1-2)

We cannot really prepare for those days because we don't know exactly what any of us will face individually. We may live in different cities and countries. There are thousands of variables. The days ahead insist that we have oil in our lamps. We must hear and know His voice for ourselves. We can prepare for what could be some of the most phenomenal supernatural encounters ever witnessed by the world by simply connecting to God in our heart and following Him every day, in every situation.

When walking through *the valley of the shadow of death* the key is to know and trust the One you are following! Too often we want to lean to our own understanding. We want to trust what we know. We are going where no man other than Jesus has gone. He not only knows the way, He is the Way and we can trust His leadership. In the original temptation man didn't intend to reject God as his Creator, only as his Shepherd and Lord. But once he was overcome with fear he wasn't willing to trust God. He began to trust his own intellect, ingenuity and understanding. The rest is a history of corruption, self-deceit, personal destruction and iniquity. Believing the truth starts with a choice. The choice brings us to personal experience and that bolsters our hope. We are never put to shame when we have true hope in God and His promises (Romans 5:1-5).

Surrendering every aspect of your life, holding nothing back, is opening the door to a relationship with Him as your Shepherd. Renewing your mind and aligning your knowledge and world view with His is another essential step in the process. Then surrendering your view and opinion to His in every aspect of life puts you in a non-antagonistic relationship with Him as Lord. As you follow His voice in your heart you will become increasingly ready and willing to follow Him in all things. You are ready to *walk through the valley of the shadow of death* with no fear or hesitation because you know the One you are following!

To learn more about the resources mentioned and for additional support material for this chapter please visit www.secondcomingguide.com.

CHAPTER 19

SECRET SOCIETIES: THE CHILD OF THE GREAT HARLOT

The signs of secret societies exist everywhere; but to acknowledge them for what they are is to be labeled the worst kind of nut... a conspiracy nut!

THE KINGDOM OF BABYLON WAS CONCEIVED UNDER THE LUCIFERIAN INFLUENCE OF SEMIRAMIS, NIMROD AND TAMMUZ. The spirit of Mystery Babylon has been at work in the world from that time until now. Mystery Babylon is the mother of **all** religions except Judaism and Christianity. However, much of her corrupt influence has been seen in both Judaism and the Church throughout history. Ironically, in a world where governments are claiming to be secular, they are, in fact, radically religious. Their faith is not in the Creator, Jehovah, the God and Father of the Lord Jesus Christ; it is in Lucifer, the one who claims to bring enlightenment as the first freethinker.

These words from *God and the State* by Mikhail Bakunin in 1871 reveal the continued indoctrination of the father of all lies as it becomes expressed in a more educated, supposedly non-religious, enlightened society.

> But here steps in Satan, the eternal rebel, the first freethinker and the emancipator of worlds. He makes man ashamed of his bestial ignorance and obedience; he emancipates him, stamps upon his brow the seal of liberty and humanity in urging him to disobey and eat of the fruit of knowledge.

He goes on to explain the second element of freedom is the revolt of the individual against all divine, collective, and personal authority.

> The first revolt is against the supreme tyranny of theology, of the phantom of God. As long as we have a master in heaven, we will be slaves on earth. Our reason and our will stand to be equally annulled. As long as we believe that we must unconditionally obey – and vis – a – vis God, no other obedience is possible – we must of necessity passively submit, without the least reservation, to the holy authority of his consecrated and unconsecrated agents, messiahs, prophets, divinely inspired law-makers, emperors, kings, and all their functionaries and ministers, representatives and consecrated servitors of the two greatest institutions which impose themselves upon us, and which are established by God himself to rule over men; namely, the Church and the State. All temporal or human authority stems directly from spiritual and/or divine authority. But authority is the negation of freedom. God, or rather the fiction of God, is the consecration and the intellectual and moral source of all slavery on earth, and the freedom of mankind will never be complete until the disastrous and insidious fiction of a heavenly master is annihilated.[i]

The enlightened world is too sophisticated to enslave itself to an imaginary god, or at least that is the propaganda. They are more than ready to side with Lucifer in exchange for secret knowledge that will provide them with wealth, power and indulgence beyond their wildest dreams. But even more significant is they feel they can do these things with no consequence.

No matter how it is packaged - enlightenment, philosophy, science or higher education - the reason that drives the world is nothing more than the

---

i http://www.marxists.org/reference/archive/bakunin/works/1871/man-society.htm

anarchist rebellion of men who do not want to live moral and godly lives. They seek the expression of the first deception: *"you will be like God knowing good and evil"* (independent of God). While inspiring man to give up any loyalty to God, these same dispensers of lies and propaganda are enslaving man to their own will. All workers of iniquity, those who exalt their opinions and views over the revealed knowledge of God, become gods unto themselves. As such, they declare independence from the true God but always feel the need to impose their will onto others. It becomes inherent in their nature to enslave others to their ideals.

Man, in his attempt at self-rule without law, brought murder, disease, chaos and suffering into the world. The more anti-God any government becomes the more it murders, destroys and manifests the true nature of its father. Just in the 20th and 21st centuries in attempts to establish the no-God Utopia millions of innocent people have been murdered. Mao Zedong killed an estimated 78 million people establishing a fair and honest government. Hitler deliberately murdered 12 million people in concentration camps and other civilian "purgings" while 3 million Russians were left to die as POWs to establish the elite race. These numbers don't take into account the casualties suffered by the allied forces fighting the Nazi regime. Leopold II in the Belgium Congo killed 8 million. Josef Stalin killed 7 million. The Ottoman Empire killed approximately 2.5 million coming to power. Pol Pot of Cambodia murdered 1.7 million. Kim Sung of North Korea slaughtered 1.6 million of his fellow countrymen. Minghistu of Ethiopia killed 1.5 million. Another 30-40 rulers of other regimes each killed a million or less.[ii] Communists in Europe, according to some estimates, have murdered as many as 100 million people imposing their ideas on others.

...in the 20th and 21st centuries in attempts to establish the no-God Utopia millions of innocent people have been murdered.

These numbers do not include the millions that have died throughout history by the Luciferian rage that has gone undocumented. What makes this so staggering is that if you ask most people the cause of more deaths than anything else they will say something like, "More people have died from religious wars than anything else." While their answer is sort of true, they don't understand

ii http://www.scaruffi.com/politics/dictat.html

what really drives religious wars. It is true that the name of Jesus Christ through the Religionists was exploited to wage war on the world. Because they called themselves Christian does not make them the Church. But even considering the carnage caused by the corrupt Church, the truth is most people died by godless, power-hungry, anti-God tyrants seeking to destroy all knowledge of God.

It is true that the name of Jesus Christ through the Religionists was exploited to wage war on the world. Because they called themselves Christian does not make them the Church.

All of these destroyer countries and all of these rulers were drunk with wine of the wrath of the fornication of Mystery Babylon (Revelation 17). Mystery Babylon is intimately connected to three world factors: economy, government and Satanism. It does not matter if those who follow the way of Satan acknowledge, worship or believe in Satan. A tree is known by its fruit. Politicians that murder, imprison, lie, cheat, slander or create chaos to ensure their seats of power are walking the path of the destroyer. As bizarre as it seems, war is critical to world economy. There have been reports suggesting the US economic system can only survive if there is constant war. Many have suggested that our involvement in Vietnam, Iraq and Afghanistan was driven by financial gain. More sinister still is that most wars within the last 200 years were inspired, financed and driven by secret societies.

With the emergence of Religionists, Nimrod cults operating in their true intention moved underground. Above ground they wreaked theological havoc through the Religionists. We see secret societies appear in a new identifiable way when Solomon built the temple. According to the Bible, master builders from Tyre and Sidon were employed to build the temple. Tyre and Sidon were the home of Baal worship, near the entry point for the fallen angels. They had never abandoned worship of the Luciferian gods. Here we have emergence of builders with a specific set of skills based on mathematics passed down by the fallen angels through the Nephilim.

Histories of these groups can be documented from Babel through Egypt, Tyre, Israel, Rome, Europe and finally, America. One progeny of this lineage is Freemasonry, a secret society based on the worship of Osiris the sun god, that exalts secret knowledge. They had knowledge of geometry and mathematics as it was passed on by the fallen angels. It was this information that made them master builders. Inclusion into their group is by secret initiation. Vows of secrecy supported by sworn self-mutilation are part of the initiation. But like all secret societies many (if not most) modern Freemasons have no real idea of the true goals and agendas of their organization. They only know what has been revealed to them at their current level of initiation. I have known many Christians, including deacons and even pastors, who participated in Freemasonry convinced it was simply a charitable, benevolent fraternity.

Freemasons had knowledge of geometry and mathematics as it was passed on by the fallen angels. It was this information that made them master builders.

In the 12th century the Knights Templar formed and were granted permission to use the Temple Mount as their base of operation. Their purpose was to protect Christian pilgrims in the Holy Land. In just a few short years they were sanctioned by the Catholic Church and grew to enormous wealth, prestige and power. In 1139, Pope Innocent II declared them free from taxation, granted them passage through any land and saw that they answered to no authority but the pope. The Order grew rapidly and spread throughout Western Europe.

Many speculate that they sought to find Solomon's gold but others say they were after something much more important, secret knowledge hidden beneath Solomon's Temple. Legend says beneath the temple at Jerusalem the Templar found two stone jars, one of which included the secret name of God. It is a common cult belief that if one knows the name of a god he can control him. The other jar included ancient scrolls with secret knowledge of the universe.

It is thought the Knights Templar began what is now called Freemasonry based on the secret knowledge found in the scrolls. According to many ancient writings the names of the organization as well as its terminology changed as it sought to find influence in different countries and cultures. Regardless of the change of name or initiation, symbols of ancient Egyptians worship of the sun god are a constant in all Freemasonry. Through the rite of initiation participants are slowly indoctrinated. Should one ever reach the inner circle of their purpose, dedication to Lucifer, the original "freethinker," the god of enlightenment becomes the absolute goal.

It is thought the Knights Templar began what is now called Freemasonry based on the secret knowledge found in scrolls.

The Templar continued to grow in power and wealth. They had a massive standing army and sought to establish their own country which made them a particular threat to King Phillip of France. By this time they were suspected of Satan worship, sexual perversion and other occult activity. On Friday 13th, 1307, under the direction of King Phillip, the Knights Templar were arrested without warning, imprisoned in the Castle at Domme, tortured and killed. The tradition of Friday 13th being unlucky was born. It is possible that the 13th was chosen because of its mystic meanings. On the walls of the castle were found carvings of Adonis, the god of harvest and male fertility, as well as a carving of Dagon, another name for Nimrod. There was evidence of a number of satanic rituals and observances.

The remaining Knights Templar loaded their ships with massive wealth and set sail for parts unknown. While it is unclear exactly where they went and where they hid their fortunes, it is known that at some point they came to the New World. That's right! Columbus wasn't first to discover the New World. We know the Nephilim had knowledge of the New World because thousands of their burial mounds complete with giant skeletons have been discovered. Many native American tribes say the giants were here when the "natives" arrived. If the Templar were operating from secret knowledge in coming to America, it is possible this knowledge was gained from the scrolls they found under the Temple Mount. Regardless of how they knew, they came to America 150-200 years before Columbus. Artifacts and rune stones have been found documenting this fact.

The Knights Templar created the first banking system. It was against the Word of God to charge interest so, like all legalists, they found a technicality to skirt around God's Word: they charged rent for money instead of interest. Their dark and questionable connection to the papacy gave them many privileges not enjoyed by others. This connection may have been the beginning of Vatican banking. If so, they would have been in competition with the papacy causing them to fall from favor. Their connection to banking, worship of

Nimrod and connection to the New World may have been the perfect combination of factors for the final launching of Mystery Babylon in the New World which would be called the New World Order. As usual there was a new name and a new face but the same eternal intent.

From this New World secret societies were beyond reach of the Catholic Church and European royalty that felt threatened by their presence. They could create a perfect society to be the last and final Luciferian launching pad for global domination under the guise of the New World Order. If history is correct, this has already transpired. After nearly 6,000 years of trial and failure Satan could use the hunger for true religious freedom to once again establish an earthly kingdom for Mystery Babylon. Mystery Babylon and its intention to create a godless world would facilitate and finance the rise of the antichrist nations. There would be just enough of God's truth to make this new country a world military and financial power; yet, there would be an unseen evil that would drive the destiny of this new nation.

> The Knights Templar created the first banking system. It was against the Word of God to charge interest so, like all legalists, they found a technicality to skirt around God's Word: they charged rent for money instead of interest.

Free enterprise (a biblical concept that did not exist in Europe) would give opportunity for the vile and greedy to take control of wealth and resources. A free economy would be the perfect cover for the Great Whore, Mystery Babylon, to nest and grow unnoticed and unchecked until such a time as she could take total control of the world through this nation and its wealth.

Many people have tried to paint America as the Great Whore. There are many problems with that concept; first and foremost is that Mystery Babylon is not a physical city. Mystery Babylon existed long before America, Wall Street or any other corrupt aspect of the American experience. To turn against a nation because of the spirit working in its corrupt citizens is short-sighted and will work against the person seeking to survive and thrive in the Beginning of Sorrows and the tribulation. Our struggle is not with flesh and blood. To focus on any group of people is nothing but a distraction from true issues.

The government is not the country. Very few Soviets were actually Communists. Not all Americans are greedy, immoral Satanists. There are always those hungry for power who claw their way to a place of control in any nation. They claim to represent the will and well-being of the people, but with a few exceptions, their claim is never true. Government is the system more than the people. The people are just the puppets of the system. Governments were originally formed by bands of murdering thieves who would attack villages, rape the women, murder the people, steal their food and burn the village. At some point they realized they would get more benefit if they sold them "protection" rather than destroy their resources. "We'll be back next year and we won't burn down your village or take all your crops. We'll even leave some of your women and children, but you'll give us the majority of what you produce."

The government is not the country. Very few Soviets were actually Communists. Not all Americans are greedy, immoral Satanists. There are always those hungry for power who claw their way to a place of control in any nation.

In time, in order to protect their investment they had to protect the villages from other raiders and looters. The goal was seldom to benefit the people; it was to protect the income of the controlling government. They didn't want anyone else to steal what they were already stealing. As villages became cities and cities grew into kingdoms the population had to be appeased in order to keep proceeds coming to the government! Centralized powers have never represented the well-being of the population. They represent only their own selfish interests. Additionally, man was never designed to be ruled by any centralized power beyond family. But man fell and we inherited the need to find a way to manage a world that God never intended for us.

America, like most countries, is a group of people who embrace certain values and cultures. Efforts on the part of government to start race wars and exalt individual cultures to the state of conflict are designed to breakdown and destroy any sense of a nation as unified. The Luciferians don't want you to have patriotic loyalty or national identity as a people; they want loyalty to the government and they intend to have it at any cost.

Demonic forces have always been at work in our country, we just have not recognized them. They are at work in every nation of the world. They will not stop until they bring about the end of all things. The irony is that the New World Order wants to control the world and the antichrist nations want to end the world. The antichrist nations can only fulfil their goal if the New World Order first cripples all nations. Satan wants nothing other than the total destruction of mankind. Antichrist nations will not stop until the destruction of all mankind. They imagine the end of the world to be the return of their god in victory over the God of Jews and Christians. The Bible warns us that there is no escaping it; this is the course of all the nations of the world. But we are citizens of the Kingdom of God.

Demonic forces have always been at work in our country, we just have not recognized them. They are at work in every nation of the world.

SPIRITUAL GUIDE

This is the time to realize your citizenship in His Kingdom. Discover what it means to be part of the family of God. Live by the laws of the Kingdom which are based on love and faith. The laws of this land will never stop the flood of iniquity; in fact, they will only serve to promote it. The more we look to the government for solutions, the more they will establish lawlessness (iniquity). Politicians cannot and will not change this. The economy improving will not solve the problem. People who know who they are in Jesus and believers who spread the love of God provide the only opportunity to make a real difference.

Jesus made it clear that His Kingdom was not of this world. He didn't try to change Rome and He didn't attack the injustices in the political system. He taught men about the Kingdom of God. He exalted every word ever spoken by God to the level of love. He revealed the true intentions of God the Father for all mankind. He understood there was no changing of nations, only changing of men as they experienced God in their own heart. We must live as citizens of the Kingdom. Our hope must be an eternal hope. We must know and walk in the way of peace.

We are *in* this world but not *of* this world so it is not ours to fight for. Only the souls of men and women for whom Jesus died can be the focus of our battle and the place of our effort. It does not matter if we have a Republican government, a Democratic government or a Libertarian government. None of that means anything in eternity, nor will it have any lasting effect on the affairs of this world. Who we elect to office may buy a little time, but that is only valuable if we use the time we've bought to spread the message and example of the gospel of the Kingdom of God to the entire world!

To learn more about the resources mentioned and for additional support material for this chapter please visit www.secondcomingguide.com.

APOCALYPSE

CHAPTER 20

AMERICA AND THE NEW WORLD

The easiest lie to hide is that which is left out in the open until it becomes part of the culture. To fight against it is to fight against the culture!

PROSPECTS OF A NEW WORLD MEANT A NEW LIFE FREE FROM THE CONSPICUOUS, OVERSHADOWING EYE OF A TYRANNICAL GOVERNMENT. Many, tired of oppression and religious persecution, were willing to sacrifice land, possessions, jobs, security and fortune for the opportunity to live in some measure of freedom, very specifically religious freedom.

King Henry VIII had broken away from the Catholic Church and declared himself to be head of the newly formed Church of England. The separatists felt the Church of England didn't go far enough in reform. They wanted the Church to be less formal, less controlling, and more like the early Church. Since the primary goals of the Church, both Catholic and Protestant, were primarily carnal and political, true religious freedom would never happen.

Separatists left England and migrated to the Dutch Netherlands where they remained for eleven or twelve years. Fear of war and loss of their children to the culture provoked them to take flight to the New World. The early colonists sought true religious freedom, not freedom for any religion but freedom to worship God the Father of our Lord Jesus as they felt the Bible presented. This was the foundation of religious freedom in America. It was not for the worship of other gods; it was freedom to worship God in true biblical fashion.

In this new world of religious freedom those of a more corrupt nature who were willing to use Christian terminology to mask their true motives and agendas could find a place to thrive, free from imprisonment, torture or death dictated by Church and state for treason, blasphemy, Satanism and sexual or religious crimes. Free from the prying eyes of Church and government they could pursue the dream of the fallen one: a new world after his corrupt image. This "new world" would be the perfect place to establish a New World Order!

By the time of the American Revolution most (if not all) of the men who became known as the Founding Fathers were members of the secret society.

By the time of the American Revolution most (if not all) of the men who became known as the Founding Fathers were members of the secret society. As Freemasons their sworn allegiance was not to the God of the Bible but to the god of their occult organization. At best there may have been a few deists involved but the secret society was the true philosophical driving political force in the revolution and founding of the new nation. Had they revealed their true beliefs and intentions the colonists would have put them to death. They were surrounded by people ready to fight and die for religious and political freedom. The occultists, more than any group, needed freedom of religion to provide the cloak of darkness to make their subterfuge and deception completely legal. Freedom of speech and religion placed them safely and legally beyond the scope of government intrusion.

Religious freedom, the motivation and cornerstone of American freedom, would provide two hundred years of opportunity for the Church to grow, flourish and reach the world. But this freedom would also allow the growth of a Luciferian shadow government that would be the ultimate downfall of this nation. It would not be until the manifestation of the New World Order that they would take total control of the nation and revoke freedom of religion. That which facilitated their rise to power is the one thing that must be completely revoked in order for them to create the utopian elitist world based on a new set of morals and values: iniquity.

What began as religious tolerance has been replaced with fierce antagonism. Those who pretended to seek peaceful coexistence sought only time to gain the upper hand. There is a strategy employed by all Luciferian groups including Muslims, Communists, gangsters, Capitalists and all greedy profiteers. Keep your true intentions secret. Claim to be peace-seeking. Be aggressive until met with superior opposition. Blame intolerance of others for your aggression. Negotiate or pass laws for peace. Then, use the time of peace to grow in power and develop new strategies. Break the peace agreement and repeat the process until total domination and annihilation of opposition occurs. This has been the way of the Atheist, feminists, Communists, Muslims, Satanists and all groups that oppose God's Word. They only believe in freedom of speech and freedom of religion when it is their speech and their religion. Lying, cheating and violence are all justifiable means to a worthy cause. Those who embrace godly values and morals play by the rules while the wicked murderously and viciously break every rule. They have crooked hearts committed to lawlessness and filled with iniquity. The innocent are like lambs led to the slaughter.

The backgrounds of our Founding Fathers, their writings and their activities provide more than enough evidence to reach reasonable conclusions about their involvement in occult activities.

The backgrounds of our Founding Fathers, their writings and their activities provide more than enough evidence to reach reasonable conclusions about their involvement in occult activities. They were openly masonic. To the naïve or ill-informed being a Freemason isn't a real problem; after all, it is simply a benevolent, humanitarian organization seeking the well-being of mankind. Since most Americans do not believe in a personal devil it doesn't matter that they have aligned themselves with Lucifer. To the ignorant it seems like a lot of fuss over nothing. Over time the establishment of new secret organizations, the use of symbols in architecture and on our money and the constant use of occult terminology make the astute observer reevaluate the nature of the founders' true goals. But more than anything, the footprint on politics and society at large make these entities undeniable regardless of whom we believe to be participants.

In 1776, right along with the birth of a new nation was the birth of the Bavarian Illuminati in Germany. It was the child of the forerunners whose corrupt logic led all the way back to Nimrod, the Garden of Eden and the rebellion of Lucifer. The word "Lucifer" in Latin means "light bearer." Like their predecessors they believed Lucifer was the light bearer that emancipated man from God, the angry Creator, who wanted mankind ignorant and enslaved. They are fully devoted to establishing Lucifer's kingdom here on earth, but to do so all belief in the God of the Bible, Jesus, or God's Word must be eradicated. In their ideology, man is only free when he is free from God.

In 1776, right along with the birth of a new nation was the birth of the Bavarian Illuminati in Germany.

The Illuminati was the satanic adaptation of the eternal goal to current culture. It was their goal to secretly influence every area of society and, by degrees, shape the morals and thereby establish a great society - a New World Order for man. The new world, America, led by occultists (Freemasons and Illuminati) on the inside, supported by numerous wealthy and powerful groups on the outside, was the great hope of a new Luciferian world. As much as this sounds like a logistical impossibility necessitating a conspiracy of millions, the reader will soon see that this is the work of a handful of people, a few powerful international organizations and millions of *useful idiots* who are not knowing participants of a conspiracy, they simply seek to fulfil their personal lust independently of God and His Word. In their ignorance they destroy the world and themselves.

A quick glance at the back of a US dollar bill reveals one of thousands of secrets laid out in the open that are meaningless to most of the population but very significant to the initiated. The pyramid on the back of the US dollar bill is obviously an Egyptian symbol. The all-seeing eye at the top of the incomplete pyramid is Osiris (Nimrod, Ra, Horus) the sun god. This seems like strange symbolism for a country supposedly Christian. Why isn't there a cross, an empty tomb or some recognizable symbol of faith in the God of the Bible? The answer is obvious: the God of the Bible is not the god of those who secretly founded and controlled this country!

The number 13 is important to the occultist. Each of the blocks in the unfinished pyramid represents a period of 13 years. Count the blocks adding them to 1776, the beginning of the new country, and it reaches the year 2012. In 2012, according to this symbol, the New World Order was expected to (and probably did) take control of our government and is finally capable of ushering in the New World Order with the Luciferian savior of the world, the one the Masons call "the great architect." This does not mean they are ready to rule by force; it merely means they have control of the government. They now have the power to usher in their god, the eye at the top of the pyramid.

In the years leading up to 2012 the American public was misinformed concerning the Mayan, Aztec, Hopi and other ancient calendars and prophesies. We were led to believe these ancient calendars prophesied the end of the world. The sensationalism was designed to misdirect our attention and anesthetize us to the real truth held in these ancient documents. They didn't predict the end of the world; they predicted the beginning of a New World Order. Illuminati, ancient Nephilim and occult astrologers all read the signs and fully expected the beginning of the New World Order when Nimrod, Osiris, Horus… Lucifer would be in a position to establish his kingdom once again on earth as he did in ancient Babel.

In the years leading up to 2012 the American public was misinformed concerning the Mayan, Aztec, Hopi and other ancient calendars and prophesies. We were led to believe these ancient calendars prophesied the end of the world.

Our country is not an antichrist nation but those who control our leaders are certainly antichrist, as are those who control the leaders of other nations. America, with all its flaws, has taken the gospel into the entire world. The time the devil used for evil God used for good. This is not the time to become anti-American. This is the time to wake up and stop living in the deception of an easy life in a country of prosperity. Don't allow your circumstances to blind you to the eternal struggle.

The time is quickly coming when there will be no compatibility or tolerance between this or any government and true biblical faith. Like ancient Rome the issue will come down to lordship. They don't mind if you have a casual relationship with Jesus, but He can't be your Lord. Lordship determines who gets to say what is right or wrong, good or evil. Lucifer, the father of iniquity (lawlessness) wants to establish a politically correct world based on the rejection of God's morals, standards, ethics and truth.

> The average man does not want to rid the world of God; they just want to rid the world of rules.

The average man does not want to rid the world of God; they just want to rid the world of rules. They see God's commands as burdensome, legalistic and controlling. They have unwittingly embraced Luciferian (the enlightened one's) doctrine. "Come on! This is the 21st century; sex before marriage isn't going to kill you." "Sexual orientation is a matter of choice." "You have to lie to do business." On and on the list goes. All those rules are antiquated and irrelevant. They only serve to limit our freedom of expression and personal fulfillment.

Our twisted definitions of sin, our perverted view of God and our own lustful desires deceive us. The Bible says the *"soul that sins shall die."* To the religious legalist, that means God will kill you if you sin. To the religious worker of iniquity that means "I'm under a new covenant that doesn't apply to me." But God is really saying, "You were created in My likeness and image, you have no capacity for that which causes you to see or experience yourself as less than completely righteous."

He mercifully points out that death starts in your soul. Sin hardens your heart which affects your understanding. Then, when Jesus is not Lord we look at compromises and say, "I don't understand the problem with this!" This journey of hardening our hearts alienates us from the voice of God, rendering us completely susceptible to the lies and destruction of the one who exists for the sole purpose of our destruction.

As the war on terror evolves it will justify the continued passing of laws that violate our freedoms. As far-fetched as it may seem, the time will come when failure to acknowledge the state as the supreme lawgiver will be tantamount to treason or terrorism. I have personally witnessed members of military being expelled from service for refusing to acknowledge the military as their supreme lawgiver. I have personally had government officials tell me the State is the only entity having the right to teach our children. I have been told they are only allowing us the freedom to teach the Bible out of the kindness of their heart. You have all unknowingly experienced the government gradually enforcing their position that your child is a ward of the state. They are seeking a "cradle-to-the-grave" control of all human life and thought. You must give them "immunizations" that have been proven to destroy their immune systems and actually cause an increase in certain diseases. You are required to put your children in schools approved by the state. You must give them the medical treatment chosen by big pharma or you will lose your child. All this is happening and people still think everything is going to turn out positively. We have to learn to be ***in*** the world but not ***of*** the world!

As the war on terror evolves it will justify the continued passing of laws that violate our freedoms. As far-fetched as it may seem, the time will come when failure to acknowledge the state as the supreme lawgiver will be tantamount to treason or terrorism.

SPIRITUAL GUIDE

Joseph, Daniel, the three Hebrew children and others thrived in anti-God nations. They didn't fight against the government and they didn't lead rebellions. Jesus, Paul and the early apostles did not focus their attention on Rome with all its injustices; they sought God and spread the gospel. But where it became "life and death" was when it was a question of whom they would obey. If a revolution would solve the problem Jesus would have led a revolution, but His kingdom (as of this moment) is not of this world!

The question for many comes down to, "Have you walked in full trust of God's Word long enough to see and experience the value it brings to your life, or have you simply clung to God while despising His commands?" The question is not, "What will I do when the New World Order takes full control of my religious freedom?" The question is, "What am I doing with my religious freedom now?"

Now we must use our time, life and resources for more than comfortable living. It is time for us to put the Kingdom and His righteousness first. We cannot surrender to pessimism and fear; we must begin living for an eternal purpose. As the nations become more corrupt and controlling we must open our hearts to God and allow Him to give us more freedom. In oppressed countries all across the world believers are multiplying the gospel, seeing miracles, having personal encounters with Jesus and thriving in the midst of persecution. We need to thrive in the freedom we have for the purposes of the Kingdom.

To learn more about the resources mentioned and for additional support material for this chapter please visit www.secondcomingguide.com.

APOCALYPSE

CHAPTER 21

THE UNIVERSALISM CHURCH

Of all the insanities of man none is as great as religion. Religion allows a man to open the pages of the Bible but never see a word that is written!

WITH A COMPLETE CHANGE OF STRATEGY SATAN'S ARSENAL WOULD NOT BE COMPLETE WITHOUT THE CORRUPTION AND MISREPRESENTATION OF TRUE FAITH IN GOD. I do not like to use the word "Christian" since it is not a word God ever used to describe His children. It is a word the world used to describe us and sadly we have incorporated into our sense of identity. We are children of God, brethren, followers of Jesus, disciples, heirs and the housed of God. We are believers in the truth of the death, burial and resurrection of Jesus. We are lovers of His Word. We are children of the light. The words God uses to describe us are more about our relationship, beliefs, identity and lifestyle. The words the world uses are more about our ceremonies and external observances.

Even the word "church" is difficult to use without others projecting their interpretations onto its actual meaning. The word "church" comes from the Greek word *"ecclesia,"* which means "the called out." The Church is the body of Christ, those who have heard and responded to the voice of God in their heart to follow Jesus as Lord. We have been born of the Spirit of God and baptized into His body. We have been made righteous through faith in the finished work of the resurrected Lord. We have become a family of believers and citizens of the Kingdom of God. The word "church" is more about individuals that comprise the group and who they are in relation to God, not the group as an organization.

> Even the word "church" is difficult to use without others projecting their interpretations onto its actual meaning. The word "church" comes from the Greek word *"ecclesia,"* which means "the called out."

Because of references in the New Testament about the Church meeting in certain houses or references to a specific group of believers, over time the concept of Church became less about the individual in relation to God and more about the individual in relation to the group, and in time it came to refer to the organization. As the Church became more of an organization and less of a living organism it tried more and more to look like the false religions of the world. In Catholicism the "church" meant the Catholic Church. Among Protestants the "church" eventually became the building where a local congregation met. A local body of believers is incredibly important. I deeply believe in the value of local churches. I am fortunate enough to visit many wonderful churches that are, in fact, very healthy and committed to Jesus' purpose in the earth.

Many believe that organizations are evil and conflict with true spirituality. While this can sometimes be true, such universally applied thinking is narrow and idealistic. Without organization within the scope of biblical purpose the Church (the called out) will not be very effective at maintaining sound doctrine or reaching the world. Additionally, there is a biblical pattern for small groups (house to house) and public gatherings. Without local churches true fellowship is rarely experienced. A list of the positive benefits of a healthy, biblically-based, local church is quite extensive. If we lose sight of the fact that the "local church" is not the building, the name on the building, or the name of the denomination but it is, in fact, the people within that group who have personally answered the call of God, then we limit our capacity to understand how the Church will flourish in the end times, in the last great revival. For the sake of clarity, when references are made to any church denomination, group or movement I am not talking about the people who comprise the membership and I am not making a sweeping statement about any particular leader. I am, however, referring to what that institution has become and embraced as part of its theology and identity.

In Matthew 16:13 Jesus asked:

> *"Who do men say that I, the Son of Man, am?" Simon Peter answered and said, "You are the Christ, the Son of the living God." Jesus answered and said to him, "Blessed are you, Simon Bar-Jonah, for flesh and blood has not revealed this to you, but My Father who is in heaven. And I also say to you that you are Peter, and on this rock I will build My church, and the gates of Hades shall not prevail against it. And I will give you the keys of the kingdom of heaven, and whatever you bind on earth will be bound in heaven, and whatever you loose on earth will be loosed in heaven."*

The Church God would build would be those who recognized Jesus as Lord. It would be to these "called out" believers that God would establish His Kingdom against which the gates of Hades could never prevail. But the criteria for this Church are to hear and respond to the call of God through the Lord Jesus, then to operate in the authority that is ours in Planet Earth. The Church is a spiritual body that organizes around the purposes of Christ.

Catholicism violated the New Testament warning against following genealogies[i] and made a vain attempt to create a monopoly on Christianity by declaring to be directly descended through the bloodline of Peter. We are the Church because we are followers of Jesus who have answered the call, not because we are follows of Peter, Paul, any man or any group.

In His statement to Peter, Jesus gave us great revelation and a congruent reminder of our authority. The called out (Church) will be built from the confession of Jesus Christ, the Son of the living God, as Lord. It would be those individuals who comprise His body over which Hades, the false god of the underworld, would never prevail. He then reminds believers of the authority we have in Planet Earth. If a matter has been settled in Heaven we have the

---

i 1 Timothy 1:4, Neither give heed to fables and endless genealogies, which minister questions, rather than godly edifying which is in faith: so do.
Titus 3:9, But avoid foolish questions, and genealogies, and contentions, and strivings about the law; for they are unprofitable and vain.

right and obligation to declare it so in Planet Earth. What we should allow or disallow is based on what Jesus accomplished on our behalf through His death, burial and resurrection. We should use our authority to stop any curse of the law from coming upon us (Galatians 3:13). Likewise, we should use our authority to call forth any promise God made to anyone (2 Corinthians 1:20). We should only allow in our lives what God has promised to Jesus. We are in Him, we are His body; therefore, we are joint heirs in His inheritance!

If a matter has been settled in Heaven we have the right and obligation to declare it so in Planet Earth. What we should allow or disallow is based on what Jesus accomplished on our behalf through His death, burial and resurrection.

Jesus, with the authority of the Son of Man, will return physically to Planet Earth, establish His Kingdom rule over the entire world, and show us how we could have functioned had we not so compromised the beliefs of our heart! [ii] But we can look at this reality as a way to prepare ourselves for the dark days ahead. Jesus has given and taught us everything we need to know to be overcomers, but religion has so misrepresented the gospels, perverted the Bible and vilified the name of God that we do not know who we are, what we have and what we can do.

The early Apostolic Church was highjacked when Constantine, who was not a believer, dreamed that if he would march his armies under the banner of the cross he could not be defeated. Following his pagan-based religious concepts of "might is right," he began to organize the pagan-Roman-state-church. Under the power of Rome, the seeds of a state church overshadowed, overpowered and subverted the true Church, those individuals "called out" of the Lord. In time the Western Roman Empire became synonymous with "the Church." It was the beginning of apostasy, Paganism, idol worship and world domination by a state cult that called itself "the church." Every aspect of the state cult was infused with Paganism, especially in reference to the sun god, Nimrod, Ishtar, Tammuz cult. The images, the rituals, the priesthood,

---

ii John 14:12-14, "Most assuredly, I say to you, he who believes in Me, the works that I do he will do also; and greater works than these he will do, because I go to My Father. 13 And whatever you ask in My name, that I will do, that the Father may be glorified in the Son. 14 If you ask anything in My name, I will do it.

the clothes worn by the priests, the buildings, the statues and the twisted theological representations of God were more pagan than biblical. The word "catholic" means "universal." It seems by "universal" they not only mean the only church, but a church that included all religions in some watered-down form. Universalism of the Roman Church led to a Roman-cult-state entity that called itself "the church."

While the Western Roman-cult-church followed the way of Constantine and his corrupt successors, the Eastern Roman Church followed more of the apostles' teachings. Instead of a corporate institution they were made up of small congregations ministering and multiplying through personal lifestyle and preaching the apostles' doctrine and ministry. The Western Church leaders were enraged that these believers would not deny their faith and join the holy Roman Church. The Eastern Church suffered persecution and martyrdom at the hands of the Western "Roman-state-cult-church."

In time Augustine emerged as a prolific intellectual and propagandist who waged a constant war of information against the Church in the East. Rome was intent on having an absolute monopoly on Christianity. They waged a relentless war against true believers of the Eastern Empire.

> Augustine was the most powerful and influential teacher of the Latin Church. Many false doctrines that emerged from Catholicism can be traced back to him. Some of these false doctrines include: infant baptism, purgatory, clerical celibacy, and predestination. Augustine also laid the groundwork for the use of **disguised** mercenaries in the age long Vatican war against the saints.[iii]

According to Arch Bishop Trent, it was Augustine who, following his cult beliefs, redefined the word "chastisement" in the New Testament to mean, "whip or beat."[iv] It had always meant to "child train," specifically the way you would train the child you favor. Augustine acknowledged its true meaning and stated that as Christians we must redefine it with this negative connotation. Rome was bent on creating an image of God more in line with their occult philosophies than with Scripture. As such they could use fear to not only control the masses, but to subtly turn them against the true, loving God.

---

iii http://www.reformation.org/vatican-and-islam.html
iv Trench's Synonyms of the New Testament

Besides the purity of the Eastern Church, the Western Empire was in decline and facing starvation without the resources of the East. The food it took to sustain Rome came primarily from North Africa. The greed for natural resources, the lust for power and the hatred of the truth drove the Western-cult-church to every possible extreme of exterminating true believers and gaining complete control of the Eastern Empire. Among many things the Vatican wanted was control of Jerusalem. The Vatican hated Jews and waged constant war against them just as they did true believers. They wanted the Holy City to be the jewel in their crown as a validation of their divine authority.

> Rome was bent on creating an image of God more in line with their occult philosophies than with Scripture. As such they could use fear to not only control the masses, but to subtly turn them against the true, loving God.

According to some historic sources, the Vatican conspired with the Arabs to wage war against Jews and Christians of the East. It would give them control of North Africa and its rich resources, and of Jerusalem. Some go as far as to say they spent years developing Muhammad to lead the mercenary armies which they financed against Constantinople. Such claims are unprovable, but possible. Regardless of how it came to be, Muhammad, a man whose family were Baal worshippers did, in fact, lead to the downfall of Constantinople, the Eastern Empire and the church.

Muhammad is the father and prophet of Islam. According to Muslim history, Muhammad's family considered him to be demon possessed because he had frequent seizures and other manifestations of what was then considered demon possession. His personal life combined with his occult upbringing and subsequent religious tutoring facilitated the perfect heart beliefs for a hate-based religion that had as its reason for existence the annihilation of all Jews and Christians. It is speculated that, in time, a deal was struck that Muslims would be financed to wage war on Jews and Christians in exchange for a peace agreement between the Catholic Church and Islam. Likewise, he would conquer Jerusalem and turn it over to Rome in exchange for financial support.[v] Since any of this information would be closely protected by both sourc-

---

v http://www.reformation.org/fall-of-constantinople.html

es, the degree of the conspiracy will never be fully discovered. According to some sources, with the backing of the Roman Church, Islam was able to destroy Constantinople and conquer Jerusalem.

Muhammad is the father and prophet of Islam.

Regardless of who or what led up to it, after Muhammad's personal visitation and possession by a spirit in a cave, he emerged with his own personal god and his own personal agenda. While in a cave a spirit (he claimed it was an angel) came on him and threatened to kill him unless he obeyed. He would henceforth call god (Baal) "Allah" and he would dedicate his life to destroying Christians and Jews on behalf of his god. But, the true follower of jihad knows that Islam is not just about killing Jews and Christians, it is about destroying this wicked world so Allah can return. Islam has an apocalyptic vision that ends with the world's destruction. There is nothing in their "holy writings" that offers forgiveness or security of salvation other than dying in jihad. The idea that Islam is a peaceful religion is a Luciferian, New World Order, Islamic lie!

As the Muslim nation grew in power they would not comply with the alleged agreement to turn Jerusalem over to the Vatican. They turned their eyes to Europe and sought permission from the pope to invade Europe. In the eyes of the pope the right of world domination belonged to him which, after all, was the real reason for starting the Roman-cult-state-church. In retaliation Rome raised an army of "crusaders" who launched a war that continued for centuries. But, according to many, the Vatican and Islam have maintained many secret alliances against Jews and true believers for centuries.

While the inter-linking history of the two religions is questionable, the link between the Vatican and Islam is becoming more evident today as the pope has declared that Islam is not a threat to Christianity. For the first time in history imams are reading the Quran and offering Muslim prayer from the Vatican.[vi] Since 1964 the Vatican has pushed the heretical propaganda that Muslims worship the same God as Christians.[vii] In what is labelled an ecumenical (worldwide or universal) movement the Vatican, Islam and the UN

---

vi http://english.alarabiya.net/en/News/middle-east/2014/06/06/Islamic-prayers-to-be-held-at-the-Vatican.html

vii http://english.alarabiya.net/en/News/middle-east/2014/06/06/Islamic-prayers-to-be-held-at-the-Vatican.html

seem to be working more and more in harmony for a one-world religion and a one-world government.

A much-debated prophecy, credited to St. Malachy, predicted the final 112 popes, beginning with Pope Celestine II (elected in 1143), to the final pope before the apocalypse. This final pope (according to prophecy) is Pope Francis. If this prophecy from within the Catholic Church is accurate, the last pope (which is the current pope) will lead the Catholic Church into a league with the antichrist. It may or may not be accurate, but it is worth considering. As we see the Vatican embracing Islam, the seat of the antichrist, it appears there may be some truth to the allegations of their twisted history. But we do not need a prophecy to recognize the historical facts. The corrupt dogma, the gross violation of Scriptures, the incorporation of idolatry and murder, and the vast corruption of the Roman-state-cult-church more than clearly indicates that from its inception was infected with Luciferian thought.

A much-debated prophecy, credited to St. Malachy, predicted the final 112 popes, beginning with Pope Celestine II (elected in 1143), to the final pope before the apocalypse. This final pope (according to prophecy) is Pope Francis.

The point of bringing this information to light is not to bash Catholicism but to show Satan's previous strategies could not work against the Church, the true believers. He is far more afraid of us than we are of him. We believe in the resurrected Jesus as Lord. The gates of Hades, the false god of the underworld **cannot prevail against us**. If Satan had launched a straight-forward, all-out attack against the Church the children of God would have immediately risen up in faith, grace and power of the Holy Spirit. We would have completely defeated him and ushered in the return of the Lord!

Satan will never have the power and does not yet have the collective authority for a head-on attack so he will continue to work his original strategy. Just as he has done from the Garden and through the advice of the godless prophet Balaam, he seeks to move man to such compromise and corruption that he has no confidence in God or himself.

Judging and criticizing Catholic believers is not the goal or the solution. We all have shades of corruption we have not identified nor shaken out of our theology. In so many corrupt institutions there are those who have answered the call of God in their heart. The Church is not the organization; it is believers who have responded to the call of God, even if they have not possessed the knowledge to identify their own corrupt religious traditions. They are the body of Christ, the true Church. We are all limited in our sense of identity, authority and power to the degree we cling to limiting religious beliefs about God. But that does not mean we are not saved; it just means we are not experiencing as much of the life of God as has been offered.

> Satan will never have the power and does not yet have the collective authority for a head-on attack so he will continue to work his original strategy.

SPIRITUAL GUIDE

As believers we should heed the words of the Prophet Isaiah, *"Awake, awake! Put on your strength, O Zion."* As believers we must awaken to the truth about what we really have in Jesus so we can put on our strength. He continues: *"Shake yourself from the dust, arise; Loose yourself from the bonds of your neck, O captive daughter of Zion!"* In other words, open your eyes; shake yourself free. We think we are free, but to the degree that we are not living as Jesus lived we are not free. We are all captive in some degree to our limiting, religious, cultural and societal beliefs and traditions. *"'You have sold yourselves for nothing, Now therefore, what have I here,' says the Lord, 'That My people are taken away for nothing?'"* Whatever benefit we have from a compromised life or the acceptance of some religious institution is nothing compared to what we could enjoy in the limitless love of God and the grace and power to be like Jesus. It is because of these things that we are vulnerable to captivity.

Isaiah points to the source of the problem: *"'Those who rule over them Make them wail,' says the Lord, 'And My name is blasphemed continually every day.'"* It is sometimes the influence of our leaders that makes us hate God. If they influence us to believe God is angry, vengeful and merciless they are destroying our ability to trust Him. If they lead us to believe Him to be the source of our pain and tragedies how can we turn to Him for help in our time of need? We are inundated with Luciferian doctrine that makes it nearly impossible to see and experience the love of God; therefore, we blame Him for every woe, every pain and every sorrow. But we have our own Bibles to read. We have direct access to God by the Holy Spirit. As we choose to look to Him instead of those who attempt to rule over us, we can know the truth. I am, by no means, implying all pastors and leaders are leading us astray; there are wonderful pastors teaching the Word of God. But if we, for social reasons, fear or unbelief choose to continually expose ourselves to those who promote unbelief it is our problem, not theirs! If we hunger and thirst for truth and righteousness we will find the truth and be filled with His righteousness. If we continue to expose ourselves to the Luciferian angry-God-doctrine we run the risk of becoming angry and bitter against God.

Many of the most vehement anti-God propagators of death to ever walk the planet started out as "Christians." They turned against God when they experienced tragedy, loss of a loved one or some personal pain that was attributed to the will of God. This very Luciferian doctrine gave birth to Communism, Darwinism, Islam and a host of cult and occult entities that torment mankind and will play a role in bringing about the Great Tribulation. They blame

God for their pain and they hate the God of the Bible, so they will throw in with anyone to overthrow the tyrannical god they were led to believe in. They opt instead to live for Lucifer in the hopes of finding the enlightenment to free themselves.

Isaiah prophesies of a day when people would relate to God based on His name, not on corrupt church doctrine. *"Therefore My people shall know My name; Therefore they shall know in that day That I am He who speaks: 'Behold, it is I.'"* He is Jehovah, the God of Peace, the Healer, the Provider, the Shepherd and much more. He connects our seeing Him as He is with the New Covenant: The Covenant of Peace![viii] God made a Covenant of Peace with the Lord Jesus. We are in Him; therefore, we share in the Covenant of Peace. When we see God as the God of Peace and when we know we need not strive to earn His love and acceptance, we will be at peace with Him and we will finally see Him as He is. Then we will say:

> *How beautiful upon the mountains Are the feet of him who brings good news, Who proclaims peace, Who brings glad tidings of good things, Who proclaims salvation, Who says to Zion, 'Your God reigns'*[ix] (Isaiah 52:1-7)!

Is there anything in you that tends to view God as the source of your pain or problems? Or do you think He is testing you or bringing bad things on you because of your disobedience? I encourage you to read *The Gospel of Peace.* It will give you the truth you need to forever establish your heart in the New Covenant: the Covenant of Peace!

As a believer the only tool the enemy has against you is deceit. If Jesus is our Lord we must base all of our beliefs on the Word of God as understood through the death, burial and resurrection of Jesus. Anything else is religion. I once heard a minister I deeply respected say something like, "Religion is like a vaccination; it gives you just enough of the real thing so you can't catch it." Don't allow tradition (culture or religion) to make the Word of God ineffective in your life!

---

viii Isaiah 54:9, For the mountains shall depart And the hills be removed, But My kindness shall not depart from you, Nor shall My covenant of peace be removed," Says the Lord, who has mercy on you.

ix The Gospel of Peace, James B. Richards, Milestones, Publishing

It is essential that your heart is established in the New Covenant. You will know that is a reality when you never question God or suspect Him of bringing harm. The Apostle Paul tells us to have our feet shod with the preparation (readiness) of mind (that comes from a thorough preparation in) the Gospel of Peace. In an attack our footing is possibly the most crucial aspect of survival. A true warrior is taught to move in such a way that no matter the direction from which the attack emerges, he will remain balanced with stable footing. We want our footing to be in the Covenant of Peace. No matter what hits us or where it comes from we will always remain absolute in the fact that we have peace with God. He is not against us and He is not the source of our pain!

The way of Lucifer is to create a problem, blame God and then offer you protection. This will be the downfall of many believers as well as other people around the world. When the antichrist emerges in a time of world crisis he will offer peace. It will be this false peace that draws the entire earth to him and, unfortunately, it will be the final downfall of many believers who were not established in the Covenant of Peace.

To learn more about the resources mentioned and for additional support material for this chapter please visit www.secondcomingguide.com.

APOCALYPSE

CHAPTER 22

ELITIST UTOPIANISM: THE GOAL OF THE ENLIGHTENED

There is no single group that can take credit for what is happening. There are many groups with many names but they all unwittingly follow the philosophies of their father, Lucifer!

IF WE ARE TO TAKE THE WORD OF GOD LITERALLY (AND WE SHOULD) ALL OF HISTORY HAS MOVED US TO TWO WORLD-ALTERING EVENTS. First, a man the Bible calls the "antichrist" will arise during a time of great upheaval and war. He will claim to be the Messiah, but he is, in fact, a pawn of the devil seeking to annihilate all knowledge of God from the earth by killing all Jews and Christians. This man of iniquity, as the Bible calls him, is Satan's final tool to accomplish the evil that was born in his heart when he attempted to overthrow God.

The next, and even more important, event is the personal return of Jesus as Lord. He will lead His followers to overthrow the antichrist and his kingdoms. He will then establish His Kingdom on earth for 1000 years before the final end of the world as we know it. At the end of the millennium there will be a final rebellion after which will be the beginning of Heaven on earth. We will reign with Him during the 1000 years of righteous rule. He will reign in complete justice and righteousness, revealing what the world could have been if man had ruled it according to God's Word instead of following the way of iniquity.

It is from these two outcomes that we must interpret all of history. All things lead to these events. Failure to interpret history based on this eternal conflict leads to a naïveté making it impossible to understand how and why things are happening in the world. Refusal to accept these facts creates a complete impossibility to prepare one's heart to overcome in any tribulation, especially the Great Tribulation. It is from these realities that conspiracy theories arise. Those who do not understand the spiritual factors look like "conspiracy nuts." They see the conspiracies but fail to see how they all merge together.

Many conspiracy theories are based completely on an over-active imagination. Most, however misplaced, may actually be based on a factual situation, but the details appear unclear. Many other conspiracy theories, however, are completely accurate. When one accepts the evil reality that Lucifer is a real being who has worked a consistent agenda since his rebellious attempt to overthrow God, it becomes easy to understand how a world-wide conspiracy is possible. While the players of the conspiracy may never have conferred with one another they have all been led by the same master, making it an even more diabolical conspiracy than has ever been considered.

The workers of iniquity are like terrorist cells. They only personally know the people in their group.

The workers of iniquity are like terrorist cells. They only personally know the people in their group. That group may be made up of banking professionals who use unethical banking practices resulting in an economic collapse similar to the events in 2008. They are simply operating from their own greed. Lawmakers who passed the laws making it possible for banks to go unchecked could not care less about money bankers make. They desire to create a panic giving them the opportunity to pass more Socialist legislation. Greedy real estate investors don't care about any of those agendas. They simply see a way to buy property for pennies on the dollar. None of these people may have ever met, but they are in a conspiracy. They are all being led by their sinful, selfish greed. They have accepted the iniquity of the evil one as satisfactory business practices and, like terrorist cells, they are attacking the average person from every side, provoking fear and discouragement, not realizing they are under the direction of the "unseen hand."

There are dozens of cults, occult groups, Satanists, witches' covens, ancient religions and secret and public political groups working the same Luciferian-inspired game plan. These groups may hate one another, they may war against one another, they may have different names, and they may have different individual objectives, but they have one thing in common: iniquity. They are against anything the Word of God says whether it is morality, civil law, definition of family, their account of history or creation. If it is in the Bible as true, they are against it. They thrive on the theory, "The enemy of my enemy is my friend." Their one common denominator is the hatred of God and His Word. This cannot be mere coincidence.

There are dozens of cults, occult groups, Satanists, witches' covens, ancient religions and secret and public political groups working the same Luciferian-inspired game plan.

To this end we see the Middle Ages forming the basis for the goal of a New World Order coming into existence by the year 2012 as prophesied by the occult, astrologers and ancient religions for centuries. The emergence of industrialized nations all vying for world domination presented the most eerie of realities: at some point in time nearly every nation in the world became guided by the same "unseen hand." A sinister, wicked, controlling world power emerged in plain sight that took control of the nations without ever firing a shot. They are influencing and, in some cases, controlling international policy of all nations. This entity is intimately connected to the Great Harlot, Mystery Babylon: The International Banking System!

Mystery Babylon, the Great Harlot, is intimately connected to three key components: economy, governments and Nimrod worship, i.e. Lucifer. When Mystery Babylon falls the only people who mourn are kings who lived in luxury, merchants and those who made their living from shipping. These are all linked to the economy. The sins of Mystery Babylon were the spiritual fornication of the nations and blood of the saints, martyrs, prophets and … the blood… of all who were slain on the earth" (Revelation 18:24). This is the mother of all wars. This spirit worked in every power-hungry, greedy, political, business and religious leader. It was the ideological, theological doctrine that justified murder, brutality and perversion. This spirit, Mystery Babylon, gave birth to the great conspiracy, one Freemasons call the Great Architect, designer of the great society, the New World Order… Lucifer.

This spirit, Mystery Babylon, gave birth to the great conspiracy, one Freemasons call the Great Architect, designer of the great society, the New World Order… Lucifer.

Early in the history of secret societies it was often forbidden to refer to their leader as Satan or the devil. Instead, he was called Lucifer, the one who enlightens. After all, it is intellectuals, scientists, philosophers, politicians, controllers of wealth and corrupt clergy who, as elitists, have come to enlightenment. Being freed from the tyrannical domination of Jehovah they are given to iniquity. They have their own forms of fairness, justice, spirituality and morality. The hypocritical irony is while they tell all men to throw off rules and laws of God, they insist they, the state, and their political or religious party should have your complete loyalty and obedience. Reject the wisdom of God (iniquity) for the wisdom of man (foolishness and lies). Jesus asks us to surrender our opinions and accept the Word of God as truth; they demand you surrender the Word of God and accept their philosophies as truth. If you don't they will reject you, torment you, tell lies about you, steal from you and when they can they will kill you!

For example, George Bernard Shaw, a famous Progressive who expressed the view of ardent Progressives, Socialists and Communists said that all people should come before an appointed board much like the IRS or any other government board about every five years and be questioned as to whether he is producing more than he is consuming. If not, he should be put to death.[i] He went on to say, "I appeal to chemists to discover a humane gas that will kill instantly and painlessly. In short - a gentlemanly gas, deadly by all means, but humane, not cruel." It is always the mark of the Luciferian spirit to use force and coercion to peddle their lies and threaten death or imprisonment for those who disagree.

---

i https://www.youtube.com/watch?v=93eir00rOho

When the average person hears or reads something like this, they can't connect it to reality; yet, history records those who do not embrace God and His truth will murder millions to support their ideologies or to simply gain control. Consider how current social justice aborts (kills) unwanted babies. They will murder whom they consider to be a threat to their political ideas in the name of terrorism. Our current Affordable Care Act, when fully implemented, will not treat the elderly, it will simply give them "comfort care;" in other words, let them die. They will attack a country killing thousands to protect financial investments of the wealthy and call it "protecting America's concerns." They will not, however, execute an individual who rapes and murders someone's wife or daughter. This is man's morality. Man's version of righteousness (how it should be) is based on the philosophy of whomever is in power. Without the Word of God there are no absolutes; therefore, iniquity abounds!

Several hundred millions of people have been slaughtered world-wide in the pursuit of the ideal government, none of which was based on God's standard of justice.

As the 20th century approached so did the world powers. The great philosophical battle between the world powers was supposedly Communism versus Capitalism. Several hundred millions of people have been slaughtered world-wide in the pursuit of the ideal government, none of which was based on God's standard of justice. But as we examine facts it becomes obvious, whether it is a Communist or a Capitalist, that many of their core philosophies are the same: the elite should rule the world and the common man should have no freedom other than that which is allotted by the state. When we look even closer, we discover that Capitalism, Communism, Nazism and, to some degree, Islam have been financed by the same group of people.

It becomes obvious the political doctrine is really just a marketing ploy. Different men who lust for power simply use the political rhetoric as a means to appeal to the masses, deceiving them into giving away their power and authority for protection from the fabricated enemy! Is Socialism worse than Capitalism? At different stages they both have legitimate complaints and reasonable solutions. In an ideal world either could work and be effective, but in a world of greed and corruption it is impossible for either to actually work. At the end of either process the middle class is destroyed, the elite control all the wealth and natural resources and the very poor exist for the pleasure and benefit of the wealthy.

The ultimate goal of Mystery Babylon is for the enlightened to rule the world and take control of its vast resources.

The ultimate goal of Mystery Babylon is for the enlightened to rule the world and take control of its vast resources. The difference between the Great Harlot and the antichrist nations is the wealth and luxury that can be offered. Remember, the devil can only kill people through other people. If he had power to kill he would have already done it. So, when people express their desire for power, money, sex or dominance he provides the strategies with no accountability. Those who want to be world leaders tend to be people who crave power, not an opportunity to serve. Even if they want to serve it will be done through establishing their agendas, which means it is still for their benefit. The goal of all groups seeking world domination whether Capitalist, Communist or Socialist is an elitist utopian society.

The purported founder of the Illuminati set out a strategy to control all media through book clubs, newspapers and every other means of communication and education. Ultimately, they also intended to gain control of the financial institutions. Their objectives and established way of fulfilling them are all but identical to the stated planks of Communism, the goal of the big American government (Republican and Democrat), Progressivism, Socialism, the UN and all organizations committed to a one-world government.

Edith Miller, in her book, *Occult Theocrasy,* lays out the objectives of the Illuminati. (A theocrasy is the merging of several different gods into one. It is not the same as a theocracy.)

1. The destruction of Christianity and all monarchical governments
2. The destruction of nations as such in favor of universal internationalism
3. The discouragement of patriotic and loyal effort branded as narrow-minded prejudice, incompatible to the universal tenants of goodwill to all men, and the cry of "Universal Brotherhood"
4. The abolition of family ties and of marriage by systematic corruption
5. The suppression of rights of inheritance and property

Add to this the original means whereby this would be accomplished: Socialism.

Take a look at the 10 Planks of Communism[ii] or the 45 goals for the Communist takeover of America[iii] and you'll find yourself saying "I can see little difference between what is said by either group." The answer is simple; they were inspired by the same philosophies of iniquity and enlightenment. Few people realize that Marx, Lenin, and according to some, Mao Zedong were all true Satanists. Socialism and Communism were merely tools they used to conquer and consolidate all control to the elite. Even if they are not pure Satanists we should understand the majority of our presidents were members of antichrist secret societies and they were educated in schools that serve as centers for Luciferian propaganda.

Regardless of their country or political affiliation, all these people need **money** in order to gain power. Political leaders need money to get elected. Their governments must have financial resources to survive and operate. They have to sustain employment for their citizens. They must create an infrastructure for physical sustainability. And above all, they must have armies and weapons. Armies provide the ability to protect their territory, expand their control and keep their citizens in check. Thus, all the kings of the earth commit fornication (spiritual idolatry) with the Great Harlot.

The Knights Templar, a secret society, was the beginning of modern banking. Through banking it was discovered one could make money without actually working or producing anything. This is why the Word of God made it against the law to loan money and charge interest. As riches became more concentrated wealthy families not only took over natural resources, they took control of banking. It is no secret that private banks have loaned money to the nations of the world to finance wars. What is seldom realized is in most cases over the last 200 years the same banks (families) loaned money to all the countries involved in the conflict. It did not matter who won, the bankers got rich. According to many public sources the Rockefellers through Standard Oil sold fuel to the Nazis and the US during World War II. The Standard Oil group of companies, in which the Rockefeller family owned a one-quarter (and controlling) interest, was of critical assistance in helping Nazi Germany prepare for World War II.[iv] Sadly, this activity was known by our own president and was made legal.

---

ii http://laissez-fairerepublic.com/tenplanks.html
iii http://www.rense.com/general32/americ.htm
iv http://reformed-theology.org/html/books/wall_street/chapter_04.htm

The Vietnam War brought massive profits for the companies that produced weapons of warfare and there were massive amounts of fuel sold to the government to keep ships, planes, helicopters, jeeps and heavy equipment moving. Many companies that profited most were from the home state of Lyndon Johnson who escalated the war after the assassination of President Kennedy. Regardless of how many people you think were involved in it, Kennedy was assassinated after threatening to expose the secret societies that actually control the government.

Through banking it was discovered one could make money without actually working or producing anything. This is why the Word of God made it against the law to loan money and charge interest.

When banks loan money to countries it usually comes with conditions that will determine what laws are passed, who gets nominated for office, how long they will stay in office and what allies we will support or abandon. Lincoln borrowed money from international banks to finance the Civil War and in exchange he agreed to create the IRS.

> The cost of Lincoln's war incurred a debt that sank the nation into the hands and control of international bankers, something from which this nation has never recovered. Our freedom was truly lost when Lincoln implemented what is known today as the IRS.[v]

Lincoln's brutality to Native Americans and his own statements about African Americans make it clear he was not a great humanitarian. The war was never about slavery; it was about taxation. In his inaugural speech Lincoln said he didn't care about slavery; but obviously he cared about money. The South was the center of agricultural wealth in America. Lincoln attempted to impose an unlawful 52% tax on the South with a threat to invade if it was not paid. Ten states lawfully seceded from the union which led to the Civil War. In other words, they did what their state and our federal Constitution says was legal. But like the many previous presidents who Lincoln modeled and who swore to uphold the Constitution, he too ignored the document when he couldn't use it to accomplish his agendas.

---

v http://www.usa-the-republic.com/illuminati/Dishonest_Abe--Lincoln%27s_War_&_the_IRS.pdf

On Apr 14, 1865, Lincoln was assassinated and Congress revoked the Greenback Law and replaced it with the National Banking Act supporting privately owned national banks. This private banking was the forerunner to the Federal Reserve, a private bank that prints our money, loans it to our government and totally controls our economy and government. When Lincoln did not follow through allowing banks to create their own money he was assassinated. Interestingly:

> There have been assassination attempts on every President who attempted to eliminate these private National l Banks. The privately held Federal Reserve Bank has not once been audited and never pays any income tax on their astonishing income. The bank is supposed to bring stability to the economy; however, almost every major market crash and war can be attributed to the Federal Reserve Bank.[vi]

The Federal Reserve is part of the Central Banking System. These banks control the money of most countries in the world. A government can't go to war, protect itself or even stabilize its own economy without the support of the Central Bank. But I have to ask myself, "If banks have money and governments have armies why don't all governments simply break the power of these banks?" Simple! It is more than money; they hold secrets of enlightenment and power. They know the secret pathway to an elitist utopia where there will be no more mention of God, no Communism and no Capitalism, just the enlightened mega-wealthy of the world who have transcended the ignorance of the religious masses by accepting true enlightenment!

On Apr 14, 1865, Lincoln was assassinated and Congress revoked the Greenback Law and replaced it with the National Banking Act supporting privately owned national banks.

The Great Harlot weakens nations with the promise of an elitist utopian world free from the mention of the superstition of God. Through greed, lust and hunger for power leaders of nations stake a claim in the world's wealth and resources for them and their heirs. After all, they are enlightened. They

---

vi http://www.libertyforlife.com/banking/federal_reserve_bank.html

deserve the world's wealth. Why should it be wasted on the ignorant? The Great Harlot is like the prophet Balaam who sought to weaken God's people through sin and compromise. In their weakened condition, they would become disconnected from God and be vulnerable to the Luciferian nations that sought to destroy them. While leaders of the world play their game of world domination, the antichrist nations are becoming more and more powerful. They will one day reach such a pinnacle of power to be able to overthrow the Great Harlot and her adulterous lovers of iniquity!

A government can't go to war, protect itself or even stabilize its own economy without the support of the Central Bank.

SPIRITUAL GUIDE

If this is true, what can we do? God warns us of all these things so we can prepare. Prepare what? Prepare our hearts. Prepare our families. If the antichrist rises to power tomorrow would you, your spouse, your children and grandchildren have a strong enough relationship with God to overcome? Do they know enough biblical truth to resist false history and science? Will they resist false religion when there are deceptive miracles and lying signs and wonders?

This is not a defeatist attitude but the **true** Church, those who are called and are following the Lord Jesus. It does not have and has never wanted world domination; it wants people to be made whole, to be prepared for eternity and to live in peace and love. We cannot establish the Kingdom of God on earth. This humanistic concept of the Kingdom of God on earth is exactly what every other power-hungry, religious tyrant has sought to do. There will be only one righteous, religious-political world leader: Jesus!

There was a time when voting wisely would have made a difference, but that time may be gone. The two major political parties are financed by many of the same people, have been educated in the same schools and many are members of the antichrist secret organizations that began to flourish in the 20th century. Maybe we need to consider what Stalin said, "The people who cast the votes don't decide an election, the people who count them do."

There have been preachers with the Kingdom Now theology claiming the Church will take over the world and get it ready for Jesus to return. If that were possible Jesus would have done it Himself. So if the Church takes over the world, what would keep us honest? Who would decide the leaders? What would we do if we disagree? What would happen if we had a corrupt leader? People who embrace such philosophies are the *useful idiots* of idealistic or power-hungry clergy. Every doctrine or philosophy that thinks that is God's plan takes on the elitist-enlightened mentality and will destroy in the name of the good they want to accomplish.

Walk in love, pray with your children and follow God in your heart. Value what God values and turn your heart away from what the world values. If you do not choose to own some part of the world it can never own you. Keep yourself free from the love of "things." Enjoy them and use them but do not become engrossed by them. Determine your identity based on who you are in Jesus, not what you possess. *Do not love the world or the things in the world. If anyone loves the world, the love of the Father is not in him. For all that is in the world — the lust of the flesh, the lust of the eyes, and the pride of life — is not of the Father but is of the world. And the world is passing away, and the lust of it; but he who does the will of God abides forever* (1 John 2:15-17).

I recommend you go through every chapter of this book with your children and grandchildren, even if you have to modify it to make it understandable. Protect their hearts from the deceptive flood covering the world. Let them get a biblical understanding of world history instead of propaganda that is vomited on them in public education. If we do not tell them God's truth they will never understand or endure what lies ahead. But with faith and the Word of God in their heart they can do great exploits. Thy can be mountain movers of the future who take the Gospel of Kingdom to the ends of the earth!

To learn more about the resources mentioned and for additional support material for this chapter please visit www.secondcomingguide.com.

APOCALYPSE

CHAPTER 23

CONCLUSION TO SECTION THREE

The goal of all secret societies and all government is a world unrestrained by the Word of God!

I MUST REMIND YOU, THIS BOOK IS PROVIDING A SPIRITUAL HISTORY OF THE WORLD AND IT IS DARK AND NEGATIVE. But the message to you is not negative. God's Word provides the history of those who lived by faith and accomplished great conquests. Seeing what was going on in the rest of the world should open our eyes to how men and women of faith have always prevailed, even when standing alone against the entire world.

Understanding what was happening on a global scale should give you great confidence in God's ability to sustain His people in times of great adversity! It should make every victory by the children of Israel and by the Church even more incredible. When the man of iniquity gathers the entire world to his side his fate will be no different than all the vain attempts of the enemy in the past. The one difference is this will be the first time in human history Christ will be present in bodily form to lead His people into an absolute victory.

In the Old Testament believers didn't have the Holy Spirit living inside them. We have the Holy Spirit empowering us with the grace of God. They did not hear the voice of God in their heart. He lives in us as our Teacher, leading us into all truth and warning us of all things that are coming. He is our Divine Strategist. They had the law gnawing away at their conscience, exaggerating every personal frailty and failure. We have been given the free gift of righteousness and we have the ongoing blood of Jesus cleansing our conscience. They were only empowered by the Holy Spirit to do the miraculous. He is in us to manifest all His gifts any time there is a need. Just imagine: they prevailed with nothing but the Word of God, faith in His Word and the occasional empowering of the Holy Spirit. We are in this earth as Jesus is right now at the right hand of God!

We have been given the free gift of righteousness and we have the ongoing blood of Jesus cleansing our conscience.

It is true the world is plunging into the greatest darkness and most horrific tribulation the world has ever seen. There is no eschatology that can with honesty explain this away. But that is only what happens in the first 3 1/2 years of the Tribulation. The last 3 1/2 years of Tribulation will be the darkest days Lucifer and his followers have ever known. They will face millions of believers just like Jesus all over the world. It will truly be his darkest day!

What makes section three of this book and the following section so challenging is their relevance to our own lives. Even though it is a stretch for some to look at how God's people were deceived in the past, it is far more challenging to admit the degree to which we are deceived. We can look at how tradition and the occult slipped into the Church through the Religionists, but it is incredibly challenging to see through the haze of our own personal religious traditions. Now we're discussing things that force us to take inventory and examine our own heart. We can no longer force the Word to say what we need it to say. We must allow it to be used as it is intended: *...living and powerful, and sharper than any two-edged sword, piercing even to the division of soul and spirit, and of joints and marrow, and is a discerner of the thoughts and intents of the heart* (Hebrews 4:12).

As we get into section four, we will be made to question all we have ever trusted. We will, for the first time, be forced to accept the dichotomy and complete incompatibility between the World's System and the Kingdom of God! We will have to question everything we have ever known and believed about our nation and the world, but it will be this very questioning that will prepare us for the two most important aspects of ushering in the return of Jesus. Once we have removed the blinders from our mind and heart it becomes much easier to clearly hear the voice of the Lord as He gently speaks in our heart. As we see the futility and corruption of this world we will finally realize the only thing we have to offer anyone is an introduction to the Kingdom of God through faith in the resurrected and soon-coming Lord: Jesus Christ!

We will, for the first time, be forced to accept the dichotomy and complete incompatibility between the World's System and the Kingdom of God!

The shift may be slow and subtle or it may be immediate, but be sure of this, it is a shift that is coming. Proverbs tells us beatings or stripes are for the back of fools (Proverbs 19:29). In other words, fools only learn by consequences. Many who read this will close their eyes so they don't see the obvious. They will close their ears to what they are afraid to hear. They will harden their heart so they do not understand; otherwise, they have no choice but to change (Matthew 13:14-15). My heart breaks for these good people who, because of fear or unbelief, will put themselves in positions to only be persuaded by the ever-increasing intensity of iniquity, tribulation and suffering brought by the evil one. Every day they remain in darkness they increase the probability of being overcome.

You can make the choice to see the truth now. You don't have to agree with everything in this book, but you do have to accept the truth of the coming tribulation, the rise of the antichrist and the return of the Lord Jesus. If you seek God with all your heart you will soon see the truth without fear. God will work in you that which seems impossible at this moment. God will personally lead you on a journey where your lamp is filled with oil and your ears are listening for the voice of the Bridegroom.

SECTION FOUR

APOCALYPSE

CHAPTER 24

INTRODUCTION TO SECTION FOUR

ONE THING THAT MUST BE REMEMBERED, NOT JUST THROUGH READING THIS BOOK BUT THROUGH OUR JOURNEY IN LIFE, IS THAT SATAN DOES NOT HAVE THE POWER OR AUTHORITY TO ACT INDEPENDENTLY IN PLANET EARTH. In other words, **he does not have authority over you**. Your personal failures do not give him your authority. If he had authority over you he would have already destroyed you and the world. God and the devil must work in this realm as God ordained it: man has authority in Planet Earth. All that will happen with God or the devil will be because man wants it, allows it or surrenders it. When man's authority is factored into the mix some biblical questions about God's timing may be demystified.

The Bible says "*...that in the dispensation of the fullness of times He might gather together in one all things in Christ*" (Ephesians 1:10). The "*fullness of times*" seems to lend itself to an idea of many factors coming together to create the perfect moment. Many factors had to come together for Jesus to come the first time. Likewise, many factors must come together for Him to return. Many of those factors may be determined by man, his beliefs and his choices. There are some scriptural statements that indicate the time of His return is not etched in stone as we have been taught. For example, Jesus said:

> *Pray that your flight may not be in winter or on the Sabbath. For then there will be great tribulation, such as has not been since the beginning of the world until this time, no, nor ever shall be* (Matthew 24: 20-21).

Jesus would not tell us to pray for something that could not be altered. Morality, faith, technology and the will of man must come together to bring about the "perfect storm" for the emergence of the antichrist as well as the coming end time revival. Both events happen as man chooses sides, makes decisions and uses his authority.

By the end of the 20th century we saw many factors come together to facilitate the rise of the wicked one: demoralization of the world, control of the central banks over the nations, a compromised and unbelieving Church, a corrupt world-wide media and world-wide social and political chaos, just to name a few. Mass media has become the public voice of the Luciferian propaganda. It has, in fact, made it possible to move the Luciferian conspiracy from the back rooms and secret meetings to the front page of the newspaper and the 24-hour news cycle. Mass media can turn a lie into a perceived, accepted truth overnight. It can turn a conspiratorial plan into a trend. It can collapse a market with one false report or inspire great confidence in another. It can turn the masses in almost any direction with just one news cycle. Of all the powers of the media, possibly the most vile is to persuade the listener to perceive evil as good and good as evil, and do it in a way that even God's people rethink their beliefs.

By the end of the 20th century we saw many factors come together to facilitate the rise of the wicked one: demoralization of the world, control of the central banks over the nations, a compromised and unbelieving Church, a corrupt world-wide media and world-wide social and political chaos...

Some would have us believe that all these factors coming together means the entire world is corrupt, but that would be a gross misconception. Remember, Elijah thought he was the only one faithful to God, but God showed him He always has a remnant (Romans 11:3-5). Through the darkness before the Flood, through the deceit of the Universal Church, through persecution and through compromise there is always a remnant. The remnant cannot be identified by any outward association; it is comprised of those who have kept themselves alive to God in their heart. They are the "called out" who have heard and obeyed. God will never be left without a witness or a remnant.

Pew Research shows that 78.4% of Americans are Christians.[i] The Christian vote is so important that candidates for public office, no matter how pagan or ungodly, seek to present themselves as Christian. Although they may hate the Church they know if their anti-God beliefs and agendas are ever exposed they cannot get elected. But on the other hand, Bible-believing, faith in Jesus is the most politically persecuted faith in America. The same politicians who call themselves Christian when asking for your votes are those passing laws to restrict our freedom while giving evermore freedom and power to Islam. We are opposed in the media, marginalized by federal and state laws and banned from public expression, but be assured the called out (Church) is alive and well in America.

The 20th century gave rise to the possibility of Lucifer's dream of a world in darkness - a world-wide mindset of iniquity. Light and darkness are opposing words, both of which have many expressions. Truth, light, life, love and godliness are not just a string of synonyms; they are a continuum of expressing God and His true character. Likewise, darkness, deceit, lies, death and iniquity are a continuum. Truth and iniquity are central to the idea of light and darkness. When there is light all the manifestations of the continuum are expressed: life, love and godliness. When darkness prevails people experience the continuum of death, destruction and iniquity. Lucifer needs man to reject God's truth and thereby destroy himself. He needs for man to do to himself what Satan cannot do to him. Remember, Satan is not a roaring lion, but *"he goes about AS a roaring lion, seeking whom he may devour"* (1 Peter 1:8-9). He needs you in darkness (iniquity). When you are in faith he can do you no harm.

Truth is more than what God said in the Word. Truth is all the word implies, as well as how it should be applied. John writes: *"For the law was given through Moses, but grace and truth came through Jesus Christ"* (John 1:17). Jesus did not do away with the law; He came to fulfil it, bring it to its full, complete and perfect expression. He did not bring a new law; instead, He brought us grace *and* truth. Truth is all the law implies; grace is God's power working in us to be able to express the law in His strength with His motives.

---

i http://religions.pewforum.org/reports

The world has rarely seen God's Word applied the way He intended, from the motive of love. Love is the fulfillment of the law[ii]. In other words, when people walk in love they will do to and for one another what the law taught. They are not doing it to earn something from God; it is an expression of their new, righteous-loving nature. In Jesus the world would see the truth that God's commandments show us how to express God's love.

Because of the leaven of the Luciferian spirit in religion the law has been used to judge, condemn and control but it has not been the standard of love.

Because of the leaven of the Luciferian spirit in religion the law has been used to judge, condemn and control but it has not been the standard of love. Everything in Jesus' life, ministry and death was an expression of God's love for mankind. He gave us the model of what it should look like and He gave us power to do it. That is why Jesus is the light of the world. Everything He did was based on God's Word, God's name and God's nature!

Darkness is when man does what he deems to be the right thing independently of God's Word. Humanism, philosophy or simple wickedness rejects God's Word as the standard of morals, ethics and love. The Luciferian mindset presented the "angry God" doctrine, thereby justifying iniquity. God was not to be trusted, could not be trusted! God was not love, He was wrath. His commandments were not going to bring freedom, they would bring bondage. Since faith works by love, man could not trust a God who did not love him. Thus, God's Word could not be trusted; therefore, man went into the darkness of reason, carnal logic, perverted righteousness and corrupt science.

There were those truly deceived by the Luciferian lawlessness and there were those who used lawlessness to deceive others. The greedy, immoral and

---

ii Romans 13:8-10, Owe no one anything except to love one another, for he who loves another has fulfilled the law. 9 For the commandments, "You shall not commit adultery," "You shall not murder," "You shall not steal," "You shall not bear false witness," "You shall not covet," and if there is any other commandment, are all summed up in this saying, namely, "You shall love your neighbor as yourself." 10 Love does no harm to a neighbor; therefore love is the fulfillment of the law. Galatians 5:14, For all the law is fulfilled in one word, even in this: "You shall love your neighbor as yourself."

power-hungry used lawlessness as means to fulfill their lusts. Trillions of dollars are made in pornography, prostitution, drug dealing, arms dealing, human trafficking and other expressions along the continuum of darkness. These corrupt sellers of flesh need a desperate, corrupt world to line their pockets. The Apostle Paul gives Timothy, his understudy, an interesting look into the psychology of man. He points out these corrupt people actually become deceived by their own deceptions. *"But evil men and impostors will grow worse and worse, deceiving and being deceived"* (2 Timothy 3:13).

There were those truly deceived by the Luciferian lawlessness and there were those who used lawlessness to deceive others.

The rejection of God's standards and values gives rise to iniquity. As man moved farther from God his inherent need for the love of God became more predominate. Iniquity moved him to vainly attempt to fill that need by giving himself to more and more wickedness. In his own deception man became more deceived. In time, man needed to disbelieve in God as a means of soothing his own compromised conscience. Communism, Islam, Atheism and all haters of morality and integrity have fought for thousands of years to bring us to this point. By the 20th century iniquity became the new norm. If anything in science, morality, medicine or psychology is remotely harmonious with God's Word it is rejected and ridiculed.

The rise of iniquity brings a unity of purpose between many groups who may have been unknowingly participating in the eternal conspiracy. Now the common enemy makes strange bedfellows of women's rights groups and Islam, Socialism and Wall Street, government and the occult. When working from the motive of evil, joining together to destroy a common enemy makes sense. "The enemy of my enemy is my friend." As short-sighted as this is, it is the prevailing logic of the conspiracy of evil. After destroying their common enemy they will attempt to destroy one another at a later, more convenient time.

One would think with so many different entities seeking to establish a godless world it would be a simple task of overpowering the people, but the problem of man's authority and free will leaves deceit and seduction as the only tools that will work against beings created in the likeness and image of God! These wicked entities must have an invitation to take over the world or their dream will never be accomplished.

The Communist plan to overthrow America, which is nothing more than a rewritten plan of the Illuminati, which is nothing more than Luciferian iniquity, is basically a philosophical series of lawless, anti-Bible rejection of God's morals, values and ethics designed to demoralize man, create chaos and deceive man into selling his soul in exchange for peace. In fact, it is called demoralization. Destroy everything God says is healthy and wholesome. Demoralization is the most important fundamental step in overthrowing a nation and the world.

What the Creator gave to keep us strong, safe, and fulfilled has been rejected as limiting, legalistic domination.

What the Creator gave to keep us strong, safe and fulfilled has been rejected as limiting, legalistic domination. The family unit, starting with marriage, is founded in archaic religion that keeps man from fulfilling his desires. Breaking down the family unit is a vital step in destroying man's ability to be emotionally whole and stable. It undermines his ability to trust, but mostly it makes the individual feel alone.

It is essential to control the media so people never hear the truth. The enlightened believe people cannot handle the truth so it is better for the "powers that be" to decide what man needs to hear. Keep them entertained and spending money and they will not get in the way of the larger plans. Let the media be the main arm of propaganda.

Make people hate the government. Corrupt the judicial system; make it slow and complicated. Make the laws contradictory and unjust. Transform the courts from being courts of justice to courts of law. Enrage the people to take the law into their own hands. Make all dealings with government frustrating and unfair, then use the media to make the population feel their vote, their word and their opinion means nothing.

Create a codependent minority. Use welfare as a means to corrupt, disempower and enslave the masses, then create a class war between the wealthy and the poor. But it will actually be a war between those who work for a living and those who do not. Those who do not work are financed by government subsidies. Those who work for a living do not have time to riot, march, protest and lobby; they have to pay their bills. Create a victims' mentality (codependence) that makes minorities feel like victims. Use minorities as a way to breakdown police protection. Make everything that happens to a minority look like an injustice caused by everyone who is of a different color or social status. Make everyone who wears a badge the enemy of the poor and oppressed, then use civil rights to make it impossible for the police to do their job. Use the media to exaggerate and tell outright lies about the facts. Enrage the entire country. Create civil war.

While people are focused on chaos and fear, destroy the economy. Create national debt and keep borrowing money and drive inflation beyond control. Use the EPA and every bureaucratic agency to make goods and services more expensive, more complicated and less effective. To further enrage and inspire cultural war blame the banks. Create a rich versus poor war in the streets. Make the future look worse than anyone can imagine. Make the problem so big that no person can consider standing alone.

> The enlightened believe people cannot handle the truth, so it is better for the "powers that be" to decide what man needs to hear.

Take away the right to personal protection and disarm the population. When people cannot protect themselves and the police are underfunded and afraid to act, deliver the final blow: create massive violent chaos. Burn houses, churches and businesses. Attack the wealthy and middle class. Create so much fear, panic and confusion that even the most rational thinker will cry out for someone to save them.

In the midst of the chaos, in steps the person who promises peace, hope and change. This person personifies the system that brought the chaos. He was among those who caused all the problems, but now he is the "wolf in sheep's clothing," offering a false peace. He will help you break the power of the wealthy oppressor. He will fight for the rights of the poor and oppressed. In Russia his names were Marx and Lenin. In China he was Mao Zedong. In Germany he was Hitler. In Cuba he was Castro … you get the point! As soon as this person comes to power he removes his "sheep's clothing" and we discover we have made a deal with the devil! This is the strategy for cities, states, nations and ultimately the world. Lucifer uses chaos as his tool to take power.

On a national level, a ruler or a ruling party is controlled by banks that are controlled by the unseen hand, those committed to and working toward the New World Order. The New World Order is the Luciferian dream for annihilating all knowledge of God. But that is actually a ruse. Once man no longer has a connection to his true God-given identity and once he no longer believes in God or blames God for his woes, then the true plan is executed: the rise of the antichrist kingdom that seeks only to destroy the world and all that God loves!

> He is the "wolf in sheep's clothing," offering a false peace. In Russia his names were Marx and Lenin. In China he was Mao Zedong. In Germany he was Hitler. In Cuba he was Castro

One reason believers are so confused about the end time tactics of the evil one is that we fail to make a distinction between the role of the Great Harlot and the role of the antichrist nations. The Harlot seduces the governments of the world. She inspires the dream of a utopian world controlled by the enlightened elitists. But it is this weakening of the nations that makes it possible for the antichrist to rise to power. They are not the same entities, but they are inspired by the same wickedness.

By the 19th century previously laid plans were occurring with increasing precision and effectiveness. All over the world nations were falling to Communism, Atheism and anti-God, humanistic thought. By the use of war and economic manipulation occultists had influenced the governments of the world to see the need for a one-world government. It would be the false promise of peace that would actually be a final step toward an elitist Utopia. All manner of governmental and non-governmental agencies were born, aimed toward foreign relations. Oddly, they were all connected to and led by those who had financed all the wars and controlled the world's economy. Thus, was born the grand idea of the United Nations: a global agency whose laws, morals and values superseded the laws of the individual countries. This agency would determine the good guys and bad guys, internationally speaking. They would do away with war, national identities… and national sovereignty.

By the 20th century the perfect storm was emerging. Every strategy of Lucifer has been to get the world to this place. God wasn't giving the antichrist control of the world; the world was giving away their rights. One person at a time, one country at a time, freedom and authority was given to godless leaders. These are the same leaders who created the problems and offered an unbiblical way to solve them. Naïve people do not understand that there can only be inflation if the government creates it. There can only be bad laws if the government passes them. There can only be massive national debt if the government spends more than it has.

None of this happens by accident. As one person pointed out, if all these things occurred by chance there would be at least a 50% possibility of getting it right. So why is it that the government never gets it right? Why does the government always sell out the people? Why do they pass bad laws? Why do the majority of politicians, regardless of their party, break the campaign promises that got them elected? Simple! Politicians are simply "front men" for those who finance their campaigns. They buy their way into office with indebtedness to those who own their careers.

Naïve people do not understand that there can only be inflation if the government creates it.

No doubt there have been many men and women who believed they could make a difference if they were elected to office, but like so many before them they came to see that even the president only has the freedom to exercise authority within the boundaries of those who actually control the world. One decision by the Federal Reserve in America or any Central Bank could plunge a country into absolute anarchy, then you and your party will be blamed. Or a war could be financed giving your national enemy the upper hand. Some do what good they can, most seem to "drink the Kool-Aid" get rich, become deceived by the entire process and knowingly or unknowingly give their authority to the Great Harlot and/or the antichrist!

According to occult prophecies and signs, the final step will occur in the 21st century. 2012 would be the year all factors needed to transfer control of the world would finally be in place. In this section we will look at 19th, 20th and 21st century history. We will examine the current world factors that are proof of what has occurred from creation until now. We will look specifically at what is happening in the United States as well as Russia, China and the Middle East. These are the world powers, the global economic forces and the key players in the New World Order. The occurrences in these nations/regions will determine the fate of Israel and the world. If, in fact, America is the launching pad for the New World Order we must grasp these factors before we can look knowledgeably at end time prophecy. We will not interpret end time prophecy based on current events, but on the Word of God and how that has played out historically.

We have endured the history that preceded us. We will overcome in the history that lies before us. The best is yet to come.

I encourage you to be like Daniel who foresaw the horrible events that would unfold from his time until the very end. Daniel did not become overwhelmed by the seemingly never-ending rise of wicked world powers, each successive government becoming more ruthless and wicked than the former. He kept looking until he saw God's final and ultimate solution. Do not be dismayed by what you have read up to this point. We have endured the history that preceded us. We will overcome in the history that lies before us. The best is yet to come… keep looking!

APOCALYPSE

CHAPTER 25

THE WORLD'S SYSTEM

The destruction of moral people occurs because they attempt to treat everyone as moral!

ANCIENT HISTORY COUPLED WITH EVENTS OF THE 19TH AND 20TH CENTURIES ACTUALLY SET THE STAGE FOR THE PERFECT EXPRESSION OF THE WORLD'S SYSTEM. When man began to consider himself enlightened he dismissed as legend or myth the ancient stories of giants and beings with near supernatural powers. God, the devil and demons were relegated to the same category as Santa Claus and the tooth fairy. In their conceit they rejected the biblical account of God, creation, the identity of man and the spiritual history of the world. They were too wise in their own eyes to believe such nonsensical stories.

Reaching these conclusions did not make the demonic beings suddenly vanish. It did not neutralize the Luciferian doctrines which had filled the earth, nor did it erase thousands of years of cellular memories that had been recorded in our bodies fueling our subconscious. No! Mankind may have made new, conscious decisions but woven into the fabric of his being was a more powerful subconscious reality. We fabricated a version of history that makes us feel enlightened and in control, but this vanity will abruptly end when mankind awakens to the godless expression of man without God: 666.

It is essential we remind ourselves that the prophecies of what will be coming on the world are not prophecies of God's wrath and judgment poured on the world because of its disobedience, but warnings of what man would do to the world and to mankind if he follows the way of the wicked one. These warnings were meant to sober our minds and awaken us from our slumber. They were a call to prevent the tribulation of the antichrist, the man of lawlessness (iniquity) who, acting upon the prevalent mindset of iniquity, will deceive the world while attempting to eliminate by any means possible all belief and knowledge of God.

The 20th century was an age of vanity, ego and self-reliance. The wealthy finally realized the dream and means of controlling the world. The systems were finally in place to completely manipulate the thoughts of mankind. The false hope to finally eliminate the knowledge of God seemed within reach. The 20th century would produce the generation that would set the world stage for the ultimate polarization of good and evil, light and darkness, truth and lies. This would occur as the World's System became the rationale of the political, educational, informational and many religious sectors of the world.

It is essential that we understand the Kingdom principle. After all, we were taught to pray *"Thy kingdom come."*

It is essential that we understand the Kingdom principle. After all, we were taught to pray *"Thy kingdom come."* Too often that was a prayer of religious repetition, not the earnest cry of a believing heart. The Bible explains there are two systems whereby all things function: the Kingdom of God* and the World's System. These two systems are motivated by completely incompatible purposes. Even when the World's System utilizes the same information as the Kingdom, the distorted motive will ultimately corrupt the outcome or expression of that truth.

The system to which something belongs is determined by its basis of absolute truth. The carnally-minded (natural) uses man's wisdom, logic and reasoning as the basis of determining truth. Even when carnal man claims to believe the Word of God it is not because he trusts God, but because he has judged God's

Word by his logic and information and deemed it believable. When God's Word does not fit his personal judgment it is rejected or relegated to the "I don't understand" category. The Religionists could twist the Word of God to justify their actions and say, "I am acting on truth," but truth is not just the information contained in Scripture; it is also intent, implied information and motive. Historically, religion has seriously misrepresented God. The Prophet Isaiah said because of leaders the people are *"taken into captivity, they wail and blaspheme God's name continually"* (Isaiah 52:5-6). Religionists have always used the Word of God to control, dominate and judge, but never in truth!

When Jesus came on the scene we are told He brought truth. *"For the law was given through Moses, but grace and truth came through Jesus Christ"* (John 1:17). Some foolishly interpret this Scripture to imply that Jesus did away with the law and brought us new truth. But Jesus said that He did not come to do away with the law; yet, Scripture tells us we are *"not under the law but under grace"* (Romans 6:14). Improperly interpreting John 1:17 will lead many believers into iniquity or rejection of the law because they do not know how to embrace God's law while living under grace.

Jesus didn't bring us new truth but He personified the Word of God, showing us what it would look like applied as God intended.

Jesus didn't bring us new truth but He personified the Word of God, showing us what it would look like applied as God intended. Religionists always use the law to control the people. By making people believe they could earn their righteousness they put mankind under an impossible, unbearable burden. But Jesus showed us how the law was God's divine prescription for loving one another. Verse 14 of John 1 makes this clear. *"And the Word became flesh and dwelt among us, and we beheld His glory, the glory as of the only begotten of the Father, full of grace and truth."*

When we look at the life and teaching of Jesus we see God's Word in the flesh, that is, in human form. We see how it should have looked from the beginning. We see what it looked like when applied from the motive of love. But the glory of Jesus as the Word was not His own; it was the glory of the Father. He didn't come to speak His own words or to glorify Himself. He came to speak and model God's Word, which was from the beginning, and thereby glorify Him.[i]

In the World's System man's opinion is the absolute and final authority. Relative morals, social justice and secular fairness determine our motives.

The Kingdom of God is an internal realm.[ii] It is a realm we enter through the door of the heart by faith. In that realm we are submitted to the rule of Jesus as Lord. We live and function based on God's Word, not in legalism but in trust. His Word applied from the motive of love is the final authority. If our intent is to help and serve others and we are truly motivated by love, God's Word provides the "how to." In the World's System man's opinion is the absolute and final authority. Relative morals, social justice and secular fairness determine our motives. Since every seed bears after its own kind, that which motivates the action produces fruit after its own kind regardless of intention.

Christians in ever-growing numbers have lost any concept of relating to Jesus as Lord. They have entrusted their soul to the Lord, but the way they do business, raise kids and manage their life is based primarily on the World's System. In time being a "Christian" seems to have little relevance in their lives and as they lose touch with God in their heart they become more a part of the world than the Kingdom. In the 1970's there was a strong revival in Southern Baptist churches as the message of Lordship swept through. The congregations were challenged, "Did you accept Jesus as Savior or Lord?" There was a powerful turning to the Lord throughout many of the churches. But Lordship has never been the primary message of the Church. Lordship is the foundation for discipleship and discipleship from a heart of love and trust is the foundation for healthy transformation. Failure to obey Jesus' commission and make disciples has caused the constant erosion of believers who started well and eventually began to struggle with their faith.

---

i John 8:47, He who is of God hears God's words; therefore you do not hear, because you are not of God.
John 17:8, For I have given to them the words which You have given Me; and they have received them, and have known surely that I came forth from You; and they have believed that You sent Me.
John 3:34, For He whom God has sent speaks the words of God,

ii Luke 17:20, For indeed, the kingdom of God is within you.

At the fall of man the entire issue at stake was Lordship. Who has the right to determine good and bad, right and wrong and just or unjust? Man rejected God's reign over his life. Since then the struggle for man has still been who is Lord, Jesus or me? Whose teaching and logic will control my life? Even after salvation the carnal-minded believer struggles with the issue of Lordship. It doesn't matter if someone is a Christian or a pagan; every person functions in the realm of the Kingdom or the world based on the source of authority and the motive driving his or her actions. In one decision they may look to God's Word, but the next may be based totally on a godless motive. When fear, manipulation or control is the motive or the method that person is not functioning in the Kingdom realm. No good comes from evil. *"The wrath of man does not accomplish the righteousness of God"* (James 1:20). The Bible warns against mixing two different seeds in the same furrow.[iii] This may have been a metaphor against mixing what is sown in our heart.

At the fall of man the entire issue at stake was Lordship. Who has the right to determine good and bad, right and wrong and just or unjust?

Using the name of Jesus or quoting Scripture does not mean a person represents God or is functioning in the Kingdom. Religionists, through a corrupt, imposter Church dominated the world by force as they murdered and tortured dissenters turning the entire world away from God, but they did it all in the name of Jesus. The carnal Church functions in the World's System under the banner of the cross. But as Scripture indicates, the World's System is not just the governments but also Religionists or anyone motivated by humanistic logic and values. The 20th century brought the world to the brink of moral collapse through iniquity - humanistic values, social justice and political correctness.

Psalm 11:3 asks, *"If the foundations are destroyed, What can the righteous do?"* *Strong's Concordance* says this refers to political and moral foundations. That's probably the question you're asking yourself now. "If it is this bad, what can I do? What hope is there?" The last thing you want is to have no hope. That is why it is so incredibly important that you apply the suggestions and

---

iii Deuteronomy 22:9, You shall not sow your vineyard with different kinds of seed, lest the yield of the seed which you have sown and the fruit of your vineyard be defiled.

alternatives listed in every chapter of this book. But it is even more important that you read until the end. I will show what Jesus said we can do to prepare for the darkness that is coming.

We have to admit and recognize the problem before we can get the help we need. We have to understand the nature of the problem lest we be deceived. Armed with the right information we can begin to ask the right questions. End time books have been written for centuries, but too many of them portrayed an unscriptural concept of God, blaming Him instead of the antichrist and his followers for the coming judgment, unintentionally propagating the same Luciferian doctrine that emerged at Lucifer's rebellion, abounded before Noah's Flood, was established in the modern world by Nimrod and has since been sustained by Religionists.

A great student of history once pointed out that civilized societies tend to fall because they relate to the world with the assumption that everyone is civilized.

If we do not clearly recognize the perpetrator of sorrows and tribulation we will blame God for the problem and, consequently, we will ask the wrong questions. Asking the wrong questions always leads to the wrong answers. If we have correctly identified the enemy and his schemes we will begin to ask the right questions, thereby facing the future armed with right answers, the answers that will equip us to not just endure but overcome when others' hearts are failing them with fear.

A great student of history once pointed out that civilized societies tend to fall because they relate to the world with the assumption that everyone is civilized. There is a willful deception in assuming the possibility of reasoning with unreasonable people. It is impossible to say why our generation has chosen not to see what is obvious in the Word of God and maybe even more obvious in world history. Some of our self-deception could have been the desire to be free from passing judgment, or maybe it is an attempt to avoid negativity or it could simply be naivety that caused us to close our eyes to the prevailing, growing wickedness of our world. In fact, part of our emotional survival mechanism has been called the "normalcy bias" which refers to a mental state people enter when facing real disaster that causes them to minimize the situation. This is what Jews did as Hitler came to power. The threat was so great it was impossible to face.

We don't want to believe the world is as bad as it is, and what we have erroneously been taught makes us feel it is judgmental to see the wrong. In Matthew 7, the chapter where Jesus warned against judgment, He also told us to examine the fruit. We do not have to assume good or evil intention of the person, but we are naïve and foolish if we do not look at the fruit and thereby know the person.

Part of our emotional survival mechanism has been called the "normalcy bias" which refers to a mental state people enter when facing real disaster that causes them to minimize the situation.

There is a tendency to assume all judgment is negative, but positive judgment is just as destructive. Negative judgment assumes that someone is working from a negative motive, therefore we relate to him or her on the basis of that judgment. Positive judgment assumes the person's behavior is coming from good intention. We must remember that judgment is to decide both good and evil, not just evil. When we wrongly pass positive judgments we trust those who intend us harm, we enter into business with the wrong people and we allow into our emotional attachments those whom we should not trust! Then we assume God let us down or didn't protect us when the evil intent is acted upon us.

It seems the Church has made a positive judgment about the World's System. We actually think there are good aspects of that system. We think the world and the Kingdom are compatible. To make such a judgment is to ignore what God tells us about unregenerate man. We have lost true perspective of the sin nature and how it works in unregenerate man. The person who does not know Jesus may occasionally employ biblically consistent methods, but they are still part of the World's System. In the end, the World's System will always defame God and demoralize man. Even in its good deeds the outcome will be corrupt. We simply do not want to see the world as it is. It is too overwhelming! Intent determines whether that which is true becomes truth. When God's Word is used from a corrupt intention it is no longer truth; in other words, it no longer reveals God's intention.

Not every person realizes they are part of a diabolical system designed to drive God's Word and name from the mouth, mind and heart of all humanity. They don't realize that education, media and government are all driven by iniquity. They do not understand they are part of a system built from a philosophical perspective which is diametrically opposed to truth. Some who recognize the conflict between good and evil foolishly think the world just wants to "live and let live." They think those of the world only want the Church to stop judging them. They do not realize that those of the world want iniquity. They don't want us to accept them as individuals; they want us to approve of their deeds. They hate the light because it exposes their deeds. The World's System is established on a set of values, morals, ethics and justice that are intentionally opposed to all that is godly.

Some who recognize the conflict between good and evil foolishly think the world just wants to "live and let live."

SPIRITUAL GUIDE

At this moment you may be on the right track more than you realize. You know what few people understand. You know God's account of history and how the world has reached this dark place. Hopefully, by now you have freed yourself from the Luciferian doctrine that blames God for all the chaos and tragedy that has befallen the world. If you still struggle with the belief of a judgmental God, you may want to consider reading my book, *The Gospel of Peace.* It will give you the full scriptural terms of the New Covenant and it will change the way you see God!

As you move forward create a deliberate awareness that we are ***in*** this world but we do not have to be ***of*** this world. We do not have to nor should we attempt to resort to the same tactics the World's System employs for success or happiness. We will build our lives, our businesses and our families on God's truth. We must choose to walk in love no matter what the standard of carnal behavior becomes. Jesus warned that as *"lawlessness abounds love will grow cold"* (Matthew 24:12). We cannot let the dishonesty and corruption of the World's System justify our turning from faith, hope and love. If we allow our hearts to become hard and insensitive we will not be able to hear and follow God's leadership as He speaks in our heart for victory and survival.

Walking in love does not make us doormats. When Jesus sent His disciples before Him to minister He said, *"Therefore be wise as serpents and harmless as doves"* (Matthew 10:16). We are to be cautious, discrete, using practical skills, yet harmless, or as the Greek implies: innocent, free from guile and single-minded. We will not allow ourselves to be envious of the wicked when they prosper through corrupt means. We will treasure God, family, peace and joy. We cannot allow ourselves to be foolish or naïve in relating to the world. Without being judgmental we cannot forsake our values.

Learning the subtle but skillful art of guarding our hearts will be one of the greatest challenges as corruption and iniquity continue to escalate. We must avoid that which has the ability to vex us. Vexation is a form of obsession. When we are vexed or obsessed we are like a drunk unable to defend himself against the weakest enemy. Our hearts are guarded with the breastplate of righteousness. This begins with persuading our hearts that we are righteous because we are in Jesus. But as the Apostle John points out, our behavior has great influence on our hearts. We can't attempt to believe one thing about ourselves while practicing something else. Walk in love and righteousness, thereby your heart won't condemn you! Keeping our hearts free from guilt and obsession frees us to hear and follow God's voice! Guarding our hearts is our secret weapon that keeps us connected to our Source of peace and power.

The following chapters reveal what we already know about the current condition of our nation and the world. Admitting these problems is not negativity or pessimism, nor is it designed to stimulate fear. We cannot ignorantly deny the depravity of mankind apart from Jesus. We cannot assume others will be fair, kind or honest. While we do not want to be rebels or dissidents we cannot deny the Word of God and the history of the world and blindly think the government exists for our good. We must finally say, "Yes, I can admit the truth about the condition of the world and know there is still hope for me, my family and those who choose to trust and follow God. I am ***in*** the world but I am not ***of*** the world. As a citizen of the Kingdom of God my life is governed by the laws of God, not the laws of man. Yet, in this world I will be a peacemaker. I will be the light in the darkness!

To learn more about the resources mentioned and for additional support material for this chapter please visit www.secondcomingguide.com.

APOCALYPSE

CHAPTER 26

CONTROL THROUGH FEAR

The first manifestation of the sin nature was not the desire to do evil; it was the tendency to fear!

CONTROL IS NEVER GODLY, NO MATTER WHO DOES IT. Even more insidious is control through fear.[i] Domination and control are a form of witchcraft and were strictly forbidden by the Lord Jesus. In Mark 10[ii] the disciples wanted to know who would be in charge after Jesus departed. He made it clear that as ministers we are never to exercise lordship or authority over anyone. Because the Religionists don't share the same objectives as the Lord Jesus, they see control as a reasonable and essential aspect of "ministry." Sadly, the entire authority structure conjured up by carnal leaders is unscriptural.

---

i If you desire to learn the art of powerful leadership free from control, consider reading volume 1 of the eBook *Leadership That Builds People*.

ii Mark 10:42-45, But Jesus called them to Himself and said to them, "You know that those who are considered rulers over the Gentiles lord it over them, and their great ones exercise authority over them. 43 Yet it shall not be so among you; but whoever desires to become great among you shall be your servant. 44 And whoever of you desires to be first shall be slave of all. 45 For even the Son of Man did not come to be served, but to serve, and to give His life a ransom for many."

It is obvious an organization needs an authority structure for management purposes, but we must never confuse that with authority over people. The only authority we have is the Word of God. Once we have ministered the Word of God in love, obedience is the choice of the hearer. We do not have the right to force them to obey. A true leader inspires, an insecure leader controls. A corrupt leader controls through fear, thereby destroying the faith (trust) he hopes to build.

The Book of Revelation gives us incredible insight into the nature and expression of sin. When describing who will have their part in the second death it provides a list of traits.

> *But the fearful, and unbelieving, and the abominable, and murderers, and whoremongers, and sorcerers, and idolaters, and all liars, shall have their part in the lake which burneth with fire and brimstone: which is the second death.* (Revelation 21:8)

I have always found it amazing that fear is the number one attribute on this list. Unbelief is number two, and then a variety of obvious sinful behavior follows. Fear is so destructive and evil because it is based on the Luciferian lie that God cannot be trusted. When fear is your core driving emotion, unbelief (no trust) is always the fruit. From these two (fear and unbelief) flows every sinful, destructive behavior. The only antidote for fear is love (1 John 4:18) and faith (trust) emerges from love. When we know God is predictably and consistently good we will always trust Him.

Corrupt, Luciferian Religionists have delivered to us many definitions of key biblical terms. Redefining biblical words has always been a ploy of cults. This has happened throughout history and is happening today on a scale I've never witnessed in my nearly half-a-century of serving God! Many words were completely redefined and some were given only a slightly different "shade." Regardless of the degree of corruption, the result always brings about a perversion of God's character, making Him either unbelievable or untrustworthy. For example, our concept of sin as constantly craving evil does not prove out biblically or in life. Behavior is the fruit of sin, belief is the root of sin, and fear is the root of sinful beliefs. The Luciferian goal is to hold man in sin, fearful and untrusting of God.

Sin entered the world not when Adam actually ate the fruit of the tree of the knowledge of good and evil, but when he entered into unbelief. When he accepted the idea that he was not like God he was firmly in the clutches of the evil one. Believing that lie altered every aspect of his identity, self-worth and self-image. All the core attributes that make us able to function as we were created are found in knowing the true identity and nature of God and believing we were created in His likeness and image. When that is missing we begin to feel lack (need or inadequacy) and we will then look beyond God's truth to resolve that feeling. From that comes all destructive behavior.[iii]

Adam's sense of lack is what drove him to eat of the tree of knowledge of good and evil. In his mind he had been deceived. He had trusted God. He thought he was created in the likeness and image of God, but after unbelief entered he no longer knew who he was. He no longer had that godly sense of self-worth that comes through believing, knowing and feeling God's love. The moment he stopped trusting God his entire world-view shifted. Instead of interpreting the world from the place of love, safety and security he began to interpret all things through the lens of fear and insecurity.

> Corrupt, Luciferian Religionists have delivered to us many definitions of key biblical terms. Redefining biblical words has always been a ploy of cults. This has happened throughout history and is happening today on a scale I've never witnessed in my nearly half-a-century of serving God!

In Genesis 3:8 God walked in the Garden in the cool of the day and called out to Adam. Now that Adam no longer trusted God he passed a judgment. Judgment is when we assume to know **why** someone does something. It is a determination of their intent as being good or evil. Adam judged God's intention as evil and hid himself from his Creator. When asked why he hid himself Adam responded, *"I heard Your voice in the garden, and I was afraid because I was naked; and I hid myself."* (Genesis 3:10)

Consider what just happened: based on wrong beliefs about God and himself Adam could no longer stand confidently in the presence of his God with whom he had communed daily. Those wrong beliefs caused him to feel fear,

iii *Breaking The Cycle,* James B. Richards, True Potential Publishing.

insecurity, inadequacy and timidity. These feelings about himself spurred several judgments. It was not God who informed him he should not be naked; that was his own heart condemning him based on his fear of God. Then he judged God's intention for calling out to him in the Garden. All of this lunged from fear and unbelief. It is this sin nature that judges self and God from the basis of fear that became the ripe, fertile ground for Luciferian doctrine: God is not good and He cannot be trusted.

Fear is the primary weapon of the World's System of religion and government. Fear drives man to look for a protector (savior) and unbelief keeps him from looking to God. The Luciferian spirit has worked in every realm of the World's System to make God unbelievable and untrustworthy while simultaneously keeping man in fear. All governments of the world know they must keep their population in fear as a means of keeping them dependent on their government.

Fear is the primary weapon of the World's System of religion and government. Fear drives man to look for a protector (savior) and unbelief keeps him from looking to God.

I was a child of the Cold War Era. I was born shortly after WWII and the Korean War. We lived under the constant threat of nuclear attack. As a first grader I remember going through emergency drills in the event of a nuclear explosion. In later years, "science" began to warn of a coming Ice Age. This was not the ramblings of a religious fanatic; it was the educated scientific body. In the 1980's there was the threat of planetary starvation. The world population was too massive to feed; we were all going to die of starvation unless we followed the government scientists' recommendations. Nevermind that the famine happening in the world at that time was mostly man-made. Over the course of time we have gone from the scientific proof of a new Ice Age to "global warming." Just like every other threat of world annihilation, the global warming trend ended nearly 20 years ago. We now know that scientists used faulty models to predict future weather trends. Any scientist who refuted the false findings was fired and censored. The governments of the world want us to be afraid!

In the book, *Healing Codes for the Biological Apocalypse,* Doctors Leonard Horowitz and Joseph Puleo discuss a study seeking to find ways to control the population once a one-world government has been established. The philosophy is if man sees the world at peace he will become difficult to control; therefore, man must always be faced with perceived threats and challenges too massive and menacing for him to face alone. He must be held in fear as a means to always be controlled by the government. Among the recommendations for fear propaganda are to create the constant threat of any of the following: war, pollution, pandemics, threats from outer space and slavery, just to name a few. According to this book, war is not really about one nation infringing on another, it is about controlling the population. Based on the report from *Iron Mountain,* "No modern political ruling group has successfully controlled its constituency after failing to sustain the continuing credibility of an external threat of war" (Page 375).

The 19th and 20th centuries became nothing less than a global propaganda effort to accomplish a few goals:

1. Make the belief in God seem utterly foolish.
2. Create false science to disprove the facts of creation, thereby disproving God.
3. Use medicine to advance Atheism.
4. Bring about global demoralization through iniquity.
5. Promote fear-based religion so those who do believe in a God see Him as negative, wrathful and untrustworthy.
6. Create massive fear through disease, war, economics, etc.
7. Destroy the Church as a relevant factor in life and society.
8. Promote unrest and chaos through class warfare.
9. Collapse the world economy.
10. Create a perceived need for a "one-world government."

All the institutions you trusted to protect you have, through ignorance, unbelief or corrupt intentions sought to destroy your faith and lead you astray. It seems too diabolical to believe. Sometimes it is just a matter of semantics. If we call it education instead of brainwashing, news reporting instead of propaganda, science instead of philosophy, economic trends instead of market manipulation, social justice instead of self-righteousness, comfort care instead of euthanasia, a fetus instead of a baby, enlightenment instead of atheistic hatred of God or religion instead of iniquity … if we just use the politically correct words it no longer sounds or feels so very evil!

SPIRITUAL GUIDE

We are ***in*** the world but not ***of*** the world. As we come to a realization of Christ in us and us in Him we will no longer feel the need to follow men. We will follow the Word of God and the voice of God as He speaks in our heart through the Holy Spirit. It is absolutely essential that we realize no one can take our freedom from us, we can only surrender it, and that is exactly the goal of those who follow the Luciferian spirit. They want you to be so helpless that you give your authority to others.

Fear has little to do with external factors for the believer. In fact, where you focus your attention determines the ability of a real threat to consume you, not on the degree of threat. Those who habitually experience God in their heart will establish a lifestyle of looking and listening inwardly when faced with threat of danger. Doing this in times of relative peace will develop a lifestyle that we carry with us into any type of tribulation.

Keep in mind, every time you see the phrase "knowing God" or "knowing the Lord Jesus" this is not a reference to intellectual knowledge alone; this knowing is about **experiencing**. The only way to experience God on a regular basis is to meditate, ponder, reflect on, worship, praise and think about your experiences with God and His promises until they bring about a shift in your emotions and ultimately in your feelings. Feelings don't go away when the emotions die down.

Heart Physics® is a program I developed to help the believer come to the abiding reality of "Christ in me." When we have the abiding sense of His presence we tend to have a feeling of limitlessness. All things become possible because we are now seeing the world through the mind of Christ, the One who conquered sin, death, the grave, the devil and the curse of the law. When our paradigm is through His experience **all things change!** Fear has no ability to hold us.

To learn more about the resources mentioned and for additional support material for this chapter please visit www.secondcomingguide.com.

CHAPTER 27

ELITE UTOPIANISM: THE NEW WORLD ORDER

There is no greater pride than a man thinking he is wiser than God!

PRIDE WAS AT THE CORE OF LUCIFER'S PERVERSION. Pride is arrogant, haughty and has a "know it all" attitude. Pride, which is always rooted in a corrupt sense of self, boosts its false sense of self by finding fault and criticism of others, thereby exalting self. Therefore, pride always goes before destruction, the destruction of self and others. Iniquity (lawlessness) is the organic logic of pride. When anyone diminishes, devalues, or disagrees with God's Word he or she is expressing their pride. Their attempts to twist or even deny God's Word as a means of self-vindication is the expression of iniquity in their heart. Even unbelief is a subtle expression of pride. There is nothing wrong with acknowledging what one does not understand; this is the way of humility. It surrenders its opinion to the Word of God even before it understands, and then seeks God for understanding. But the moment an individual says. "I don't believe that," or "that's not how I see it" or "I have a better way," they are in the same arrogance of Lucifer. The only difference is he saw the heavenly realm and still exalted his opinion over God's. Lucifer is the ultimate fool.

1 Timothy 3:6-7 gives insight into the dynamics of pride. Paul is providing Timothy with guidelines for developing leaders. He says, *"not a novice, lest being puffed up with pride he fall into the same condemnation as the devil."* The phrase *"not being puffed up with pride"* has at least two interesting and important concepts. Both concepts present the idea of a slow burn without much light and the concept of being enveloped in smoke depicting the state of arrogant, vain imaginations that exalts itself against the knowledge of God.[i]

First is the idea of slowly burning.[ii] Pride and the process toward iniquity is a "slow burn." It starts with a temptation, a compelling that leads to the process of extrapolation. Extrapolation is a process of reasoning that starts with a fact or a truth but then, through corrupt logic, it goes beyond the original truth, thus is no longer true. In Ezekiel 28:17 the KJV says of Lucifer, *"Thine heart was lifted up because of thy beauty, thou hast corrupted thy wisdom by reason of thy brightness".* This passage was addressed to the king of Tyre; it may be well to remember Tyre and Sidon are in the area of Mt. Hermon where the rebellious angels (watchers) crossed over. It is also the center of Baal worship. It is completely reasonable that this is directed to the spiritual power of Tyre.

"Thine heart was lifted up because of thy beauty, thou hast corrupted thy wisdom by reason of thy brightness".

The passage tells us this was a perfect being until iniquity was found in him (Ezekiel 28:12). In other words, through his pride he chose his opinions over God's. He judged good and evil for himself; therefore, through default he judged against God. This is exactly what we do when we choose our opinions over God's. We put Him on trial and find Him guilty of untruth. Paul, as well as all the Scriptures, seems to indicate that the eternal quest of Lucifer began with pride. The passage indicates he was a glorious created being that was filled with wisdom. But his wisdom became corrupted when through pride, looking at his own greatness, he began the process of corrupt reasoning. Through corrupt reasoning and extrapolation we follow in Lucifer's path

---

i 2 Corinthians 10:4-5, For the weapons of our warfare are not carnal, but mighty through God to the pulling down of strong holds;) 5 Casting down imaginations, and every high thing that exalteth itself against the knowledge of God, and bringing into captivity every thought to the obedience of Christ (KJV)

ii The process of burning slowly, with accompanying smoke and relatively little glow - 'to smolder, to flicker. (from Greek-English Lexicon Based on Semantic Domain.) Copyright © 1988 United Bible Societies, New York. Used by permission.) NT:5187

when we look at our own intelligence or greatness and feel this somehow qualifies us to reach our own conclusion independently of God's Word or God's wisdom. Corrupt reasoning is always the product of a crooked (froward) heart.

The second meaning of the phrase in Timothy means to be "enveloped in smoke." There are many dynamics to which this could potentially contribute. The slow, subtle burning in his own heart gave rise to a smoke that distorted his view of reality. A created being looked at his splendor and worshipped himself instead of his Creator. That is exactly what man does and extrapolation is always the process. It starts with a reality and then, because of our corrupt logic, it leaves the realm of reality and reason. In fact, it usually ends by denying the very element of truth it used to start its reasoning process.

Iniquity begins by twisting truth in one's heart. Truth is synonymous with light so if the heart is crooked light that enters into it will bend. Thus, the clear, pure light now changes colors. *"A crooked heart cannot find good"* (Proverbs 17:20).[iii] It loses its capacity to find good in the Word of God. Because he did not guard his heart what began as a thought, opinion or imagination slowly burned and smoldered through the process of extrapolation to a lie, to an exaltation of self, to rebellion… to hating God.

Iniquity begins by twisting truth in one's heart. Truth is synonymous with light so if the heart is crooked light that enters into it will bend.

The warning goes on to say, *"lest being puffed up with pride he fall into the same condemnation as the devil."* The word "condemnation" can mean "to judge, to condemn, or to decide." There is theological debate over the exact use of this word in this passage. At first glance the thought would be a reference to Satan being judged by God for his pride; but the context may suggest something more specific. It is obvious that the devil has been judged and cast out of Heaven. But in this context Paul is teaching Timothy how to train leaders who will not lead the believers astray. Therefore, without rejecting the early definitions, the context seems to be a warning about the pride that leads to

iii OT:6141 crooked, perverse. (from Theological Wordbook of the Old Testament. Copyright © 1980 by The Moody Bible Institute of Chicago. All rights reserved. Used by permission.)

iniquity - judging good and evil from one's own opinions.[iv] The condition of the world today is the product of an escalation in man exalting his opinion over God's. Then, because religion blames God for the problem, man hates God for the destruction he brings upon himself. He is enveloped in a cloud of smoke that distorts his perception of reality, but in his pride he chooses good and evil for himself. In this context the condemnation may be the judgment man passes against God.

During what is called the "Age of Enlightenment" man reached a new dynamic in iniquity and a never before known pinnacle of pride.

During what is called the "Age of Enlightenment" man reached a new dynamic in iniquity and a never before known pinnacle of pride. What Satan could not fully accomplish through religion he now did through education, specifically, false science. Man began to think his "science" was so advanced he now understood all things. The Age of Enlightenment is also referred to as the Age of Reason. This was not about man coming to a place of true knowledge; it was about throwing off the shackles of God and government. Man considered himself to be so educated and enlightened that he could finally think for himself… independently of God.

Enlightenment is actually nothing more than iniquity disguised as education; man being smarter and more righteous than God. Even if God were the horrible being they try to sell, they can justify control, domination, euthanasia, abortion, war, rioting and eugenics as it fits man's new scientific-moral model. Almost all concepts of God up to this point were based on the Luciferian lie of sovereignty: God (the gods) is in control of everything. This heretical theology was adapted by the Religionists and was the basis for church and government leaders to declare themselves appointed of God with unlimited, unquestionable authority. If it were not God's will it would not be so! This became the justification for every corrupt thing imaginable. In the name of God and the king one could be tortured, killed or made homeless. And if it happened, it must have been God's will.

---

iv NT:2917, 'to judge legal cases,' 56.20) the authority or right to judge guilt or innocence - 'the right to judge, the authority to judge.' (from Greek-English Lexicon Based on Semantic Domain. Copyright © 1988 United Bible Societies, New York. Used by permission.)

In the Book of the Wisdom of Solomon the writer reveals the corrupt logic of the wicked in their affliction of the righteous who hope in God.

> *Let us see if his words be true: and let us prove what shall happen to him in the end. For if the just man be the son of God he will help him and deliver him from the hand of his enemies. Let us examine him with despitefulness and torture that we may know his meekness and prove his patience.* (Proverbs 2:17-19)

To the wicked, whether they are religious or not, the doctrine of sovereignty makes it possible to justify any treatment of mankind and make God responsible. The world was sick of religious oppression, but in their foolishness they turned to the author of oppression.

Since enlightenment was based on iniquity, the rejection of God's Word was the standard of morals, values and integrity. If it opposed God's Word it was considered a valid probability.

The Age of Enlightenment was the ground which grew the seeds of the Rosicrucians, Illuminati, Atheism, Satanism, Communism, Socialism, Darwinism, Progressivism, Keynesian Economics, the Robber Barons, Ancient Astronauts Theorists, Edgar Cayce, Skull and Bones and other new cults (some claiming to be Christian), the United Nations, the Bilderbergers, the Trilateral Commission, the Council on Foreign Relations, a host of secret societies and even more political groups committed to a one-world antichrist government. Since enlightenment was based on iniquity, the rejection of God's Word was the standard of morals, values and integrity. If it opposed God's Word it was considered a valid probability.

The fuel behind this "new enlightenment" was nothing new at all. The secret societies were the impetus for iniquity. The classics provided the literary information and the Religionist Church provided the excuse. All the while the wicked-hearted capitalized on the rebellion, misery and confusion. But the same spirit that inspired the Nimrodian, tyrannical, totalitarian, anti-God, one-world government was the lifeblood of this "new intellectual movement": the father of all lies, Lucifer. The irony of enlightenment was the idea that through intellectualism the world was finally escaping the smothering grip of religion. But every facet of the Luciferian logic of enlightenment *was* religion. Despite the reasons why "useful idiots" did what they did, the money and power that drove the reasoning was Luciferian iniquity.

Enlightenment gave rise to the philosophy of elite utopianism. Believers in the God of the Bible were considered ignorant and superstitious.

Enlightenment gave rise to the philosophy of elite utopianism. Believers in the God of the Bible were considered ignorant and superstitious. Not only were they in darkness, they were the problem with the world. The elite were the enlightened, those who did not believe in the God of the Bible. Only by freeing society from the foolishness of faith could the wars and world struggles cease and a utopian world emerge. Utopia was a mystical land where a totalitarian government implemented the principles of Socialism to create a perfect world. Since religion had been blamed for all the woes of man, if all religion could be eliminated there would finally be peace on earth.

A new enlightened government would replace religion. Allegiance to the state would be the central requirement. The state would determine each citizen's profession. There would be no ownership. The state would own everything. All people would be equal and happy and there would be no more tyranny from those controlling laws and commandments of God.

Somehow these people convinced themselves that the enlightened would do what religion, kings and monarchs had never been able to do… be fair and just. The definition of fair and just would, however, be determined by the government. So, now, after centuries of revolution and war from Europe to Asia no group has ever been able to make this theory work. The only people who believe it will work are the ones who hope to be in charge and the "useful idiots," the idealists who have little real-life experience. There have been hundreds of names given to hundreds of groups seeking to mask their true agenda who have killed hundreds of millions of people in the name of this new enlightenment, this new justice, fairness and equality. So far, the rich just keep getting richer and the poor keep getting poorer while more and more people suffer and die for the cause.

The Illuminati and the Communists have probably laid out their goals in the most succinct form to which we now have access. But all of the anti-God groups have the same agenda and they are all playing from the same handbook. The intention is to take total control of education, political parties, religious organizations, moral definitions and world view. Eliminate the traditional family, take control of the economy and eliminate all freedom of speech, freedom of religion and ownership of property. In this new enlightenment it will not be enough that everyone obeys the state, they also have to think and believe what the state requires. Ultimately, based on one's value to the state, who lives, who dies and length of life are all determined by the state.

One goal of these enlightened groups is control of world population. The Georgia Guidestones state the goal of reducing world population to 500,000,000. For this to happen would require 6.5 billion people die. Anyone who believes any group would be willing to murder 6.5 billion people is considered an absolute "nut job." As I have previously presented in this book, ego-driven idealists have murdered millions in the past and would have murdered millions more if they had not been stopped. But if you believe the Bible you must believe *"the thief comes only to steal, to kill and destroy"* (John10:10). So how many do you suppose the devil is willing to kill? EVERYONE! The Book of Wisdom once again gives us insight into the mind of the wicked.[v]

> *FOR the ungodly said, reasoning with themselves, but not aright, Our life is short and tedious, and in the death of a man there is no remedy: neither was there any man known to have returned from the grave. And our name shall be forgotten in time, and no man shall have our works in remembrance, and our life shall pass away as the trace of a cloud, and shall be dispersed as a mist, that is driven away with the beams of the sun, and overcome with the heat thereof. Come on therefore, let us enjoy the good things that are present: and let us speedily use the creatures like as in youth. Let us fill ourselves with costly wine and ointments: and let no flower of the spring pass by us: Let us crown ourselves with rosebuds, before they be withered: Let none of us go without his part of our voluptuousness: let us leave tokens of our joyfulness in every place: for this is our portion, and our lot is this. Let us oppress the poor righteous man, let us not spare the widow, nor reverence the ancient gray hairs*

---

v I am not implying the Book of Wisdom is inspired or in any way equal to the Holy Scriptures. But I view much the same as any historical book like Josephus.

> *of the aged. Let our strength be the law of justice: for that which is feeble is found to be nothing Worth* (Proverbs 2:1, 4, 6-11).

The philosophy of the wicked is that they must get all the pleasure they can while they are here because this is all they have. They do not believe they will give an account of their life before the Lord; therefore, they will oppress the poor, the widowed, the helpless and the righteous. They will enjoy it to their fullest capacity and pass it to their heirs. In order to assure that all the world's resources will be enjoyed by them alone there are at least two lies that must be perpetrated upon man. First, there must be the illusion of limited resources. Second, this lie must extrapolate into population control.

Population control is simply the politically correct way to say "mass murder." To echo the words of Stalin, "One death is a tragedy; one million is a statistic." Many who are in government or powers behind government have talked of population control and mass elimination for generations. Americans fail to realize the eugenics practiced by Nazis was an American idea. Planned Parenthood was originally created to eliminate babies of minorities. Abortion, euthanasia, eugenics and comfort care are all masks for population control. Population control has always been one of the primary goals of Communism, Socialism, Progressives, Nazis and the New World Order. The idea that we cannot support world population is a myth that grows ever more diabolical and irrational as governments take control of food sources and limit the right of citizens to produce their own food.

Population control is simply the politically correct way to say "mass murder." To echo the words of Stalin, "One death is a tragedy; one million is a statistic."

Creating food and energy shortages is nothing more than a shell game designed to direct your attention to one hand while the other hand moves the pea! There is only a food shortage if government wants a food shortage. In the name of fairness and equality the US government can take any of your food stores or your garden. Bureaucratic regulations are making it almost impossible for small farms to survive. One would think if there were food shortages everything possible would be done to encourage development of personal provisions. There is more than enough land to raise more than enough food for the entire world's population.

When enough *useful idiots* buy into the deception they will, in fear of loss of their own life, join the resonating cry, "if there is not enough food we must reduce the population!" The only question is, how will it be done and who gets to decide who lives and dies? But food shortages and population control only work within the boundaries of a particular nation. It is a slow and tedious process of elimination. The best global form of population control is war.

> Creating food and energy shortages is nothing more than a shell game designed to direct your attention to one hand while the other hand moves the pea!

Andrew Breitbart, a former insider with the extreme left, spent many years of his short life exposing the philosophy and plots of those who seek to dominate the world. He explained how those who control finances and governments desire to promote war as if it were a chess game. War transfers massive amounts of wealth to a smaller group of people in the shortest period of time, but it also serves to eliminate the "useless eaters." It is almost the perfect form of population control.

Just imagine a scenario like this orchestrated by a small group of international financiers. Fund radical Islam and allow them to destroy Israel, much of Christianity around the globe, as well as any Muslims who will not go to jihad. If only marginally successful that could eliminate a few hundred million. Initial focus would be annihilation of those who know God. Then as the Middle East becomes chaotic and weakened, imagine what would happen if China, the world's fastest growing economy which desperately needs oil, were to go to war to take over the Middle East. They could eliminate the jihadists. Step by step, religions are being destroyed and populations are being reduced.

Then what if Russians were emboldened to attack China? What you have is a chess game where nation after nation, led by a maniacal, power-hungry, narcissistic leader with a vision for world domination, is manipulated to eliminate millions of people through war. Eventually, those powerful countries would be decimated to a point that a small One World Government seeking to finally bring an end to war could seize power of the entire world to the adulation of a world population living in the terror and destruction of war and alienated from God, who would welcome a man of peace! I am making no claim this is exactly how it will happen; I am simply revealing the mindset of those who seek to control the world will stop at nothing because the real goal is not to govern the world; the true Luciferian goal is to destroy the world. In the upcoming chapters we will see how the 20th century gave near total control of all of man's intellectual influences to the Luciferians and Religionists. But in each chapter we will continue to identify steps we can take to rise above the fray, have light in the darkness and overcome the evil one!

> Those who seek to control the world will stop at nothing because the real goal is not to govern the world; the true Luciferian goal is to destroy the world.

A group of self-proclaimed "enlightened people," either Atheist or Luciferian, intends to eliminate Christians and Jews who inconvenience their plans with talk of morality, honesty and justice. They have followed the way of their father, their hearts are filled with pride, they hate God, His Word and His righteousness and they love their wickedness. They intend to create a world in their own image… a world without you or me… unless we could be made into passive, hard-working slaves living only to fulfil their pleasure!

SPIRITUAL GUIDE

How does one prepare for the future I have described? As Jesus said, *"With men this is impossible, but with God all things are possible"* (Matthew 19:26). It seems that the Church looks at everything Jesus said about the end and continues to think that a natural solution can be found. The natural mind cannot process an end as the Bible describes it. But if we attempt to find a solution to the problem with the same mindset that got us into the problem, we will only make the problem worse.

It is time we, as individuals, return to a life filled with, empowered by and dependent on the Holy Spirit. I am extremely evangelistic and have devoted much of my life to winning the lost; so, I understand the need to be seeker-sensitive. But that can translate into simply compromising to attract a larger crowd or it can translate into becoming a "more relevant" church. Much of the Church has become such an ingrown subculture it is nearly impossible for an uninitiated person to walk in the doors and make sense of what they see, hear and experience.

In our attempt to be seeker-sensitive we became so compromised that we had nothing to offer the crowds we attracted. *"The Kingdom of God is not a matter of talk but of power"* (1 Corinthians 4:20, NIV). My friend, Leon Fontaine, has coined the phrase "Spirit Contemporary,"[vi] emphasizing the fact that we must be contemporary in order to reach our generation, but we must still operate in the gifts of the Holy Spirit. We must minister as the Lord Jesus modeled. We have nothing to offer this world if we exclude the Holy Spirit as the power by which we live this life and overcome the powers of darkness.

"Greater is he that lives in you than he that is in the world" (1 John 4:4). It is by the One who lives in us that we overcome the world. We cannot face the times ahead devoid of the leadership, power, strength, grace and wisdom of the Holy Spirit. Making this connection cannot be taught. It can only be learned in the heart of a believer who is submitted to the Lordship of Jesus and lives a life of openness and sensitivity to the voice of God speaking in their heart. This is our only viable key to preparation for the future: **walk with God now!**

---

vi http://www.spiritcontemporary.com/

All the gifts of the Holy Spirit will be essential tools as we seek to take the Gospel of the Kingdom to the world, usher in the return of the Lord Jesus, and overcome the strategies of the Great Harlot and the antichrist! As we yield to Him more we will find ourselves walking where those of great faith walked in the past. We will be the ones who demonstrate the life and power of God to a dark and dying world! We will show them what they needed to have seen all along. We will be Spirit Contemporary, in touch with their needs and in touch with the power of God!

To learn more about the resources mentioned and for additional support material for this chapter please visit www.secondcomingguide.com.

APOCALYPSE

CHAPTER 28

THE ILLUSION OF FREEDOM

The masses will always believe the lie, truth is too frightening!

19TH CENTURY AMERICA SAW A MONUMENTAL SHIFT IN POWER AS MASSIVE WEALTH WAS TRANSFERRED TO A SMALLER GROUP WITH WHAT SEEMED TO BE A LIMITLESS LUST FOR WORLD POWER. The ambition and greed of a handful of men labelled the "Robber Barons" provided the opportunity for the few to rule over the many. It would be good at this point to remember through the spiritual delusion of the Great Whore the economy of a nation became justification for all manner of evil legislation. Anything could be justified in the name of keeping the economy strong.

Selfish ambition was cloaked in commercial and humanitarian accomplishments. Ambition doesn't have to be a negative attribute. To serve, heal or to make the world a better place are all worthy ambitions. The problem is that ambition not built on the Word of God and defined by the love of God will always become corrupt. Ambition that is not rooted in serving our fellow man based on God's ethics, morals and values is always a reflection of a deep need. This ambition becomes self-serving. Iniquity makes it possible to hide any agenda. If we define morality and ethics for ourselves all we need to do is create new definitions and the most barbaric actions are now deemed acts of philanthropy.

The American countryside was decimated, millions of buffaloes were killed for their tongues, and an entire continent of people was ruthlessly murdered to make it possible to travel across the country by train.

The American countryside was decimated, millions of buffaloes were killed for their tongues, and an entire continent of people was ruthlessly murdered to make it possible to travel across the country by train. This opened the door to an entirely new continental marketplace. The government either passed laws or turned a deaf ear to the natural and human atrocities. Identical hideous deeds were occurring across the industrialized world in the same manner. Governments were controlled by the economy, which was controlled by a handful of wealthy profiteers.

The Book of James was written to a church filled with strife and conflict. The members tried to create a spiritual rationalization for the problem. They claimed their hardships were tests from God. But James made it clear that the source of all their strife was their own selfish willingness to destroy one another to get what they wanted. In chapter 3 verse16 James zeroes in on the problem. *The Amplified Bible* does a wonderful job of translating this verse. *"For wherever there is jealousy (envy) and contention (rivalry and selfish ambition), there will also be confusion (unrest, disharmony, rebellion) and all sorts of evil and vile practices."*

The word "envy" which is used in the KJV, comes from the same Greek word translated as "zeal." This word presents the idea of heat or passion[i] and is very much akin to "jealousy." This word is about a need to succeed or have one's way because they are driven by jealousy or other negative emotions.

---

i zelos (dzay'-los); from NT:2204; properly, heat, i.e. (figuratively) "zeal" (in a favorable sense, ardor; in an unfavorable one, jealousy, as of a husband [figuratively, of God], or an enemy, malice):KJV - emulation, envy (-ing), fervent mind, indignation, jealousy, zeal. (Biblesoft's New Exhaustive Strong's Numbers and Concordance with Expanded Greek-Hebrew Dictionary. Copyright © 1994, 2003, 2006 Biblesoft, Inc. and International Bible Translators, Inc.)

We are then told that when *zelos* is present it will always be accompanied by a host of other destructive motivators: contention, rivalry, self-ambition, confusion and disorder, unrest, disharmony, rebellion and all sorts of evil and vile practices. This second word "strife" in the KJV or "contention" in the Amplified has to do with "day laborers," people who will demean themselves for gain like prostitutes.[ii]

The zeal Paul speaks of is exactly what drove the Jews to crucify Jesus (Romans 10:2). He identifies it as a sign of carnality (1 Corinthians 3:3). In Galatians 5:20-21 the KJV translates it as "emulations" which Paul identifies as a work of the flesh on par with *idolatry, witchcraft, hatred, variance, emulations, wrath, strife, seditions, heresies, envyings, murders, drunkenness, revellings,* and the like. In fact, it was this very zeal that moved Paul to persecute the Church (Philippians 3:6).

This, accompanied by systemic greed, was the driving force behind the Robber Barons' cruelty and dishonest dealings. This list of ultra-powerful, ultra-wealthy men included the likes of J.P. Morgan, Andrew Carnegie, John Wayne Gates and John D. Rockefeller. History reveals they were ruthless in the pursuit of wealth and power.

These men, along with a few from Europe, like the Rothschilds, were the wealthiest in the world. To accomplish their goals in industry it was incumbent upon politicians to pass laws to facilitate their plans; after all, money wins elections. It was the way of the world that in a country where there was freedom, that freedom would be abused. As men of mega wealth emerged onto the field dominating the economic scene, politics took on an entirely new dynamic. No matter how it is explained it was pretty simple: money bought elections and the elected were obliged to those who had money!

---

ii "to work as a day-laborer"; this has to do with the work or disposition of the day-laborer. 2. It then comes to denote the attitude of self-seekers, harlots, etc., who demean themselves for gain. As a complex term in everyday usage, it can be given different senses according to context. "Contentious" is perhaps too specialized in Romans 2:8, where it refers to the "despicable nature" of those who do not obey the truth but seek immediate gain. This also fits the context in 2 Corinthians 12:20; Galatians 5:20; Philippians 1:17; 2:3. The idea is "base self-seeking," the "baseness" that cannot shift its gaze to higher things.
(from Theological Dictionary of the New Testament, abridged edition,)

The poor and middle class were only a cog in the wheel of wealth and power. They were an irritating necessity. After all, someone had to perform the actual labor. Allowing the poor and middle classes to actually have a voice in government was unthinkable. The elitist mentality was fueled by selfish ambition and the corruption it brings. The wealthy considered themselves "enlightened." Their wealth gave the assumed right to make the rules. They would create a country and a world that gave their heirs a rightful inheritance: the world's resources.

The poor and working class were a bother, but also a necessary evil. These people needed to be appeased so they would continue to function in their roles as workers and servants. Therefore, it was incumbent on the wealthy to create a system that provided the illusion of choice and freedom but actually only served the goals of selfish ambition. As government became more controlled by the wealthy, the middle class required the illusion of having a voice in government.

The birth of the two-party system, regardless of the true intentions of the founders and validity of choice it offered, grew into what we now recognize as the Republican and Democratic parties. Like almost all things that start with good intentions, if left in this world long enough it succumbs to the intentions of those who have money and influence. The two-party system leaves no room for any real competition or variety in the choices, but it does allow the illusion of choice.

There is an ancient philosophy that says once something reaches an extreme it transforms into its opposite. Night reaches its ultimate darkness and begins to morph into day. Physical energy gives rise to movement which expends energy which collapses into fatigue. Fatigue brings one to sleep which gives rise to energy. As a result we see the continual process of exchange that keeps all living things alive. Thus were the Robber Barons and the rise of the two-party system.

As the wealthy took control through free enterprise and Capitalism, it became obvious they could only hold that control through Socialism. Our country was never a democracy; it is a republic with a democratic process. A republic is based on a constitution as the final and absolute rule of law. The democratic process means we have the right to choose our government. Their job is to be sure the country is governed based on the Constitution; thus, the fundamental part of their oath of office is to uphold the Constitution. Through the democratic process we not only have the right, but the freedom to remove them from office should they fail at that one fundamental responsibility.

Our founders knew our experiment in freedom would only last as long as men were moral. Just as all things cycle into an extreme and collapse, democracy always cycles into mob rule, which brings us back to a few wealthy influentials controlling the masses. Wicked people of power offer benefits to the poor who are always perfect pawns. On the basis of voters receiving benefits in exchange for their votes, those seeking the votes are, in fact, buying them.

Benjamin Franklin said, "When the people find that they can vote themselves money that will herald the end of the republic." I fear his prophetic insight was not only correct but has come to pass. Government officials soon become more concerned with job security and control than serving people and protecting the republic, thus the transformation into politicians. Politicians are more interested in keeping their party in control of the government than anything else. The surest way to accomplish this is to get the people to "vote themselves money." In other words, make the vote about "what government will do for you" and ultimately the masses will be led by their selfishness.

The concept of being a "party" is, at its core, designed to motivate people through greed, power and selfishness. Most voters in America vote "party" regardless of the candidate, regardless of his or her track record and regardless of how they destroy the Constitution. In the KJV, *heresy* is identified as a *work of the flesh.* Interestingly, according to Strong's Concordance, this word can mean "party spirit." A party spirit is more than being a member of a party; it is about following the party vote, the party decision or the party doctrine. This is not only a reference to governmental parties, but includes the idea of following denominational doctrine.

A little closer look at this word and its original use, however, delves even deeper into the true attitude behind the party spirit.[iii] The *Theological Dictionary of the New Testament* reveals this party spirit is motivated by the "right to choose." Human beings have absolute freedom of choice. God provided us

---

iii NT:139, On the basis of hairéœ , the senses are "seizure," "choice," "resolve." Choice of opinion led to the philosophical use for "teaching," "school," with the associated ideas of delimitation from other schools, the authority of the teacher, specific doctrine, and the private character of these features.
(from Theological Dictionary of the New Testament, abridged edition, Copyright © 1985 by William B. Eerdmans Publishing Company. All rights reserved.)

with the Operator's Manual (the Bible) so we would have the information necessary to make choices that did not bring death, chaos and destruction. At the heart of iniquity (lawlessness) is the need to be gods unto ourselves. Making our own choices independently of God's Word about good and bad, right and wrong, fair and unfair, etc.

The rebellious do not want to be answerable or accountable; they only want to move their opinions forward. The writer of Proverbs says it best:

> *He who willfully separates and estranges himself [from God and man] seeks his own desire and pretext to break out against all wise and sound judgment. 2 A [self-confident] fool has no delight in understanding but only in revealing his personal opinions and himself.* (Proverbs 18:1-3, AMP)

Whether in politics or faith, the proud and rebellious have no interest in following rules. Rules are for everyone else. The lawlessness in government is an outgrowth of lawlessness (iniquity) against the Lordship of Jesus and the authority of God's Word. By becoming the party that does "this" for a special group, that special group will sell their votes in order to get what they want with no consideration for the Constitution, the well-being of our nation or the Word of God.

By the 19th century the New World had the political framework, the natural resources and would very soon have the military might to make the quantum leap toward the dream of the secret societies: the New World Order. But more than anything else, the massive wealth concentrated within a few power-hungry families would finally give rise to the Great Harlot, Mystery Babylon. The wealthy controlled America. Once America became a super power it would be de facto controller of the world.

By the 20th century the probability of a true choice in national elections was little more than an illusion, especially in presidential races. Winning a national election is so expensive that the choice no longer is in the hands of the average citizen; it is in the hands of corporate donors. While there are many wealthy idealists who only contribute to their own party, the truth is the mega-wealthy, those who truly control the destiny of our country, contribute to both political parties. They want to ensure they have influence, if not control, over either candidate.

Lack of choice does not end with national politics. Many opposing candidates are members of the same secret societies: the Freemasons, the Bilderbergers, Skull and Bones or any one of dozens of organizations committed to a New World Order. So it doesn't matter who is elected, they will pursue the same ultimate goals. In the 2004 election both John Kerry **and** President Bush were members of Skull and Bones. To the American public these secret societies are harmless fraternities, but to become a member one must swear an allegiance to the order that supersedes and nullifies any other commitments.

> By the 19th century the New World had the political framework, the natural resources and would very soon have the military might to make the quantum leap toward the dream of the secret societies: the New World Order.

Here is where it gets tricky! Democrats run on the class warfare ticket. They are going to "make the wealthy pay." Yet, it is the very wealthy they say will pay that support them and get them elected. Why would bankers, Wall Street tycoons and titans of Capitalism support Democrats and even speak out in favor of socialistic policies? It is because what the public believes about Socialism and what Socialism really is are completely different.

When the wealthy talk about sharing the wealth they are talking about sharing **your** wealth, not theirs. Since they are enlightened, they are the only ones truly deserving of wealth and control. The unenlightened, especially those who hold any religious belief, can never be trusted with power. These groups own many, if not the majority of, politicians. The ones they do not own are owned by their party or they are powerless to accomplish much without powerful financial allies. The political parties are basically only different in their rhetoric.

Consider this: Republicans usually come to power after a period of excessive Democrat spending. So they run on the rhetoric (sales pitch) of bringing out of control spending back within bounds. But history reveals some interesting facts. They seldom, if ever, reverse any of the obscene laws they so vehemently opposed during their campaign. They usually stabilize funding for the laws Democrats previously enacted. They all appoint cabinet members and other bureaucratic positions from the same pool of people, very often from the

Council on Foreign Relations or some other organization laboring to bring about a One World government. They seldom do any of the things promised during their campaign. The most telling anomaly is the fact that our national debt and size of government keeps growing under both Republicans and Democrats.

So, a politician publically debating "the issues" is little more than a slight-of-hand distraction designed to capture our attention while the true global goals of a New World Order inch forward. Since major media is almost exclusively controlled by the "unseen hand"* they are experts at keeping our attention on frivolous social and political issues, providing cover while we are destroyed by tactics that are practically out in the open. If the middle class fight against Socialism and win they will put the same people in power under a different name. If Democrats fight against Capitalism and win they too will put the same people in power under another name.

Sadly, the Church has been swept up in the illusion of freedom of political choice to the degree that it has all but abandoned its true mission here on earth: to make disciples for the Lord Jesus Christ. This is the only effort, the only struggle, the only battle worth fighting; it is the only issue that means anything in eternity.

Socialism is false hope extended to desperate people that seduces them into giving away their freedom. The poor live under the illusion that money will make them happy. The wealthy live under the illusion that wealth gives them privilege. The middle class live under the illusion that if they work hard and are honest they can have a secure future. The rich get tax breaks, the poor get entitlements and the middle class actually pay the bills for everyone. Ironically, the middle class is the least represented part of the population in Washington. Each group is so engrossed in the demands of their class they are all blinded to the reality.

Here is one simple slight-of-hand performed by both Republicans and Democrats. Each party uses its talking points to justify its actions and they both criticize the other party for these very actions. We have had both Republican and Democrat bailouts. When America got sick of the rich getting richer the term was changed from bailout to "quantitative easing," which is just a "bailout" by a different name. This was supposed to have helped the economy and eased the financial suffering of the middle class and the poor, but the money was given to the same banks and companies that had mismanaged us into the financial crisis. And what did they do? They gave themselves large bonuses and pay raises.

The bailouts did nothing for the average citizen. If they had wanted to stimulate the economy they would have given the money to the people who could have paid off their mortgages, hospital bills and other serious debt. That would have provided income to the banks, automotive manufacturers and other suppliers and businesses as people spent money. The people would have directed their money to the companies of their choice, meeting the most demanding needs in their life. The economy would have been stimulated, the banks would have received the money owed to them and the suffering of the poor and middle class would have been resolved. But the truth is that the bailout wasn't about helping people. It was a reward to the banks, Wall Street and other money suppliers who had financed both the Bush and Obama administrations.

> On one side of the ledger we see that the big banks are bigger than ever, more than 90% of the gains in GDP in the past four years have accrued to those in the top 1% of the income distribution, and **total Wall Street pay is still near record highs despite a sharp drop in employment**. On the other side we find that median net worth fell by 40% since 2007; real median income is still 8% lower than in 2007, there are still more than 7 million fewer full-time jobs than in 2007, and there have been at least 4 million foreclosures, many of which could have been prevented through investor-friendly government policies.[iv]

It would be somewhat soothing if the bad news stopped there, but it doesn't. By twisting the numbers the government is able to disguise the truth that America is in a depression worse than the Great Depression of the 1930's. As people drop off the unemployment rolls, go on welfare or age beyond the parameters of research they are no longer counted in the unemployment numbers. You might ask, "Then why aren't we seeing bread lines and soup kitchens?" We are! They just have a new name: welfare, entitlement, government assistance and food stamps. There are more people living off the government now than ever, even during the Great Depression, which means they are jobless, contributing nothing to the economy and doing nothing to solve the problem. The same banks that were rewarded for their corruption

---

iv http://www.economist.com/blogs/freeexchange/2012/10/americas-bank-bailouts

through the bailout are still involved in identical practices that brought about the collapse. Yes! It's all going to happen again! Who passed the laws to make that possible? It was the very party that said they were going to make Wall Street pay.

Worse than all the above is that our country is enslaved by Keynesian economics, an anti-biblical ponzi scheme where the government and central banks print worthless money to manage inflation and create a false economy. The more entitlement programs we have the more bailouts, the more quantitative easing, the bigger government gets, the more we go to war, the more we give money to foreign aid and the more money we borrow from the Central Bank. Get the picture: we borrow money to give away. The Federal Reserve, which is a private bank, prints worthless paper money. The more money they put into circulation the more our money is devalued. As our money is devalued we pay the FED higher interest on the money we borrow. No one benefits from this except the Federal Reserve Bank, which is private and bank-owned and controlled by those who are fully invested in taking control of the entire world. The only winners in politics are those corrupt mega-wealthy people who control the economy. It doesn't matter who becomes president; they will control him or kill him. Sadly, history reveals that regardless of who gets elected to federal office nothing really changes.

The only winners in politics are those corrupt mega-wealthy people who control the economy.

SPIRITUAL GUIDE

Since Ronald Reagan was in office Christians have believed we could turn America to righteousness through the political process. I do think that believers should be responsible citizens and voters; however, it is complete naiveté to think we can make any real difference at the polls unless it is accompanied by reaching our nation and the world with the Gospel of the Kingdom. The Gospel of the Kingdom is not about getting people saved, it is about bringing people into a relationship with the King! It is about making disciples, not converts. Remember, Christians supported Hitler and have supported many other ungodly, destructive political choices that have shattered our nation.

"How could that happen?" you might ask. "How could they consider themselves to be Christians?" Maybe you should ask: "Do I raise my children in the Word of God?" "Do I vet every politician based on his voting record and lifestyle?" "Do I handle my money the way God said?" "Do I even have a sense of how the Word of God would fit into my practical life?" "Am I a Christian or a disciple?"

America may be a Christian nation as far as percentages go, but it has never been a nation of disciples. The Word of God has had little meaningful influence on the way "Christians" vote. Most still vote party!

This may sound hopeless to you, but it is time to realize Jesus said all this would be coming. If we were disciples, people who lived their lives, made their decisions and voted based on the principles of the Word of God, we would not be in the situation we're in. Jesus did not call us to be Christians; He called us to be disciples. The questions you must ask are: "Am I really a disciple of the Lord Jesus?" and "Do I have a clue what my life would look like if all my business dealings, all my relationships, and all my political decisions were made based on the Word of God?"

Become a disciple today; it is simply a choice. Then, read the Word of God from the perspective of application, not legalism, not attempting to earn something from God, but because you believe God is smarter than you, because you believe He is good and only good and because you believe His Word is a divine prescription for a great life. Learn how to be a disciple without being a judgmental, religious nut!

The essence of being your own god is the right to choose good and evil for yourself, independently of God's Word. Surrender your right to choose Jesus as your Lord. God will never force you to choose His Word. It will only be done because you trust Him and believe He loves you.

The masses will always follow those who offer them things they think they need for survival and security. Changing politicians is not the important factor in the equation; changing the hearts of the people through a relationship with Jesus is their only hope, and the only hope of any nation. When people are having their deepest needs met through the love of God they will no longer be blinded by the lies of those who seek to use and destroy them.

Political freedom is always an illusion. The only true freedom is in Jesus. All governments of the world, no matter how true and sincere their intention, operate on the principles of the World's System. Only the Kingdom of God ruled by the Lord Jesus will show us what a just and righteous government looks like. Come quickly, Lord Jesus!

To learn more about the resources mentioned and for additional support material for this chapter please visit www.secondcomingguide.com.

APOCALYPSE

CHAPTER 29

EDUCATION: THE PATH TO ENLIGHTENMENT

There is nothing more important or strategic for the future of mankind than raising a generation of children who know Jesus as Lord!

THERE WAS A TIME WHEN ENSURING YOUR CHILD A GOOD EDUCATION WAS THE HOPE OF EVERY AMERICAN FAMILY. It was a way to safeguard their future. But today higher education is sometimes more a course in propaganda than an education in a particular subject or discipline.

Public education has become the most uncensored, anti-God, anti-government, systematic, brainwashing system in the world and we, as parents, think the best thing we can do for our children's future is get them a better education… and by better we mean **more**. Every day good parents who think they are doing their children a service send them off to have their minds and hearts overtaken by deliberate, systematic brainwashing.

Many Christian families do not actually pray together or teach their children the Word of God. Between the demands of work, school and extracurricular activities there is not even enough time to eat together. The Bible is seldom used as a positive, proactive resource for solving problems and teaching children God's wisdom. Too often, when the Bible is used it is primarily a means of negative, legalistic rules which affirms the Luciferian concept that God allows no freedom or fun. Then, when our children turn their backs on God we feel God has failed us. We do not realize that our children have been subjected to a lifelong process of programming and demoralization.

From a constitutional perspective it is a violation of our First Amendment rights to forbid representation of the biblical account of creation. "Congress shall make no law respecting an establishment of **religion**, or prohibiting the free exercise thereof; or abridging the freedom of **speech**..." When neither teachers nor students are allowed to express their religious freedoms on government property or in any public place we have already lost freedom of religion. When Creationism or even intelligent design cannot be taught as a viable probability this is tantamount to laws that prohibit both freedom of speech and freedom of religion.

Those who seek to control the minds of future generations know it is only possible if they have control of the education system.

Stalin said, "Education is a weapon whose effects depend on who holds it in his hands and at whom it is aimed." Lenin said, "Give me four years to teach the children and the seed I have sown will never be uprooted." Those who seek to control the minds of future generations know it is only possible if they have control of the education system. From at least the first grade through twelfth grade someone is shaping your child's life paradigm more than their parents or pastor. They are directly or indirectly being led to believe there is no God. Immorality is just a lifestyle choice. Society, not the individual, is responsible for the actions of the person. They are being swayed in their understanding of what comprises a family. They are being influenced about their political ideology. And it is all systematized iniquity (the rejection of God's morals, values and standards). We must remember the Luciferian doesn't care what is taught or believed as long as it opposes the Word of God.

I will be the first to say, being a teacher is a selfless job. There are many wonderful teachers who truly seek to serve their students. Yet, in my more recent experience with teachers, administrators and parents seeking advice I am seeing an increasing number of *useful idiots* becoming teachers. Many teachers are not only baptized into Socialism, they have no aptitude to teach or work with children. More and more teachers have the "I am the government and I am in control" mentality which is the typical bureaucratic, socialistic attitude. There is no reason we should expect anything else. Anyone who is under 40 and attended public school, went to college and then earned a post graduate degree has been programmed with ideals of Communism, Socialism and Luciferian thought. Unless they have a strong Bible knowledge and faith it is nearly impossible to become a teacher without becoming a Socialist. The one exception would be for those who grow up in a family that has a good understanding and experience in free enterprise.

How did the entire educational system take a deep decline in such a short period of time? Simple! When the federal government becomes involved in anything this is what happens. The true goal behind big government is systematic brainwashing and control on a national level. In my life I have never seen anything taken over by the federal government improve. Once a cabinet level Department of Education was established under the Carter administration the die was cast. This would be the standardizing of not just the educational process but of the individual student.

How did the entire educational system take a deep decline in such a short period of time? Simple! When the federal government becomes involved in anything this is what happens.

Nikita Khrushchev, Communist leader of the Cold War Era, boldly declared, "Comrades! We must abolish the cult of the individual decisively, once and for all." School is no longer about education; it is about conditioning, brainwashing and destroying the individual. God told man to *be fruitful and multiply.* In other words, a person was to go out, do what he or she felt inspired to do and have individual success. There is no room for individualism in a Luciferian world. For years the National Education Association has been reported to make comments that acknowledged their lack of concern for children's education; they exist to take care of teachers, not students. In the 1970s a Teachers' Union representative said, "We don't care if Johnny can read, we just care who has control of Johnny."

The Teachers' Unions have taken control of the educational system away from parents, away from local governments and even away from Washington. It is nearly impossible to fire a bad teacher. Across America there are teachers guilty of crimes ranging from sexual misconduct to violence. These teachers should have been imprisoned, or at the very least fired. Instead, they continue to get paid every week to do nothing. There are 700 in New York alone[i] who are not allowed in a classroom but still get paid, costing the state millions of dollars annually. Thousands more across the country are unable to teach because they are tending to union business during school hours.

> The Department of Education pays about 1,500 teachers for time they spend on union activities and it pays other teachers to replace them in the classroom. It's a sweetheart deal that costs taxpayers an extra $9 million a year to pay fill-ins for instructors who are sprung — at full pay — to carry out responsibilities for the United Federation of Teachers. With Mayor Bloomberg calling for thousands of teacher layoffs to balance the 2012 budget, critics say it's time to halt the extravagant benefit.[ii]

A Google search of "teachers paid to do nothing" reveals millions of dollars per year that could be applied to education is being paid to teachers who not only do nothing, but also are a threat to the safety of students. It does not take a genius to realize we are spending millions on unqualified teachers who are unable to prepare students to pass standardized evaluations. And even worse is that we are not allowed to evaluate them or their performance. We spend millions on teachers that do not work!

Many students do not have textbooks. Some teachers are paying for school supplies out of their own pockets, yet the schools construct buildings, buy computers and have massive sports programs. A teacher with tenure cannot be fired, yet students graduate every year who can hardly read or write

---

i http://www.huffingtonpost.com/2009/06/22/new-york-teachers-paid-to_n_219336.html

ii http://nypost.com/2011/02/27/1500-teachers-paid-to-do-union-business-and-miss-class/

a complete sentence. But, make no mistake, the true goal is being accomplished: students are being turned into godless workers of iniquity.

Across America there is moral and philosophical indoctrination not supported by city government or parents. New textbooks make mass murderers appear to be social pioneers of justice and freedom. Christianity is attacked and belittled while Communism, Socialism and Islam are exalted. The question we have to ask ourselves is "How does this happen across the country and around the world at the same time? Can this really be just a coincidence or social trend?" It is not a coincidence; it is a strategy that can be discovered by anyone with a computer. Communists and Socialists have publically presented their strategies and philosophies for over a century. They took control of our schools of higher education and, in time, those graduates became the teachers, principals and politicians of this generation. This is not a conspiracy where everyone attends meetings and plans together, but a conspiracy of a few well-placed people who have the opportunity and intention to influence the minds of students.

Teachers are authoritarian influences and as such their word is often accepted without question. Most people trust the government and those in positions of authority thinking they would never allow something to be taught that is untrue. Most think what teachers say is fact and once something is accepted as fact it is no longer questioned. Once something becomes a part of standardized education the "educated" ("indoctrinated") become propagators who duplicate the process of generating *useful idiots* who leave the world of true science and honest academia for ego bolstering by repeating what the experts say. When you say what the expert says, by association you are an expert. Some studies indicate once a thought or point of view is incorporated into a group for three generations people are born into the world hard-wired with a propensity to believe that same point of view. It is now part of our sense of self and we must fight to preserve it no matter how irrational the information may be or how contradictory the facts.

Teachers are authoritarian influences and as such their word is often accepted without question.

To control a nation all one has to do is control the educational system. The leftist, atheistic view of the world has increased exponentially with every graduation ceremony of brainwashed students. Education is the primary path of demoralization by minimizing God to nothing more than myth and superstition through false science. It is the place where children are prepared to be participants in the New World Order even if those words are never used.

In school a student could have as many as 20 years of Luciferian brainwashing. Besides the academic influence there is social influence that comes from being in an environment where acceptance of the group is dependent on agreeing with the group. Just think of it, our children are taught as fact unscriptural, philosophical concepts, many of which have never been proven, much less succeeded. The medical model of man, which is completely atheistic, presents the Reductionist theory of the mechanical man. So how we manage our health has been programmed.

In school a student could have as many as 20 years of Luciferian brainwashing.

Our understanding the mind and mental health is deeply rooted in the teachings of Freud who, by his own admission, was a godless Jew. Much of Freud's research is known to be fraudulent. In other words, he had his own opinions and lied about his research to make his opinions appear to be correct. At the center of his equation for mental health was the corrupt concept of absolute rejection of morals and standards and the pursuit of personal gratification. Freud's obsession with sex revealed his perverted presuppositions. Then, of course, there were others who taught that man was not responsible for his action; society was responsible. Since society was the problem the individual never took responsibility for his action and never changed his life. The cure was that society had to change. So now they have an anti-God idea of mental health and personal responsibility!

Socialism is touted as the answer to man's every social and political issue. Chairman Mao, Lenin and Stalin are presented as cultural heroes. Capitalism is presented as the cause of all evil in the world. The romanticism of a world with no one in charge is appealing to young idealists who have little or no life experience. The rich are vilified. Rebellion and anarchy are promoted as healthy responses to injustices; thus, you have the leftist-inspired, student-led riots that began taking place in the 1960's. But the truth is they are not led by students, they are led by professional agitators and community organizers, many of whom are participants in organizations like ACORN that are subsidized by the US government. So now their political views are shaped.

Keynesian economics is a Socialist concept embraced and possibly inspired by the Illuminati that has never worked. It is totally opposed to free enterprise and fully committed to an economy controlled by the government. It has failed in every Communist nation in the world and it is failing all over the world now. If it were not for the economy of the United States Communist and Socialist nations would have failed years ago. Contrary to the ridiculous logic, someone has to keep generating and spending money for there to be an economy. When the economies of the US and China fall there will a global economic collapse. But students graduate from college misinformed about who and what is actually causing all the economic instability. They are completely overlooking the reality that if the government has control over money, they control everything. And who is to say there is anyone on this earth who could have that much power and not be corrupted?

Keynesian economics is a Socialist concept embraced and possibly inspired by the Illuminati that has never worked. It is totally opposed to free enterprise and fully committed to an economy controlled by the government.

Of course, Darwin's theory of evolution is the lynchpin of nearly all anti-God education. There is not, however, one concrete piece of evidence in the fossil record proving evolution; it is just a theory, and a poor one at that! Even Darwin encouraged his readers to ignore the fossil record; yet, it is the cornerstone of Atheism. There are hundreds of geological and anthropological proofs of the accuracy of the Bible. Yet, because this information is suppressed none of those actual proofs will ever be admitted into a classroom. In years gone by, because of the limitations of science and lack of information, this knowledge was excluded on the basis that it was not scientifically proven. But the bias of secular science is obviously suppressing that which affirms creation and falsifying concepts that seem to support evolution. In 1909, Charles D. Walcott, director of the Smithsonian Institution, discovered a very rich fossil record proving there had been no slow progressive evolution of phyla into other life forms. But you may ask, "Why is evolution still taught in school as an absolute fact?" Walcott hid his finding of more than 60,000 fossils for over eighty years. Just like the scientific proof of biblical giants, the Smithsonian is part of the unspoken conspiracy.

Today, although much of the Bible has been scientifically validated, it has been excluded simply because it is in the Bible. The misrepresentation of separation of church and state is so deeply ingrained that if scientists looked through a telescope and saw Jesus coming to Planet Earth it could not be publically stated because it would violate separation of church and state.[iii]

Today, although much of the Bible has been scientifically validated, it has been excluded simply because it is in the Bible.

Darwin is the holy grail of Atheism; therefore, nothing will be permitted into academia that allows a reasonable idea concerning Creationism or intelligent design. More than anything, in order to totally control the human race the fact that man was created in the likeness and image of God must be eradicated. If we knew the truth about God, His true nature and who we are in relation to Him it would be impossible to seduce us into giving the government our authority. And let there be no doubt, the very government that rejects all religion and must have separation of church and state will be the very government that one day demands our surrender to the antichrist to form a new religion.

The antichrist is also called "the man of iniquity" or "lawlessness."[iv] In this modern world iniquity is enlightenment. Education has become the authoritative voice of truth. The educational system is controlled by the enlightened.

---

iii The entire current concept of separation of church and state is not in the constitution and was never the intention of the founders.

iv 2 Thessalonians 2:7-10, For the mystery of lawlessness is already at work; only He who now restrains will do so until He is taken out of the way. 8 And then the lawless one will be revealed, whom the Lord will consume with the breath of His mouth and destroy with the brightness of His coming. 9 The coming of the lawless one is according to the working of Satan, with all power, signs, and lying wonders, 10 and with all unrighteous deception among those who perish, because they did not receive the love of the truth,

Those who only sought to learn math, economics or other valuable life skills are indoctrinated into Satanism under any number of names. In their attempt to cast off religion they have been thoroughly indoctrinated into Luciferian religion. As the "educated" take control of the world they unwittingly play a role in the demoralization of humanity and prepare the way for the man of iniquity, the antichrist. The only way for the man of lawlessness to come forth is for lawlessness (iniquity) to abound. Satan has worked frantically for this very moment. Freedom that once made our nation great is the very freedom through which the spirit of iniquity worked to bring us to this place.

A social order, which culminated in the 19th and 20th centuries, has been carefully crafted throughout history. A group of people slowly and subtly cultivated what would be taught. One man determined the first accredited schools. They received accreditation, which meant they qualified for grants only if they taught the approved curriculum. Schools needed money so they agreed. To the uninformed it seemed simply like a move to provide better education, but it was actually a move to control information.

The process was so slow and calculated the public never noticed. This group convinced the government to fund its efforts through taxes. So the people paid for it, but they eventually lost any meaningful say as to what happened in the schools because of the unions. Then the government taxed the people even more to create a nationwide bureaucracy to make sure what was taught in schools complied with the ideas of the controlling group. This brings us to the true goal of government: controlled education. The government wants to define truth independently of God. They want to create a society of enlightened individuals who have thrown off the ignorant superstition of God and morals through education. Once the government has defined truth it must protect citizens from lies; therefore, if it is not true, according to the State, it is a lie and cannot be taught.

You must be trained in accredited schools to become a teacher. You must become a participant in the official version of truth. If you disagree you could be ostracized and never given the opportunity to teach in an accredited school. The group is self-taught, self-governed and self-regulated. They define truth and evaluate all information based on their own definition of truth. If it does not comply with their definition of truth it cannot be taught in an accredited school. Furthermore, anyone who embraces an unapproved idea is rejected, ridiculed and considered an uneducated idiot.

The final and ultimate blow is when it becomes law that your children must be taught by these accredited schools. The taxpayers pay for the schools and teachers and, by extension, we pay for them to be members of the union. The union (which now has millions of dollars to funnel into campaign donations) buys politicians, so directly or indirectly they control the curriculum, the teachers and the classroom. The NEA (like the AMA) has become a self-governing organization that actually answers to no one. It polices itself and always finds itself innocent. But most tragically, it has the ability to decide what each generation of children will consider to be true and false.

The final and ultimate blow is when it becomes law that your children must be taught by these accredited schools. The taxpayers pay for the schools and teachers and, by extension, we pay for them to be members of the union.

As parents we would like to think we could resolve this disaster and restore a valid educational system through the political process, but that is foolish idealism. Yes, we should be politically involved, especially on a local and state level; after all, these people will be future national leaders. More than that, local politics is easier to influence and brings the most immediate benefit to our cause. But to put your hope in the political process is delusional reasoning.

SPIRITUAL GUIDE

There is no substitute for teaching our own children. Unfortunately, we think of teaching as purely academic. One of the reasons we have young adults graduating from college without really knowing how to do anything productive is the abandonment of the tried and true process of mentoring. God's wisdom for teaching our children is not a classroom; it is *"when you sit in your house, when you walk by the way, when you lie down, and when you rise up."* [v] (Deuteronomy 6:7) This is talking about influencing our children in the process of real life. As parents and grandparents we should be life coaches for our children. If we can teach them how to live and to accept God's values and morals as the way to a great life, they can sift through the propaganda without becoming poisoned.

We can develop our children in the way of wisdom. Sadly, few people seem to want wisdom. Because of the historical Luciferian influence in Christian thought we tend to take more of a mystical perspective than one based on faith. The occult (secret knowledge that comes by initiation) works from formulas: saying the prayer properly, performing the right set of works, etc. These mystical Religionist approaches to prayer and faith are taught as "spirituality." In fact, much pop-doctrine is so inundated with the formula concept they think wisdom is not of faith.

Wisdom is always about practical application. If I trust God's love for me and trust the wisdom of His Word I will experience grace to put it into practice. The key is "put it into practice." Wisdom answers the question, "How does this work in real life?" This is what needs to be modeled to our children. Our children need to see what it looks like when we put God's truth and our faith to work in a practical way that benefits our life.

We have all heard the Scripture: *"Train up a child in the way he should go and when he is old he will not depart from it"* (Proverbs 22:6). For many parents this means take him to church, make him do right, and even if he backslides when he is old he will come back. The *Amplified Bible* provides a little better insight when it says: *"Train up a child in the way he should go [and in keeping*

---

v Deuteronomy 6:6-9, "And these words which I command you today shall be in your heart. 7 You shall teach them diligently to your children, and shall talk of them when you sit in your house, when you walk by the way, when you lie down, and when you rise up. 8 You shall bind them as a sign on your hand, and they shall be as frontlets between your eyes. 9 You shall write them on the doorposts of your house and on your gates.

with his individual gift or bent], and when he is old he will not depart from it." This seems to be more in line with the original language.

We should be observant parents who listen and discover our child's interests and passions - their particular bent. Then we should show, disciple or train them in walking in God's Word to fulfill their dreams. If people connect living their dreams to walking with God it will be hard to separate them from God. This, of course, means it is how you must live your life.

I highly recommend reading a chapter of Proverbs every day with your children in a translation they can understand and teach them how this wisdom applies to their lives. Don't limit your spiritual modeling to just praying for their needs; nothing is as devastating to a child as an unanswered prayer. Pray for them and then show them God's principles for walking into their truth. Let them see you listen to the Holy Spirit and get good results. Show them how to apply God's Word from the motive of love. You be the light in their world of darkness!

Not everyone can afford it, but obviously one of the greatest gifts you could give your child is to place him or her in a good Christian school. Be sure when placing your child in a Christian school that it is not just a school for kids who have been kicked out of public school; you don't want them in a reform school. Find a school that takes a positive approach to walking with God. They don't need to be turned off to God by extreme legalism.

One solution for funding attendance in a private school is the "voucher system." This is the only thing that will break the socialistic monopoly forced on the educational system. Let your city, county, state, and federal representatives know you want them to support the voucher system. If the opportunity ever arises for a presidential candidate who is willing to dismantle the Department of Education, the voucher system would be worth supporting. But even the perfect educational system doesn't replace personally mentoring our children to walk with God!

The Apostle Paul said, *"Imitate me, just as I also imitate Christ"* (1 Corinthians 11:1). Living the kind of life you want your children to live ensures that if they imitate you they will be imitating Jesus.

To learn more about the resources mentioned and for additional support material for this chapter please visit www.secondcomingguide.com.

APOCALYPSE

CHAPTER 30

SCIENCE: THE NEW RELIGION

The only problem with science is scientists!

PURE, UNADULTERATED SCIENCE IS A WONDERFUL FIELD OF RESEARCH. There are few things that reveal the wonders of God like physics. The scientist whose heart is a blank slate gazing into the window of the unknown will daily participate in an adventure that is unparalleled. He or she will see and grasp things known by few. This person allows "what is" to shape their thoughts and be instructed by God's revelation in His creation. Of all people in the world who should be ardent worshippers of God, scientists deserve top of the list.

But modern science has become a belief system itself with all the prejudice, dogma, corruption and blind faith of which it accuses religion. It has become the rod of Atheism, the teaching arm of the New World Order. What should and could be pouring daily revelation concerning the glories of God into the world has the information base for all that is unholy. Sadly, not many scientists see God in His creation. They do not look at creation allowing their minds to be a clear slate. They do not allow that which "created" to speak to them. Instead, they speak to what is created and tell it what it must say. Scientists (at least the ones whose observations will be accepted by the

"System") look at creation with a predetermined opinion seeking a desired outcome with the prejudice of unbelief. While science itself is wonderful, scientists are burdened with the temptations, fears, ambitions and corruptions of mere mortals. In the end not everything called science is actually scientific.

The Apostle Paul addressed the Luciferian influence over those who studied creation from the earliest of times down to the scientists of our day.

> *...unrighteousness of men, who suppress the truth in unrighteousness, ...For since the creation of the world His invisible attributes are clearly seen, being understood by the things that are made, even His eternal power and Godhead, so that they are without excuse, because, although they knew God, they did not glorify Him as God, nor were thankful, but became futile in their thoughts, and their foolish hearts were darkened. Professing to be wise, they became fools... who exchanged the truth of God for the lie, and worshiped and served the creature rather than the Creator* (Romans 1:18-23. 25).

From this Scripture we realize anyone who mindfully observes creation, the laws of physics, without prejudice would see and understand the attributes of God. Instead, they suppress the truth in their own unrighteousness. Rather than worshipping and acknowledging God, they worship or idolize the creation. The moment we eliminate the possibility of the Creator we have elevated creation to a self-made, self-perpetuating entity. We honor the wisdom of the universe or the universal mind instead of the mind and wisdom of the Creator.

In verse 25 of Romans 1 there is a subtle but very significant truth. It does not say they exchange *a truth* for *a lie.* They exchange *"the truth"* about God for *"the lie"* that leads one to worship the creation instead of the Creator. The definite article "the" means this is talking about a specific truth and a specific lie. When scientists observed creation they saw and understood the infinite love and wisdom of God as the Creator. They saw how all things were created to sustain life. The meticulous attention to the smallest detail reveals the love and wisdom of God in creating a perfect world for mankind. They deliberately chose to not just reject that truth; they hold or suppress it because they have accepted *"the lie"* about God from the father of all lies. They close the door of truth about God to the entire world. Eventually these very "scientists" who claim there is no God will bow their knee by choice or force to the one whom they already ignorantly bow their knee today: Lucifer.

When we abandon the truth about God as Creator it produces a continuum of corrupt logic. All calculations and conclusions are only as reliable as the assumptions from which one begins. Beginning with the assumption, "There is no God," changes the entire process of observation. In fact, based on the quantum theory of an interactive universe, it may even change what creation reveals to the individual. When observing the subatomic world scientists have discovered that what is observed is dependent upon the observer. Thus, the observer alters the experiment.

The "no God" theory then rejects the importance of Planet Earth to God's eternal plan. The true identity of man as the one created in the likeness and image of God is rejected. Besides this corruption of our faith, this facilitates the moral basis for abortion, eugenics, euthanasia, and genetic modification, the mechanical model of man, no absolute morals and values and almost any corruption of the human imagination. All of this is nothing more than an essential precursor for the escalation of iniquity leading to the rise of the antichrist. When man no longer sees himself as created in the likeness and image of God he surrenders his authority, dignity and worth. Consequently, only the wicked who actively seek to undermine it actually realize the truth about man's authority. To fulfill their plan for Planet Earth that is a truth they cannot afford for you to know. They will give their authority to the antichrist while Christians pray for God to do for them what they alone can do for themselves.

When we abandon the truth about God as Creator it produces a continuum of corrupt logic. All calculations and conclusions are only as reliable as the assumptions from which one begins.

Christians have bought into the lie of "leaving these things to the experts." The Church has ignored the basic reality that the unrighteous will bend the truth about anything as a means to accomplish their godless goals and agendas. Because iniquity is in their hearts they will, by nature, twist the truth to support the bent of their own heart. We have trusted Atheists, murderers and Luciferians to establish our understanding of reality on nearly every plane of human existence. They tell us how the world randomly came into existence, denying creation. Man's God-given identity and subsequent authority is lost through the unproven theory of evolution. God's wisdom for managing our emotions is perverted as the basic nature of man and his emotional struggles are redefined by the experts. We raise our children to be rebellious workers of iniquity because the professionals know best how to raise and discipline them. Our judicial system is a complete inequitable process of fraud and injustice because we reject God's standards of justice. The list of rejecting God's wisdom and accepting the fraudulent lies of carnal man is endless. The Bible is no longer a book whereby we live our lives based on the wisdom of God, it is something we read out of religious obligation, violate its teaching and vainly call Jesus our Lord. Then as the world around us descends into complete chaos we wonder why God has failed us.

The scientific community was already corrupt beyond imagination, but a quantum leap of corruption occurred at the end of World War II. While the Nuremburg trials made a pretense of bringing justice to pacify the world, many of the masterminds behind the most hideous crimes against humanity, the doctors and scientists that murdered millions of people and sought to enable Hitler to overthrow the world, were secretly smuggled out of Germany into various countries of the world. It was called Operation Paperclip. Instead of being punished for their atrocities they were rewarded with a new identity, immunity, wealth and prestige. These sadistic, narcissistic, sociopaths helped launch our scientific, military and medical communities into entirely new levels of corrupt logic and Luciferian philosophy. These are the "great minds" we trust to tell us how to live, eat and raise our children, as well as what we believe about God. We trust them more than the witness of the universe, more than the written Word of the Bible and more than the inner voice of the Holy Spirit.

The scientific community was already corrupt beyond imagination, but a quantum leap of corruption occurred at the end of World War II.

The seduction does not occur because these people openly oppose our faith or verbalize their antagonism toward God. It slowly and subtly occurs because we elevate the opinions of these men above the Word of God. We do not know we are elevating them above God because we are not diligent enough to guard our hearts and minds and we are not knowledgeable enough of the

Bible to recognize the lie. Once I have accepted science as my trustworthy, reliable, authoritative source, I accept what it says with little or no realization of how that affects the rest of my beliefs.

The World's System, through government controlled education, has created a closed circuit, self-perpetuating, intellectual loop that initiates the lie, sustains the lie and enforces the lie. The world has created an educational system that determines its own truth and its own rules of philosophy and logic. Their truth is determined by a set of absolutes that have no knowledge of God and, moreover, is committed to destroying all faith. That set of absolutes is based on "science." Science reaches conclusions that it then determines to be absolutes and all theories must be judged by this set of absolutes. It is like playing poker with someone who stacked the deck. Regardless of how good your hand may be, you will still lose. Education is based on science and science is validated through education. Anyone who disagrees with the information or the conclusions is ostracized, vilified, persecuted, sometimes imprisoned and occasionally murdered. Two things a scientist cannot do and maintain his standing are support any concept of intelligent design or do anything that would take wealth and control from the hands of the mega-wealthy.

Science reaches conclusions that it then determines to be absolutes and all theories must be judged by this set of absolutes.

***Science has thousands of unanswered questions. There are many contradictions to its view of reality. These questions cannot be answered because they reach beyond the capability of modern science but, more significantly, they reach beyond the will of modern scientists to accept the truth they so vehemently reject. The ultimate question that cannot be answered and neither will it be rationally discussed is, "Where did all things begin?" Until the 1970's science was adamant that the universe had always been. Then with the advent of quantum mechanics and the "big bang" their unreasonable dogma which had been based on nothing more than philiosophy, went up in smoke. The laws of science prove there was a very specific beginning. Without an apology, an admission of error, a change in the science text books or even the willingness to consider the facts, they conveniently ignore the true science when it is not to their liking and move forward to concoct more unprovable theories to lead man away from faith in his Creator.

At the end of the equation all current "scientific" theories of creation and humanity can be nothing more than theory because they cannot answer the first and most important question. It does not matter if you believe in evolution and the big bang, you are still left with the fact that something cannot come from nothing unless it does, in fact, have a beginning. Nor can one ignore the fact that our universe is not old enough to randomly create human life from nothing. If the first assumption of any theory is incorrect, regardless of how many supporting facts are correct the conclusion will never be accurate, especially when the conclusion is determined at the outset, regardless of facts. The World's System hates God and it hates the truth that proves God's Word to be absolutely correct. They will lie, twist the facts, cover the evidence and even murder those who expose their sinister intentions.

Nor can one ignore that fact that our universe is not old enough to randomly create human life from nothing.

The very idea of a random universe violates the second law of thermodynamics. Order does not come from chaos. Our current understanding of quantum theory says the universe is interactive and cannot exist without an intelligent observer. If it requires an intelligent observer it must require an intelligent Creator! If we take into consideration that all things must start somewhere, added to all that we currently know about quantum mechanics, factored in with all the known scientific contradictions and remove that which is simply theory, the World's System would have absolutely no answers for creation of the world or human life. They would have what they have now… many unproven theories; and unproven theories that are advanced as truth are lies. Actually they are more hideous than lies; they are conspiracies to conceal the truth.

The theory of evolution upon which all Atheism hangs its proverbial hat cannot be proven. But now we know, based on the greatest scientific equations of the greatest scientific thinkers in the world, that the world was created in six 24-hour days. Our universe is expanding and as it expands, time elongates. In this universe time moves according to your perspective of it or the point from which you observe it. What God did in the beginning is six 24-hour days from that point in time, but is measured differently from our point in time. Based on the current scientific knowledge the universe is a little over 15 billion years old and only about 6000 years old at the same time. It's all a matter of perspective. Are you measuring from the beginning when time was very condensed or from today when the universe (space and time) have continually expanded?

Astronomers calculate that the universe has expanded since the beginning at a rate of one million squared. Gerald L. Schroeder arrived at this incredible insight by dividing the 15¾ billion years old universe by one million squared and arrived at roughly six days. Even more amazing is the fact that based on these mathematical calculations each aspect of creation actually happened on the exact day it is recorded in Genesis. This is not based on the calculation of an extremist using strange math. This is a scientist using the best information from the best books in the best library at MIT. This is information that all scientists, teachers and politicians could know if they wanted to know it. But to acknowledge these facts would validate God's Word. The accuracy of God's Word completely undermines the Luciferian agenda.

> Based on the current scientific knowledge the universe is a little over 15 billion years old and only about 6000 years old at the same time. It's all a matter of perspective.

The biblical absolutes in the creation and genealogy of man, validated by scientific proof, displace all misinterpretations and misrepresentations of God's Word. The absolute essential deception of the Luciferian doctrine is rooted in the opposition to man being created in the likeness and image of God. For the believer this will be key to maintaining your faith when the world as you know it begins to unravel. It is in this very reality that we have the authority of man: we were created in the likeness and image of God and we were given dominion. This is the deception wherein Planet Earth makes it possible for the man of sin, the lawless one, the antichrist to rise to power. If we don't know who we are in relationship to our Creator, we have no authority. If science has proven the Bible is little more than a religious myth, you are now a slave to the System.

Science blinks its eyes at the thousands if not millions of factors that must be in perfect harmony in order for man to live on Planet Earth. The trillions of cells in our body and the billions of activities that occur every second require a perfectly balanced world and a precision of organized function that could never have evolved by chance. If it did evolve the estimated age of Planet Earth is not old enough for all of these factors to emerge at the right time and sequence. Then the absurdity that our bodies would randomly develop into such a complex, yet perfectly organized organism defies the parameters of actual scientific fact or reasonable logic.

The trillions of cells in our body and the billions of activities that occur every second require a perfectly balanced world and a precision of organized function that could never have evolved by chance.

When we factor in the mind which interacts with the body and the subatomic world in ways that are near miraculous, there are more questions than can be answered by the prejudiced, atheistic, scientific parameters of thought. The mind/body connection has never been adequately explained or reasonably discussed. The emerging science of psychoneuroimmunology and new breakthroughs in epigenetics are proving what has long been known in Oriental Medicine, *thoughts and emotions transform the body.* Our overall health lies primarily within the realm of our mind and emotions. Like the universe, our bodies are interactive; they are not the random development of non-intelligent observation. All these facts are ignored and unanswered by the science that controls the way we see the world and understand God. Science cannot even come up with an adequate explanation of consciousness.

Those who embrace the theory of evolution cannot explain and will not even acknowledge the discovery of the remains of giants all across the globe; this would obliterate their already unprovable theory. The idea that there was advanced technology thousands of years before Christ that cannot be duplicated today does not fit into the idea of a slowly-evolving intelligence. Then there is the pesky detail of man somehow leaping from a subspecies and living like a primate, to having astounding intelligence, knowledge of the cosmos, astrology, medicine, geometry, anatomy and structural engineering seemingly overnight. Combine all these anomalies with the fact that there is not one piece of concrete evidence supporting evolution and it only comes down to one possibility: *"They are blind because they say they see."* They have decided what they want to see and that is all that will be seen. But long before the present day intellectuals reached these conclusions their predecessors were seduced by Luciferian thought; thus, the intellectually superior are the *useful idiots* of the enlightened.

So-called "science" born from Luciferian, Nephilim knowledge fueled with an anti-God prejudice has always had as its fundamental premise that the Bible is not true so we must not, in any way, support or agree with it. However, today "scientific information" that is released to the public has become controlled by the System. It is more about making money and controlling humanity than discovery. Scientists, who are human beings with opinions and prejudices, control the core of education, medicine and psychology. Science in itself is not good or evil, but the basis of Luciferian knowledge was to show man how to live independently of God. Knowledge, therefore, is neither inherently good nor bad; but the person who uses knowledge does so for good or evil based on the condition of his or her heart. Neither the universe nor science is evil but the suppression of truth and the intention to support a false premise are evil.

> There is the pesky detail of man somehow leaping from a subspecies and living like a primate, to having astounding intelligence, knowledge of the cosmos, astrology, medicine, geometry, anatomy and structural engineering seemingly overnight.

One major twist in scientific thought is to diminish the idea that Planet Earth is unique. Everything about our universe is not only unique but it is thoughtfully designed to sustain human life. The distance of Earth from the sun, the distance of Earth from the other planets, the gravitational field of Earth, and thousands of other factors tell us that Earth and our universe are incredibly unique and came into being by intelligent design. For example, every day there are more than 7,000,000 lightning strikes. These lightning strikes keep the frequency of the atmosphere between the surface of the earth and the ionosphere balanced at just 7.83 Hz or higher harmonics which is the exact frequency required to sustain functions of the human body and a peaceful mind. There are thousands of occurrences that happen in nature that support this uniquely designed eco-system, specifically for man's healthy existence.

Planet Earth is incredibly unique in ways that not many Christians even seem to realize. Planet Earth will be the abode of New Jerusalem.[i] Heaven will not be off in the clouds on some far away planet; it will be here on a recreated Planet Earth! This is what makes global destruction through pollution or annihilation a primary Luciferian goal. Most people believe we are over-populated and the earth cannot sustain life. All of this is a discredit to the Creator. It even causes Christians to question the wisdom of God. Some seem to think God has failed in His design of Earth or these events are the consequences of divine judgment, but both of these conclusions discredit and undermine our confidence in God. Even more importantly, they make us believe we must rely on the knowledge of scientists and the benevolence of government to save the world.

Heaven will be here on a recreated Planet Earth! This is what makes global destruction through pollution or annihilation a primary Luciferian goal.

To bring the greatest pain to God Lucifer must destroy what God loves, mankind and the place of God's eternal dwelling, Planet Earth. Angels were created to be servants of mankind. It was to us authority of Planet Earth was given, not to the angels. It was we who were created in the likeness and image of God. It is the human race that has the unique capacity to know and feel God's love. Lucifer's pride would not let him be a servant of man. He wanted all man had including rule of Planet Earth. His jealousy and pride drives him to destroy what he cannot control, but it has to be done through deception. Man must not trust God; he must surrender his authority through ignorance, unbelief or choice. Nothing works quite as well as creating a global crisis that threatens Planet Earth and all of humanity, then forcing the submission of a world to a false savior!

In the World's System politicians pass laws that define morals and scientists manage the information, which defines truth. So the combination of politics and science is the key to controlling all thought, logic and faith. In other words, it is from the theories of scientists that we establish and justify the moral behavior that has been determined by the politician. Thus, science and

---

i Revelation 21:1-2, Now I saw a new heaven and a new earth, for the first heaven and the first earth had passed away. Also there was no more sea. 2 Then I, John, saw the holy city, New Jerusalem, coming down out of heaven from God, prepared as a bride adorned for her husband

politics form a godless religion with all the dogma, bias and blind loyalty of religious zealots. And now the government has gone as far as to suggest anyone who does not embrace the scientific world view is a danger to society. There have been discussions of imprisoning or eliminating those who do not agree with global warming… another theory that has never been proven and, for all practical purposes, has been disproven. Yet, it is the truth of the "enlightened." The governments of the world have probably murdered more of their own citizens for disagreeing than have been killed by opposing armies in all wars.

We must have government and we must have science. The problem is that humans with agendas are involved in the process.

We must have government and we must have science. The problem is that humans with agendas are involved in the process. Humans have lusts, insecurities and egos which always lead to agendas, and they will use government and science to fulfil them. Believers, in the meantime, are like sheep led to the slaughter. They want to believe the government can be trusted and scientists are always scientific, but that is delusional. We trust them because we have never really trusted God with all our hearts. In our sense of lack and insecurity we are looking to science and government to give us what can only be found in our hearts from God alone.

I recently heard a women's rights advocate explaining how she answers conservatives who ask her how she can support the murder of millions of babies. Her response was, "I do not support the murder of babies and if you can show me where that is happening I will take your side and help you stop it. I do know women are eliminating fetuses; but according to science, fetuses aren't babies so no babies are being killed." Science determines the truth and government passes the laws defining morals. Then we accept it as our standard of right and wrong, good and evil.

Eugenics, which was seriously studied and encouraged by Progressives in America, was the science Hitler studied to justify eliminating millions. Based on the theory of evolution only the strongest species survive; therefore, he was not only doing the world a favor by eliminating the inferior species of Jews and other races, he was actually working with the laws of nature. Government determined what was legal and science determined the humane way to execute them; therefore, his hands were clean. When scientists become the authors and definers of truth and government becomes the definer of morals anything can be declared legal and moral if it is the will of the government.

Like all things in the World's System the only funded research is that which supports and promotes the accepted premise. Researchers are funded by groups that need science to reaffirm their position. Researchers repay the system by validating their opinions, thus, giving them more power, influence and, of course, affluence. It is an endless cycle of "the blind leading the blind." Everyone makes money while deceiving the world and advancing their causes.

Eugenics, which was seriously studied and encouraged by Progressives in America, was the science Hitler studied to justify eliminating millions.

SPIRITUAL GUIDE

As believers we should never reject science. It has been this reaction to science that caused the Church to look controlling and ignorant. Science is not the problem; it is the misinterpretation of facts. Likewise, do not make the same mistakes made by many labeling information as evil because it came through a pagan culture. Nothing in creation is inherently evil. God is good and all He created is good. Religionists tend to observe the world through a "secular or sacred dichotomy," then through a series of judgments determine good and evil based on their judgments. We all share pretty much the same information, so the question is not, "Who discovered it?" The question is "How do we understand it in light of God's Word?"

Few believers have a sound enough understanding of the Word of God to look at the same information a scientist looks at and understand how that could be interpreted from a biblical perspective. Science can often do incredible research, but without a good comprehension of the Word of God neither they nor we can reach a healthy conclusion. God's Word is the greatest history, science, sociology and psychology book ever written. But the way we read it closes our mind to the treasure it holds. If we have already accepted the world's explanation of all things we are not looking for those answers in the Word of God. We remain blind because we insist that we see. I have spent the last 40 years studying science, medicine, psychology and the Bible. I have not changed my understanding of the Bible because of new scientific or medical discoveries, but many times I have changed my understanding of the "sciences" because of what I saw in the Word!

The Apostle Paul explained, *"To the pure all things are pure, but to those who are defiled and unbelieving nothing is pure; but even their mind and conscience are defiled"* (Titus 1:5). At the end of the equation all we need to have accurate information, regardless of where it comes from, is to have a good enough knowledge of God's Word to find the proper conclusion. Likewise, we need a pure heart, free from selfish agendas, that yields to the wisdom of the Holy Spirit. When Jesus said, *"Blessed are the pure in heart, For they shall see God"* (Matthew 5:8), He may well have been echoing the fact that he who has a crooked, twisted, froward or perverse heart cannot find good because they cannot find God.[ii] A pure heart can find the "God element" wherever it exists, but the religious, biased, prejudiced, bigoted, hardened or unbelieving heart cannot find God and they cannot find the good.

---

ii Proverbs 17:20, He who has a deceitful heart finds no good.

Never fall for the deception that any part of creation is bad or evil. That is an indictment against God as Creator! We must always be aware that corrupt people will use what God has given for our benefit for some evil purpose. That does not, however, mean God's creation was evil.

At the end of the process we who believe in God and see Him as Creator of all things worship Him. We are enamored with the creation only to the degree it reveals the glory and wisdom of the Creator. The key difference between a believer, Religionist or Atheist is we not only see God's hand in all of creation, we give Him the glory for all of creation!

To learn more about the resources mentioned and for additional support material for this chapter please visit www.secondcomingguide.com.

APOCALYPSE

CHAPTER 31

MEDICINE: THE ULTIMATE CONTROL

He who controls your healthcare also controls your life by using your greatest fear as an ally!

PROBABLY THE MOST CONFLICTING AREA WHERE OUR LIVES ARE BEING SYSTEMATICALLY STOLEN FROM US IS MODERN MEDICINE. So many doctors are deeply compassionate and caring individuals who truly desire to help people. But, possibly more than any other professionals, they are caught in a system that allows little freedom. Among the insurance companies, the AMA, government controls, massive school debt (which demands an unrealistic patient load) and big pharma, there is little room for them to fulfil their passion. But as with all things, the real problem is not the doctors but the system that trains and controls them.

If we were to compare the various bureaucratic branches of government the FDA would, no doubt, be complicit in more deaths than all other branches put together, including the military. To keep this in perspective we must remind ourselves that more people die or are maimed annually due to medical mistakes than all who die in war and terrorism. Yet, all this goes unquestioned and unchallenged by the government or the general population.

Medical science, like all other science, rejects God; thus, it rejects the premise that man is created in the likeness and image of God. Based on the theory of evolution, man is simply a higher evolved animal; therefore, in the eyes of some, he requires no higher moral treatment than any other animal. By rejecting any form of intelligent design, body parts that have been previously understood were simply removed. There is little concept of assisting the body to heal itself. There is only a god-like complex that feels no respect for the human body or how it was created.

Certainly the influence of Nazi scientists brought to America after World War II has swayed that train of thought. Through Operation Paperclip, Nazi war criminals who had performed all manner of godless experiments on those in prison camps were brought to America, given new identities and played a major role in shaping American medical thought.

In the "science of medicine" man is a machine that works on outdated, disproven Newtonian concepts of cause and effect.

In the "science of medicine" man is a machine that works on outdated, disproven Newtonian concepts of cause and effect. None of the knowledge of quantum energy has been applied to medical treatment by those who control the science. Interestingly, diagnosis is done employing energetic quantum theory, but the body is treated with drugs based on outdated Newtonian theory. The fact that modern diagnosis uses advanced techniques lets us know that this is not a problem of ignorance, but a problem of choice. As usual, huge profits for drug companies drivesthe choice of treatment.

One researcher working to find a cure for diabetes was involved in an interaction with a drug company representative. When his boss began to propose a new direction of research to discover a cure for diabetes the idea was rejected even though it had merit. The reason given by the representative was, "There is no money in curing diabetes." Diabetes is a "business" worth $245 billion annually. The same is true with cancer and many areas that get billions of dollars each year for research. Finding a cure would only put them out of business. Many drug companies were probably started by someone who had a passion to cure a disease, but like all things that fall prey to the World's System, they cease to exist for a cure, instead they exist for a profit. After all, investors are not necessarily looking for a cure; they invest to make money.

We now know the body works from electromagnetic energy. Healthy cells must have a specific voltage to be healthy. The voltage in a cell determines its degree of oxygen. In the absence of voltage, disease begins. When they dysfunction and the disease process begins it is always a matter of low voltage. These are facts that can be found in many medical papers, but the drug companies (who supposedly desire to find a cure) accept no research that does not support the need for more allopathic medicine. In other words, they will allow people to die from the disease or from the side effects of treatment before losing profits.

With the knowledge of quantum energy and sophisticated equipment, treatment could easily and inexpensively be developed that would restore energetic balance to the cells, thus facilitating the body's ability to heal itself with little or no side effects. The only hospitalization ever needed would be for accidents, an occasional rare need for surgery, advanced disease and to facilitate the dying. But this would upset a $1.6 trillion industry! Modern medicine is based on the outdated theory of determinism.

With the knowledge of quantum energy and sophisticated equipment, treatment could easily and inexpensively be developed that would restore energetic balance to the cells, thus facilitating the body's ability to heal itself with little or no side effects.

Determinism means that we are victims of a fateful universe, and we have no power to change the outcome of events. In medicine the two deterministic principles are genetic determinism and the germ theory of disease. Genetic determinism means we are victims of our own genetic heritage where disease runs in the family and there is nothing we can do to change our genetic fate. The other deterministic model is the germ theory of disease, and that we are victims of germs, bugs, bacteria, viruses, etc. and modern medicine "tries" to come to the rescue with antibiotics and vaccines to kill these invaders (we'll see in this chapter just how wrong these outdated notions are).[i]

Determinism has deep roots in Darwinian Theory. But we now know that very few (if any) diseases are genetic. Long known medical research reveals

---

i PEMF The Fifth Element of Healing, Bryant A. Meyers, 2014 Bryant A. Meyers, Balboa Press, Bloomington, IN that most disease is, in fact, environmental. Dr. Joel Wallach, who did groundbreaking research using thousands of human and animal autopsies, says there are no genetic birth defects. According to Dr. Wallach "birth defects" are nutritional deficiencies. Most of these birth defects have been eliminated in animals through veterinary nutrition, but these same proven principles will not be applied to humans because of the massive loss of profits.

> Determinism has deep roots in Darwinian Theory. But we now know that very few (if any) diseases are genetic. Long known medical research reveals that most disease is, in fact, environmental.

This is not an indictment against the average doctor who is in practice helping patients, but the drug companies, insurance companies, the FDA and the corrupt doctors who do their bidding for a price. According to some research over 70% of all costs associated with healthcare are due to preventable conditions. In other words, if we were taught honest, simple nutrition we would avoid most diseases that plague our family and our nation.

We have learned that the idea of germs and bacteria attacking our body from the outside is antiquated and inaccurate. Our bodies do not "catch" diseases as much as they create them.

We now know, through the use of dark field microscopes, that microorganisms are pleomorphic (from latin pleo = "many"; morph = "form") that they can often change forms. A virus can become a bacterium, which can mutate into a yeast or fungus. Pleomorphic research reveals that healthy cells actually morph into bacteria and viruses based on the environment surrounding those cells. The idea of pleomorphism is that bacteria and viruses change depending on the environment. The type of organism is a result of the chemical environment.[ii]

Based on the biblical and alternative principles of diet and emotional management we create the environment that determines the development of our cells for life or death. The biblical wisdom for diet and emotional management as it relates to health was rejected because of the predominance of

---

ii ibid

Luciferian philosophy as the attempt of an angry God to control our lives and steal our happiness. The Church of Rome made it illegal for Christians to observe the wisdom of God's Word. It was against the law for a Christian to rest on the Sabbath, they could not observe any of the feasts and God's laws (divine prescriptions) for health and abundant life were not just rejected, they were punishable by imprisonment or death. God's wisdom was replaced with the foolishness and philosophies of man and occult teachings of Luciferian thought.

> Based on the biblical and alternative principles of diet and emotional management we create the environment that determines the development of our cells for life or death.

When I teach God's wisdom for health a well-intentioned but ignorant believer will often say, "All of that is under the law, so it doesn't apply." It is as if the human body changed from the Old to the New Covenant. Our bodies (which were created by God) did not change nor did His wisdom for managing our physical health. We are not under law; none of those divine prescriptions makes us more acceptable to God. Jesus is our righteousness. But those insights from our Creator provide the basic wisdom to manage our own health.

On the scientific front this ancient wisdom is dismissed as ridiculous superstition. I cannot tell you how many times I have heard "medical experts" say, "It does not matter what you eat" or, "Taking vitamins will just create expensive urine." It is the absence of organic vitamins, minerals and other nutrients that causes the massive degree of disease that makes us dependent on their toxic medicine with all its side effects. Remember, medical research is only considered valid if it fits into accepted scientific parameters. When the basic premise of those parameters is wrong the research itself, while not being completely wrong, will still be incompatible with human physiology, thus creating all the side effects.

The entire drug industry is operating on a disproven theory that was never completed when it was accepted as fact. Why was it accepted? It facilitated a theory that made man believe he was a victim who needed to be rescued. Louis Pasteur, father of the germ theory, as it turns out was an ambitious, dishonest fraud. He plagiarized his research from Bechamp's uncompleted research. Bechamp went on to prove that germs were the consequence of disease and not the cause. On his deathbed Pasteur admitted "The germ is nothing, terrain is everything." In other words, most of the disease is in us. It is activated when the body's oxygen and voltage levels drop. The diseases don't attack us as much as we create them in a body that is toxic from following the teaching of modern medicine.

> The entire drug industry is operating on a disproven theory that was never completed when it was accepted as fact. Why was it accepted? It facilitated a theory that made man believe he was a victim who needed to be rescued.

Even the long held "scientific" idea that DNA controls our health and longevity is now known to be incorrect. Cutting-edge epigenetic research reveals how our thoughts and our environment can actually activate chemical switches in the body that regulate gene expression. In other words, it is not that you have static programmed DNA; we all have the same potential. But our DNA is programmed by switches that are turned on or off by our emotions, beliefs and diet. Amazingly, in contradiction to years of dogma, we know that cells have the ability to reprogram their own DNA. Since all of this is known to the medical research community why don't they change their theories? Why are we still treating disease the same way it was treated one hundred years ago? The answer is easy to find: just follow the money!

In the absence of the biblical model of man, the human is reduced to a mechanical model made up of independent parts. Therefore, medicine works from the reductionist theory which can have advantages for some situations. But reductionism tends to look at each individual function of the body independently of the whole. Its approach to treatment seldom considers the damaging effects of the treatment on other aspects of the being. Even worse is denial of the power of a more holistic approach to healing that considers man in his entirety: spirit, soul and body. Holistic medicine considers the effect any treatment has on the whole being, therefore, serious side effects are rare.

The side effects (while being many and deadly) are of little concern in allopathic treatment. Side effects simply mean more profits for the drug companies. They will sell you a medicine for the side effect. Allopathic means "to oppose or attack a disease or symptom." Thus, surgery and drugs are all that are offered by allopathic treatment. There is no concept of working with the body so it can heal itself. Allopathic treatment could be described as a group of terrorists seizing a shopping mall taking hundreds of shoppers hostage. So, the military, who sees its role only as eradicating the terrorists, decides to bomb the mall. It will kill the terrorists but it will also kill the hostages. Based on the definition of their role, although they kill all civilians it is a successful mission if they kill the terrorists. This does not mean all allopathic medicine is bad, but when it is the only legal choice it becomes diabolical, even in the hands of someone who truly wants to help the hurting.

In the absence of the biblical model of man, the human is reduced to a mechanical model made up of independent parts. Therefore, medicine works from the reductionist theory which can have advantages for some situations.

There are many wonderful physicians who are fully committed to helping mankind. But the more government (FDA), insurance companies and the AMA get involved in medicine, the less these dedicated people can do. The journey to the current state of affairs was a road filled with questionable motives. Medical schools were the first to begin accreditation. As the Rockefellers and Carnegies began to invest in allopathic medicine, the entire process of medical training and philosophy changed. What may have begun as a philanthropic endeavor dwindled into a profit-driven venture. One of the strategies employed by corrupt, wealthy families has always been to increase profits by eliminating competition and taking control of the market. There are few places where humanity is more negatively affected by the greed of the World's System than the monopoly of the drug companies in the practice of medicine.

Abraham Flexner was employed by Carnegie to investigate all medical schools. New standards were placed on medical schools making it nearly impossible for them to survive on the tuition of the students. Doctors were required to have a college education before entering medical schools. Medical schools had to become part of universities. Medical research was focused more on the laboratory than the clinic. It became impossible for medical schools to exist without grants. The grants came from drug companies and drug companies existed to make a profit. Profits are not made by making people healthy or by preventing disease but by people being sick! I am not implying this to be the intention of doctors, but it is clearly the intention of big pharma.

Once insurance companies entered the race for profits and government saw it as a means of buying votes, the hands of good doctors were tied and the hands of the greedy and corrupt were loosed. As more people bought insurance they failed to understand that two things would happen. The price of medical care would skyrocket to such an extent that you had to have medical coverage, but even worse, now the insurance companies would determine your treatment. That's right! You can only get the treatment covered by your insurance company unless you are able to pay for it yourself. As we move toward a more socialistic government it will soon be illegal to purchase the treatment of your choice.

There are many wonderful physicians who are fully committed to helping mankind. But the more government (FDA), insurance companies and the AMA get involved in medicine, the less these dedicated people can do.

The FDA (Food and Drug Administration) is supposed to be protecting us from bad food and drugs. Ironically, the research upon which the FDA makes its determination is done by "scientists" employed by the companies producing the food and drugs. Many of those employed by the FDA were former politicians who pushed drugs or foods through the system with little or no research. Their reward is a nice-paying job when they leave political office. So we can trust neither the FDA nor the drug companies. Then there is the AMA, the most powerful trade union in America. It is doubtful that a president can win an election without the backing of the AMA. Like any union, it does not exist to protect the consumer but to protect the income of its members.

The AMA (American Medical Association), like the NEA (National Education Association), is a closed unit, a self-contained system that makes its own rules, governs itself and polices itself. It seeks to make all other forms of medical practice illegal, not for the benefit of mankind, but for the benefit of investors in drug companies. If a doctor treats a patient who gets well with anything not approved by the AMA he could not only lose his license, he could go to prison. If he were to treat or advise a patient whose claim is being paid for by an insurance company in any natural or alternative procedure other than what the insurance company approves, he could lose his license and go to jail.

> The AMA (American Medical Association), like the NEA (National Education Association), is a closed unit, a self-contained system that makes its own rules, governs itself and polices itself.

So, the people controlling your health-care are not the doctors who treat you but the politicians, the insurance companies and the AMA. It might be understandable if they had a better track record; but consider this information published by the World Health Organization and the Center for Disease Control in 1990, taken from *Hell's Kitchen* by J.D. Wallach, BS, DVM, ND and Ma Lan, MD, MS, Lac.

- America is ranked 17th in longevity compared with the top thirty-two industrialized nations. By 2000 we had dropped to number 24 and 26th in 2005.
- The entire world spent $2.7 trillion on health care; the United States alone spent $1.6 trillion, more than the rest of the world combined.
- A Harvard School of Public Health survey showed that 180,000 Americans are killed each year in hospitals alone as a result of medical negligence.
- According a 1998 Center for Disease Control report 1.3 million are physically injured each year as a result of medical negligence.
- 2,000,000 Americans are infected in hospitals each year by negligence and 90,000 die.
- According to the Institute of Medicine, 1999, medical mistakes ranked as the 8th top killer in America.
- In December of 2002 a Johns Hopkins study elevated the medical mistakes to the number three cause of death in America killing 250,000 each year.
- In 2004 the Center for Disease Control listed poly-pharmacy as the cause of bad drug reactions to 2.2 million Americans, 140,000-200,000 resulted in death.

Each year 5.8 million American casualties, killed, wounded or infected are perpetrated against hospitalized patients by medical doctors, yet no one seems to care – an unbelievable score that dwarfs the horrors of all terrorism and wars.[iii] Did you get that? More people are killed or injured by medical treatment than ALL WARS AND ALL TERROISM, yet no one seems to notice. Why? Because doctors are all but exempt from charges of murder. It is called "malpractice," another area where insurance companies line their pockets. And it is very difficult to find an attorney or a medical expert who will help you file a lawsuit against a doctor.

The irony gets worse. This organization that kills more people than any other single cause or entity wants to control all forms of medicine and medical practice. Let one person die from an herbal reaction and that herb will be outlawed. If an alternative practitioner has any type of medically-related accident he will be vilified by the full force of the AMA and prosecuted, if possible. Control is always the way of the Luciferian spirit. Control the information to establish a new truth, control the market so there is no competition, control the laws to instill fear (and punish any dissenters), control the media to vilify the competition and exalt the powerful, control the educational process to control the individual's thoughts, and finally, control the power of life and death in order to control the person. Is there anything in this process that remotely represents godliness, freedom or love for your fellowman?

> Today we are all required by law to have insurance. We cannot choose our doctors and we cannot choose the type of treatment we want. We can only get the treatment covered by our insurance plan.

Once it becomes profitable for people to be sick, those who are in it for money do not want you well. What actually reaches the news outlets reveals greedy pharmacologists selling expensive prescriptions only to replace the real medication with an artificial. But this is not even the tip of the real iceberg. Patients regularly receive unwanted and unnecessary treatment. Furthermore, what we do not know is how deeply big pharma, the government and insurance companies are plotting together to control population growth, eliminate dissidents, control races and use profits

---

iii Hell's Kitchen, Dr Joel Wallach, Dr Ma Lan and Wellness Publications, 2004, Wellness Publications, LLC, Bonita, CA

from our suffering to finance global political goals. Sadly, the honest doctor is like the honest preacher attempting to truly help people in the seedy shadow of those who are so corrupt.

> We will, for the first time, be forced to accept the dichotomy and complete incompatibility between the World's System and the Kingdom of God!

I have personally encountered a situation where a man with cancer was declared completely cancer-free; consequently, he opted not to go through chemo. He was informed by the insurance company that should he not complete the prescribed treatment he would be charged for his treatment up to that point and would not be covered in the event of future reoccurrence. I am also personally familiar with another case where a child was dying. He was prescribed a treatment that would cause him much suffering. The irony was that the doctors told the parents the treatment would not improve his condition, but it was the only thing they knew to do. In light of the horrible prognosis the parents elected to refuse the treatment. They wanted his remaining days to be as enjoyable and sickness-free as possible. Even though the treatment was not going to work, they were forced to put their son through this horrible experience or the State would take the child into protective custody. All of this is because of the power of the AMA who, like all unions I have encountered, is more interested in flexing their muscle to prove control than in actually reaching a fair outcome.

Today we are all required by law to have insurance. We cannot choose our doctors and we cannot choose the type of treatment we want. We can only get the treatment covered by our insurance plan. If children are involved and we refuse treatment we could lose our children. We are not far from being forced to take whatever treatment the government requires, the AMA prescribes and the insurance covers. The government already uses force to accomplish this corrupt agenda. It has already started with vaccinations, but who knows where it will end?

One case in Europe actually proved the extent to which Socialism forces itself on every level of our freedom of choice in order to maintain "fairness." There was a woman with a disease so rare the medical companies in that country could not afford to develop a treatment. After suffering for years, a drug was developed in the United States. The drug company offered to provide the drug for her. Her country refused her the drug because it would not be fair for her to get this when it was not available to others. When the government talks about equality and fairness it is talking about everyone being equal to the poorest. They are opposed to the Bible teaching that those who work hard have the right to earn a better quality of life. When all people are equally poor and destitute the government has complete control of human life.

Why are people not up in arms about the atrocities occurring in our nation and the world? Why are people sitting passively as the government takes control of our lives?

Why are people not up in arms about the atrocities occurring in our nation and the world? Why are people sitting passively as the government takes control of our lives? Why does the Church not do something? Questions like these are, on one hand, very legitimate, but, on the other hand, reveal an extreme naivety. Our citizens as a whole still believe you can trust the government. When they see a politician do something incredibly unacceptable and later apologize, people think he really is remorseful and repentant. The general public fails to realize that the apologetic politician is simply doing what is necessary to salvage his career, although he or she may continue in the same destructive behavior. How many thousands of times have I heard someone say, "The government would never let that happen." as a statement made in reference to some atrocity? So many times they failed to see the government was not only already letting the atrocities occur, they were complicit in the very acts.

Lenin said, "Socialized medicine is the keystone to the arch of the Socialized State." People's fear of death, the legitimate suffering of humanity, plus the plagues, diseases and coming pandemics created by governments produce a codependent need for a medical savior unlike any we have ever known. We have been conditioned to believe we cannot survive without regular doctor/patient interaction. When the government controls the science, the medicine and the treatment, for the most part, they control the individual.

Atheistic eugenics is the goal of socialized medicine. The antichrist governments, after convincing the world that there are not enough resources, will convince the population of the need for government-controlled abortion, sterilization, euthanasia and the elimination of what they have called "worthless eaters." A "worthless eater" is one who contributes less to society than he consumes. To a world that believes it is starving to death, elimination of undesirables makes sense as long as you are not one of the undesirables.

But it may be that our need for so much medical treatment is more of a conditioned neuroticism than an actual fact. Once, after a very serious surgery, my doctor taught my wife how to give me the needed treatment for recovery before he sent me home. He said, "If you stay in the hospital you could die." It could be that his wisdom is statistically supported. It may be in the case of modern medicine "less is better."

A "worthless eater" is one who contributes less to society than he consumes. To a world that believes it is starving to death, elimination of undesirables makes sense as long as you are not one of the undesirables.

The June 10, 2000 issue of the *British Medical Journal* reports on an interesting statistic that has occurred in Israel. It seems that three months ago physicians in public hospitals implemented a program of sanctions in response to a labor dispute over a contract proposal by the government. The article stated that the Israel Medical Association began an action in March to protest against the treasury's proposed imposition of a new four year wage contract for doctors. Since then, the medical doctors have cancelled hundreds of thousands of visits to outpatient clinics and have postponed tens of thousands of elective operations.

To find out whether the industrial action was affecting deaths in the country, the *Jerusalem Post* interviewed non-profit making Jewish burial societies, which perform funerals for the vast majority of Israelis. Hananya Shahor, the veteran director of Jerusalem's Kehilat Yerushalayim burial society said, *"The number of funerals we have performed has fallen drastically."* Meir Adler, manager of the Shamgar Funeral Parlour, which buries most other residents of Jerusalem, declared with much more certainty:

> *"There definitely is a connection between the doctors sanctions and fewer deaths. We saw the same thing in 1983 when the Israel Medical Association applied sanctions for four and a half months."* [iv]

I have dedicated more space to the corruption of the medical system than to any other aspect of the World's System because in the near future it may become one of the greatest determining factors for receiving the mark of the beast. What will you do if your child is sick and will only survive with medical treatment, and that treatment is only available to those who have received the mark? Today is the time to work through such serious issues, not later when you are faced with life-and-death situations.

We do not know what the government and the drug companies are doing to create the pandemics of the future. It could very well be that the plagues of the Book of Revelation are just another aspect of the antichrist's tribulations. We know that the first 3½ years of tribulation are horrors that are manmade.

---

iv http://www.qcc.cuny.edu/SocialSciences/ppecorino/MEDICAL_ETHICS_TEXT/Chapter_3_Moral_Climate_of_Health_Care/Reading-Death-Rate-Doctor-Strike.htm

SPIRITUAL GUIDE

If the cutting-edge research supported by biblical wisdom is true we should begin taking charge of our health management now. As you read God's laws pertaining to health, rest, diet and emotional management do not approach them legalistically. The Apostle Paul said the law is good as long as it is used lawfully.[v]

Always approach God's Word by faith. Even in the Old Testament the righteous lived by faith. Faith is our response of trust to what God has said, done or promised. Works is the behavior we exhibit to get God to respond to us. We know we are righteous through Jesus. We are not seeking to earn God's approval by our obedience to His Word. Conversely, because we trust Him and His Word we obey it - put it into practice.

The first law of health is, "do no harm." If you want to feel well and have energy, stop polluting your body with artificial, processed and/or dead foods. Begin eating organic, chemical-free food. Drink filtered, chemical-free water. It is essential that you remove fluoride and chloride from your drinking water to stop the destructive effects on your thyroid and all the other negative effects. Get plenty of fresh air and sun. One of the most important things you can do is have a lot of physical movement. It doesn't have to be strenuous exercise, just full body movement.

One of your primary goals should be to get your "ph" balanced. Complete lists of acid and alkaline foods are available online. Physically, there are few things as important to living disease-free as balancing your ph; therefore, eliminate acidic, disease-causing "dead foods" from your diet. Eat a lot of dark green foods. Most people should avoid glutens because of their tendency to cause inflammation. Be sure to avoid GMOs. This is just another area of godless arrogance that ignores how man was created and, as such, needs natural, organic foods.

One of the worst lies imposed upon the American public is the low fat diet. We know from modern research that almost everything we were told about low fat diets was incorrect. Our body needs fat for energy and cell development. Avoid trans-fats, heated fats and canola oil. Eat vegetable and animal fat. Be sure your meats are hormone and antibiotic free. If you have good

---

v 1 Timothy 1:8, But we know that the law is good if one uses it lawfully,

digestion a moderate amount of animal fat and protein is very good for you. The whole "vegetarian" line of thinking is just another aspect of iniquity. God told us to eat animals and man decided he was smarter than God!

The children of Israel wandered the desert for 40 years, yet when they came into the Promised Land there was not one sick among them. But they did not eat unclean foods, got plenty of good nutrition, drank chemical-free water, breathed fresh air and had daily physical movement. It may also be good for you to follow God's prescription and take a day a week for rest, relaxation and family. A vital part of our health/spiritual life should be daily meditating on God's promises of His love, peace and provision. We should establish our hearts in the Word of God. If this is a foreign concept go to www.heartphsyics.com and discover the biblical secrets to establishing your heart.

Trusting God's Word for wise, practical application does not negate the fact that Jesus died to set us free from sickness. Sickness is a curse of the law and we have been redeemed from the curse of the law. But it is utter foolishness to neglect the wisdom of His Word, abuse our bodies until we are sick and then seek a miracle. It is always easier to employ God's Word for protection than it is to seek a miracle in the face of life-threatening hardship.

As you renew your mind (not just in information but also in attitude) realize any information that makes you feel helpless is a Luciferian ploy. It does not matter if it comes from the church house or the White House. Codependency is the emotional state needed to be controlled and dominated. Always trust and learn to experience God's empowering truth through the Holy Spirit in your own heart. Make this a way of life today. As the Prophet Jeremiah forewarned those who put off preparation:

> *If you have run with the footmen, and they have wearied you, Then how can you contend with horses? And if in the land of peace, In which you trusted, they wearied you, Then how will you do in the floodplain of the Jordan* (Jeremiah 12:5).

Let's enjoy health now so we do not have to rely on a corrupt system designed to control our lives and steal our resources!

To learn more about the resources mentioned and for additional support material for this chapter please visit www.secondcomingguide.com.

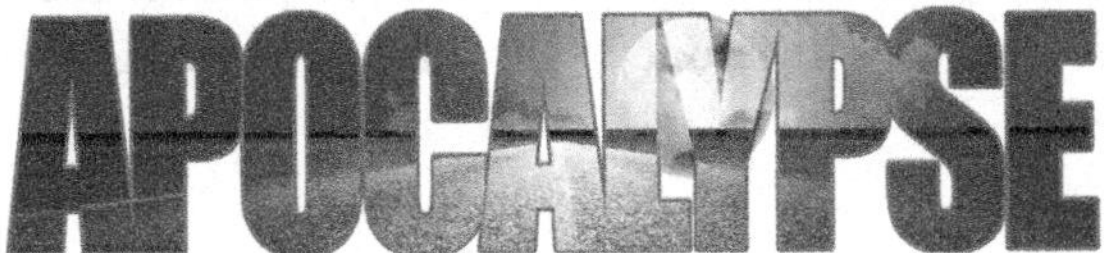

CHAPTER 32

CONTROL THE MONEY AND CONTROL THE WORLD

The borrower is always servant to the lender; he who controls the money controls the world!

THE CATCH PHRASE MADE POPULAR BY THE 1976 MOVIE *ALL THE PRESIDENT'S MEN*, "FOLLOW THE MONEY," HAS TURNED OUT TO BE VERY ACCURATE. When you want to know who is in control, who is benefiting from something or where the corruption is in any given scenario, simply *follow the money.* The trail of money leads to an understanding of true motives in many situations.

A "con" can only be successful if the target has greed or lust. In other words, once people become blinded by their own desires they become blind to that which would be obvious to any casual observer. The Great Harlot is only successful at deceiving leaders of nations because of their great and selfish ambitions.

Of all the topics in the Bible money is mentioned more than anything else. That does not mean Jesus always talked about money. It does mean the issue of money and how we relate to it is so central to Kingdom living that it provided the perfect metaphoric concepts that go straight to the heart! In Jesus' strongest warnings about money He used a word the KJV translates as "mammon." To most people mammon is synonymous with money, but mammon is actually more about avarice, the insatiable desire or need for wealth. But more than that, it points to selfishness, greed and possibly the lust for power and control associated with money. Our relationship with money tells a lot about our heart.

The Bible does not actually say "money is the root of all evil."

The Bible does not actually say "money is the root of all evil." Lenski translates the original language to read more like, *"money-love is the root of all the evils"* (1 Timothy 6:10).[i] It is very probable that "money love" is a throwback to what Jesus taught about people who trust in money. For those who trust in money it would be easier to pass through the eye of a needle than to enter the Kingdom realm. Money, for many, is their source of security, power and influence. This mindset positions their heart in direct opposition to the way of the Kingdom.

The definite article makes this read *"the evil."* This is not just a general reference to evil. It references the specific evil that corrupts men more deeply than any other, the evil that will drive you to choose the World's System over the Kingdom of God. In Matthew 6 Jesus teaches what has been reduced to a series of individual lessons about various topics. But when kept in context it is a message that conveys one of the most powerful lessons about *"the evil"* in the New Testament. In verses 19-21 He discusses our treasure, those things we consider precious or important, that to which we give our time, energy and attention. He explains that whatever we value takes control of our heart. Then in verses 22-23 He explains that the light, insight, revelation, understanding and even our perception are affected when our eye is not *"single."* When our eye isn't single our heart is divided between two, which brings us to this strong warning, *"No one can serve two masters; for either he will hate the one and love the other, or else he will be loyal to the one and despise the other. You cannot serve God and mammon"* (Matthew 6:24).

---

i The Interpretation of St Paul's Epistles to the Colossians, to the Thessalonians, to Timothy, to Titus and to Philemon, R.G.H. Lenski, Augsburg Publishing House, Minneapolis, 1961

In Luke 6 Jesus puts forth a parable wherein He explains if we cannot be trusted in this issue of mammon, we will never be trusted with true riches. This issue of mammon or what we trust[ii] determines values, morals and ethics. It determines loyalty and forces us to choose between God and the thing that we actually trust to make us feel safe and secure or gives us an identity. The concept of mammon can, like any root, branch out in any number of directions. For some it is a simple matter of trying to be confident in life. For others it is a means to control. Because the World's System was birthed by the Great Whore, Mystery Babylon, wealth is a means to control, seduce, manipulate and destroy.

Nowhere in the Bible is God opposed to wealth or success. All of the patriarchs of the Old Testament were wealthy. Wealth (when used for godly purposes) is a powerful, positive force for good. But wealth can easily corrupt someone's heart, which is why God has dozens of Scriptures about how to manage money. God's wisdom for managing money, giving and generosity are not rules whereby we manipulate Him into giving us prosperity; they are the foundation for guarding our heart so that wealth will not corrupt us. Failure to know and apply God's divine prescriptions (commandments) concerning money is why so many of God's people suffer from lack and poverty.

Nowhere in the Bible is God opposed to wealth or success. All of the Patriarchs of the Old Testament were wealthy.

The Old Testament has very clear commands against loaning money out for interest. Likewise, it has a number of warnings to the desperate and foolish about acquiring debt. I personally see this most clearly expressed in this Proverb, *"The rich rules over the poor, And the borrower is servant to the lender"* (Proverbs 22:7). In order to get the financial backing needed to win elections politicians make "agreements" with corporations. As a means to pay bills individuals compromise their life and dreams for their employer. Countries make treaties and alliances based on financial gain. Economy becomes the justification, cause and goal for almost all war. But at the end of the day, the person with money rules over the one without money or the one who borrows money. Simply said, people with money pass laws that benefit them and oppress those without money. We have already discussed the

---

ii NT:3126, what is trusted, from Thayer's Greek Lexicon, PC Study Bible formatted Electronic Database. Copyright © 2006 by Biblesoft, Inc. All rights reserved.

corrupt connection of world domination through banking and finance. Since, however, finances and greed are at the heart of the power of the Great Harlot's ability to corrupt and control governments, we must look briefly at this system once again. Remember, "If you want to know who's doing what, just follow the money." Mammon is the way, the means, the power and the treasure of government. When it is all revealed in the light of day, *"no one will be able to buy or sell anything except they have the mark of the beast of the number of his name"* (Revelation 13:17). The economy politicians use to buy votes will be the last great ploy of world domination by the antichrist.

Federal debt is the ultimate proof of the wisdom of this Scripture: *"The borrower is subject to the lender."* Nowhere is this truth more clearly seen than in nations that go into debt.

Federal debt is the ultimate proof of the wisdom of this Scripture: *"The borrower is subject to the lender."* Nowhere is this truth more clearly seen than in nations that go into debt. Chaos happening around the world is linked to nations spending more money than they should. The world crisis generated by the Great Harlot will weaken the nations of the world, especially America, to such a degree that it will usher in the antichrist. The work of the Harlot revolves around the economy and national debt and the rise of the antichrist is facilitated by the inability of nations to provide military and police protection. Interestingly, the sin that gets the entire world to this place is "iniquity." Politicians of all countries buy votes through unscriptural concepts of fairness and entitlement. They overtax the working class, provide loopholes for the wealthy and purchase the loyalty of the poor. The day will come when all those people who are on entitlement programs and have no ability to create finances will lose all those benefits. This will result in riots, mass destruction and the justification of military force against citizens. At this point I want to remind you, the majority of players in this Luciferian conspiracy are not players by intent or even by choice. They are simply caught up in a world that is far out of balance, without the truth of God's Word, the wise direction of the Holy Spirit and the grace of God to empower them and they do not feel they have a choice. I am sure the majority of them feel they are doing a service by keeping the world economy relatively stable, even if it is a false economy built with borrowed money.

This is where ignorance and defiance (iniquity) toward God's Word factors into the mix. The Luciferian philosophical/religious influence convinced man that God was untrustworthy, harsh and legalistic. God's law was twisted into a system of works righteousness instead of wisdom, practical application and divine prescriptions. Mix that with man's underlying greed and God's Word is seldom, if ever, considered as a practical solution to national or global problems. God's Word had built into it an economic system that made it impossible for families to ever permanently lose their land or be permanently crippled by debt. But what wealthy person would ever agree to cancel debts on a regular basis or allow property to return to the original owners? The Year of Jubilee was a national recalibration of the economy. It protected the poor and middle class against domination by the wealthy.

Violating God's warnings against loaning money with interest is the road that paves the way for the antichrist. Banks were started from a practical need but, as always, the need was used to justify corruption and iniquity. The first banks were started by the Knights Templar. In connection with the Catholic Church they violated God's Word and loaned money at interest. The Church skirted around the issue by saying they were not charging interest but charging rent for the money. At this point it is worth saying, if man had followed God's economic laws there would be no recessions or depressions and it would be close to impossible for the rich to rule over the poor. Banking, in violation to God's Word (iniquity), became the legal vehicle for transferring the wealth of the world into the hands of the few wicked in the world.

Violating God's warnings against loaning money with interest is the road that paves the way for the antichrist.

It is important that we understand how banks work. Let's say you are a farmer and you raise potatoes. You take your potatoes to the market and trade with people who raise or make other goods. The problem is, the people who have what you need may not need or want potatoes. And when you transport your possessions, whether food or precious stones, you always run the risk of being robbed. So you need something that keeps you safe and protects your wealth. Additionally, you need a way to obtain the products you desire even when the people who have those products do not want what you produce.

Let's say Bob starts a bank. It is a way to secure your money and protect yourself from being robbed. In exchange for the gold or precious assets that Bob holds and protects for you he gives you a piece of paper, a "note," that records the value of your goods. You can use this note to purchase goods in the market place. It doesn't matter whether people want your potatoes or not, they will take your note or coin. This seems to work pretty well. It stimulates the economy and everyone is happy.

America and most nations operated on the "gold standard" which basically required there be enough gold to back the amount of money being printed. This provided some degree of accountability to the banking system.

So Bob, the banker, has an opportunity to make money without having to work, produce anything or even have a craft. He can now loan (at interest) paper money that can be spent in the marketplace. But, Bob really isn't loaning his money; he is loaning *your* money. This means Bob may take risks and make deals he would never make with his own resources.

As time goes by, Bob has more and more opportunities to make a profit by loaning these pieces of paper that are backed by the precious stones and other resources you have in Bob's protection. But Bob doesn't really have enough precious resources to guarantee the value of his paper money. But no one really knows that except Bob. Soon Bob is becoming wealthy loaning out pieces of paper that actually have no real value, but these loans give Bob, the banker, power over people's property and other valuables. Bob can now take away your land and your wealth and leave you destitute should you fail to meet his demands.

Let's say Pete, the politician, wants to maintain power by offering the people some benefit, especially the poor and uneducated. But he doesn't have enough money to purchase the goods he will use to buy favor with the people so he goes to Bob. In exchange for a loan at a higher-than-usual interest rate Pete, the politician, also makes a side deal to pass some laws that makes what Bob is doing legal. Remember, Bob, the banker, is not loaning *his* money and Pete, the politician, will not repay the loan with *his* money. Pete does not mind paying exorbitant interest rates with someone else's money; he will just raise taxes. In time Pete and Bob cannot exist one without the other. They provide the basis for one another's power, but the innocent people are paying the bill to both of them. We, the people, are paying for the ridiculous, irresponsible spending of the politicians with our tax dollars.

There was a period of time when America and most nations operated on the "gold standard" which basically required there be enough gold to back the amount of money being printed. This provided some degree of accountability to the banking system. America, however, was taken off the gold standard so an illegal organization called the Federal Reserve could print worthless paper money. The Federal Reserve or the FED, as it is referred to, is not part of our federal government; it is actually a privately owned bank that began in the shadows of corruption and secrecy. The Federal Reserve provides a way to shift all of the nation's resources to the wealthy, destroy the middle class and eventually bankrupt the economy resulting in all citizens being completely dependent on the government. Does it sound like something too horrible to ever happen? It has happened in every Communist and Socialist country in the world.

Through the World Banking System nations are overthrown without a "shot being fired." The mega-wealthy take control of nations through the banking system.

Through the World Banking System nations are overthrown without a "shot being fired." The mega-wealthy take control of nations through the banking system. They loan worthless paper money to governments. As the governments get deeper in debt they pay more and more interest to the bank by raising taxes. The increase in taxes eventually destroys the economy. After destroying the economy the mega-wealthy buy all the resources for pennies on the dollar with pieces of paper that have absolutely no value. This entire system is promoted through Keynesian Economics. This economic system was purportedly started by the Illuminati and adopted by Socialists, Communists and Progressives as a means to concentrate the wealth of the world in the hands of the enlightened and thereby accomplish the goal of a One World Government. This system of economics has never worked anywhere in the world but is taught in most major colleges and universities. It is a philosophy that rejects free market principles and gives government the power to regulate the economy through its relationship with the world banks. Communist and Socialist countries of the world needed the US to survive for a period time; after all, we financed their efforts toward world domination. But the international bankers need all the super powers. They need arms races, continual uprising and wars. All of these events cost money which is borrowed from the banks. As previously mentioned, the banks basically determine the winners and losers of all wars based on their global goals for the New World Order.

It is essential to this cause that the wealth of America now be destroyed. It isn't rocket science; anyone who can add and subtract knows our continual deficit spending will lead to economic collapse. No one in government doubts that. There are, however, those who understand and participate in the plan and those who understand and fight against it without ever actually saying what is happening; then there are those who do not have a clue, idealistic *useful idiots* at the highest level.

Banks basically determine the winners and losers of all wars based on their global goals for the New World Order. It is essential to this cause that the wealth of America now be destroyed.

Few of these calamities are a surprise to those who are making the decisions. Although many of these decisions are not actually those of the politicians they are decisions made by those who own the politicians. In the mind of the politician they often make compromises to remain in office and do what little good they believe can be done. Many political decisions come down to the lesser of two evils.

For example, right now the US dollar is the international reserve currency. It is the currency all countries use in every international transaction. This is particularly essential to the oil trade. US currency is also considered the "petrodollar."

> In an effort to prop up the value of the dollar, Richard Nixon negotiated a deal with Saudi Arabia that in exchange for arms and protection they would denominate all future oil sales in U.S. dollars. Subsequently, the other OPEC countries agreed to similar deals thus ensuring a global demand for U.S. dollars and allowing the U.S. to export some of its inflation. Since these dollars did not circulate within the country they were not part of the normal money supply,

> economists felt another term was necessary to describe the dollars received by petroleum exporting countries (OPEC) in exchange for oil, so the term petrodollar was coined by Georgetown economics professor, Ibrahim Oweiss.[iii]

The Arab world knew it needed protection from the Islamic extremists, specifically from Iran. The US, who for decades was the world's leading consumer of foreign oil, stayed active in the Middle East to maintain stability in exchange for the US dollar being the "petrocurrency." It was the only way to inflate our economy by continually printing worthless paper notes. However, this current administration has violated that agreement and empowered radical Islam throughout the region. Now we are compromising in our stance toward Iran and allowing extremism to flourish.[iv] This violation of our agreement coupled with the fact that other parts of the world are now consuming massive amounts of oil means other countries are negotiating for their currency to become the petrocurrency. When that happens the US dollar could (and probably will) devaluate by 50% overnight. No country will want our money. We will no longer be able to borrow at discounted interest rates. It will be the unfolding of a global financial crisis that will affect every nation in the world.

You might ask, "So who will then be in charge of the country?" It will continue to appear that we have a government and for some time the illusion of our votes making a difference will be allowed. But in the end our government will be totally controlled by the Great Harlot. The Bible warned us, *"the borrower is servant to the lender."* The private organization controlled by a handful of wealthy families will own the American government. They will force laws to be passed destroying our autonomy and giving power to the UN. International law will supersede national, state and local laws. In the beginning it will happen smoothly; after all, we have been demoralized as a nation. While according to some polls, 80% of the American population claims to be Christian most reject God's laws, ethics, values and morals. Governmentally, we have allowed politicians to disregard our Constitution for generations. The truth is, most people are so ignorant of our Constitution and so out of touch with God they will invite the government to take charge of their lives.

---

iii http://en.wikipedia.org/wiki/Petrodollar

iv I am not expressing an opinion about what we should or shouldn't do. I am merely stating the facts.

There are those who want to believe the US will not be part of the world collapse. They hope we will somehow escape the tribulation of the antichrist, but that is just not what the Bible says. It clearly states the entire world will be affected by this end time rise to global power by the wicked one. I fear many of our doctrinal concepts of the end time are born more out of fear and subsequent normalcy bias than biblical certainty. In order for the antichrist to rise to power the US must either be a supporter of the antichrist or an insignificant world power.

There are those who want to believe the US will not be part of the world collapse. They hope we will somehow escape the tribulation of the antichrist, but that is just not what the Bible says.

SPIRITUAL GUIDE

Those who recognize the coming financial collapse are trying to make plans for the days ahead. I believe we should be prepared for financial collapse. I think we should always take steps to preserve ourselves and our family through crisis. But when the end comes there will be no safe place for your retirement, your bank account or your food storage. Even if we have money, the time will come when we cannot buy or sell without the mark of the beast. In the early days of the collapse we will buy a short time of survival through diligent preparation, but in time those who overcome will be the ones who know, trust and follow God's voice in their heart. Any plan that looks to hiding wealth and food could lead to the mammon issue. We could find ourselves trusting our natural resources more than trusting God. I am, by no means, saying it is wrong to store and prepare, but that cannot be where we put our hope and trust.

Current laws originally passed by Republicans, then reinforced and expanded by Democrats give government the right to seize all of your resources. You can be placed on a potential terrorist list just for storing food. Those who push for "food justice" will make it illegal to grow your own food or to have any means of survival. Regardless of their motive, these iniquitous, *useful idiots* will knowingly or ignorantly make it impossible for anyone to survive beyond the will of the government. That is… for those who do not know the God that can feed you manna in the wilderness and get water or honey from a rock. It is time believers stop looking at these historical events of God's protection, provision and deliverance as children's Bible stories. We should prayerfully read and meditate on these biblical events until we can see these miraculous events happen for us.

God is Jehovah-Jireh, the Lord that provides. We must personally know Him as the Provider. Our trust for survival must be rooted in Him. Our confidence in eternity must be the anchor for our soul. We cannot wait; we must disconnect from the Great Whore in our heart and in our way of thinking. While there are things we can do on an external level, the key is what happens in our heart. Is God our Source? Is Jesus our life? Is our treasure in Heaven or are we seeking something in this life to give us what can only be found in Him?

The Religionist would have you believe that money itself is evil. But as you know, the determining factor that makes anything evil or good is how it is used. Luciferian doctrine would make you believe God wants you poor. But abundant life and complete provision is a benefit of the New Covenant.

Being *in* this world but not *of* this world is deeply related to our attitude toward material possessions. God gave the children of Israel the wealth of the Egyptians before they left the country. The wise men brought precious, costly gifts to Jesus at His birth. In both examples these were the resources that provided for them on their journey.

Do not develop a poverty mentality. Do not succumb to a legalistic, Luciferian poverty doctrine. God may make you a financial source for others. Enjoy the wealth you currently have at your disposal, but be sure and use it wisely and for Kingdom purposes. More than anything, make God your absolute Source! Be able to *"walk through the valley of the shadow of death"* with complete peace because you trust the One you follow.

If you struggle with your beliefs about God's desire and willingness to help you prosper and provide for you in times of famine, you may want to read my book, *Wired for Success, Programmed for Failure*. I wrote this practical, how-to book to help people prepare their hearts for what we will face in the future!

Regardless of what happens in the world, we are under a better covenant than the children of Israel. We have better promises and our promises are sure because they are secured in Jesus. We should expect to have God's leadership and provision every day through every circumstance!

To learn more about the resources mentioned and for additional support material for this chapter please visit www.secondcomingguide.com.

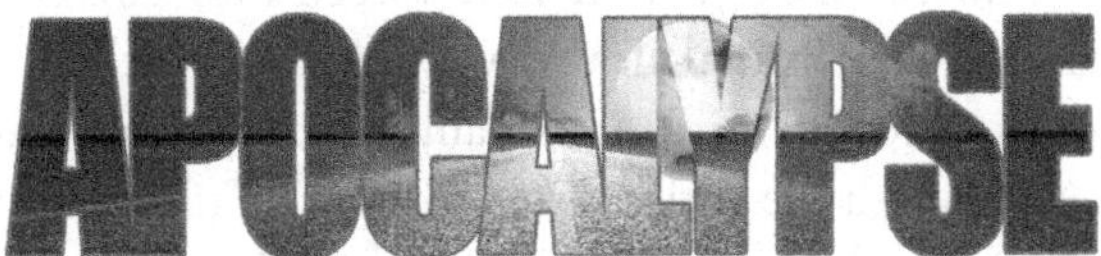

CHAPTER 33

CONCLUSION TO SECTION FOUR
The Normalcy Bias

Admitting the evil doesn't make it worse, but it does make us capable of taking intelligent action!

I REALIZE AT THIS POINT THINGS MIGHT SEEM COMPLETELY NEGATIVE AND OVERWHELMING. Part of what causes the feeling of hopelessness is when we see how others have so miserably failed. But there is also the tendency to see the problem as being so massive we can do nothing about it. That is true if you want to change the World's System or if you think changing government will make any long-lasting difference. In other words, if you think you can change the system you are thinking from the world's perspective and the task is impossible.

We must follow the example of Jesus, our Lord. He lived and ministered during one of the most oppressive times in history. The brutal, pride-filled, supremist Roman Empire ruled the world. Rome hated Jews. They demanded supreme loyalty to the emperor and unless you were a Roman citizen you had very few judicial rights. Besides the overbearing Roman government there was the intolerance of the Sanhedrin, the ruling body of the Jewish religion. They were so legalistic and controlling the average Jew lived in abiding fear of displeasing God. They had hundreds of rules to obey daily in order to maintain their righteous standing before the religious leaders. Failure to do so could not only result in condemnation in their own heart, but could sometimes end in death.

Rome was an immoral society. Men were forced into slavery and made to fight as gladiators. Their brutal deaths were entertainment for the masses. Public executions were part of Rome's daily entertainment. Infanticide was legally practiced through the entire Roman Empire. Full-term, unwanted babies were smothered and their bodies often thrown into the garbage dump or sewers. Other babies were often abandoned alive, left to die by the elements or by wild animals. Occasionally, a live baby would be found and saved to be raised as a slave. Then there was child sacrifice occurring at various places throughout the Empire.

In following Jesus' model I am not writing this book to tell you how to change the government or the world, but to show you how we got here and give us a chance to learn from the past.

The list of horrors, atrocities and religious practices of the Roman government could fill a book. There were temples for prostitutes. Slaves were sexually abused. The poor were oppressed and government was intolerably corrupt. Yet, Jesus brought incredible hope to His followers. Jesus refused to "take on the system." His solution for a corrupt world was a pure heart and this only occurred one person at a time with those who accepted His teaching, believed on Him as Lord and surrendered their lives to follow Him. He didn't try to change the Roman world or the Roman government. He brought change to **people**. They entered a kingdom in their hearts that provided a freedom that could never be provided nor taken away by any outside source.

In following Jesus' model I am not writing this book to tell you how to change the government or the world, but to show you how we got here and give us a chance to learn from the past. But most importantly, I want to remind you of how Jesus taught us to prepare for the coming end times. Up to this point we have only studied history. We can do nothing about history other than learn from it. If we do not learn from it, history is meaningless. That is why in each chapter there are simple truths we can learn from each segment of history.

But the true hope is what follows in the next segment as we look at Jesus' very clear teaching about how to prepare for what lies ahead.

Prophecy tells us what is coming and history makes us realize the validity of the warning. Teaching based on prophesies, history and the words of our Lord tell us how to prepare, but history also reveals that people often refused to believe the prophecies, acknowledge the signs or heed the warnings. Sometimes refusal to obey or follow the warnings come from a misplaced passion to help others as in the case of the Apostle Paul. Sometimes, however, it is simply fear.

The Apostle Paul did not land in jail because it was the will of God. He landed in jail because he did not heed the warnings sent by God. Paul received many warnings of which we do not have the specifics, but this warning was recorded for our benefit.

> *And as we stayed many days, a certain prophet named Agabus came down from Judea. When he had come to us, he took Paul's belt, bound his own hands and feet, and said, "Thus says the Holy Spirit, 'So shall the Jews at Jerusalem bind the man who owns this belt, and deliver him into the hands of the Gentiles* (Acts 21:10-11).

At that point Paul should have either turned and gone the other direction or spent time seeking God's will for his life. Instead he made an incredibly stubborn statement that we take out of context and turn into a virtue.

> *I go bound in the spirit to Jerusalem, not knowing the things that will happen to me there, except that the Holy Spirit testifies in every city, saying that chains and tribulations await me. But none of these things move me* (Acts 20:22-24).

Paul's misplaced passion for his Jewish brothers cost him his life and may have even limited his scope of ministry. One positive lesson to be learned from what seemed like a fatal mistake is, despite his disobedience, God still used him as much as possible.

When Paul arrived at Jerusalem God continued to warn him.

> *Now it happened, when I returned to Jerusalem and was praying in the temple, that I was in a trance and saw Him saying to*

> *me, 'Make haste and get out of Jerusalem quickly, for they will not receive your testimony concerning Me.' So I said, 'Lord, they know that in every synagogue I imprisoned and beat those who believe on You. And when the blood of Your martyr Stephen was shed, I also was standing by consenting to his death, and guarding the clothes of those who were killing him.' Then He said to me, 'Depart, for I will send you far from here to the Gentiles'* (Acts 22:17-21).

Instead of obeying, Paul was arrested while trying to explain to Jesus why his personal plan would succeed!

People do not want to see what they fear, what they are not prepared for or that which disrupts their way of life.

For most of us it isn't passion to win our fellow man that paralyzes us; it's fear. Time after time biblical history has recorded events where people who did not like the warnings God gave them about the future brought about their own self-destruction by refusing to listen. It is as if listening and obeying will make it come to pass. So, people do what they are so good at - **denial**. "If I deny this situation it isn't real; it will not happen!" When Israel was going into captivity God warned them of impending disaster. Suddenly these people whose corruption brought them to this point of destruction were going to have faith. They began to prophesy protection and deliverance. They assumed speaking in God's name and believing in His power would alter the course of events... but nothing could have been farther from the truth.

This not only occurred repeatedly in the Bible, it has continued throughout history right up until this day. People do not want to see what they fear, what they are not prepared for or that which disrupts their way of life. People specifically do not want to see that which is overwhelming. One of the times when this was most clearly demonstrated was in pre-Nazi Germany during the rise of Hitler.

Hitler made his feelings and intentions concerning Jews public; it was part of his political platform. He stirred racism and hatred toward Jews. Ironically, only about 200,000 Jews fled Germany before he implemented his diabolical plans of confiscation of property, imprisonment, slave labor and mass murder. This refusal to accept and prepare for the obvious cost millions of Jews their lives. Why? Some say it is a condition called the "normalcy bias!"

> The **normalcy bias**, or normality bias, refers to a mental state people enter when facing disaster. It causes them to underestimate both the possibility of a disaster occurring and its possible effects. This may result in situations where people fail to adequately prepare for a disaster…[i]

Right now world events are unfolding that, true to Jesus' warning, will cause men's hearts to fail them for fear. While we still have freedom of speech and internet access we can find the speeches and documents that map out the murderous plan for millions of Americans as the Elitists fulfill their Utopian dream. This news goes ignored by the masses. Our ignorance of history and the blatant facts cause us to shut our eyes to the fact that Islam and the antichrist nations are fully committed to destroying Israel, killing every Christian who refuses to convert and destroying America. We will not accept the biblical reality that our nation spending more than it produces will destroy our economy, catapulting the world into a spiral of financial crisis. We turn a deaf ear to the threats of atheistic educators destroying the minds of our children. And most of all we are oblivious to the fact that more end time prophecies are being fulfilled now than any time in history.

Right now world events are unfolding that, true to Jesus' warning, will cause men's hearts to fail them for fear.

Believers, godly people, have closed their eyes - probably because the truth is so overwhelming it seems impossible to face. We hope we can change it politically. We try to pray it away, but the train is still speeding down the tracks. We are surely in what the Bible calls "The Beginning of Sorrows," with the likelihood of the rise of the antichrist being a reality within just a few years. "It just can't be! These things can't happen, especially in America. We're a Christian nation! After all, every generation has believed Jesus would return in their lifetime!" And so the reasoning goes. We do not want to believe we

---

i https://en.wikipedia.org/wiki/Normalcy_bias

could be the generation that will actually face the greatest tribulation the world has ever seen.

We should be prepared to be here another thousand years, but live as if He is returning tomorrow; it is the only way to keep an eternal perspective.

In Jesus' parables He taught much about the need to keep an expectant attitude of His return. Many see that as delusional thinking considering it has been 2000 years since He left and so many past generations believed He was returning in their lifetime. But I think His emphasis was on the expectant attitude more than the belief that He would return during any particular generation. People who maintain an attitude of expectancy have a tendency to govern their lives from more of a Kingdom perspective. Those who lose sight of His return often become complacent. We should be prepared to be here another thousand years, but live as if He is returning tomorrow; it is the only way to keep an eternal perspective.

The day of the Lord will be *"like a thief in the night"* to some and *"like a sounding trumpet"* to others. Your willingness to observe the signs and keeping your heart alive and sensitive to God are the main actions that will determine into which category you fit. But these days will be just as it was in the time of Noah. People will close their eyes and continue in normal activities. There will be an increase in those who ridicule the warning of the end and the promise of His return. Sadly many of those will be Christian leaders. 2 Peter 3:3-4 gives this warning:

> *...scoffers will come in the last days, walking according to their own lusts, and saying, "Where is the promise of His coming? For since the fathers fell asleep, all things continue as they were from the beginning of creation.*

This logic emerges partially from the fact that we just do not want it to be true and we do not know how to prepare for such cataclysmic events.

In these times we will be more flooded than ever with propaganda from the news media. Our view of current world events will be shaped by those to whom we listen. An entire segment of this book could be committed to the corruption of the media; but suffice it to say, with few exceptions the media, news, television, movies and bloggers are nothing more than a combination of *useful idiots* and intentional propagandists. If your sense of what to do is shaped by these outside sources you will not hear the voice of God leading you into the protection and provision He has in store for you.

In these times we will be more flooded than ever with propaganda from the news media.

Jesus also warned of false prophets, teachers and lying signs and wonders, all of which are designed to overwhelm you with fear, pushing you to surrender to the "caring arms" of the government. There will be an increase in UFO sightings and at some point the government and some religious institutions will claim to have contact with alien beings. There will be a religious push toward the idea that we were created by aliens. There is already an endless flood of ancient alien theorists attributing to the aliens what we know were the works of the Nephilim and their descendants. It will all seem plausible because it comes from the media, the government and some religious sources. Movies and sitcoms will have more of a political message than an entertaining message. But do not follow those false signs. The entire world will know when the true Messiah comes. You do not have to fear being deceived. Simultaneously, you must guard your heart so it does not become vexed with the deluge of propaganda. In the next section we will look with great clarity at exactly what Jesus told us to prepare for what is coming. You will be equipped to choose whether you will be deceived, endure (survive) till the end or be an overcomer!

The fact that you have made it to this point says you are like Daniel who saw all the terrible things that would come upon the world. It seemed there would be no good, but he kept looking until he saw the Kingdom of God and the return of the Messiah. You are still looking, you are still seeking… and you will find the answers you need!

SECTION FIVE

CHAPTER 34

INTRODUCTION TO SECTION FIVE
From the Beginning of Sorrows to the Millennium

We have asked the wrong questions; therefore, we have gotten the wrong answers!

BEING A CHILD OF GOD IS AN INTIMATE, TRUSTING RELATIONSHIP BUILT ON LOVE. Religion is little more than spiritual politics. Religionists, like politicians, specialize in answering the questions no one is asking. Since religion and the World's System are driven by the same spirit, the characteristics of both are the same; the only real difference is the terminology. Both love to create a "straw man" to deflect attention away from important issues. The World's System introduces iniquity as a form of moral high ground. It is simply deceit by philosophy. Religion, however, introduces iniquity through legalism, mysticism and personal revelations. The most deadly form of iniquity is subtly abandoning Jesus' teaching. While using Christian terminology they pervert our values and push us into asking ourselves the wrong questions. While we agonize over completely irrelevant issues we lose confidence, intimacy and trust. Our faith becomes all about words and is devoid of power.

In the early years of the Church of Rome there was an aggressive movement to alienate believers from the Word of God and true faith in the Jesus of the Bible. We call on Jesus by faith. Faith is not belief He will answer; faith is trust based on everything the Word says about Him. The Roman government as well as the Roman Church hated Jews and hated the Bible. They relentlessly persecuted Jews. Much of early anti-Semitism was propagated by the Church of Rome.

The move against the Jewish faith was more than a misunderstanding about doctrine; it was a deliberate ploy to alienate believers from the Word of God. Keep in mind, the Bible to an early Christian was what we call the Old Testament. Those who knew the Bible saw Christ in the sacrifices, feasts and commandments. It was not only the Bible of the early Church, it was also the Bible from which the apostles based all their doctrine, teaching and ultimately the epistles (letters) they wrote to the early churches.

The move against the Jewish faith was more than a misunderstanding about doctrine; it was a deliberate ploy to alienate believers from the Word of God.

The New Testament as we know it was not canonized until about 397 AD. To understand God, for centuries people relied on the Old Testament which most Gentiles did not understand. There were the fortunate churches that had copies of some of the apostolic letters which helped them resolve many issues. Believers did not have the gospels or the epistles so they attempted to sort out the differences in the Old and New Covenants for themselves. In the very beginning Paul was not saved, and even after he was he spent 14 years developing himself in his calling as he grew in God and in the knowledge of God. But we forget that Paul's revelations of the identity of Christ and the New Covenant were based on his knowledge of the Old Testament feasts and sacrifices.

Failure on the part of the Church to recognize what God was doing in the New Covenant provided the basis for the first big doctrinal struggle. Most of the early epistles addressed the error of the Judaizers, which is the basis for much of modern legalism.The Judaizers taught that one should have faith in Jesus to be saved but obey the law to be made righteous. Paul taught against this misuse of the law. The law was still true, but it was not the basis for our righteousness. This paradox was and still is the stumbling stone of the gospel (Romans 9:30-33).

The misinterpretation and misuse of the law facilitated the opportunistic philosophy of Luciferian doctrine resulting in legalism. Believers could not intellectually grasp the fact that God's law is still the basis for morality, ethics, judicial law and love but was not the basis for righteousness. The law describes what righteousness looks like in application, but righteousness is the result of faith in the finished work of Jesus, not the works of the law. This is still a struggle for millions of believers.

Paul identifies faith righteousness as the stumbling stone of the gospel.[i] Paul's warning and Church History reveal the issue of faith righteousness is still the greatest doctrinal conflict in the Church. The legalist makes righteousness something that has to be earned while the inclusionist makes righteousness simply a state of existence that produces nothing in real life. The writer of Hebrews explains that a person who is not able to comprehend the word of righteousness is still a babe and has not yet established himself in the foundations of the faith.[ii]

> The failure on the part of the Church to recognize what God was doing in the New Covenant provided the basis for the first big doctrinal struggle.

Two significant events occurred that laid the groundwork for what would become the way of iniquity that has hastened the Church and the world toward the appearance of the man of iniquity. As the gospel was taken to the Gentile nations the doctrinal battle for the Church shifted. Converted Jews had knowledge of God from the Old Testament. They grew up studying the

---

i Romans 9:30-33, What shall we say then? That Gentiles, who did not pursue righteousness, have attained to righteousness, even the righteousness of faith; 31 but Israel, pursuing the law of righteousness, has not attained to the law of righteousness. 32 Why? Because they did not seek it by faith, but as it were, by the works of the law. For they stumbled at that stumbling stone. 33 As it is written: "Behold, I lay in Zion a stumbling stone and rock of offense, And whoever believes on Him will not be put to shame."

ii Hebrews 5:13-14, For everyone who partakes only of milk is unskilled in the word of righteousness, for he is a babe. 14 But solid food belongs to those who are of full age, that is, those who by reason of use have their senses exercised to discern both good and evil. For a free course in the Foundation of Faith please visit http://www.impactministries.com/self-development/foundations-of-faith/

Pentateuch, the five books of the Bible that had been dictated from God's lips to Moses. But their enslavement to legalism led them down the Luciferian path of the angry God doctrine. They struggled to make the shift from seeing the law as the way of earning righteousness to God's wisdom, definition and description of righteousness.

> The Gentile converts' concept of God, morality, ethics and fairness were based on idolatrous Luciferian doctrine and humanistic philosophies. They were rooted in Occultism, Polytheism and Roman culture.

The Gentile converts, however, had an entirely different struggle. They did not know the Old Testament. Their concept of God, morality, ethics and fairness were based on idolatrous Luciferian doctrine and humanistic philosophies. They were rooted in Occultism, Polytheism and Roman culture. So, their tendency was to impose their Luciferian doctrines and philosophical concepts onto the gospel. Rather than using the Old Testament sacrifices, rituals and holy days as a basis to understand what happened at the cross of Christ they mixed the gospel they heard with Luciferian philosophy. This gave rise to Gnosticism, Antinomianism (organized, doctrinal, iniquity) and, to some degree, played a role in the early development of Islam.

Rome's hatred of Jews made it essential that the Church distance itself from them. This was not a simple persecution and rejection of Jews; it was a rejection of God's Word. They distanced themselves from God's historical revelation of Himself through His Word, which is the basis for our revelation of Jesus. Roman religion, which was very performance-oriented, demanded that the practitioner pray enough and make satisfactory sacrifices to appease the wrath of the gods. Might was considered right. If I can kill you it means my god is more powerful than your god. Thus, force and hierarchy of authority became the model for the Roman Church. The Church of Rome laid a corrupt foundation that, to some degree, has served to corrupt almost all of Christianity since that time.

The early Church failed to pursue Jesus' commission to preach this gospel to the world; instead they stayed in Jerusalem continuing to pray in the temple. Persecution, not passion, scattered the early Church which resulted in evangelizing the world.[iii] Even more interesting is the fact that it was the "laity" more than the apostles who preached the gospel to the world. Failure to preach the Gospel of the Kingdom to the world is monumental considering it is one task to be completed before the return of the Lord. Two areas where the Church has historically failed are in this very issue. First is the failure to preach to the entire world, and second is the failure to preach the Gospel of the Kingdom which, by its very nature, involves making disciples.[iv] Failure to make disciples unto the Lord Jesus has given rise to iniquity in the Church, thus making the Church an impotent force in the world.

Failure to focus on Jesus' teaching clouds our understanding of end time events. As the signs Jesus spoke of become evermore obvious we look everywhere except the teaching of Jesus for an understanding of how to prepare for what lies ahead. One of our main tendencies is to interpret the Bible by current events instead of understanding current events from the Bible. For example, there were people during World War II who believed Mussolini was the antichrist. A book with irrefutable facts was published declaring it to be so. Just after the first publication of books rolled off the presses Mussolini was killed. Hitler, Lenin and Stalin were all believed and declared to be the antichrist at one time or another. In modern times Henry Kissinger was thought to be the antichrist. There have been numerous predictions about certain years being the return of the Lord. In 1988 thousands of believers' lives were set off course because of a booklet entitled *88 Reasons Why the Rapture Will Be in 1988.*

Failure to focus on Jesus' teaching clouds our understanding of end time events.

All of these failed predictions resulted from at least three primary factors:

- There was lack of understanding of some of the most straight-forward Scriptures about the return of the Lord.

---

iii Acts 8:1, At that time a great persecution arose against the church which was at Jerusalem; and they were all scattered throughout the regions of Judea and Samaria, except the apostles.4, Therefore those who were scattered went everywhere preaching the word.

iv Matthew 28:19, 20, Go therefore and make disciples of all the nations... teaching them to observe all things that I have commanded you.

- There is what seems to be a total disregard for Jesus' teaching concerning the end.
- In the vacuum of biblical knowledge we tend to interpret Scriptures based on current events.

This last indictment is part of the spirit of iniquity that has infected the Church since the beginning. There is a general tendency to make the Word of God fit our preferences in nearly every area rather than adjust our thinking to conform to His Word.

While we may use the information we have, if we don't have the foundational truths we are only guessing at who is doing what and what will happen next.

Our attempts at understanding the end times are like those people mentioned previously. Much of the 21st century Church lacks an understanding of biblical history which provides the only basis for reaching a clear, simple, accurate and understandable grasp of the future. It is as if we have walked into the middle of a mystery movie. There are multiple characters and we are attempting to understand the plot without having seen the first half of the movie. While we may use the information we have, if we don't have the foundational truths we are only guessing at who is doing what and what will happen next. Since we have only seen a few minutes of the movie we are guessing based on what is happening now; in other words, we are attempting to interpret world events based on current events rather than biblical history that identifies all the players. If we don't know the Old Testament we have missed the first part of the movie which identifies all the players and their intentions.

Keep in mind, everything about the World's System has programmed us to ask the wrong questions. We are seeking intellectual answers to spiritual truth. Even if we get the correct answers they will not bring us peace. When you ask the wrong questions you always get the wrong answers. Knowing who the antichrist is, what country he comes from, what will happen to America and if or when there is a rapture will not prepare us to overcome in times of great tribulation. The answers to these questions will not make it any easier for us to endure (survive) or overcome what lies ahead.

Jesus taught us what we would need to do to prepare, but it seems very few are interested in what He said. We want our irrelevant questions answered. We think we can get the intellectual answers to our questions, prepare a carnal strategy and all will be well. But in my observation, most of what people are doing to prepare only adds to their fear and confusion. Only applying what Jesus taught about the end can prepare us for what is ahead, keep us from confusion and equip us to play our role in ushering in the return of the Lord!

Jesus taught us how to recognize the signs. It is only when we try to force these simple signs to be what we want them to be that they become confusing or contradictory.

Jesus taught us how to recognize the signs. It is only when we try to force these simple signs to be what we want them to be that they become confusing or contradictory. He taught us how to prepare for eternity, but our eyes are focused on the tribulation. We are trying to escape pain, not reach the world. When we think what He taught is not enough we become driven by fear and desperation, resorting to extreme measures to find security. He taught us what we need to be able to do in order to follow Him through the upcoming tribulation, but we may have never applied these teachings to current life so we cannot seem to understand how they will benefit us in the future.

Section five of this book focuses mostly on the concrete factors Jesus taught us to prepare for the times that lie ahead. We will also clarify some of the confusion the Church has created by its many versions of the end times and we will prepare to connect to our Savior and Lord and ask the right questions! Since this last segment is all about solutions, there will not be a **Spiritual Guide** section at the end of each chapter.

As we consider the teachings of the Lord Jesus we must be constantly aware that there will be four categories of believers in the tribulation:

- Those who deny their faith and submit to the antichrist
- Those who die for their faith
- Those who merely survive (endure)
- Those who overcome

There are no other choices. There are two primary factors that will determine in which category we will find ourselves. The first factor is our knowledge and trust in God's Word. Those who do not know and trust God's Word will succumb to iniquity the soonest. It will all sound fair, reasonable and genuine to these easily-deceived believers. The second factor is our willingness and capacity to hear, trust and follow the Holy Spirit. These are capacities we can develop now.

APOCALYPSE

CHAPTER 35

THE PRIMARY MESSAGE OF THE END

We may not understand anything else, but we know for sure He will return and we know how we should live our lives!

> *Now as He sat on the Mount of Olives, the disciples came to Him privately, saying, "Tell us, when will these things be? And what will be the sign of Your coming, and of the end of the age."* (Matthew 24:3)

Taken in context this conversion actually began in the previous chapter when, after rebuking the Pharisees for giving themselves fully to religion and abandoning the purpose of God, Jesus began to lament for Jerusalem. Then in Matthew 23:37-39, He says:

> *How often I wanted to gather your children together, as a hen gathers her chicks under her wings, but you were not willing! See! Your house is left to you desolate; for I say to you, you shall*

> *see Me no more till you say, 'Blessed is He who comes in the name of the Lord!'*

We can assume the destruction of Jerusalem and His final return were both issues the disciples did not discern from the Scripture, nor did they yet understand it from His teachings. Like most Jews they had only been taught of a victorious coming of the Messiah and had completely missed the descriptions of two separate events, the suffering Messiah and the conquering Messiah. In their minds, Jesus would at some point overthrow the Roman government and establish Jerusalem as the capitol of the world from where He would reign. So they had to question how it was possible that Jerusalem would be destroyed and He would come again before the end. This resulted in them pointing out the buildings that were part of the rebuilt temple.

In both Old and New Testament eschatological idealism there had always been a tendency to long for a kingdom that would be established by man in the name of the Lord. While this is a lofty goal, it is supported by neither the Old nor New Testament Scriptures.

In both Old and New Testament eschatological idealism there had always been a tendency to long for a kingdom that would be established by man in the name of the Lord. While this is a lofty goal, it is supported by neither the Old nor New Testament Scriptures. Jesus made it clear to His disciples they would not have the right to exercise authority over one another. There would be no hierarchy of power whereby the Church rules over others. This question was settled by Jesus when the disciples argued about whom among them would have most authority.

> *You know that those who are considered rulers over the Gentiles lord it over them, and their great ones exercise authority over them. Yet it shall not be so among you; but whoever desires to become great among you shall be your servant. And whoever of you desires to be first shall be slave of all. For even the Son of Man did not come to be served, but to serve, and to give His life a ransom for many.* (Mark 10: 42-45)

There is something inherently unhealthy and seductively appealing in the carnal concept of spiritual authority.

Concerning Jesus' statements, the disciples wanted to know three things:

1. When will these things occur?
2. What will be the sign of Your coming?
3. What will be the sign of the end of the Age?

It is important to realize the Greek text clearly connects the end and the return of the Lord Jesus. The truth is, after reading these verses there are many things still as unclear as before Jesus answered.

There is much debate about the following verses. Are they referring exclusively to the soon-coming fall of Jerusalem? Did the abomination of desolation occur when Antiochus Epiphanes sacrificed a pig on the altar of the temple or when Titus defiled the temple? Is the end of this age also the end of the Jewish Age? Almost any argument can be somewhat rationally justified concerning these Scriptures. Because of the events that befell Jerusalem in 70 AD, Preterists believe all end time prophecies were fulfilled. Futurists, on the other hand, point out many of these statements and other prophecies are yet to be fulfilled. Some point to the idea of a "double fulfillment," which, to some degree, has logic based on Old Testament prophecies that often have double fulfillment.

> Regardless of your end time point of view, any attempt to develop a congruent eschatological doctrine from passages of Scripture alone is short-sighted, scripturally limited and missing the primary point of Jesus' teaching.

In my opinion, regardless of your end time point of view, any attempt to develop a congruent eschatological doctrine from these passages of Scripture alone is short-sighted, scripturally limited and missing the primary point of Jesus' teaching. My assumption is that when Scripture seems to present conflicting points of view I obviously do not grasp its full meaning and when Scripture is vague it is presenting something about which I do not require specific details to get the point of the passage. But even more importantly, I am fully convinced that if we are open to the voice of God in our heart, all the things we need to understand will be made plain and simple when the time comes. We must remember there are some things God sealed until the time of the end (Daniel 12:4-9). To debate over the nonessential is to be drawn away from those things Jesus made clear and important.

Proper interpretation of any Scripture must include:

1. Context: How is the Scripture to be understood within the context it was stated?
2. The whole counsel of God: How is this passage to be understood in light of all that God's Word says about the matter?
3. Original language: What is the proper translation of the original text, specifically the (common Greek)?
4. Manners and customs: Do I understand the terminology, examples and actions taken in light of the manners and customs of the times?

Until all of these agree I must accept and be comfortable with my limited understanding but, in the end, all of this must point to an applicable truth. God's Word and the revelation of the Holy Spirit should always bring us to wisdom which is the practical application of the God's Word. After I have walked through a responsible process of interpretation as a disciple I must ask, "What does this mean to my life and how do I apply this truth?" Until we are committed to application it is all just intellectual and egotistical self-indulgence.

We must remember there are some things God sealed until the time of the end (Daniel 12:4-9). To debate over the nonessential is to be drawn away from those things Jesus made clear and important.

In many of these passages of Scripture it is unclear whether Jesus is referring to the imminent destruction of Jerusalem, talking about the events prior to His return, or possibly making a double reference. But the common theme on which Jesus focused, regardless of the theological interpretation, is vigilance and service.

This vigilance seems to be two-fold. As He continues in His lengthy sermon it becomes evident He is talking about being able to recognize and respond properly to the signs, which are all external factors. Even more important is the emphasis on being able to hear God in your heart, which is all about internal events. Secondly, is how we are living our lives as it relates to the Kingdom of God. If we miss these two factors of vigilance and servanthood it really doesn't matter what we extrapolate from these verses concerning the end times. No matter how accurate our interpretation, unless we are attentive to God and serving our fellow man, we have still missed the crucial points.

He is talking about being able to recognize and respond properly to the signs, which are all external factors. Even more important is the emphasis on being able to hear God in your heart, which is all about internal events.

In the teachings of Jesus, I will point to these two main messages. I will clarify some Scriptures that have long been taken out of context, thereby complicating our ability to grasp the message of the end. But what we need to know is how to heed the warnings and live responsibly as children of the Kingdom living in Kingdom rule. These two factors will move us from fear and uncertainty of the future to a place of intimate interaction and empowering of the Holy Spirit. As we listen to God's voice we will be like the Prophet Elisha. It will be as if we are eavesdropping on what the enemy says in his private chambers. We will know what is happening and how to prepare (2 Kings 6:12).

Read each of the following chapters asking the right questions. Do not ask "When will Jesus return?" "How bad will the world become?" "Will I go through persecution?" "What will happen to America?" Instead ask yourself, "Am I living as those who are described as wise stewards, faithful servants and wise virgins?" If not, align your life and, more importantly, your heart with your Lord and be about His business. Choose to live an eternal-minded existence for the benefit of the Kingdom of God. Begin to live your life for the two main priorities Jesus emphasized: sensitivity to the Holy Spirit and servanthood.

"Am I living as those who are described as wise stewards, faithful servants and wise virgins?" If not, align your life and, more importantly, your heart with your Lord and be about His business.

Remember, this entire passage of teaching began by Jesus rebuking the religious leaders who had stopped using the Word of God as a means of serving, encouraging and developing the people of God. Instead they forced the people to serve the law and the leaders. To some degree this entire passage is drawing a comparison between the failure of those who were previously called to serve God's people and those Jesus is now calling. We do not want to repeat their failure!

APOCALYPSE

CHAPTER 36

THE LAST GREAT DECEPTION

Satan is like the playground bully; he has the least power but the loudest voice!

AT THIS POINT WE MUST ONCE AGAIN REMIND OURSELVES WHY DECEPTION IS THE TOOL OF THE ENEMY. **He does not have the ability (authority) to force anything on anyone!** One of the great Luciferian lies is the idea that man gave his authority to Satan at the Fall. Even if that were true (which it isn't), Jesus clearly received all authority at the resurrection.[i] Unless Satan can seduce a person into yielding their authority (rights) to him he cannot act upon it; therefore, deception is his only real tool. This is why he is the father of lies. Lies are the power of deception. Negative emotions that emerge when we believe lies become the false verification that lies are true! Unbelief in God's truth facilitates fearful feelings that give rise to these false witnesses.

Just as Jesus could only come to the world in the *"fullness of times,"* the wicked one can only make his last great move in the fullness of times. I am not

i Matthew 28:18, And Jesus came and spoke to them, saying, "All authority has been given to Me in heaven and on earth.

referring to the timing of God; I'm talking about the timing of man. Man must be ready to give his authority to someone who will make him feel secure and safe. All factors must be ripe for Satan and his followers to "thrust in their sickle!" Religion has corrupted faith. Science has corrupted knowledge. Governments, because of their collaboration with the Great Harlot, have deceived the world and made mankind feel powerless. There is a great vacuum in the world facilitating a desperate need for leadership just as there was in pre-Nazi Germany. Desperate times for the masses are times of opportunity for the wicked to seize power. It has always been the way of governments to create crisis and desperation then offer a solution that transfers more power to the elite. The world is rapidly becoming so desperate mankind is ready to give loyalty to whoever offers the greatest hope of prosperity and safety.

Jesus' words spoken to His disciples in response to their questions were applicable for the soon-coming fall of Jerusalem and for any future persecution, but especially for the time of the end.

> *And Jesus answered and said to them: "Take heed that no one deceives you. For many will come in My name, saying, 'I am the Christ,' and will deceive many. And you will hear of wars and rumors of wars. See that you are not troubled; for all these things must come to pass, but the end is not yet. For nation will rise against nation, and kingdom against kingdom. And there will be famines, pestilences, and earthquakes in various places. All these are the beginning of sorrows."* (Matthew 24:4-8)

The capacity to resist deception is among the warnings issued by Jesus concerning preparation for the end. All the works of darkness, like disease, are opportunistic. If we do not allow in our heart that which facilitates temptation, confusion, sin or deception then it cannot grow. But a crooked heart, a heart willing to twist the truth of God's Word, is a heart set to facilitate deception. It will always be confused, doubting, struggling, walking the wrong path, and/or denying the truth.

The Bible warns, It is *"the little foxes that spoil the vine"* (Song of Solomon 2:15). Our conditioning for mass deception begins with small, daily issues. We foolishly think twisting truth to facilitate one area of compromise will only affect us in that single area, but every compromise is a step down the road to deception.

The writer of Hebrews warns that the deceitfulness of sin is a hardened heart![ii] A hardened heart is one that becomes calloused and insensitive. It no longer feels or perceives the gentle leading of the Lord. The voice of the Holy Spirit becomes less perceptible the more we expose our hearts to sin. A calloused heart is just like a calloused hand; it protects the instrument from abuse. It is a survival mechanism that protects us, as much as possible, given the circumstances. The person who continually gives over to sin eventually moves from the place of a somewhat passive participant to an inventor of sin. As their heart becomes harder they not only lose the capability of hearing the voice of the Holy Spirit, at some time they can no longer hear the voice of their own conscience.

The deception of the evil one is to entice you to choose selfish gratification instead of love. The pathway of deception is iniquity, the rejection of God's morals, values, ethics and fairness. The justification of selfishness is temporary fulfillment. The need for transgression is refusal to believe the promises of God. There is nothing wrong with desires, we all have the same ones. The problem with desire is when we seek to fulfil it the world's way. When we believe God is good and His promises are sure the World's System will not corrupt us. This is the way of faith. We trust God to lead us into the perfect fulfillment of every desire in a way that preserves our heart and our relationship with Him. When we know His promises are true and are freely given in Jesus, we look to the promises of God. The Apostle Peter said that it is through God's promises we escape the corruption of the World's System which works by our desires.[iii]

The deception of the evil one is to entice you to choose selfish gratification instead of love.

Once the world's way of seeing, defining and understanding truth, morality, justice and love are our standard we are deceived. We don't simply wake up one morning and decide, "I'm not going to follow God anymore." Little-by-little, day-by-day, we entrench ourselves in carnal logic until we are *carnally minded.* The carnal mind sees and interprets all things based on the logic of Humanism. The carnal minded are not attentive to the words and wisdom of

---

ii Hebrews 3:13-14, but exhort one another daily, while it is called "Today," lest any of you be hardened through the deceitfulness of sin.

iii 2 Peter 1:4, ... precious promises, that through these you may be partakers of the divine nature, having escaped the corruption that is in the world through lust.

the Spirit. They are alive to their carnal desires.[iv] Because they cannot experience the life and peace of God through this process, they become more and more lustful for the fulfillment of their desires; thus, their mind facilitates the infectious deception. Now they are lovers of mammon. They seek to fulfil their lust and greed by trusting the World's System.

Jesus warned there would be *"wars and rumors of wars."* This is not the end, but "The Beginning of Sorrows." The world has been at war since the time of Christ. Rome conquered the world through continuous war. Then Muslims (The Ottoman Empire) conquered the last of Roman territory. The final collapse of Rome was at the hands of the Muslim caliphate. Local wars have continued endlessly. By the 20th century war became a necessary strategy of the Great Harlot. Through organized effort wars would be fought that would have a global impact. The global economy must have war to survive. It is the constant state of war that fulfils Lucifer's lust to kill all that God loves. But more importantly, it is the constant state of war that paves the way for the antichrist. He cannot seize power in a world of peace. Plagues, cultural (race) wars, pestilence and famine are the tools that promote uncertainty, fear and unbelief. It is this constant chaos that gives rise to the cry for a deliverer, but not a deliverer who will establish Kingdom rule!

Jesus warned there would be *"wars and rumors of wars,"* this is not the end, but "The Beginning of Sorrows."

In a time of incredible chaos, especially in the Middle East, the ultimate end time deception will be the man of peace, the antichrist. He will make peace between Israel and Islam based solely on deception. His basis for peace will be the carnal, humanistic, politically correct, iniquitous logic of the world. His wisdom and spirituality will be hailed by the antichrist religion of Islam.

Everything the Book of Revelation says about the antichrist is twisted by Islam. Everything our Bible says are evil attributes of the antichrist, Islam declares to be godly traits. He will offer the choice of beheading or conversion. He will declare Allah (Nimrod/Baal) as the only god. He will make a seven-year peace treaty with Israel and break it in 3 1/2 years. The one our

---

iv Romans 8:5-7, For those who live according to the flesh set their minds on the things of the flesh, but those who live according to the Spirit, the things of the Spirit. 6 For to be carnally minded is death, but to be spiritually minded is life and peace.

Bibles calls "the false prophet" will be a man who arises declaring himself to be Jesus. He will work miracles and force the world to worship the antichrist. He will convince the world he is Jesus who has come back to set the record straight. He will declare he was never crucified and he never said he was the Son of God. He will be so convincing, according to Islam and the Bible, that millions of Christians and Jews will accept his words and worship the beast... the antichrist!

The basis for identifying Islam as the antichrist religion is not a prejudiced, personal opinion. It is based on what Muslims believe, what is written in the holy books and what the world governments already know but refuse to tell you in the name of political correctness. The absolute written intention of Islam is to destroy Israel, the Christian faith and America, and prove Jesus was not the Messiah. This is all deliberately being withheld from America and the world.

The fact that the antichrist religion will follow the false prophet is proof of his true intention. Since the world is already deceived into believing Islam is a religion of peace, they will not consider that to lead this religion he must be committed to destroying Israel and Christianity. Once the world has rejected God's standards of values and morals it will be unable to recognize the dangerous threat the man of false peace brings. The absence of God's Word and wisdom creates a vacuum filled by man's logic.

Prior to the fall of Jerusalem there were those who declared themselves to be prophets and messiahs. History reveals that many were led astray believing that God would provide supernatural protection by following these corrupt leaders. One difference between what happened at the fall of Jerusalem and what will happen in the end is that there will be false leaders, prophets, teachers and christs within the Church as well as those outside the Church. This is why we must heed Jesus' teaching to develop our heart and our relationship with God to be able to hear, know and trust His voice in our heart. This must be rooted in a renewed mind that knows the Word of God.

We must pause for a moment and deal with the idea of false christs within the Church. We know there will be an antichrist, someone who will actually claim to be the Messiah. But one may wonder, "How could this actually happen inside the Church? If anyone comes claiming to be Jesus we'll all know he is false!"

Inside the Church the problem will not be those claiming to be Jesus; it will be those claiming to have special anointing they can get from God for you, those things that Jesus has already freely given. In some areas of charismatic thought there are extreme teachings about the anointing. The word "Christ" or "Messiah" comes from a Greek word that means "anointed." So the logic is based on a slight twist of the truth. We are in Christ and we share His anointing. But this logic goes off the rails when it advances to "I have His anointing so I can apply any Scripture about Christ to me or my ministry." It is true that we are in Christ and we **all** share in His anointing, but it is a leap from reality to take any Scripture with the word "Christ" in it, translate it as "anointing," and then apply it to ourselves or our ministry.

You are as anointed as anyone who has ever believed on Jesus. You may not, however, have made it a life practice to yield to that anointing. It is essential that you know, live and move in the reality that you are in Christ. As He is so are you. You have what He has. You can do what He can do. Unless this is your reality, when tribulations come, you will be like the foolish virgins who go searching for oil. You will be searching for someone who can hear from God for you, pray for your protection or tell you what you should do. Surviving and overcoming is predicated on what's in your heart, not what's in someone else's heart!

Among a large portion of believers there is the idea of "special anointing." This is an Old Testament concept that was extrapolated by the Gnostics and refuted by the Apostle John. He told us to abide in the anointing we received and allow that anointing to teach us.[v] The Gnostics taught that there were a series of anointings one received by obtaining special revelation from a teacher who had a special anointing. A variation of this teaching has been widely accepted in Pentecostal and charismatic circles. It is now very popular in Universalism and Inclusionism, with the idea of personal revelation being equal to God's Word!

Where teaching about the anointing becomes misleading is when leaders tell us we receive special blessings by sitting under, giving to or, in some way, partaking in their anointing. I do not believe deception is the intention of

---

v 1 John 2:26-27, These things I have written to you concerning those who try to deceive you. 27 But the anointing which you have received from Him abides in you, and you do not need that anyone teach you; but as the same anointing teaches you concerning all things, and is true, and is not a lie, and just as it has taught you, you will abide in Him.

those who preach this doctrine, but in the hearts of fearful, codependent people this becomes a substitute for hearing from God for themselves. While there will always be great leaders yielding to the anointing of Christ who will play key roles in leading the Church through the dark days ahead, their desire will be to help you. They have no intention of becoming a mediator between you and Jesus. This history of codependent Christianity will render many incapable of hearing from God for themselves; they will be at the mercy of wolves.

At this very moment there is a sect within the Catholic Church prepared to accept an alien as the true Jesus.[vi] This sect has long held to the Illuminati's secret teachings. Since the time of the ancient Sumerians in Mesopotamia it has been taught that the Anunnaki were a race of aliens that created mankind. According to their lore, in the beginning there was no end to the lifespan of man. Thus, they had to create plagues and eventually the flood to cut man's life shorter and end their suffering.[vii] To those who do not know and believe the truth about the fallen angels and the Nephilim, the idea of extraterrestrials is the only explanation for all the anomalies that occur in secular, atheistic anthropology, geology and evolution.

At this very moment there is a sect within the Catholic Church prepared to accept an alien as the true Jesus. This sect has long held to the Illuminati's secret teachings.

There is a likelihood that governments will create UFO scares as a means to manipulate the masses. There is the possibility of demonic manifestations of aliens and alien abductions. All of this will be fodder for the anti-God media. Proof of aliens will seem irrefutable. Just as it was before Jerusalem fell, there will be delusional prophets and false messiahs who will offer protection and deliverance that will end in tragedy. Then there will be the "wolves," those who see the opportunity to seize power and self-exaltation, but none of this will move those who experience God in their own hearts.

You must know God for yourself! In chapter 25 of Matthew, Jesus teaches us how to prepare. He uses the parable of the ten virgins. They were all virgins, in other words, they all belonged to God. The only difference between the

vi Exo-Vatican, Cris Putnam &Tom Horn, 2013 Tom Horn, Crane MO 65633
vii http://aliens.wikia.com/wiki/Anunnaki

two groups was that five were wise (attentive, practical, alert) and five were foolish (dull, heedless and inattentive). Both of these groups were looking for the return of their master. The five wise virgins kept their lamps full of oil so as to be ready at any moment. The five foolish planned to wait until there was a need and then fill their lamps.

While there can be subtle nuances to the typology of this parable, the most scripturally consistent is the fact that oil represents the Holy Spirit. The five wise, because they were attentive, kept themselves filled with (yielded to, under the influence of) the Holy Spirit.

Many foolishly embrace a fatalistic theology that states, "Because I'm in Christ, everything just happens automatically." In fact, they would go as far as to say, "Any efforts on our part to further connect to Christ would be dead works." This doctrinal position overlooks and denies hundreds of Scriptures. It specifically denies Jesus' teaching about preparedness for the end times. We are not seeking to earn anything from God by our attentiveness; we are seeking to simply be attentive to the voice of our Lord and Savior.

Many foolishly embrace a fatalistic theology that states, "Because I'm in Christ, everything just happens automatically."

There is no substitute for a life of prayer, worship, meditation and obedience. I am not talking about a legalistic obedience that seeks to earn from God, but a loving trust that seeks to follow God! The Lord is a Shepherd, not a slave driver. He walks before and calls out to us. If we are attentive we hear His voice. If we are disciples we follow. This is the way of the Kingdom!

APOCALYPSE

CHAPTER 37

THE BEGINNING OF THE END

The end of the World's System is the beginning of Jesus' rule on earth; based on where your hope lies it will either be a time of great joy or great sorrow!

JESUS' DISCIPLES ASKED HIM MULTIPLE QUESTIONS. *"Tell us, when will these things be?"* and *"What will be the sign of Your coming, and of the end of the age* (Matthew 24:3)*?"* There is an attempt by Preterists[i], Historicists[ii] and Futurists[iii] to force Jesus' reply as a single answer to a single question, thereby enabling the intention to make His answer support their predetermined doctrine. This attitude toward Scripture will drive many believers to seek doctrinal answers rather than life answers as their means of preparation for the end. The result will be whether Preterist, Historicist or Futurist will still not be adequately equipped for the end. Even if they happen

---

i Preterism is an eschatological that interprets all end time prophecies as events which have already happened

ii Historicist believe in a literal, progressive and continuous fulfillment of prophecy. This is the viewpoint of almost all Protestants.

iii Futurism interprets portions of the Book of Revelation, Daniel and other prophecies, as future events in a literal, physical, apocalyptic global event. This was probably the earliest view of eschatology held by the earl church.

to be doctrinally correct, they are still focusing on the wrong issues for security. *"The Kingdom of God is not in word (talk) but in power."* (1 Corinthians 4:20) Winning the argument has never empowered anyone.

The power of God manifests in us internally as grace and is synonymous with the power of the Holy Spirit. Grace makes us able to do and be who we really are in Jesus. Only those believers who can experience grace, the power of the Holy Spirit, will have any hope of being overcomers. We will never be victorious then or now in our own strength. But many have done with grace what eschatologists have done with end time Scriptures; they have twisted it into a doctrine they argue instead of a power wherein they live.

The power of God manifests in us internally as grace and is synonymous with the power of the Holy Spirit. Grace makes us able to do and be who we really are in Jesus.

Technically, the opposite of grace is legalism. Over the years there have been many kinds of legalism. In the traditional sense we understand legalism as an attempt to be made righteous by works of the law. While that is a correct concept, legalism is actually more inclusive because it is not actually the law that is bad or destructive, it is the way we approach it. In my 40 plus years of walking with God I have seen many different movements come and go. Each of them tended to turn their biblical insights into laws they observed to give them a sense of security that comes from being right. I have not, however, seen anyone live in the Spirit who was depending on a doctrine. Living in the Spirit is more about being alive to, aware of or sensitive to the Spirit. Depending on a doctrine tends to lend itself to being in the flesh.

Catholic, Church of Christ, some Pentecostal and even some Baptist denominations claim to be the only ones who are actually going to Heaven; they think they are the only true church. These groups have categorically ignored Paul's warning about tracing genealogies and other mystical means of claiming superiority. Every group has a tendency to turn some or all of their security to some legalistic formula or performance.

The early Faith Movement had what I called the "confession police." They were "hyper-spiritual," legalistic people who corrected your every sentence to ensure you were stating things as you should in order to maintain the blessings. Some of my Pentecostal friends were adamant about what must be said over you at baptism. If you did not observe the right formula your baptism was invalid. I had relatives who insisted all prayers must end with, "...in the name of Jesus and for His sake we pray"; otherwise, God would not hear your prayer. Then there were my Baptist friends who insisted that you must believe "once saved, always saved" or you were in works. Today there are the "grace people" who must at every point prove they are in grace. They believe every Scripture must have a secret grace meaning. While I believe every person has the right to listen to their own conscience in the application of truth, I also recognize what Paul said about people who must have certain observances; they are weak in the faith (Romans 14:1-4).

Legalism is not just the observance of a rule or law to earn righteousness; it is the use of any rule, law, doctrine or custom as a means of security. That which gives us security makes us feel righteous. We use these feelings of self-righteousness as a substitute for the righteousness of Christ. Jesus and His work on the cross must be our security. We see the Scripture juxtapose law and grace so the immature believer thinks rejecting law is the pathway to grace. Rejecting law is not the pathway to grace; it is the pathway to iniquity! Grace and law (legalism) are not **root issues** they are **fruit issues** which emerge from faith or unbelief. Grace works through faith.[iv] Legalism, ritualism and dead works of any kind emerge when you don't have an absolute trust in the finished work of Jesus for your righteousness.

The reason believers tend to ask the wrong questions when studying eschatology is often rooted in the desire of finding a doctrinal answer that will give them the hope and peace they are not finding in relationship with Jesus! Conversely, even if your doctrine is right, it will not make you feel secure when walking *through the valley of the shadow of death.* The Book of Revelation gives the one formula for those who can overcome the devil in any situation, persecution or confrontation. *"And they overcame him by the blood of the Lamb and by the word of their testimony, and they did not love their lives to the death"* (Revelation 12:11). This cannot be done in your own strength; it must be a work of grace experienced through your intimate connection with Jesus as your Lord and your righteousness.

For two 2000 years people have faced and overcome the wicked one by this very life stance. In America, since we have avoided persecution this seems

iv Ephesians 2:8, For by grace you have been saved through faith, and that not of yourselves; it is the gift of God,

like more than we can ever bear, but much of the rest of the world has faced persecution, humiliation, torture and murder for their faith and they have won. Even if they died, they died in victory. Because we have not seen real grace to live in a supernatural realm, we don't really know what it looks like in real application. We will, however, experience more and more grace as the darkness grows because *"where sin abounds grace does much more abound"* (Romans 5:20).

Do not set you concerns on what lies ahead. Live in your grace and righteousness today. Corrie Ten Boom, who suffered under Nazi occupation, told the story of going to the city with her father. It wasn't until they were ready to board the train that her father would hand her the ticket which allowed her passage. She likened this to her fear of facing persecution at the hands of the Nazis. When she expressed her fears to her father he reminded her of their travel. He told her he did not give her the ticket until she was ready to board the train. In the same way he told her God will give her the power exactly when needed. If we are consumed with fear about tomorrow we will not walk in faith and grace today. Consequently, when the challenges come we will not be equipped. But if we trust God and experience His grace to live in victory today we will be ready for anything tomorrow presents.

Until this part of Jesus' answer most of what He said would be first applied to the imminent fall of Jerusalem. But there seems to be a shift in His primary emphasis to answer other parts of their question. He now focuses on the persecution of Christians. These persecutions are not the end but they are the beginning of the end. *"Then they will deliver* ***you*** *up to tribulation and kill* ***you****, and* ***you*** *will be hated by all* ***nations for My name's sake"*** (Matthew 24:9, emphasis mine). Jews would not be persecuted and hated by the world for His namesake; they did not believe in Him. Today, believers who follow Him as Lord are hated the world over.

Christians throughout the world have nearly always faced persecution of some kind. The Roman government persecuted Christians. Then, when Christianity became the State religion of Rome, the Religionists persecuted true believers. Islam has murdered Christians and Jews since its inception. Based on the teachings of Muhammad this is the only real purpose of Islam and the only way a Muslim can go to Heaven: die in jihad! Communism has murdered tens of millions of believers. Socialism is diametrically opposed to the Word of God and hates true faith. Today Islam has gained enough wealth and power through the Great Harlot to restart what they believe is their final world-wide campaign of jihad, killing anyone who is Jewish, Christian or any other religion. They are so demonically driven they even kill other Muslims who are not radical enough.

"And then many will be offended,[v] *will betray one another, and will hate one another"* (Matthew 24:10). This passage, no doubt, refers to people in general betraying one another, but it may even point more specifically to believers betraying other believers. Intimidation always happens when government becomes too powerful. An invasive government always uses fear and intimidation to get people to spy and report on others. One of the greatest fears when Communists or other extreme groups take over a country is you never know who to trust. Neighbors and family members spy on and betray one another. Studies show that when people are made to view others as lower class and when they have a sense of unrestrained power, they become incredibly cruel. There is no reason to think it will be different in the future. But as we will soon see, the cause for the betrayal and cruelty points back to the very reason Lucifer chose to rebel: iniquity.

An invasive government always uses fear and intimidation to get people to spy and report on others.

One thing that happens as a precursor to total domination of faith is a State-approved Church. Some Christian leaders in Germany, the Soviet Union and under other oppressive regimes have always been seduced into yielding to a State Church. Some do it as a way to keep their job and others do it out of fear and ignorance. Sadly, many believe it will be a means to help people to some degree. But a State Church can only preach what the state approves. So in the end it becomes obvious that one can never stay true to the gospel in a church that does not have full freedom to preach the Word of God. The most dangerous minister in the future will be the one who has drifted so far from the Word of God as its basis for truth that he or she actually believes the Church will be better off without these "radical Christians." They will side with the State against believers who believe the truth. These, along with

---

v Offended: NT:4624, kandali/zw; from NT:4625; to entrap, i.e. trip up (Biblesoft's New Exhaustive Strong's Numbers and Concordance with Expanded Greek-Hebrew Dictionary. Copyright © 1994, 2003, 2006 Biblesoft, Inc. and International Bible Translators, Inc.)

those of the antichrist religion, will believe they are doing God a service by silencing you![vi]

Many believe this could never happen in America, but the truth is we are already far down that road. It is against the law to pray in school or on any state property. Public expressions of Christianity are banned in most states. In many cities it is against the law to have Bible studies in your own home. Yet, our Constitution guarantees freedom of religion and restricts Congress from making **any** laws that would diminish this freedom. Neither the IRS nor any government agency has any constitutional right prying into your church or ministry, but it happens every day. What few people realize is the current administration has sought the power to define and control ordination of ministers. That is in direct contradiction to our Constitution and to the Word of God. Make no mistake; the State intends to take control of your religious rights!

What ministers fail to understand is once you incorporate as a 501-c-3 you are no longer a church; you are a non-profit corporation.

I do not know how this came about, but the IRS tax code clearly states that all churches are tax exempt and need not apply for a 501-c-3 tax exemption. A 501-c-3 is not church tax exemption; it is a tax exemption for non-profit corporations. At some point accountants began urging churches to become 501-c-3. Then banks started refusing to loan money to churches that were not incorporated as such. What ministers fail to understand is once you incorporate as a 501-c-3 you are no longer a church; you are a non-profit corporation which means the State can revoke your tax exempt status if you refuse to follow the laws for a non-profit.

It will be a simple task for the government to vilify and make a church or ministry that does not comply look dishonest. In fact, the word for people becoming offended means to scandalize and entrap. Just as the Roman Church scandalized and persecuted believers in the Eastern Empire, well-meaning

---

vi John 16:1-4, "These things I have spoken to you, that you should not be made to stumble. 2 They will put you out of the synagogues; yes, the time is coming that whoever kills you will think that he offers God service. 3 And these things they will do to you because they have not known the Father nor Me. 4 But these things I have told you, that when the time comes, you may remember that I told you of them.

Christians will do the same to believers in the future. They will believe the propaganda, the twisted news media and the governmental deception.

"Then many false prophets will rise up and deceive many" (Matthew 24:11). In the midst of the persecution there will be false prophets who will arise and deceive as many as possible. 2 Thessalonians 2:3 foretells the two great events that must happen before the day of Christ: the great falling away (the apostasy) and the revelation of the man of sin (the antichrist). All of these horrors emerge upon the earth because it is the fruit of iniquity (lawlessness,) not God's judgment.

People who are not steadfast in God's Word as their basis for wisdom, insight, morals, values and ethics will slowly be shifted to political correctness and social justice. Because they do not hold the truth in their hearts they have no stability. The Holy Spirit has nothing to work with when seeking to bring them deliverance.

Verse 12 of Matthew 24 brings us to the cause of the world's calamities and the reason many will not endure or overcome. *"And because lawlessness will abound, the love of many will grow cold."* In the absence of God's true justice in a world of betrayal, persecution and disappointment, love disappears. It is important to remember everything God's Word teaches about how to treat one another is based on love or value. God's Word protects the innocent, the widows and the fatherless. It requires restitution and justice for the violator. God's justice always conveys value for mankind, rewards responsibility and corrects lawlessness.

The social justice leading us to a godless world vilifies the hard-working and responsible and it vilifies any degree of personal success. It rewards wickedness and mocks any form of godliness. Through evolution and Atheism it destroys the value of human life and undermines the God-directed process of dignity and worth. When man no longer loves (values human life) murderous chaos reigns.

The Bible tells us, *"faith works by love."* In other words, when we believe that God truly loves us we are able to trust Him. When fear increases love decreases and subsequently faith evaporates. Besides the disloyalty of people and government, the massive sense of betrayal will come from the false prophets declaring all this evil as God's judgment on man. As Isaiah pointed out, people *"blaspheme God continually"* because of those who rule over and lead them.[vii] When people are made to believe God is the source of their suffering they not only doubt God, they grow to hate Him.

Who will trust a God they believe to be causing so much death and destruction? Remember, the Luciferian lie that began with Lucifer's pride was that God is not good. Lucifer's way (iniquity and rejection of God's Word) is presented as the true light. The greatest false prophets that will entrap God's people are those of judgment and wrath. They will make the world hate God. In the Book of Revelation when God's wrath is really loosed on the antichrist and his followers (not on the earth in general and not on the Church) people don't repent, they curse God (Revelation 16:11). Wrath has never been God's tool to bring people to repentance. It has always been *"the goodness of God leads you to repentance"* (Romans 2:4).

The word "repent" means "to have a change of mind." The major area where we need a change of mind is in the fact that God is good, loving and trustworthy. Isaiah goes on to say there will be a day when people will see God as He is because they will hear and believe the gospel of peace (Isaiah 52:6-7). They will finally accept the Covenant of Peace (Isaiah 54:10) God made in Jesus. This is the covenant God made with Jesus, the New Covenant. Because we are in Christ we share His righteous; therefore, we have peace with God. He will not do anything to us that He would not do to Jesus.

The prophets of doom point back to the terms of the Old Covenant completely oblivious to the New Covenant we have in Jesus. They would have us believe our failure to observe the law is the reason God is pouring His judgment on the nations. While they do an excellent job at explaining the feast and the requirements of the law, they unintentionally deny the provision of the cross. We are delivered from the curse of the law (Galatians 3:13). We are qualified for the inheritance (Colossians 1:12). Every promise God has ever made is "yes" for us (2 Corinthians 1:20). Then they completely ignore the fact that the first 3½ years of tribulation are the tribulation of the antichrist, not the wrath of God. The Beginning of Sorrows is the constant war driven by the Great Harlot conducted by wicked governments. As long as we falsely accuse God there will be little basis of hope for anyone.

---

vii Isaiah 52:5, "Those who rule over them Make them wail," says the Lord, "And My name is blasphemed continually every day."

Verse 13 of Matthew 24 promises *"But he who endures to the end shall be saved"* (healed, delivered, blessed, prospered, protected and set apart). When preparing His disciples for what lay ahead He told them *"But when the Helper comes, whom I shall send to you from the Father, the Spirit of truth who proceeds from the Father, He will testify of Me"* (John 15:26). We are not left alone as orphans; we have a Helper. This is, of course, intimately connected to the parable of the five wise virgins who kept oil in their lamps. The Holy Spirit is here to lead us and give us power beyond our own so we can endure and overcome.

The ultimate question is: Today, under no pressure or persecution and minimal hardship, are you developing your capacity to hear, recognize and follow the Holy Spirit? I'm not talking about what you do in church services; I'm referring to how you make decisions when you get a gentle nudge to do something differently like stop what you are doing, drive home a different route, go by and see a friend or give a helping hand to someone in need. In other words, do you follow His leading?

The ultimate question is: Today, under no pressure or persecution and minimal hardship, are you developing your capacity to hear, recognize and follow the Holy Spirit?

In counseling with thousands of people who have faced tragedy the vast majority has always been able to pinpoint an exact moment when they knew in their heart they should either take action or make a specific decision that would have averted the tragedy. That is a hard thing to face, but it is the only way we will ever learn to follow the Holy Spirit without hesitation. Jesus speaks to us through the Holy Spirit and He never leaves us or forsakes us. There is never a time when the Holy Spirit is not attempting to lead us away from trouble and into absolute victory.

In John 16:13 Jesus says, *"When He, the Spirit of truth, has come, He will guide you into all truth."* Truth is not just the Word; it is all the Word implies and entails. Jesus showed us how to walk in God's Word. He showed us how to heal the sick, cast out demons, minister to the hurting, stand up against Religionists and function in a realm where all things are possible. He took everything God ever said and showed us what it looks like in people of faith. You may not be walking in this right now, but it should be your goal. You should have yourself in training for hearing and following the Holy Spirit, and this is what Jesus said would prepare you!

Finally He says, *"These things I have spoken to you, that you should not be made to stumble"* (John 16:1). In order to protect us from stumbling Jesus had to warn us of what was coming. Sadly, many believers take the words Jesus gave to prevent our stumbling, obsess on the warnings and ignore the instructions. That which was given to help us makes us stumble because we are focusing on the warning as if it is a punishment or threat. For those who are not experiencing the comfort and direction of the Holy Spirit the warning is so overwhelming they cannot endure what they read. If He had not warned us we would be taken totally by surprise, but because He warned us, as it comes to pass we can know that everything else He told us is true and reliable. *"But these things I have told you, that when the time comes, you may remember that I told you of them"* (John 16:4).

He told us it would be people who did not really know God who would do this (John16:3). Thus, we know it is not God doing all these evils; it is godless people, the very ones who reject God's Word. We can also be comforted by the knowledge that He has gone before us to prepare a place where we will dwell with Him eternally. He sent the Holy Spirit to us and He will never leave us, forsake us or fail us (Hebrews 13:5 AMP). If we focus on His promises and follow His instructions we will not only endure, we will overcome. We will be among those who take the Gospel of the Kingdom to the ends of the earth. We will be vessels through whom God manifests His glory.

The war and chaos of the ungodly is the beginning of the end. It has been going on for centuries. It is walking in grace, following the Holy Spirit and spreading the Kingdom during this stage of conflict that we equip ourselves for the end. As you live in victory today you have the assurance that you can live in victory no matter what tomorrow brings!

APOCALYPSE

CHAPTER 38

THE ANTIDOTE TO DECEPTION

Believers will finally reach the world and usher in the return of Jesus when we embrace His mission and His message!

ONE OF THE GREAT EARMARKS OF THE TIME JUST BEFORE THE RETURN OF JESUS IS MASSIVE DECEPTION. There will be deception in the world that replaces God's morals, values and standards with new morals, political fairness and Luciferian justice. Inside the Church there will be a rise of false teachers. One main emphasis of these false teachers will be their "personal revelation." They will teach that godliness has no value. They will offer freedom that is nothing more than a cover for lawlessness (iniquity). They will dismiss, corrupt and ultimately reject the teaching of Jesus.

It is more than obvious that the only antidote to deception is truth. But we must realize every person reaches their own idea of truth by starting with that which is true, that is, the Word of God. Based on some process of reasoning they reach an interpretation of what the Word means in real life. Just because we start with what is true does not mean we reach a conclusion that is truth.

Truth is when what is true, what has been stated is made understandable, applicable and functional. In Hebrew thought there is no concept of truth that does not result in action. The rabbis took upon themselves the job of interpreting God's Word. In other words, they would read God's Word and attempt to explain how it should be applied in life. For example, one rabbi may take the command to do no work on the Sabbath and interpret that to mean you can only walk two miles on the Sabbath and anything beyond that point will break that particular command. Another rabbi may interpret that same command to mean you can walk five miles. In other words, instead of allowing each individual to take what was plain and straight-forward in God's Word and listen to their own heart, it was interpreted for them.

When a rabbi developed his interpretation and application of the Word it was called his "yoke." Thus, to follow that rabbi was to accept his interpretation and application of the Scriptures as the yoke one would take upon them. This would be their attempt at living in a way pleasing to God. The problem was these men had never seen God for themselves. They had their own issues and culture bias which all became part of their interpretation of God's Word. Their yoke was never an exact representation of God's intentions.

When Jesus came on the scene He was uniquely qualified to reveal the true intentions of God. He had seen God the Father. He was God. He was with God in the beginning. All things were created by and through Him. He was the first man qualified to say, "This is what the Word of God means in application. This is what it looks like in real life. This is what God intended when He said these words." Yet, since the earliest of times teachers of iniquity (lawlessness) have sought to alienate us from the only One who could show us the perfect representation of God (Hebrews 1:3) and empower us to live in true intentions.

When Jesus came on the scene He was uniquely qualified to reveal the true intentions of God. He had seen God the Father. He was God.

His invitation to take His yoke upon us was the first and only time in history we could finally see God and His Word as He intended. It was the first time we would be free from a mediator or teacher claiming to show us the truth about God. Yet, false teachers build their ministries around their "private interpretations" of what God's Word means and how it should be interpreted, subtly alienating us from Jesus, our Lord.

Jesus' last words were instruction to make disciples by teaching all nations to obey everything He commanded (Matthew 28:18-20). When Jesus is Lord we trust what He has done for us through the cross; thus, we are able to fully commit to Him as Lord. This means we accept His yoke, His interpretation of God's Word and how it should be applied. As disciples and believers we look to His life and teaching to understand, interpret and apply every Word of God. One cannot follow Jesus as Lord, be His disciple or protect his or her heart from deception while rejecting His teaching and His life example.

If you desire to understand anything God ever said or anything written in the epistles, look at the life and teachings of Jesus. He taught it. He lived it. He was God in the flesh. He is our model, our perfect example!

Jesus was not a teacher of the law as many claim. He was a Teacher of the Gospel of the Kingdom of God. He taught men the truths, the principles embedded in everything God ever said. In His parables of the Kingdom and His life He showed us not just what the Word said but all that it implied and intended. Sadly, these principles were soon perverted by the Religionists as prescriptions for going to Heaven instead of how to function in this realm called the Kingdom of God. This twist made the parables appear to be formulas for earning salvation. This perversion of truth made Jesus' teaching irrelevant to the believer. For this reason some groups reject Jesus' teaching claiming He was a teacher of the law which results in Jesus' teaching being completely disconnected to the New Covenant; but nothing could be more inaccurate or farther from the truth.

Jesus was the Living Word of God… the Word made flesh! As such, He personified, lived, taught and modeled exactly what God's Word would look like and sound like if applied from the true intention of God's heart. He brought truth. Truth is more than what is true; it is all that was intended. God intended that His every command be applied from a motive of love. While the law was all true, it had an inherent weakness: the flesh. In other words, man perverted the law, its meaning and its intention to suit his preferences. All that Jesus did was based on God's Word. He never spoke anything of Himself.

He had no private interpretation of God's commands. Jesus' every word and action brought us the "truth," all that was implied and intended in God's law.[i]

Many claim the Old Testament teachings are totally irrelevant. It is as if Jesus changed God's Word. Jesus did not bring a new Word; He was the same Word that was with God in the beginning. The Apostle John said we are declaring that which was *"from the beginning,"* not something new (1 John 1:1). In the Gospel of John we are told that no man had ever seen God, not the religious leaders and not the Religionists who forced men to carry heavy legalistic burdens. Jesus is the only One who has seen God and He declared Him to us (John 1:18). The word "declare" can mean to "unfold." The true nature of God had actually been concealed through man's twisting of the law into religious legalism. Jesus unfolded the Word, so for the first time man could comprehend a good and loving God.

It is important to keep Jesus' message about the end in context. This sermon began by Jesus rebuking the religious leaders for the heavy religious, legalistic burdens they placed on the people. He said they *"shut up the kingdom of heaven."* It was not that they kept people out of Heaven as much as they kept people from entering the Kingdom realm in this life. Through His entire discourse He warned the disciples not to become like those religious leaders who had abandoned God's intentions for man.

So, we have now progressed to Jesus' warning of great deception by false prophets and false messiahs. At this point it seems that Jesus' statement about the gospel being preached in the entire world is almost out of context; but not so! He is telling us what will be the only antidote for the world-wide deception as well as the basis for the last great world-wide revival. But we must realize the great end time revival will not be because God decides to pour out a special anointing of the Holy Spirit. It will be because the Church finally preaches and believes the truth it was commissioned to teach.

This Kingdom message may well have been the message that prevented the world from escalating so far out of control. As people respond to this they

---

i NT:225, The Original Greek Usage and Its Differentiations. Etymologically al¢¡theia means "nonconcealment." It thus denotes what is seen, indicated, expressed, or disclosed, i.e., a thing as it really is, not as it is concealed or falsified. al¢¡theia is "the real state of affairs," (from Theological Dictionary of the New Testament, abridged edition, Copyright © 1985 by William B. Eerdmans Publishing Company. All rights reserved.)

will experience what we could have had all along. We will experience the Kingdom realm. But what does that really mean?

In verse 14 Jesus declares, *"And this gospel of the kingdom will be preached in all the world as a witness to all the nations, and then the end will come."* There are four relevant factors in this statement.

1. Not just any gospel will be preached, but the Gospel of the Kingdom.
2. It will be preached to the entire world.
3. It will serve as a witness to all nations.
4. After all this the end comes.

Attempts to relegate all of Jesus' teachings to the fall of Jerusalem do not reconcile with the many times He points out the immediacy of the end following these events.

What is the Gospel of the Kingdom? We should start by reminding ourselves that "gospel" means "good news." Until the time of Jesus' appearance on earth everything the people heard of the Kingdom was negative, external and based solely on obedience to the law, independent of love. The law was seldom presented as a means to treat your fellowman with dignity and worth. It was universally viewed as a way to keep God happy which stemmed from the Luciferian concept of pleasing the angry gods. This religious approach perverted every aspect of the Word of God; there was practically no good in it at all.

What is the Gospel of the Kingdom? We should start by reminding ourselves that "gospel" means "good news."

The law was meant to be the wisdom of God so man could have an incredible quality of life while awaiting the coming of the Lord. But the sin nature, man's inability to see himself as he really is in relation to God, always drives him to self-righteousness - dead works of the flesh. He wants to feel he is earning his way to God. In the absence of faith righteousness, Religionists tend toward works righteousness. That tendency twisted all God said so that which was given for our good turned to death![ii]

---

ii Romans 7:11-12, For sin, taking occasion by the commandment, deceived me, and by it killed me. 12 Therefore the law is holy, and the commandment holy and just and good.

Performance is an external substitute for an internal reality. God always wanted man to relate to Him and His Word from his heart (Deuteronomy 30:10). The Word in our hearts will produce fruit in our behavior free from the flesh. Our righteous behavior is a matter of faith, not works. Jesus proclaimed *"the Kingdom of God is within you"* (Luke 17:21). Faith, as a matter of the heart, makes all things related to God internal realities while externals are the fruit of those realities. When we trust God with all our heart the driving force in our life is internal.

Performance is an external substitute for an internal reality. God always wanted man to relate to Him and His Word from his heart (Deuteronomy 30:10).

The Kingdom of God is an internal realm where Jesus rules as our Lord.[iii] The difference between living in the World's System and living in the Kingdom of God all comes down to Lordship. If Jesus is Lord, we follow His teaching and example of the Word of God. We take on His yoke, not Paul's, Peter's and certainly not some self-proclaimed teacher of private revelations.

Until now some of the Church has preached salvation through belief on the resurrected Lord. At this point many have detoured into righteousness by legalistic works, which is the same as the Judaizers. Others have delineated into security through the intellectual agreement of some doctrine or rite. These are Religionists. A few have taught Lordship but only in the sense of obedient loyalty. Very few have believed the Covenant of Peace which God made with Jesus. Even in obedient loyalty few seem to experience Jesus as our "everything" and from that basis enjoy a life of faith-filled, love-based discipleship.

Jesus said the way we would be identified as His disciples was by the love we have one for another.[iv] Even though it is talked about, Bible-based love is never seen in the religious world. Most groups who emphasize love tend to be more humanistic, departing from the Word of God. They seem to have

---

iii NT:932 This term refers to the being or nature or state of a king, i.e., his dignity, and secondarily the expression of this in the territory he governs. (from Theological Dictionary of the New Testament, abridged edition, Copyright © 1985 by William B. Eerdmans Publishing Company. All rights reserved.) NT:932 royal power, kingship, dominion, rule (from Thayer's Greek Lexicon, Electronic Database. Copyright © 2000, 2003, 2006 by Biblesoft, Inc. All rights reserved.)

iv John 13:35, "By this all will know that you are My disciples, if you have love for one another."

little capacity to grasp the congruence of the commands of God and love. But when love is rooted in Lordship, we accept that God's Word is the basis for true love. His commandments while completely incapable of making us righteous, show us the only way to express His love.

The Gospel of the Kingdom will not be a message of God's judgment on the world. It will be one of His love that can be accessed no matter what is happening in the world. It will reveal what Jesus expressed in His teaching of the Kingdom. It will expose mankind to life principles in God's Word and the power to live it. It will portray Jesus as Lord, Teacher, Model and Master. These believers, so overflowing with God's love, will be compelled to take this message and this way of life to a world that is ruled by iniquity, enslaved to sin and living in the desolation of both. This message will be the true peace in a world offering false peace.

The Bible tells us the only thing that matters in relation to what we do for God is, *"faith works by love"* (Galatians 5:6). Faith is trust. When the world hears and believes the love of God they will trust Him and His Word. When believers truly believe that God loves the world they will know He wants them whole and well and they will understand He is willing to manifest His promises on their behalf. Believers will explode into miracle-working agents of God's love. But for possibly the first time in Church History it will not be miracles for the purpose of showing God's power; it will be miracles for the purpose of expressing His love.

It is difficult to talk about the role of the Church in this end time revival. Our concept of the Church is so fixed in what we have known it is almost impossible to see the Church as God sees it, a body of people who, like the cells of the human body, are interconnected on so many levels it is hard to comprehend. We tend to simply see the local church. There are some incredible local churches in the world and I have been privileged to visit and know of many of them. But with the changes in the political arena it is unlikely the Church in the end will look anything like it does today. It will be more like the underground churches in China and other persecuted countries. Being a Christian will mean risking your life for something more precious than anything else.

Like the early Church, this will be the witness to the world. We will, *"overcome him by the blood of the Lamb and by the word of their testimony, and they did not love their lives to the death"* (Revelation 12:11). But this will not be a formula we work to overcome the evil one. It will be the fruit of lives that are completely in love with, totally sold out to, entirely trusting and thoroughly experiencing the life and love of God. This will be a radical love walk that defies reason and cannot be controlled or stamped out! Like Stephen, the first martyr, we will work signs and wonders and they will *"not be able to resist the wisdom and Spirit by which we speak"* (Acts 6:10). Like the martyrs under Communist regimes, the love we have for them will never escape their minds even if they kill us! Many will be like Phillip who experienced supernatural transportation from one part of the world to another (Acts 8:39-40). For some who experience this miracle of transportation it will be for spreading the gospel and for others it may be a means of deliverance from persecution! A Church (the body of Christ) that is fully committed to the Word of God, the love of God and the Lordship of Jesus will be an irresistible witness, a ray of hope and a guiding light to a dark, perishing world!

It may be that for the first time in history the Church will use the keys of the Kingdom bestowed on us by our Lord. We may finally, out of a revelation of the love and goodness of God, realize we don't need a special revelation, anointing or word of knowledge to act on God's promises. If God declared something illegal in Heaven we can declare it illegal on earth, and if He has declared it legal in Heaven we can declare it legal on earth![v] While for many love will grow cold and their hearts will fail them, multitudes will discover the love of God and their hearts will burn for their Lord and for the hurting world.

These words help us understand why in previous chapters Jesus' two primary factors for preparation to endure is sensitivity and yielding to the Holy Spirit and for believers to be about the Father's business of rescuing a hurting world. The parable of the talents contrasts those who use their resources for Kingdom purposes versus those who do not. In this parable we also have the reminder that when we do anything for His children we do it for Him, but when we refuse to do anything for them we neglect Him. This parable does not emphasize the importance of how many talents you have and it doesn't even emphasize the results you get from investing your life for the Kingdom; it simply points out the need to be willing. I am fully convinced that if the man with one talent tried and failed, his master would have given him more talents.

---

v Matthew 16:19, "And I will give you the keys of the kingdom of heaven, and whatever you bind on earth will be bound in heaven, and whatever you loose on earth will be loosed in heaven."

Regardless of when you think Jesus will return or when or if you think there will be a rapture makes no difference. Most end time doctrines are mere possibilities based on variables that cannot be concretely proven. On the other hand, the truth that cannot be escaped is Jesus' instructions concerning our preparation for the end. We are to live intimately connected to the Holy Spirit and make disciples of the entire world by preaching and teaching the Gospel of the Kingdom. To reduce this to an argument of times, sequences or dispensations is, at the least, avoidance and, at the most, foolishness. We are here to **be disciples** and **make disciples** unto the Lord Jesus Christ.

We are to live intimately connected to the Holy Spirit and make disciples of the entire world by preaching and teaching the Gospel of the Kingdom.

Could it be that believers actually believing the message of the Kingdom, lordship and the true authority of the believer is the key factor in the return of Jesus? I believe there is much we do not understand about how authority works, but we do know all that happens on Planet Earth does so because of the beliefs of mankind. It seems there is a synergism in belief. In other words, if a group believes something, it has more of a global effect than an individual believing the same idea. It could be that for the first time in history the body of Christ comes into agreement and actually desires the return of the Lord.

When the entire world is influenced with the Gospel of the Kingdom the Church may become a united body. It seems believers have historically been deceived about just how wicked the world could become. If history as presented in Scripture is correct we have been incredibly naïve about the ruthless, wicked intention of the evil one. We have dismissed as foolishness the idea that some of mankind has entered into a conspiracy of darkness to accomplish Lucifer's abominable goals. As such, it is questionable how many believers would join together at this moment and use their authority to usher in the return of the Lord today. Those who have never seen the underbelly of the serpent just cannot conceive how heartless and ruthless the wicked can be.

When wickedness reaches its ultimate crescendo and every government in the world is complying with the antichrist we will finally see the personification of wickedness. Believers will finally wake up and realize this cannot be changed through the political process. Not only can government do nothing about the problem, we will finally see that governments are the problem! The total dissolution with the World's System juxtaposed against the hope in the righteous reign of Christ may, for the first time in history, unite the body of Christ around the desire, hope and faith in the imminent return of the Lord Jesus. The Gospel of the Kingdom is not only the antidote to false prophets, it is the antidote to false understanding of the believer's role in the destiny of Planet Earth!

Near the end of the Book of Revelation it says, *"And the Spirit and the bride say, 'Come!' And let him who hears say, 'Come'"* (Revelation 22:17). Believers who are alive to the Spirit of God, living in divine purpose and finally influencing the world with the Gospel of the Kingdom may be the deciding factor when the Lord Jesus returns. Jesus said after the Gospel of the Kingdom is preached to the entire world then the end will come.

Finally, the believers will pray *"Thy kingdom come, Thy will be done on earth as it is in Heaven"* and really mean it! Our Lord will return to personally defeat the antichrist and his followers, then His Kingdom will be established in the physical world. This will be the end of the rule of man and the World's System and the beginning of the reign of the Lord Jesus and the Kingdom of God on earth!

Hold fast to Jesus! The early Church overcame incredible persecution and reached most of the known world, not because they had all manner of deep revelations. They had the testimony of Jesus - His representation of God. They took on His yoke and clung to Him personally. Let us hold fast to Him. Do not allow anyone to become your teacher who gives you a new yoke. The moment you allow someone to provide you with a private interpretation they have become your mediator. Remember the words of our Lord, *"Behold, I am coming quickly! Hold fast what you have, that no one may take your crown"* (Revelation 3:11).

APOCALYPSE

CHAPTER 39

WHAT NO ONE SAW COMING!

There has always been a tendency to create end time doctrine to fit current events instead of interpreting current events by end time prophecy!

AS MUCH AS ANY OTHER FACTOR IT IS OUR PREDETERMINED IDEAS THAT CLOSE OUR EYES TO OR DISTORT OUR UNDERSTANDING OF TRUTH. Anyone who finds security in their doctrine will forever seek validation of their position. Even if they are correct in their doctrine, true peace will still evade them. No one has ever found peace by being right; yet, many believers still seek peace and validation through their doctrines. Once we put our security in that doctrine we must defend it. If someone disproves our doctrine they have taken away our security.

Once we decide how something "should" be it affects what we perceive and understand. A teacher of the law came and asked Jesus what he must do to *"inherit eternal life."* Like so many people asking questions he wasn't really seeking an answer, he was seeking to justify himself. Jesus asked the man two questions. *"What is written in the Law?"* he replied. *"How do you read it?"* (Luke 10:26) Our struggle with truth is never with what God has said; it is the way we read or interpret it. Because of the way the rabbis read and interpreted the Scripture few people recognized the Messiah for which they longed and prayed.

At the time of Jesus' crucifixion and for hundreds of years after, Rome was the manifestation of evil in the world. Rome was a ruthless, merciless oppressor. It abounded in immorality, including homosexuality, sexual dominance of slaves and even sexual occult worship. It was a polytheistic religious state that incorporated the gods of the countries they conquered into their vast array of gods. They hated Jews and Christians for their monotheistic beliefs and their refusal to comply with Roman religion.

This clearly demonic, governmental manifestation, along with the idolatry of the Roman Church, became the basis of nearly every eschatological doctrine for hundreds of years.

This clearly demonic, governmental manifestation, along with the idolatry of the Roman Church, became the basis of nearly every eschatological doctrine for hundreds of years. The confusion is not simply the doctrine put forth by the Roman Church, it was also the doctrine presented in reaction to the Roman Church's official doctrine. Everything about Rome seemed to be close enough to fulfilling end time prophecies that even if Scriptures* had to be twisted a bit it was a near perfect fit. The tendency to create circumstantial theology based on the hatred of Rome and the Catholic Church blinded many theologians, but the bigger cause for confusion may have emerged from the attempt to create theological explanations before it was possible to know the facts. Remember, there are some facts that are sealed until the time of the end!

Jesus' next words in His discourse about the end form the basis of one of the most significant events in eschatological history. *"Therefore when you see the 'abomination of desolation,' spoken of by Daniel the prophet, standing in the holy place (whoever reads, let him understand...)"* (Matthew 24:15). Just the fact that the phrase *"whoever reads, let him understand"* should have been ample indication this would be difficult to sort out.

According to the Apostle John there have been many antichrists but that does not mean they were THE antichrist. The Apostle Paul said the *"mystery of iniquity"* was always at work and would continue until the time of the end. As we have discussed, there have been many persecutions and much tribulation, but that does not mean it has been THE Tribulation. Every major theological position of which I am aware, if adhered to, will prevent believers from preparing for the end in the way Jesus instructed because it is predicated on accepting a particular doctrinal theory of eschatology. Some believe the tribulation has already occurred. Others believe we will all be forcibly snatched away to escape any persecution. Both of those positions have to twist a lot of Scripture and thinly interpret historical facts to maintain their illusion of scriptural premise. To hold either of those positions is your choice, but do not let it interfere with living your life the way Jesus warned and taught. It really matters little if we are right or wrong in some of our eschatological positions as much as it matters that we have our security in following our Shepherd, not in choosing the path we walk.

According to the Apostle John there have been many antichrists but that does not mean they were THE antichrist. The Apostle Paul said the *"mystery of iniquity"* was always at work and would continue until the time of the end.

Before we consider the abomination of desolation we need to acquaint ourselves more with what no one saw coming. Early theologians could not see the threat and last days' prophetic fulfillment in Islam. After all, Islam was only publicly preached by Muhammad in the early 7th century. The first attempts at interpreting end time Scriptures was a typical effort to make God's Word fit into a limited perception. Current events, not the Word of God, took preeminence in scriptural interpretation. Rome was the clearest picture of false Christianity. Rome was persecuting true believers. They had mingled every imaginable idolatrous doctrine with Scriptures. How could Rome not be the false religion? From this predetermined position everything one read about the end times was tainted.

Like the early theologians, American theologians have attempted to craft a picture of the end times based on American culture. The Church in America has tried to make America the centerpiece of end time events. It has been these twists of Scripture that have brought about the many theological overreactions that continue to create so much confusion and provide so little comfort. Very little of what has been taught about eschatology for the last 100 years has been consistent with the larger scope of Scripture. I don't think any tried to deceive, I think, like those who had gone before, they were simply acting with limited information.

Not until recently has the average American had even a glimpse of what religion and geographic part of the world the antichrist will emerge. Almost all any American knows about Islam is the politically correct, deliberately deceitful propaganda put out by our government and the media. The greatest interpretation problems, however, have been the tendency to overlook what Jesus said was important. We have made our theories more important than His teaching!

American theologians have attempted to craft a picture of the end times based on American culture. The Church in America has tried to make America the centerpiece of end time events. It has been these twists of Scripture that have brought about the many theological overreactions that continue to create so much confusion and provide so little comfort.

It has only been in recent years that Americans have had any knowledge of the potential threat Islam poses to the world. We were led to believe that a few extremists are giving Muslims a bad name. As true as that is, the extremists may give other moderate Muslims a bad name, but they do not give Islam a bad name. Those called "radical" are the ones actually obeying their Islamic scriptures. Based on the Quran and Hadith, those identified as moderate Muslims are compromisers who (according to "radical" Muslims) do not deserve to live. This is why ISIS and other terror groups kill moderate Muslims along with Christians and Jews. Unless a Muslim is willing to go to jihad they are traitors to Allah.

It is difficult to identify what Muslims truly believe because their writings are full of contradictions. So, how they are represented is all based on which passage you quote. Adding to the confusion, in Muslim faith, whatever was written last is considered the truth. When seeking to appear moderate and peace-loving, a jihadist will quote from earlier, more moderate Islamic writings even though they have no intention of following those teachings. The second problem in understanding Islam comes from a practice called *Kithman. Kithman* is a command to deliberately conceal ones beliefs.[i] Muslims are commanded to use deceit to gain the upper hand when negotiating with infidels. Thus, it is impossible to get the truth from a group who is seeking world domination, believes they are doing Allah a service when committing acts of terrorism and are instructed to lie. While what is written here obviously does not apply to all Muslims, it does apply to the teaching of Islam because it is all based on their own writings.

All of Muhammad's family considered him to be demon possessed. Muhammad had an encounter with a "being" who claimed to be the Angel Gabriel in a cave where the entity choked him to force him to comply with its will. Three times Muhammad had this type of encounter until he complied, went into a trance and wrote the Quran. This entity demanded him to worship Allah (another name for Baal) as the only true god. The purpose of this religion was to destroy Christians and Jews and bring about the forced domination of the entire world. Even Muhammad originally thought himself demon possessed. Those who heard him preach his message thought him to be insane.

Early in his attempts to gain a following in Yathrib, he presented himself as a teacher of Judaism.[ii] When Jews rejected him and his teaching, he and his followers stopped praying toward Jerusalem and began to pray toward Mecca. He stopped recognizing the Sabbath and declared Friday to be the holy day. He began conducting raids on caravans and helping the poor of Yathrib which slowly increased his following. At some point he had a subsequent visit from a being who now told him those who went to war with him could keep portions of the spoils for themselves and they could take slaves. This was particularly inviting with the idea of taking sex slaves. Interestingly, some sources point out that Muslims tended to take more female slaves than male because females also became sexual slaves.

Islam, like all cults and the occult, has a base of deep sexual perversion. For an entire year in Muhammad's life he had sex with entities he thought to be his wife, but were not. In Islam the laws that govern men's sexuality are far more permissive than those governing women. Islam is a chauvinistic belief system that has little respect for women. For example, if a man rapes a woman it will usually be the woman who is put to death for tempting the man. Today in the Middle East women and young girls are forced to be sex slaves of ISIS

---

i The Islamic Antichrist, Joel Richardson, 2009, Los Angeles, WorldNetDaily

ii http://www.fsmitha.com/time/ce07.htm

fighters. They are married for one night at a time, so it doesn't count as adultery for the jihadists. Additionally, homosexuality and pedophilia is rampant in extreme Islam.

> Islam, like all cults and the occult, has a base of deep sexual perversion. For an entire year in Muhammad's life he had sex with entities he thought to be his wife, but were not.

Islam is not a religion of love, peace or ethics but one of war and oppression. It offers no sure promise of forgiveness or Heaven unless a Muslim dies in jihad. By definition this is an antichrist, anti-Jehovah religion that exists only to extinguish all knowledge of Jehovah as God and all biblical knowledge of Jesus from the earth. Some Christians foolishly believe "Allah" is another name for "Jehovah." They think this religion emerged from Ishmael, but it didn't! It descended from the worship of Nimrod who declared himself as the sun god. It is the offspring of the conflict that has existed between the children of God and the children of Lucifer since time began.

There are several factors unique to Islam that are exact biblical descriptions of the false religion, the antichrist and the false prophet. This collection of factors has never been present in other groups of people. The exact biblical description of the antichrist, his nations and their goals are the stated beliefs, intentions and Islamic prophecies concerning the end time. There is no religion in the world that, from its own writings, declares itself to be everything the Bible describes as the last great antichrist deception.

There are five things one **must** believe in order to be a Muslim:

1. One must believe in Allah, which is a rejection of Jehovah as God and Jesus as His Son.
2. One must believe in the last days. Committed Muslims live to bring about the end times. They do not desire to rule the world, they desire to end the world and bring about the judgment of Allah.
3. One must believe in angels. The very basis of Islam is a message from an angel that contradicts the Bible as God's authoritative Word. The Apostle warned, *"But even if we, or an angel from heaven, preach any*

other gospel to you than what we have preached to you, let him be accursed" (Galatians 1:8).

4. One must believe in Muslim scripture. This requires the rejection of God's Word. Muhammad, under the influence of a spirit, becomes your rabbi. You must accept his interpretation of the scripture. You must take his yoke upon you.
5. One must believe in the prophets. The prophets wrote the additions to the Quran. It is these prophets that are provoking and inspiring world-wide terrorism.

Other than belief in Allah the Muslim prophecies related to the last days are the true driving force of Islam. They exist for the purpose of bringing about the last days. There are several unique factors concerning their end time beliefs.

First, they believe it is incumbent upon them to fulfil the prophecies. In other words, to be a good Muslim they must make the prophecies happen. This is why war and terrorism will never end until Jesus Himself returns and conquers the antichrist nations. No matter what treaties and concessions are made they will never stop plotting the destruction of the entire world. Everything happening in the Middle East today is a deliberate attempt to fulfil prophecies and facilitate the manifestation of their Mahdi* (our antichrist).

Other than belief in Allah the Muslim prophecies related to the last days are the true driving force of Islam.

Second, the majority of their end time prophecies are exactly like those in the Christian Bible with the exception of a role reversal of good and evil. They intend to fulfil all prophesies applicable to the antichrist, yet they believe they are serving Allah in doing all those things we see as evil. Our antichrist is their savior. Our false prophet is their Jesus. The Ottoman Empire that overthrew Rome is the nation (beast) that died and has come back. But they claim Christians twisted the Book of Revelation. They intend to fulfil all the evil in the Book of Revelation yet claim it is we who worship Jehovah who are evil.

Third, jihad is the means of ushering in their savior and fulfilling the Islamic last days' prophecies. They must go to war against Israel and Christians in order for their Mahdi to reveal himself. Therefore, we in the West must realize there are no negotiations for peace that will succeed until the antichrist, their Mahdi comes forth. As a result of conflict between (old) Syria and Egypt he will negotiate a false peace with Israel. But according to Islamic teaching this peace will only be a strategy for gaining the upper hand. In both the Book of Revelation and Islamic prophecies this peace treaty will be broken in 3 ½ years.

Jihad is the means of ushering in their savior and fulfilling the Islamic last days' prophecies. They must go to war against Israel and Christians in order for their Mahdi to reveal himself.

Many religions have offered the false hope of a counterfeit savior, but only the lineage of Nimrod has attempted to create a false Jesus. Semiramis concocted a fake supernatural conception giving birth to the false messiah after the death of Nimrod. In the end, Islam will not just present a false savior; they will present an antichrist and a false Jesus - one who claims to be Jesus of the Bible. The Muslim messiah will be the Mahdi. He will be the one who unites the Muslim world in a caliphate* and leads them in a war of annihilation against Israel and the world. He is considered to be Allah's representative on earth.

He will be followed by another beast, the false prophet. According to Islam, what the Bible calls the false prophet will be Jesus, who was not really crucified but taken to Heaven alive. He is returning to say that He is not the Son of God, He was not crucified and He is not the Messiah. Both the Book of Revelation and Muslim prophesies talk of this man's ability to call fire down from Heaven and work great miracles.[iii] This man will lead the war against Christians, giving them the opportunity to convert or die by beheading. He will set up the image that has the power to kill those who do not worship the false Christ. Among the many events that will deceive the world includes finding secret books of the Bible that support his deception and supposedly finding the Ark of the Covenant. It could be this very act that leads Jews to

iii Revelation 13:13-14, He performs great signs, so that he even makes fire come down from heaven on the earth in the sight of men.

believe him to be their long-anticipated messiah. He will lead many Christians and Jews into deception.

He will also be a co-conspirator in the abomination of desolation. Many believe Titus' destruction of Jerusalem and the temple was the fulfillment of the prophecy in Daniel as well as Jesus' warnings about what would befall Jerusalem. Titus, an evil man who was no doubt driven by the antichrist spirit, does not fulfil many of the qualifying requirements of the antichrist. The list would be too long and would distract from the point. But the main thing we must realize is the Bible makes no reference to 70 AD being the time the Kingdom of God is taken from the Jews and given to the Church; that occurred at the resurrection with Christ, the Head of the Church, taking His rightful place at the right hand of God.

> According to Islam, what the Bible calls the false prophet will be Jesus, who was not really crucified but taken to Heaven alive.

We know, according to the Books of Daniel and Revelation, the antichrist will make a seven year peace treaty with Israel, something Titus did not do. This is also what the Muslims prophesy will happen. It has been assumed that during this time Israel will rebuild the temple and resume the sacrifices. I can't comment on that; it is yet to be seen. But what we do know is the Dome of the Rock is a holy place for Muslims which now stands on the Temple Mount, the place where the Jewish temple once stood. According to the Bible it will be in this very place where the Mahdi breaks the covenant and declares himself as God. It may be at this place the false Jesus (false prophet) honors the Mahdi (antichrist) and begins working to force the world to worship him. This is the abomination of desolation.

As we walk through the rest of Jesus' warnings we will see how His words cannot be completely fulfilled until the antichrist takes very specific steps. We will see that Jesus Himself will come personally and physically return to the earth, overthrow the antichrist and his armies, and set up His Kingdom rule for 1,000 years. And we will see how the simple command to *"watch and pray"* lies at the heart of absolute victory for every believer. We will clearly see what is coming and how to read the signs. The thing that will ensure we recognize the signs as they unfold is the source of our security. Our hope will not be based on the fact that we have it all figured out; it will be in the fact that we know and trust Jesus as Lord. Our security will be founded in the deep, intimate connection we have with our Lord, Savior and Shepherd.

> We will see that Jesus Himself will come personally and physically return to the earth, overthrow the antichrist and his armies, and set up His Kingdom rule for 1,000 years.

The world never saw the resurrection of the Islamic Empire, nor was it aware of its vehement pursuit of the destruction of Israel, Christianity and America. But your eyes are open. We will not allow our preferences or eschatological ideas to force us to interpret the Bible in any predetermined manner. We will follow Jesus with our whole heart and we will overcome!

APOCALYPSE

CHAPTER 40

WHAT HAPPENS NEXT?

There is nothing confusing about Jesus' teaching until we try to make it say what we want it to say!

JESUS DIDN'T FORETELL THE END SO WE WOULD LIVE IN FEAR. He foretold the end and all the events leading up to it so we would feel safe. Knowing He sees the end from the beginning (Matthew 24:25, John14:29) is a major source of hope for many reasons. When things begin to unravel just as His Word describes, we can look to the promise and realize, just as sure as the Tribulation has come the deliverance will also come! Additionally, when things do not take us by surprise it is easier to stand. Nothing throws us off balance more than being taken by surprise. Knowing what is coming gives us the opportunity to prepare for the attack. Knowledge of the future is not, however, just a defensive benefit. If we take Jesus' teaching seriously our preparation will be more about facing and conquering than just surviving. Those who experience His return as a thief in the night are not reading the signs. They will not only be surprised, they will most likely become despondent, fearful and deceived.

It is incumbent on us as believers to know that even after mankind has given their authority to the evil one and turned their backs on God, He has not turned His back on us. And we should know that when the evil one, along with evil men, musters all of his most destructive, diabolical resources, our Savior is our still our Deliverer. He is able and willing to do for mankind what He wanted to do and probably would have done at any time we chose the Kingdom of God over the World's System. But we didn't trust God. We didn't heed His warnings. We didn't even pay attention to history. We (the human race) wanted the World's System to give us what only the Kingdom of God could provide.

After giving a warning to those who are in Jerusalem when persecution comes, He makes this very defining statement. *"For then there will be great tribulation, such as has not been since the beginning of the world until this time, no, nor ever shall be"* (Matthew 24:21). Later in the Book of Revelation the specifics of that tribulation are described. While there have been very obvious similarities to these tribulations in the past, none have ever fulfilled the complete biblical description of the last and greatest, world-wide tribulation. In order to understand what's going to happen we will review the players and how we got here.

When revealing the precise identity of the antichrist kingdom John said these words:

> *Here is the mind which has wisdom: The seven heads are seven mountains on which the woman sits. There are also seven kings. Five have fallen, one is, and the other has not yet come. And when he comes, he must continue a short time. The beast that was, and is not, is himself also the eighth, and is of the seven, and is going to perdition.* (Revelation 17:9-11)

This verse gives us an historic and prophetic combination that makes it impossible to confuse the antichrist religion and nation.

The Great Harlot rode on a beast with seven heads and ten horns. This shows a temporary dominance of the Harlot over the beast until the time when the beast destroys the Harlot. The ten horns were kings that had not, at the time of John's vision, received a kingdom (verse 12). Like the ten toes in Daniel's vision, these are ten kings that will all reign at one time, not consecutively (Daniel 2:41). Again this points to the fact that this prophecy has not yet been fulfilled. These were ten future kings that emerged from the seven heads (previous nations). The kings and their kingdoms are the source of the antichrist's power and authority. *"These are of one mind, and they will give their power and authority to the beast"* (verses 13-14). We are once again reminded it is not God who gives the antichrist his authority to destroy; it is the synergistic agreement of not only evil kings but also of entire nations committed to and believing for the same things. This will be the ultimate expression of man's secret (occult) powers attempting to overthrow and destroy what God loves.

The seven heads which shall comprise the ten last days kings arise from the seven nations which all have certain factors in common:

1. They have not only dominated the known world
2. They have all ruled over Israel
3. Each nation successively overthrew the previous nation
4. They had a distinct hatred for Jews and ultimately for Christians
5. Their spiritual heritage links back to Nimrod and Babylon

These previous five nations, which had all fallen by the time of the writing of Revelation, were Egypt, Assyria, Babylon, Persia and Greece.

The kingdom in power at the time John penned Revelation was Rome. Rome had a hatred for both Jews and Christians. Titus killed 1.1 million Jews when he invaded Jerusalem and enslaved more than 97,000.[i] Under Rome's dominion Christians were burned alive, fed to wild animals and murdered in the coliseum for entertainment. Their bodies were used to make torches. But the fierceness and brutality of Rome is only a type of what will be seen in the fulfillment of the final antichrist. It is clear that Rome cannot be the antichrist kingdom because there is a seventh kingdom that must surface, and it will be from that kingdom the antichrist emerges and reigns.

So the next kingdom was *"not yet."* It is essential that rather than jumping to conjecture or extrapolation we continue with the mind that has wisdom, that is, God's way for identifying the nation that will later emerge as the antichrist nation. *"The beast that was, and is not, is himself also the eighth, and is of the seven, and is going to perdition"* (17:11). This beast was "not yet," in other words, it could not be Titus of Rome because Titus of Rome was already in power. Some, however, believe it will be a resurrected Roman empire. Taking that position violates the scriptural explanation for identifying the antichrist

i Wars of the Jews, VI, ix, 3

and his kingdom. Before we can identify the eighth and final kingdom we must identify the seventh kingdom to overthrow its predecessor, rule over the previous territories and rule over Jerusalem. This seventh kingdom will become the eighth resurrected kingdom - the antichrist and his false religion.

Some, looking to the fact that Rome fell to the Germanic tribes in 410 AD, were able to extrapolate the doctrine of Hitler being the antichrist. Of course, others who focused on Rome predicted Mussolini was the antichrist. What they failed to consider was that the Roman Empire did not end with the fall of the Western Empire by the Germanic tribes. The capitol of Rome was moved to Constantinople which was overthrown by the Turks in 1453 AD. The Turks were made up of the Muslim caliphate.[ii] Germany never ruled over Jerusalem, but the Turks (Muslim caliphate) conquered Jerusalem as well as the Roman Empire. The Muslim caliphate was officially abolished in 1923. This qualifies the Ottoman Empire as the nation that was to come after Rome. The seventh nation from which the eighth, the antichrist nation, will emerge is the ancient Muslim caliphate.

ISIS fights under a black flag to fulfil the Islamic prophecy of an army carrying black flags that will invade Israel and bring forth the Mahdi (the antichrist).

At this very moment ISIS, Al Qaeda and a few other terrorist organizations are aggressively attempting to fulfil their Islamic prophecies by overthrowing all the nations of the Middle East and reestablishing the caliphate. ISIS fights under a black flag to fulfil the Islamic prophecy of an army carrying black flags that will invade Israel and bring forth the Mahdi (the antichrist). Some scholars say the insignia worn on the bandanas and armbands of the jihadist followers is the 666 sign. At this moment this so-called religion of peace which will bring forth the man of false peace, has nearly 400 terror groups responsible for 90% of all war and terrorism in the world. This does not include the thousands of cells in countries around the world that continually agitate, steal and kill to further its cause and to wreak havoc and destabilize the economy! These cells are not only ready to activate upon order of their leaders, they are being encouraged to wage their own independent jihad. We

ii A caliphate is a form of Islamic government led by a caliph —a person considered a political and religious successor to the prophet Muhammad under which all Muslim nations and people are ruled.

are seeing this happen in America and all over the world as individuals and small cells murder for the sake of murder. These atrocities are not just acceptable in their religion of hatred; they believe they will be eternally rewarded for their jihadist acts of violence.

For years nations of the world have catered to the demands of Islam. Some seeking to be politically correct, some because of oil or other economic considerations and many because of fear of reprisals have compromised the well-being of their own citizens. In some countries Sharia law is enforced even though it violates human rights and the laws of those countries. Muslims are treated as a minority and given special privileges while officials' hands seem to be tied in investigating their known terrorist connections and activities. Through the UN and other New World Order initiatives, news agencies and liberal universities the world interprets the constant attacks by radical groups against Israel as justified and honorable while any effort by Israel to protect itself is broadcast as an act of terrorism. The brutal beheadings of Christians and destruction of churches is overlooked. The seduction of the Great Harlot has bewitched the world; thus, she drinks a cup filled with the blood of martyrs (Revelation 17:6).

Make no mistake! The time will come when the caliph (Mahdi, antichrist) will call for a world-wide jihad by all Muslims.

Make no mistake! The time will come when the caliph (Mahdi, antichrist) will call for a world-wide jihad by all Muslims. A Muslim who believes the teaching of the Quran, follows the example of Muhammad, but especially believes failure to act will result in eternity in Hell will act. Many moderate Muslims will realize if they fail to act they will be targeted by jihadists just as surely as Jews and Christians are targeted. If, by that time, the leftist governments of the world have disarmed their citizens, mankind will be helpless against a well-armed, vicious army on a holy quest of religious fanaticism. But it will be the revelation of the wickedness of Islam that will open millions of Muslims to the truth about Jehovah and salvation through Jesus. While on one hand wickedness and violence will abound, on the other hand millions will turn to Jesus.

The United States, along with other governments, developed foreign policy that has facilitated the rise of ISIS and other extremist groups. The Middle Eastern nations we have supported and the ones we have neglected seem very clearly to be part of a deliberate plan to hand all of the Middle East over to the emerging caliphate. These are all signs that anyone who reads the Bible should see and understand. Jesus said this:

> *Now learn this parable from the fig tree: When its branch has already become tender and puts forth leaves, you know that summer is near. So you also, when you see all these things, know that it is near — at the doors! Assuredly, I say to you, this generation will by no means pass away till all these things take place. Heaven and earth will pass away, but My words will by no means pass away.* (Matthew 24:32-35)

Sadly, this simple parable has been twisted into something so far from its straight-forward message it has lost its meaning. Some groups take this logic: the fig tree represents Israel, so this passage is talking about when Israel was restored as a nation. Thus, the generation alive when Israel became a nation will not pass away before the end. While there may be some validity in such an interpretation that I do not see, I can tell you what I do see. Jesus is simply saying, just as surely as the budding leaves of a fig tree indicate summer is near, when all the signs begin to appear we too can know the end is near. This is not referring to the end of Jewish dominance of the Kingdom of God; it is a clear reference to the end of man's rule and the beginning of the rule of the Messiah on earth!

Why is this important and how can we prepare for it? As previously mentioned, concerning the two most prominent eschatological beliefs, if they become your hope they will prevent you from following Jesus' instructions. It is normal and acceptable to have an opinion about the end; however, that opinion cannot interfere with our diligent adherence to the words of Jesus. We must prepare our hearts and we must reach the world with the Gospel of the Kingdom.

A quick read of Islamic prophecies reveals that Muhammad took the Book of Revelation and flipped its meaning. Every Scripture the Bible applies to the antichrist, Muslims see as their caliph (Mahdi, 12th Imam - the Muslim messiah). The Scriptures that apply to the false prophet they apply to their version of Jesus who returns, works miracles, denies that he was ever crucified and denies he ever said he was the son of God. But because they reject the authenticity of the Book of Revelation they say all the Bible says about the antichrist are lies, that he is, in fact, the true messiah of the world. It is this belief about their savior, our antichrist, that drives them to a furious intent to bring about an end to the world.

The accuracy with which Muslim last days' prophecies will be fulfilled will seduce many Christians, Jews and unbelievers. Little will the biblically ignorant know, they are only accurate because they were copied from the Bible. The Luciferians have been masters at taking a biblical truth, proving its validity and then treating it as their revelation and proof of their legitimacy! This falls back to Paul's warning of those who use God's creation to seduce people to worship the creation instead of the Creator.

The Book of Revelation has lost validity in the life of most believers. It has been so mystified and twisted it seems impossible to understand and the two major eschatological doctrines make it even more irrelevant. One says it has already taken place and the other says it does not matter; we will all be forcibly raptured. The Book of Revelation is not that complicated when we do two simple things: interpret the Bible with the Bible and do not try to use current events to interpret the Bible. Do not be concerned about what you do not understand. If we follow Jesus' instructions for preparation for the end we will know what we need to know when we need to know it.

Jesus' teaching does not change when it comes to the end times. His words give us direction to face and conquer any tribulation. Everything He taught is 100% applicable 100% of the time. But the application of His teaching does become more essential to survival as we approach the end. There is probably not a more relevant time for this teaching.

> *But seek first the kingdom of God and His righteousness, and all these things shall be added to you. Therefore do not worry about tomorrow, for tomorrow will worry about its own things. Sufficient for the day is its own trouble* (Matthew 6:33-34).

Seeking the Kingdom today is far more important than worrying about the tribulations that may come tomorrow. The experience we develop in walking with God today will prepare us for walking with Him when our lives depend upon it.

Do not be amazed or perplexed as governments of the world become more illogical, permissive and ungodly. Don't be surprised as more countries make more allowance for jihadists and obvious Muslim propagandists. We must realize that for generations iniquity has led us to believe society is the blame for people's violent, irrational behavior. This anti-God philosophy was crucial in bringing us to this moment in history. In the name of social justice, society will be influenced to believe jihadists are only that way because of how their forefathers were treated by the crusaders. They will have us believe, as one US representative recently implied, if we just get them all jobs they will end the violence. Those who embrace socialistic philosophy, the young who have been seduced by the rubbish taught in universities and those who are so afraid of conflict they will do anything to appease this tidal wave of violence will go along with any plan that would appease jihadists. But the real problem is the fact that the nations of the world have been fed a steady diet of iniquity for generations. The world is ignorant of God's Word concerning human nature. Furthermore, we have been lied to concerning Islamic beliefs. We think our concessions will diminish their fervor to destroy Israel, Christianity, the US and then the world.

Do not be amazed or perplexed as governments of the world become more illogical, permissive and ungodly.

But we must turn our eyes to Jesus and His imminent return. We must find comfort in God's consistent historical model of deliverance for those who look to Him. We should envision and look forward to a world of true peace and righteousness. We should experience the comfort of the Holy Spirit in times of trouble and follow Jesus' admonition:

> *Let not your heart be troubled; you believe in God, believe also in Me. In My Father's house are many mansions; if it were not so, I would have told you. I go to prepare a place for you. And if I go and prepare a place for you, I will come again and receive you to Myself; that where I am, there you may be also. And where I go you know, and the way you know* (John 14:1-4).

APOCALYPSE

CHAPTER 41

READING THE SIGNS

Reading the signs isn't possible for a person who has already decided what the signs will be!

ONE THING THAT SEEMS TO MAKE IT DIFFICULT TO UNDERSTAND JESUS' TEACHING ABOUT THE END IS THE TENDENCY TO CONFUSE AND OVERLAP THE ACTIONS OF THE GREAT HARLOT AND THOSE OF THE TEN ANTICHRIST NATIONS. These entities are the two primary players in moving us to the end times but they both have very different, yet significant roles. If we confuse or overlap their roles in history we will not only complicate the signs of the end, we will make it so overwhelming that it is easier for people to simply ignore what is happening.

The Great Harlot, Mystery Babylon seems to seduce the entire world through trade, finance and economic systems (Revelation 18:3, 9-14)). She is the seducer of kings through whom she has influence over all the people of the world (Revelation 17:15). By her harlotry the kings of the earth reign and make policy. It could be that the Great Harlot, through the economic system, is the basis for the rationalization that seduces and blinds the kings (leaders) of the earth to allow the antichrist's rise to power.

Recently I heard the head of the International Monetary Fund (IMF) explain how striking the proposed nuclear deal with Iran will help global economy. There are few things that have happened in my life as obviously destructive to the world as allowing Iran to pursue nuclear power. They are the number one propagator and financier of jihadist terrorism. They have been more publically committed to the destruction of Israel and hatred for America than any other group. They have made their intention to bring forth the Mahdi (antichrist) clear for years. It is impossible that everyone in the US military, congress, the news media and the administration do not know Iran's agenda. These people are not stupid. But they are committed to a plan that will never be publically admitted until it is too late for America and the world. The world leaders who may not be complicit in the Luciferian agenda are so preoccupied and consumed with wealth, power and expansion they are blinded to the threat posed to the world.

US military, congress, the news media and the administration do not know Iran's agenda. These people are not stupid. But they are committed to a plan that will never be publically admitted until it is too late for America and the world.

Mystery Babylon is also the mother of all cults and occults. It is the spirit that gave birth to Nimrod and Semiramis which were the forerunners of all false doctrine, all false religion and all false Christs. Through the lies of the fallen angels perpetuated by the Nephilim, sustained by religion and advanced through secret societies every perversion of God's identity and nature has been integrated in the secular world and the religious doctrines of man. But *"greater is He who is in us than he who is in the world."* We may be outnumbered but we are not out-powered. We are the winners in the end time scenario. We must never lose sight that the end of the World's System is the beginning of God's system - the Kingdom of God!

Mystery Babylon sustained and inspired all iniquity among men and is probably the spirit of iniquity (lawlessness) mentioned by the Apostle Paul in 2 Thessalonians 2:7. The antichrist spirit was at work in Gnosticism which was addressed by the Apostle John in his first, second and third epistles. It is the same spirit of lawlessness which works in groups today that reject God's law, minimize the warning of the effects of sin and weave New Age philosophy throughout their biblical doctrines.

In these last days Mystery Babylon seems to be the power working through the New World Order attempting to overthrow and oppress the world through humanistic governments built around greed, deception and the concentration of wealth among the elite. Mystery Babylon seems to be the force (spirit) that works in Europe and the Americas while the true threat grows in the Middle East.

By combining the actions of these two demonic entities working together for the same cause, most of the Christian world still has its focus on Europe and Rome. This confusion, mixed with preconceived ideas, has most of the world considering the pope to be the false prophet, Catholicism the false religion and the European common market as the antichrist nations. Based on circumstance it would be easy to start with this idea and then attempt to superimpose it onto Scripture. It seems these entities and their actions are most certainly the work of the Great Harlot, but clearly do not fit the biblical description of the antichrist nations. It may even be the Church's tendency to focus on Catholicism and Europe that has captured our attention thereby blinding our eyes to the obvious that is happening in the Middle East.

Mystery Babylon seems to be the force (spirit) that works in Europe and the Americas while the true threat grows in the Middle East.

In reading the signs there are some factors that are so clear they are undeniable. Even if we are wrong about one or two of these prophesies we have enough irrefutable truth that it does not change the prognosis. The clarity of these factors once again brings us to the painful reality that had we been willing to accept the prophecies as they are written we could have seen all of this coming and we could have altered history. We may have even hastened the return of the Lord.

Daniel provides the clearest and easiest end time prophecies to understand. As we walk through these prophecies what we need to understand from the Book of Revelation becomes obvious and what we do not understand is not essential to preparation and survival.

Four of the five fallen nations John refers to are also mentioned in Daniel's prophecies. Then he flips through the prophetic pages of future history with an accuracy that is beyond comprehension. With those accurate prophecies we receive the model to understand the identity of the end time's nations.

Now we will take a quick look at some of Daniel's prophesies. In the Book of Daniel, chapter 2, Nebuchadnezzar dreams about a statue with each body part descending from the head being made of an inferior metal. Through the Holy Spirit Daniel interprets the dream to be the successive kingdoms that will come. The head of gold is Babylon, Media Persia is represented by the chest of silver, the loins of brass represent Greece, the legs of iron represent Rome, and the ten toes represent the ten last days' kings that will give their power to the antichrist. Finally, he saw a stone cut out without hands, meaning it was not the work of man. This stone destroyed all the kingdoms of man. Because Daniel was looking into the future from his specific time in history he did not identify Egypt or Assyria. They had already fallen and were not pertinent to the future. However, when John looked to the past he saw five kingdoms that had already fallen because he was looking all the way back to Egypt.

In Daniel, chapter 7, he sees four beasts rise up out of the earth giving him even more understanding of those kingdoms that would emerge. This as an expansion of what he saw in the vision of the statue. The beasts were a lion with eagle's wings, a bear with one side raised and three ribs in its mouth, a leopard with four wings and four heads, and a dreadful, terrible beast that subdued and destroyed. After these four he saw ten horns from which emerged a little horn. These are the ten last days' kings and their kingdoms. This little horn represents the antichrist. It says that before him three of the horns were plucked up by the roots. This seems to indicate that the first three nations he overthrows will be by force. Evidently the others will follow him by choice. This little horn was given eyes like a man and a mouth speaking pompous things, thus depicting that he is a man (the antichrist) communicating with the world. We have a tendency to interpret each end time prophecy as a separate individual event. Many of these prophecies are actually a different perspective on a previous prophecy.

After this little horn Daniel sees everything set for judgment and the coming of the Son of Man with the earthly establishment of the Kingdom of God. Once the antichrist appears everything is set for judgment. Many, in seeking to establish a philosophical concept of God's love, cannot grasp the idea of a judgment. This is the result of humanist love replacing God's definition of love. The argument sometimes goes like this. "Since Jesus died for the sins of the world, man cannot be judged of sin." There is not enough space to explain all the biblical contradictions embedded in this position, but suffice it to say, even after man's sins were paid for by Jesus and righteousness was offered as a free gift, many rejected God's righteousness and opted to trust in their own definitions of righteousness. In the Great White Throne Judgment people will be judged by their works because they rejected the free gift of righteousness through the blood of Jesus. This gives a whole new meaning to the concept of trampling underfoot the Son of God and counting the blood as nothing (Hebrews 10:29). We who accept Jesus as our righteousness will not participate in the Great White Throne Judgment. We do not stand before God on the basis of our works; we stand confidently before God because of the finished work of the Lord Jesus (Revelation 20:11)!

Once the antichrist appears everything is set for judgment.

Once again, Daniel not only saw the future, he saw the characteristics of each of the coming kingdoms, but this time we have the first mention of the antichrist that emerges from the ten last days' kingdoms. The details of Daniel's vision of history to come are so detailed that "scholars" refuse to accept it was the writings of one man. Rather than go into all the details of accuracy revealed in Daniel's vision we will jump ahead to his prophecies that reveal the most about the last days.

In chapter 9 we find Daniel studying the prophetic writings of Jeremiah in order to understand how much longer Judah would remain in captivity (verse 2). We see that Daniel's insights were inspired by his combination of prayer and studying the Word of God. In chapter 9, verse 24 the angel, Gabriel, comes to deliver the answer which Daniel seeks. He tells him 70 weeks, or as the original says, *"70 7's are determined on thy people to accomplish six specific goals."* It is interesting to note that not all of these goals were fulfilled by the beginning of the Church Age. This is a reference to seven periods of seven totaling 490 years.

> *Know therefore and understand, That from the going forth of the command To restore and build Jerusalem Until Messiah the Prince, There shall be seven weeks and sixty-two weeks; The street shall be built again, and the wall, Even in troublesome times.* (Daniel 9:25-27)

Daniel had been reading the scrolls of Jeremiah. As one who used God's Word to read the signs he realized the time was approaching for their captivity to be fulfilled. Since he prayed about years it only makes sense that God answered him in years; thus, each week or period of sevens is referring to a seven year period of time. From the decree to rebuild Jerusalem until its fulfillment was seven sevens or 49 years. This was not the edict of Cyrus. The edict of Cyrus was to rebuild the temple. This was the order given by Artaxertes. This was all done in the troubled times we can read of in Nehemiah. From this passage he knew how much longer it would be before Judah would return to Jerusalem.

"And after the sixty-two weeks Messiah shall be cut off, but not for Himself" (26). After the forty nine years of rebuilding Jerusalem there would be a period of sixty two sevens or 434 years until the Messiah would be cut off. This passage of Scripture is why Herod's occultist astrologers were looking for the sign of the Messiah which resulted in the death of all the male babies. Just like Nimrod was reading the signs for the coming of a deliverer (Abram) **those who opposed the coming Messiah were also reading the signs**. Jesus would have cost the priests their power and, moreover, their livelihood. The kings were afraid the Messiah would depose them. In general, Jesus was not the messiah they wanted, so they closed their eyes, twisted doctrine and did with His first appearing exactly what we are doing as the time approaches for His last appearing.

"And the people of the prince who is to come shall destroy the city and the sanctuary. The end of it shall be with a flood, And till the end of the war desolations are determined" (26). This obviously happened with Titus in AD 70; however, verse 27 did not happen with Titus and the destruction of the temple. This means that Titus did not fulfil the end time aspect of Daniel's prophecy.

> *Then he shall confirm a covenant with many for one week; But in the middle of the week He shall bring an end to sacrifice and offering And on the wing of abominations shall be one who makes desolate, Even until the consummation, which is determined, Is poured out on the desolate* (27).

Daniel's periods of sevens are clearly broken into three: seven sevens, sixty-two sevens, and the last seven which is a covenant made and broken. The only logical explanation of this verse (if we allow Scripture to interpret Scripture) is the several mentions of a 3½ year period in the Book of Revelation concerning the antichrist. *"And he was given a mouth speaking great things and blasphemies, and he was given authority to continue for forty-two months"* (13:5-6). There are several Scriptures that refer to a unique 3½ year period of time[i] all of which seem to point to the antichrist. These passages indicate that desolations will continue until the final judgment of the antichrist which begins when Jesus returns. Contrary to religious teaching, Jesus is not returning to destroy the world and punish all the wicked. Jesus is returning to save the world from the destruction of the wicked one. He will establish His Kingdom and for 1,000 years all of mankind will have the opportunity to see the righteousness of God implemented in Planet Earth.

From these passages of Scripture both Preterists (all end time prophecies have been fulfilled) and Futurists (pre-tribulation rapture) extrapolate what they consider to be absolute proof of their doctrinal positions. Again, we must conclude four things:

1. Both positions have at least part of the truth.
2. When different positions can be clearly established there is some key truth neither side is seeing.
3. We must also conclude some things are unclear and possibly not yet revealed.
4. The extremes each side defends are not essential facts or lessons we should be learning.

What I want us to see are the clear, simple signs Israel had concerning the coming of the Messiah, yet through their personal agendas, justified through religious agendas, they failed to recognize or receive their Messiah. I want us to see the accuracy of prophetic ministry, specifically so we can look at Daniel's next prophecy and get the intended benefit. I want us to follow Daniel's example of studying Scripture to gain understanding about relevant historical issues (Daniel 9:2). And last of all, if Daniel's seventieth week is the last seven years of history it gives us the clearest way to know when the seven year clock, the peace treaty made with Israel by the antichrist, the false peacemaker, is set.

Daniel, chapter 11, provides what I believe to be the most detailed prophetic preview of history ever written. We will not go through each element, but Daniel sees explicit details of the rise and fall of all nations he previously

---

i Daniel 7:25, 9:27, 12:1,7; Revelation 11:2-3, 12:6, 14, 13:5-7

saw through Nebuchadnezzar's dream and subsequently through his personal dreams and visions. He goes into detail about how the rulers will die and how their kingdom will be divided. He even describes the treachery of Cleopatra and the eventual Maccabean revolt. In verse 10 he begins to discuss Antiochus III and his descendants which leads to Antiochus Epiphanes. One incredibly important fact established by these Scriptures is that when the Bible talks of the King of the North it is referring to Syria. Likewise, the King of the South is, without a doubt, Egypt. This is one of those places we must allow Scripture to interpret Scripture.

Verse 35 takes us to the time of the end in a clear description of the antichrist. The events mentioned in these verses were not accomplished by Antiochus Epiphanes or subsequent conquerors. Given the detailed specifics of these prophecies it is unlikely he would suddenly get vague. The strange god of this evil oppressor mentioned in verse 39 could well be Allah, but the most important sign we should look for is found in verse 40 and following.

> *At the time of the end the king of the South shall attack him; and the king of the North shall come against him like a whirlwind, with chariots, horsemen, and with many ships; and he shall enter the countries, overwhelm them, and pass through. He shall also enter the Glorious Land, and many countries shall be overthrown; ...the land of Egypt shall not escape* (Daniel 11:40-42).

The conflict that finally consummates the beginning of the end will be between Egypt and Syria. This could be when the antichrist (little horn) plucks up the first three nations by force. It could be the subsequent treaty that facilitates the other seven nations giving their authority to him. The thing, however, that is so clear is the antichrist will come from the territory of ancient Syria which now comprises more than one country. This could be the war between the Sunnis and the Shiites that finally consolidates the Islamic world under the caliph.

So the final invasion of Israel is the fruit of internal conflict in the Muslim nations. This is completely logical considering the centuries old violent war between Shiites and Sunnis. Egypt is the nation that was nearly overtaken by the Muslim Brotherhood in the Arab Spring, but the moderates recaptured their country and ousted the Muslim Brotherhood. They have maintained peace with Israel and the US for years which, according to jihadists, is reason for their annihilation. Egypt has even sought to protect its Christian population.

Verses 44 and 45 go on to tell us:

> *But news from the east and the north shall trouble him; therefore he shall go out with great fury to destroy and annihilate many. And he shall plant the tents of his palace between the seas and the glorious holy mountain; yet he shall come to his end, and no one will help him.*

At this point Jerusalem becomes the head of the antichrist governmental base, the false prophet will come on the scene and world-wide dominance and worship will be required by the antichrist. There is much speculation about the news from the North and East. That is not a crucial sign we need to understand to identify the antichrist; it will become obvious when it happens.

Here are events we know will happen, but this is not necessarily the order.

- There will be wars, famine and pestilence.
- A caliphate will be established with the head of it claiming to be the Mahdi, caliph (antichrist).
- The Great Harlot will be destroyed (possibly the world economy).
- The Islamic Jesus will appear working miracles and forcing the world to worship the antichrist (the false prophet).
- The antichrist will emerge from Old Syria.
- There will be war in the Middle East, especially Egypt and Syria, resulting in the invasion of Israel.
- The antichrist will bring peace to the Middle East through a seven year treaty.
- The king of Syria will sweep down through Israel because of conflict with Egypt.
- The Gospel of the Kingdom will be preached unto the ends of the earth.
- The antichrist will declare himself to be God in the dome of the rock.
- Jesus will return and deliver the world from the antichrist.

Jesus made it clear that after the Gospel of the Kingdom is preached to all nations the end will come. The "end" is the end of man's rule on earth and the beginning of Jesus' personal rule as Lord and King over all the nations of the world.

The tribulation of the antichrist, which will last for 3½ years, is met with the wrath of God against the antichrist and his followers.

There are many Christians who believe all the horrible things that occur on Planet Earth are the product of God's wrath for the sins of mankind. Those teachings are based on legalism and religion. The tribulation of the antichrist, which will last for 3½ years, is met with the wrath of God against the antichrist and his followers; **but we are delivered from wrath!** We will not be punished by God for the sins of the wicked. Unless we accept the Covenant of Peace we have in Jesus we will, at best, be able to endure whatever part of this we must endure. Those whose hearts are established in the Covenant of Peace and know their God will overcome and do great exploits. I encourage you to read my book, *The Gospel of Peace* and free yourself of all guilt, condemnation and negative concepts of God. Establish your heart in the Covenant of Peace and live your most fruitful life at a time when the world needs us most!

What our protection and deliverance means and what that will look like I cannot say, but the preparation Jesus instructed is: Do not allow yourself to be deceived, do not give in to fear, watch and pray, and be about the Father's business. This is the time that Daniel says those who win souls are wise and shall shine like the stars, but he also says the book will be closed until the time of the end. In other words, many things will not be understood until they occur (Daniel 12:1-4). But be assured, God can be trusted and those who listen to God will read the signs and recognize what to do as these apocalyptic events occur. This we can trust:

> *...for He [God] Himself has said, I will not in any way fail you nor give you up nor leave you without support. [I will] not, [I will] not, [I will] not in any degree leave you helpless nor forsake nor let [you] down (relax My hold on you)! [Assuredly not!]* (Hebrews13:5, AMP).

APOCALYPSE

CHAPTER 42

WAR WITH THE LAMB

The final battle reveals the utter weakness of the wicked one against God and His children!

TOO MUCH OF OUR CONVERSATION AND FOCUS OF ESCHATOLOGY IS CENTERED AROUND THE GROWTH OF DARKNESS AND EVIL. It is absolutely necessary for us to be aware of these factors, but it is a gross error to focus on the evil one and fail to bring it back into perspective by focusing on the victorious return of our Lord, Savior and Deliverer.

At the end of the eternal struggle it all comes down to a war Satan knows he can't win; thus, the source of his great fury. This will be the ultimate destruction to those who have determined to ally with him against Jehovah and His followers, those who loved lawlessness, the lust of the flesh and power.

> *These will make war with the Lamb, and the Lamb will overcome them, for He is Lord of lords and King of kings; and those who are with Him are called, chosen, and faithful* (Revelation 17:9).

If we meet Him in the air prior to this war we may be the ones who return with Him to make war against the beast. We know that after this victory we will rule and reign with Him!

Armed with an eternal mind-set, the believer knows that no matter what happens on earth, and even though it may appear for a brief moment that the dragon will win, he will not! Patience is the ability to stand under pressure and not waver. It is the secret weapon of overcomers. Because we look at the world through an eternal awareness our hope is greater than any immediate threat. We don't flip-flop and shift emotions or lose confidence with every new challenge. It is essential that we have a very clear picture of the outcome of this final great struggle. *"If anyone has an ear, let him hear. He who leads into captivity shall go into captivity; he who kills with the sword must be killed with the sword. Here is the patience and the faith of the saints"* (Revelation 13:9-11). In the end all the wicked one has ever imposed on mankind will be revisited 100 fold!

Among the eschatological doctrines there are some who believe mankind will establish God's Kingdom on earth and deliver it to the Lord Jesus. In this theological concept "the end" Jesus spoke of was the end of the Jewish Age and the beginning of the Church Age. This would mean the tribulation has already occurred and the antichrist (Titus) has already been manifested. Thus, all end time prophesies are fulfilled. As much as I would like to believe that, it is a scriptural impossibility.

Jesus said,

> *Immediately after the tribulation of those days the sun will be darkened, and the moon will not give its light; the stars will fall from heaven, and the powers of the heavens will be shaken. Then the sign of the Son of Man will appear in heaven, and then all the tribes of the earth will mourn, and they will see the Son of Man coming on the clouds of heaven with power and great glory. And He will send His angels with a great sound of a trumpet, and they will gather together His elect from the four winds, from one end of heaven to the other.* (Matthew 24:29-31).

This did not happen immediately after the persecution of Titus. Furthermore, Titus never fulfilled all the prophecies concerning the antichrist.

By AD 50 there were erroneous teachings that Jesus had already returned. In 2 Thessalonians Paul warned:

> *Now, brethren, concerning the coming of our Lord Jesus Christ and our gathering together to Him, we ask you, not to be soon shaken in mind or troubled, either by spirit or by word or by letter, as if from us, as though the day of Christ had come. Let no one deceive you by any means; for that Day will not come unless the falling away comes first, and the man of sin is revealed, the son of perdition, who opposes and exalts himself above all that is called God or that is worshiped, so that he sits as God in the temple of God, showing himself that he is God* (1-4). *For the mystery of lawlessness is already at work; only He who now restrains will do so until He is taken out of the way. And then the lawless one will be revealed, whom the Lord will consume with the breath of His mouth and destroy with the brightness of His coming. The coming of the lawless one is according to the working of Satan, with all power, signs, and lying wonders, and with all unrighteous deception.* (7-10)

There are things that Paul says must happen before the return of Jesus. First there is a *"gathering together to Him"* that occurs before the coming of the Lord. The pre-tribulation rapture theology teaches that this happens almost simultaneous with the manifestation of the antichrist.

Second, there is the *"falling away."* This falling away isn't just a backslidden Church; it is a world that is turning to a false religion and a false god – *"the man of sin revealed."* Since Titus did not meet all the requirements for the antichrist Jesus did not personally return to defeat him, the believers were not gathered to Him and the judgment of God did not immediately occur, we know the man of sin has not been revealed and Jesus has not yet returned.

Among the eschatological doctrines there are some who believe mankind will establish God's Kingdom on earth and deliver it to the Lord Jesus.

Neither Titus nor anyone else *"sat in the temple as God,"* and worked *"signs, lying wonders, and with unrighteous deception."* And last of all, Titus nor anyone else has been consumed with the *"breath of His mouth and destroy(ed) with the brightness of His coming"!* When Jesus returns every eye will see Him. It will be like lightning from the east to the west. This will not be a hidden event known only to the Church.

While I strongly disagree with many points of Preterist doctrine I feel it is probably a safer misunderstanding than the Futurist who is convinced of a forced pre-tribulation rapture. This escapism mentality will be devastating for those who do nothing to prepare their heart. Because of their beliefs the Preterists will at least have a compelling to be about the Father's business. However, like most polarizing doctrines, the truth probably lies somewhere in the middle of these two extremes.

> There are things that Paul says must happen before the return of Jesus. First there is a *"gathering together to Him"* that occurs before the coming of the Lord. Second, there is the *"falling away."*

Jesus' teaching about preparing for the end revolves around two main factors: being open and sensitive to the Holy Spirit and His leading, and being about the Father's business. We should be winning the lost, making disciples and serving the brethren. I personally believe this renewed urgency to preach the Gospel of the Kingdom to the ends of the earth will play a role in hastening the return of the Lord.[i] The Apostle Peter tells us we can hasten, urge or speed this day coming, but he says this will be done by those who are looking for the promise of a New Heaven and a New Earth. The great end time revival will be coupled with a renewed eternal awareness. Believers who read and understand the signs will passionately serve mankind with the gospel. Believers in great numbers will finally understand what it means to live for the King and His Kingdom.

---

i 2 Peter 3:11-13,herefore, since all these things will be dissolved, what manner of persons ought you to be in holy conduct and godliness, 12 looking for and hastening the coming of the day of God, because of which the heavens will be dissolved, being on fire, and the elements will melt with fervent heat? 13 Nevertheless we, according to His promise, look for new heavens and a new earth in which righteousness dwells.

As I have previously stated, up until the time of the tribulation the Church has been so immersed in the world's way of thinking it had no intention of hastening the return of the Lord. Part of the problem was we didn't know how to be ***in*** the world but not ***of*** the world. We, like Lot, were vexed by this corrupt world. Another part of the problem is we thought we could change the world. We thought if the right laws were passed or if the right politicians were in office, or if… or if… or if… But the truth is the world has never been redeemable. It has been loosely manageable but never redeemable by man. Individuals are redeemable but the world or individual nations are not.

The hope of the Church taking over the world is a vain illusion. As long as there are wicked people anywhere in the process, the process becomes wicked. As long as believers cling to the same values as the ungodly the process will be corrupted. The rise of the wicked one will open our eyes to two startling, overly-obvious realities: first and foremost, we need to focus on making disciples of individuals. We need to lead people into a trust and dependency on the Lord Jesus like the world has never seen. Second, we need Jesus to return to rule in true righteousness and justice. Man needs to see the world as God intended.

Jesus made this statement about the end: *"And unless those days were shortened, no flesh would be saved; but for the elect's sake those days will be shortened"* (Matthew 24:22). I have pondered that statement thousands of times and I have come to believe that at least one factor in those days being shortened will be the body of Christ using its faith and authority to hasten the return of the Lord Jesus. At some point the cry, "Come quickly, Lord Jesus," will become our heart's song. What begins as a desperate plea to escape the tribulations of the antichrist will turn into a true joyous anticipation of seeing His righteousness and justice. It will be the call of the bride to the Bridegroom!

We are called to be like Jesus, not just imitate Him, but be like Him from our heart.

When we see the utter collapse of this World's System and when it is revealed for what it has always been, we will love the truth of God's Word. We are called to be like Jesus, not just imitate Him, but be like Him from our heart.

Jesus loved righteousness and hated iniquity. The day will come when we finally see that His every commandment was a divine prescription for a better life. What we once turned to legalism will be the way we want to live because we love and trust God. We will love people based on His Word instead of our humanistic philosophies and social justice. *"Here is the patience of the saints; here are those who keep the commandments of God and the faith of Jesus"* (Revelation 14:12). These are not legalists; these are people who finally trust God's love and consider His wisdom to be precious!

From the very beginning of God revealing the end to men it has been clear that Jesus Himself would win the battle.[ii] All prophecies of the Lord's victory are just that: the Lord's Victory! Not man's victory! Daniel saw a stone cut without hands that would crush the feet of the image that represented the ten last days' kings. The fact that it is without hands indicates it is not man's doing. Man will get no glory for this final victory. Revelation says it like this:

> *Now out of His mouth goes a sharp sword, that with it He should strike the nations. And He Himself will rule them with a rod of iron. He Himself treads the winepress of the fierceness and wrath of Almighty God.* (Revelation 19:15-16)

Jesus Himself is our Hope!

> *And I saw the beast, the kings of the earth, and their armies, gathered together to make war against Him who sat on the horse and against His army. Then the beast was captured, and with him the false prophet who worked signs in his presence, by which he deceived those who received the mark of the beast and those who worshiped his image. These two were cast alive into the lake of fire burning with brimstone. And the rest were killed with the sword which proceeded from the mouth of Him who sat on the horse. And all the birds were filled with their flesh.* (Revelation 19:19-21)

---

ii Daniel 2:44-45, "And in the days of these kings the God of heaven will set up a kingdom which shall never be destroyed; and the kingdom shall not be left to other people; it shall break in pieces and consume all these kingdoms, and it shall stand forever. 45 Inasmuch as you saw that the stone was cut out of the mountain without hands, and that it broke in pieces the iron, the bronze, the clay, the silver, and the gold — the great God has made known to the king what will come to pass after this. The dream is certain, and its interpretation is sure."

While there are many factors about this that I do not see clearly, I do know that believers who have been gathered together unto the Lord will come with Him as His army. We will be transformed, supernatural beings who will be impervious to death.[iii] After we participate in the annihilation of the anti-christ, the false prophet and his armies we will rule with Jesus during the 1,000-year reign of righteousness.[iv]

We can hasten the day of the Lord now. We do not have to wait until things become so unbearable that we finally surrender our grip on the world. Live like someone who is preparing to enter eternity. Love people like their eternal soul depends on it… it does! Keep oil in your lamp now through an intimate, prayerful, meditative connection to Jesus in your heart. Be about the Father's business now! Spend time meditating and ponder living in a new world with no death, no sickness, no pain and not even one tear. Get a clear mental picture of Jesus defeating the evil one and casting him into the bottomless pit. Create such a sense of a victorious eternity that your connection to this world fades away.

Prepare yourself to participate in the world's greatest praise gathering to our Lord. We will finally see why His mission to earth was so important. Having seen the intention of Lucifer upon men we will love salvation more than we ever imaged. We will sing this song of praise:

> *Alleluia! Salvation and glory and honor and power belong to the Lord our God! For true and righteous are His judgments, because He has judged the great harlot who corrupted the earth with her fornication.* (Revelation 19:1-2)
>
> *Alleluia! For the Lord God Omnipotent reigns! Let us be glad and rejoice and give Him glory, for the marriage of the Lamb has come, and His wife has made herself ready.* (6-7)

As a matter of fact, you can begin this joyous event now. The Bible says we will eventually look at a defeated Lucifer and question, *"Is this who made the*

---

iii Joel 2:1-32

iv Revelation 20:5-6, This is the first resurrection. 6 Blessed and holy is he who has part in the first resurrection. Over such the second death has no power, but they shall be priests of God and of Christ, and shall reign with Him a thousand years.

earth tremble?"[v] In other words, when we see him as he is we will be amazed that we ever feared him. The more you see and experience Jesus' absolute victory over the wicked one, the more you will live in victory over him today!

Live like someone who is preparing to enter eternity. Love people like their eternal soul depends on it… it does!

We don't have to wait until the final battle to see the truth. Lucifer's defeat and expulsion from Heaven is a victory of the past. If we embrace what Jesus really did at the cross we can see Satan as he is now: a defeated, rebellious, foolish angel. You may want to consider my book, *Satan Unmasked* to get a more scriptural perspective of the victory that is already yours in Christ.

v Isaiah 14:16, They that see thee shall narrowly look upon thee, and consider thee, saying, Is this the man that made the earth to tremble, that did shake kingdoms;

CHAPTER 43

A THIEF OR A LIGHTNING BOLT?

The condition of my heart determines if Jesus' return will be as a thief or as lightning flashing!

THERE ARE TWO COMPLETELY OPPOSING TRUTHS CONCERNING THE PERSONAL RETURN OF THE LORD JESUS. In one version His return is as a thief in the night and the other says He will come with great announcement. In the latter, it is described as lightning from the east to the west and the great sound of the trumpet of the Lord. In fact, Jesus taught His return will be so clearly realized no one will be deceived if they wait for this event.

The mood of the world will be one that is inattentive and unaware. In all likelihood the factors that cause tribulation will also cause men to be in pursuit of any pleasure to distract them from the events of the world; therefore, many will not recognize the obvious as it unfolds. Jesus compares the mind-set of the people with those before the Flood in the days of Noah. The Flood was not a mere act of wrathful judgment of mankind; it was the destruction of the Nephilim who posed an eternal threat to mankind. For those who listened and obeyed the Flood was salvation from the cannibalistic murderers seeking to dominate and destroy mankind. Likewise, the return of Jesus and the war between the antichrist and his armies is not God judging the world; it is God saving the world. He will do the one thing that mankind could never do, bring the perfect balance of love, power and justice. There will be no corrupt agenda, just pure love for His people who have suffered since the beginning under the deception of the wicked one and his followers.

Jesus describes the awareness of those immersed in the World's System with these words. *"But as the days of Noah were, so also will the coming of the Son of Man be"* (Matthew 24:37). Noah and Enoch had warned the world of the Flood for hundreds of years. In fact, Enoch named his son "Methuselah" which means "when he is gone it shall come." Everything about Enoch's life was a message calling people to the awareness of what would happen to the world. Everyone heard the message about the coming flood and could have prepared. The Book of Enoch tells us that many heard and "crossed over" in peaceful death and avoided the coming tragedy. In their hearts they must have stayed open to the voice of God!

God wanted men to repent, to change their mind, prepare and escape what was coming. As Peter reminds us, God is not slack in what He warns through prophecy.

Methuselah lived longer than any other person to ever live, which indicated God's long-suffering and patience. God wanted men to repent, to change their mind, prepare and escape what was coming. As Peter reminds us, God is not slack in what He warns through prophecy. He is patient and merciful! Every preacher that is paying attention and knows what to look for is, to some level, warning or preparing his listeners for the days that have come upon us. Some are preaching more about the end times and others are acutely aware of how current events fit into end time prophecy and continually sound the trumpet of warning. Others are consumed with the passion to evangelize the world. Each leader is using his gifting and skills in the way God is leading him or her, but the key is this: the Church is being warned. There are even secular news and talk radio hosts warning of a coming apocalypse. Those who are not hearing this message in church are being prepared by believers who are winning them to Jesus and helping them on their journey of personal discipleship.

Many, however, are oblivious to what is going on in the world. Among believers who refuse to listen it may be because of the normalcy bias. Among the lost it is clearly ignorance or unbelief. We cannot presume to judge the reasoning, but just as it was in the days of Noah, people are going about their daily business getting married, starting families and businesses, etc. In other words, people will live with no awareness of what is happening in the world, of the imminent return of our Lord, or what they should be doing to prepare unless they are warned by believers.

As trouble in the world grows, knowledgeable believers will be the only ones who have the answers to what is happening. Those who preach these events as God's wrath being poured out on the world will reach some but will turn many away. Four times in the Book of Revelation when the antichrist followers are experiencing the plagues and hardships of the world *"they repented not."* It is not the wrath of God that brings people to repentance; it is the goodness of God (Romans 2:4). Wrath is not the core nature of God; love, mercy, faithfulness and patience reveal more about His nature. After all, when you get to the most holy place man can reach with God you don't find the judgment seat, you find the mercy seat! Knowledgeable witnesses will help people understand how the world got where it is and what God offers as the solution.

It is not the wrath of God that brings people to repentance; it is the goodness of God (Romans 2:4).

As believers the only antidote to unawareness is to *"watch and pray."* This is the single solution Jesus offers concerning the timing of the most monumental event to occur on Planet Earth until now. There are no other solutions. This is not the kind of religious praying where one talks endlessly and thinks for his many words he will be heard (Matthew 6:7). This is where we will return to a more biblical pattern of prayer and intercession: pray, wait, listen and obey. As part of the family we are the true elite who have personal instructions and preparation.

There is no one-size-fits-all plan. Each person should pray and follow what they feel God is leading them to do. The country, state and city where you live and what God is leading you to do to help others are all variables. Where God will lead you to go for protection may be completely different than where He leads me. You may have skills and gifting He wants to use in some way that is completely different than what I will be called upon to do. Unlike the Luciferian Religionist approach that tries to impose one formula for all, each person will need to seek and know God for themselves. One variable we must consider is whether or not we are among those who will be eliminated first. Certain people will become "high-value targets" for a world that is seeking to eliminate all knowledge of and the security Jesus brings. This means preachers of the gospel will be among the most threatening to the Luciferian plan. There are thousands of variables in how and what God will lead each individual to do. In many countries, when Communism or Islam came to power, ministers of the gospel were among the first murdered or imprisoned. There is talk among certain mind-sets that says people who disagree with or even question global warming should be imprisoned or put to death. The Progressives and elitists have long stated that the masses do not deserve the air they breathe and should be "mercifully" eliminated. If they are seeking the legal means to kill us for disagreeing or even questioning their social and political views now, what do you think will happen when governments are required to and rewarded for killing Christians and Jews? It will be like the Romans who blamed and murdered Christians for enraging the gods and causing chaos to come upon Rome. They will believe they are doing God a service to kill us. Our survival will not depend on a brilliant master plan, but on a heart that is hearing and following the voice of God!

We must remind ourselves that everything Jesus said about preparation for the end revolves around our sensitivity to the Holy Spirit and our willingness to reach and serve others.

- *Watch therefore, for you do not know what hour your Lord is coming. Therefore you also be ready, for the Son of Man is coming at an hour you do not expect* (Matthew 24:42, 44).
- *But if that evil servant says in his heart, 'My master is delaying his coming,' and begins to beat his fellow servants, and to eat and drink with the drunkards, the master of that servant will come on a day when he is not looking for him and at an hour that he is not aware of, and will cut him in two and appoint him his portion with the hypocrites. There shall be weeping and gnashing of teeth* (Matthew 48-51).
- *And the foolish (virgins) said to the wise, 'Give us some of your oil, for our lamps are going out. "Watch therefore, for you know neither the day nor the hour in which the Son of Man is coming"* (Matthew 25:8, 13).
- *"But his lord answered and said to him (the one who did nothing with his talent), 'You wicked and lazy servant, you knew that I reap where I have not sown, and gather where I have not scattered seed.So you ought to have deposited my money with the bankers, and at my coming I would*

have received back my own with interest. So take the talent from him, and give it to him who has ten talents (Matthew 25:26-28).

- *I was naked and you clothed Me; I was sick and you visited Me; I was in prison and you came to Me* (Matthew 25:36).

There has been serious theological debate among many about the meanings of these warnings as it relates to the eternal security of the believer. Many, seeking to validate their theology, simply reject Jesus' warnings as teachings of the law which do not apply to us. But to reject Jesus' teaching simply because we do not know how to reconcile it with our theology (or for any reason) is tantamount to choosing lawlessness. If Jesus is our Lord we must follow His teaching. One can apply this legalistically or as a disciple who accepts the seriousness and importance of anything with such strong warnings. It comes back to a systemic flaw in the thinking of those who have no intention of being a disciple. Instead of obeying and following the Word of God, they seek to validate and thereby find security in their own doctrine. However one tries to explain the warnings away, they are still warnings about what we should be doing to reach and serve others.

This brings us to the question of protection for the believer during these hard times. There are some things we know about God's protection. We should comfort ourselves with these absolute truths without attempting to stretch them into our preferences. Here is what we know for sure:

We are delivered from God's wrath.

- The last 3 ½ years of tribulation is the wrath of God; therefore, we know that wrath will not be poured upon us, we will either be protected or delivered.
- *For God did not appoint us to wrath, but to obtain salvation through our Lord Jesus Christ, 10 who died for us, that whether we wake or sleep, we should live together with Him* (1 Thessalonians 5:9-10).
- …Jesus who delivers us from the wrath to come (1 Thessalonians 1:10).
    - *Much more then, having now been justified by His blood, we shall be saved from wrath through Him* (Romans 5:9).

From these and dozens of other Scriptures we should find comfort in the fact that we are in Christ and we are delivered from the wrath of God. It only stands to reason that when He does pour out His wrath He will find a way to protect and deliver His children.

We also know there will be a gathering together of believers. We know we will meet Him in the air. Many details about this may be unclear, but the fact that it is going to happen is abundantly obvious.

- *Now, brethren, concerning the coming of our Lord Jesus Christ and our gathering together to Him* (2 Thessalonians 2:1).
- *And He will send His angels with a great sound of a trumpet, and they will gather together His elect from the four winds, from one end of heaven to the other* (Matthew 24:31).
- *For the Lord Himself will descend from heaven with a shout, with the voice of an archangel, and with the trumpet of God. And the dead in Christ will rise first. Then we who are alive and remain shall be caught up together with them in the clouds to meet the Lord in the air. And thus we shall always be with the Lord. Therefore comfort one another with these words* (1 Thessalonians 4:16-18).
- *Behold, I tell you a mystery: We shall not all sleep, but we shall all be changed —in a moment, in the twinkling of an eye, at the last trumpet. For the trumpet will sound, and the dead will be raised incorruptible, and we shall be changed* (1 Corinthians 15:51-52).

As believers we should be like the five wise virgins. They had oil in their lamps and they were ready to go the moment they heard the call of the bridegroom.

As believers we should be like the five wise virgins. They had oil in their lamps and they were ready to go the moment they heard the call of the bridegroom. When Israel was in Egypt they had become enslaved to Pharaoh. Egypt has typically been seen as a "type" of the world. God sought to free His people, but Pharaoh would not listen to Moses. The plagues that God poured on Egypt were the instrument He used to deliver His people.

The children of Israel would be protected from the plagues on Egypt if they trusted and obeyed God. They were to sacrifice a lamb and sprinkle the blood on the door posts. When the angel of death came to Egypt he would see the blood and "pass over" the children of Israel. The Passover is another clear historical event where God delivered His people from wrath. But it is important to notice they had to hear and obey.

The next day they were delivered from the Egyptians. They made bread but were not allowed to put leaven in the bread. When they left Egypt they carried their unleavened bread. The feast of unleavened bread celebrates this deliverance from Egypt. Like all the feasts, it had many messages that conveyed God's eternal truths; however, one of the most interesting messages of unleavened bread is the fact that they were delivered from Egypt (the world) so quickly they didn't even have time to put leaven in their bread.

The Passover is another clear historical event where God delivered His people from wrath. But it is important to notice they had to hear and obey.

From Passover and unleavened bread I see three powerful truths. I see that God's deliverance is not forced upon us. We must trust and obey what God says. I also see that we are not subject to God's wrath, He will protect us. Last, but by no means least, I see that our deliverance from this world will be instantaneous. It will happen so quickly all will be amazed.

Another certainty of which we can be sure is when the Lord comes He will come with His army of believers.

- *I have commanded My sanctified ones; I have also called My mighty ones for My anger — Those who rejoice in My exaltation* (Isaiah 13:3,).
- *The Lord of hosts musters The army for battle* (Isaiah 13:4).
- *The Lord gives voice before His army, For His camp is very great; For strong is the One who executes His word. For the day of the Lord is great and very terrible; Who can endure it* (Joel 2:11)?
- *Thus the Lord my God will come, And all the saints with You* (Zechariah 14:5).

This army will be made of the resurrected and probably the transformed believers who have met Him in the air. The very people the Harlot and the Beast persecuted and murdered will execute justice on him and his followers.

The previously listed facts are supported by far more Scriptures than those listed above, but here is the point: our faith is in what we know, not in what we do not know. When it comes to end time events a combination of many religious teachings coupled with our own fears can push us toward our private interpretation.

There should be ample comfort in the words of Jesus and in these Scriptures. The greatest comfort should come from the realization that the tribulation is not God's fury on Planet Earth.

> We should be prepared to be here another thousand years, but live as if He is returning tomorrow; it is perspective.

There have been many legalistic extrapolations presenting the idea that God's wrath will be poured out based on the world violating the law, not allowing the land to rest and many other Old Covenant stipulations; but we seem to forget we are not under the Old Covenant! While those things may be spiritual factors in the overall plan the Luciferians used to destroy the world, they lead us back to the idea that the tribulation is God's wrath. The first 3½ years of the tribulation is the tribulation of the antichrist. The last 3½ years is the wrath of God against the antichrist and his followers. It is literally God's deliverance for those who remain. WE ARE DELIVERED FROM GOD'S WRATH BECAUSE WE ARE IN JESUS! If you lose this reality you will struggle to endure until the end, nevermind living as an overcomer.

The word "rapture" comes from the phrase "caught up" in 1 Thessalonians 4:17. There is no doubt there will be a catching away of believers to meet the Lord Jesus in the air; however, none of these Scriptures specifically explain or pinpoint the exact time of the rapture. There are some truths we can safely deduce, but I think it is unwise to put my hope for the future in something about which the Scripture is so unclear.

The idea of God delivering believers certainly does have precedence. God delivered Enoch by supernaturally transporting him from one realm to another. *"And Enoch walked with God; and he was not, for God took him"* (Genesis 5:24). Lot is another example of a believer being delivered before God's wrath is poured out (2 Peter 2:7). Then we have individual cases of deliverance with the prophets of old. But in all of these instances I see one common denominator: personal response to God's prompting.

Enoch walked with God. He had an intimate relationship with God. He responded to God's call to cross over. God sent angels to deliver Lot who barely escaped, primarily because he had become vexed with the sins of the city. We have Moses who went up on a mountain and viewed the Promised Land but never crossed over. Like Enoch, it seems he was transported. But Moses didn't resist, he didn't insist on saving his life. He heard and he obeyed!

When speaking about that day there is usually a warning about being clear-minded, not being overtaken with the cares of life and keeping oil in our lamp. It makes me wonder if there will be an event where God calls and those who harken are transported. After all, we have no precedence for God forcibly taking anyone. The idea of hearkening to God's call is congruent with every example in the Old Testament. And, it makes Jesus' teaching about our hearts being prepared, watching and praying and all the other types of listening relevant. For me the most important question that needs to be answered concerning the rapture is not when it will occur. Instead, the most import question is, "Am I listening to the voice of the Lord? Will I hear and will I hearken?"

For me the most important question that needs to be answered concerning the rapture is not when it will occur. Instead, the most import question is, "Am I listening to the voice of the Lord? Will I hear and will I hearken?"

In Luke 21:36 Jesus says, *"Watch therefore, and pray always that you may be counted worthy to escape all these things that will come to pass, and to stand before the Son of Man."* At first glance this sounds like a works statement but we know that cannot be the case. We understand this a little more correctly when we look closer at the phrase *"counted worthy."* It seems a better translation would be, "to be strong enough to prevail."[i] *We must be strong in the Lord*

---

i Worthy: to be strong to another's detriment, to prevail against; to be superior in strength; to overpower:(from Thayer's Greek Lexicon, PC Study Bible formatted Electronic Database. Copyright © 2006 by Biblesoft, Inc. All rights reserved.)

and the power of His might, strong in faith, and strong in grace! [ii] Those who are strong and will do great exploits are the ones who know, or if we put it in the present tense, "are knowing" (experiencing) their God. Regardless of the timing, we want to prevail in our confidence in God. We want to be ready when we hear that still, small voice that says, *"Come away my love I'm waiting"* (Song of Solomon 2:10-13).

We have no clear-cut evidence of a pre-tribulation rapture but it is certainly a possibility. We have types and possibilities, but these types are more about deliverance from the wrath of God and are dependent on the believer's response. So there is an equal possibility of rapture at the 3½ year mark when God's wrath begins. My only reason for bringing this out is so you will not become distraught. The key is to not put all of your hopes in a specific time, the key is to do what Jesus taught, watch and pray, prepare your heart and be ready to go at a moment's notice.

Some have put forth an interesting possibility of what they call "firstfruits rapture." 1 Corinthians15:23-26, when making reference to the gathering unto Him says:

> *But each one in his own order: Christ the firstfruits, afterward those who are Christ's at His coming. Then comes the end, when He delivers the kingdom to God the Father, when He puts an end to all rule and all authority and power. For He must reign till He has put all enemies under His feet. The last enemy that will be destroyed is death.*

There is no punctuation in the original language so the question that begs an answer is: "Is this saying Christ, then the firstfruits, and afterward those who are alive at His coming?" If this is the case this references two different raptures. Or, is this identifying Christ as the firstfruits and then those that are alive at His coming? There is a reference to firstfruits in Revelation 14:4. The term firstfruits was used in the Old Testament concerning that which

---

ii 2 Timothy 2:1-2, You therefore, my son, be strong in the grace that is in Christ Jesus.
Ephesians 6:10, Finally, my brethren, be strong in the Lord and in the power of His might.
1 Corinthians 16:13-14, Watch, stand fast in the faith, be brave, be strong. 14 Let all that you do be done with love.

belonged to God first. The idea of all offerings was that what we give to God should be before anything else.

Maybe we need to develop a heart to a firstfruits offering to the Father. In other words, we should be the ones who, before anything, prepare ourselves to serve mankind in the gospel and be among those who hasten His return. Like all theories of the rapture, those who hold a different point of view have their Scriptures whereby they will seek to prove their point and disprove yours. But all of that means nothing if we cannot hear the voice of God when He calls.

Regardless of when He calls us to meet Him we should develop a heart that loves His appearing. Maybe it is time we turn our friends and family into disciples of the Lord that are ready to help us reach the world and ready to meet Him when He calls. We can determine if our family and friends will be surprised by a *thief in the night* or if they will hear the Bridegroom call because they watch and pray. Here are some suggestions for accomplishing this goal:

- Read this book with your family and friends. It would be great for a book club. It will be an excellent tool to lead others in asking the right questions and opening their eyes to our true history. This is the only book I have ever written that I will ask all of my children to read and discuss with their children.
- Make sure they are born again. Do not assume anyone is born again. Through the natural course of discussing these details you can ask a person if they are ready to meet Jesus. If they have any response other than a definitive "yes," then you can simply share.
- If you don't know how to lead a person to Jesus read my book *Supernatural Ministry.* It will take you step-by-step through the practical steps of personal ministry. You can also go to my website and watch the very short video *Creation to Calvary.* This is the most effective closing I have ever heard for leading others to Christ.
- Teach them the signs so whether they happen in your lifetime or theirs, they will understand what is happening in the world.
- Warn them about the deceptions. This book lays out the spiritual history of the world. Understanding the deceptions of the past prepares one for the deceptions of the future.
- Help them discover the authentic voice of God. There is no greater protection from counterfeit than an intimate knowledge of the

authentic. *"This is life to know* (experience) *God and Jesus Christ whom He has sent"* (John 17:3).

- Teach them to meditate and hear the voice of God in their heart. Those who are not stabilized by hearing the voice of God in their heart will be moved by all the voices in the world.
- Teach them value for the Word of God. They must learn to always apply the Word from the perspective of love. This will give them experience with how effective it is in real life situations. Trusting the Word through life experiences is the only antidote to lawlessness (iniquity).
- Teach them to trust in and walk in love above all things. The person who stays connected to love will always be able to trust God in all situations because faith works by love.
- Teach them to enter a life of obedience to the voice of God. This is not a legalistic obedience; it is an obedience that knows following God's leadership always leads to a life of abundant fulfillment (John10:10).
- Teach them to eliminate personal distractions. Sin and carnality cannot separate us from the love of God, but they can keep us from noticing where the love of God is leading.
- Teach them to prepare to cross over. Create an eternal perspective in your children, grandchildren and everyone whom you help disciple. Meditating about entering into eternity is the most effective action one can take to prepare to be with Him. Remember, part of the wisdom for overcoming is when we *"love not our life unto the death."*

There is no greater honor or more important mission than preparing those we love for an eternity with the Father! Knowing your family is secure in their faith will remove one of the major fears and concerns that could interfere with your ability to hear and follow God!

APOCALYPSE

CHAPTER 44

WINNING OVER EVIL

The most foolish thing a person can do when facing even a remote possibility of danger is refuse to prepare!

IT SEEMS THE HISTORIC VIEW OF WINNING OVER SIN IS TO WANT SOMETHING TERRIBLY BADLY AND BY SHEER GRIT WE MANAGE TO PRAY, FIGHT AND FINALLY PULL AWAY FROM IT, EVEN AS ITS CLAWS ARE RIPPING THE FLESH FROM OUR BACK WE SOMEHOW PULL FREE AND ESCAPE. Then there is the religious concept of God's deliverance. We imagine that He only comes to help after we have taken all we can stand; then at the last minute when we are about to break He shows up. These are Luciferian concepts that have emerged from perverted doctrines of demons designed to distort and corrupt our view and opinion of God.

Our view and opinion of God tends to be based on a subjective interpretation of circumstances rather than an objective reliance on Scripture. The only reason God seemingly shows up at the eleventh hour is because we have spent ten hours and fifty-nine minutes trying to solve the problem without following God and His Word, that is, His divine prescription for victory. We have tried to hold to the world and find God's deliverance. We have often refused to walk His path and enjoy the quality of life therein[i]; instead we have chosen to walk the path of the world, carnal logic and sometimes iniquity all the while calling to Him to come and walk our path and bring His blessings. We tend to resist following the Shepherd and instead search for some formula to coerce the Shepherd into following us.

The Book of Revelation talks of the promises, process and importance of being an overcomer. Beginning with the messages to the seven churches of Asia and through to the end we are reminded of the benefits of overcoming. But we need to first realize an overcomer is not someone who simply endures. One who endures is someone who stays under, has fortitude, or persists and perseveres through the trials.[ii] It is better than failing, giving up and giving in, but there is a better way, the way of the overcomer. An overcomer is someone who has supremacy, victory or success, and they actually conquer.[iii] Sadly, many people will only endure what lies ahead when they could be overcomers. But being an overcomer versus one who endures is the choice of the believer. That choice is exercised by preparation. Being an overcomer in daily life is the pathway to being an overcomer in the grandest sense.

In the first chapters of the Book of Revelation Jesus addresses the seven churches of Asia. Those who debate theology and eschatology argue about the relevance of those Scriptures as they apply to us and the end times. We somehow forget that every Word of God is addressed to us. Even if it is addressed to us as an example, it is still to us.[iv] If we reject these words on the premise of them being for those churches, then we must dismiss every New Testament epistle because they were all written to specific churches addressing

---

i Proverbs 12:28, In the way of righteousness is life, And in its pathway there is no death.

ii hupomeno (hoop-om-en'-o); from NT:5259 and NT:3306; to stay under (behind), i.e. remain; figuratively, to undergo, i.e. bear (trials), have fortitude, persevere: (Biblesoft's New Exhaustive Strong's Numbers and Concordance with Expanded Greek-Hebrew Dictionary. Copyright © 1994, 2003, 2006 Biblesoft, Inc. and International Bible Translators, Inc.)

iii [to conquer, overcome], ník¢ [victory], níkos [victory], hypernikáœ [to be more than conquerors] Usage outside the NT. This group denotes "victory," "supremacy," or "success." It is assumed that the success is palpable and achieved by an action, but two questions remain,
(from Theological Dictionary of the New Testament, abridged edition, Copyright © 1985 by William B. Eerdmans Publishing Company. All rights reserved.)

iv 1 Corinthians 10:6, Now these things became our examples, to the intent that we should not lust after evil things as they also lusted.

specific issues. Then we would reject the teachings of Jesus because they were teaching for the people of His day… oh, wait; this is already being done by a number of groups and denominations!

The messages to these seven churches, like all Scripture, should be read and applied in a manner that gives them relevance to our lives today. Each of these churches was facing issues that related very specifically to the Luciferian issues that were prominent in the iniquity, idolatry, sin and deception that permeated the culture of their cities and the demonic religions they hosted. Not only does this have a general relevance to the Church, it is specifically important for the end times as the Luciferian, antichrist iniquity overtakes the entire world! A simple study explains the occult practices of their cities and how they affected the churches as well as the specific issues Jesus confronted.

But for our purposes, the two most significant factors addressed to all the churches were the fact that people could choose to be overcomers; it was not determined by their environment or circumstances, and that being an overcomer is intimately linked with having *"ears to hear what the Spirit is saying…."* Regardless of the conditions of these geographical church bodies, individual believers had the right and responsibility to hear from God for themselves, and follow His voice based on Jesus' teaching, so shall it be in the end, as well! Watch and pray!

I meet many believers who desire to hear and follow the Spirit but it never seems to materialize as a functional wisdom that leads them in the practical path of life. It is easy to understand why our current model does not work in real life. Our approach to following the Spirit is mystical and far removed from the scriptural model. Jesus told us He did not speak His own words, He spoke the words of the Father.[v] If He spoke His own words He would not be one with the Father. It was the fact that He spoke the Father's Word that gave His words authority. The writer of Hebrews tells us Jesus was the exact *"representation of the Father."*[vi] He is the Model of how to walk in the Word as well as walk in the Spirit because in truth you cannot do one without the other.

---

v John 14:10-11, Do you not believe that I am in the Father, and the Father in Me? The words that I speak to you I do not speak on My own authority; but the Father who dwells in Me does the works. 11 Believe Me that I am in the Father and the Father in Me, or else believe Me for the sake of the works themselves.

vi Hebrews 1:3, who being the brightness of His glory and the express image of His person

The Holy Spirit never leads or speaks anything to us that is different than what God has already said. When we were born of the Spirit all of God's laws and all they imply were written on the deep part of our heart (Hebrews 8:10). The deep part of the heart probably refers to our spirit, since it seems the heart is part spirit and part soul.[vii] It is the responsibility of the believer to renew his or her mind with the Word of God. The mind is the realm of the soul. When we renew our mind we are aligning our intellect, thoughts and emotions with God's truth that has been written on our heart. When the mind and the heart come into harmony we have immovable faith!

Some movements consider the Word to be archaic, others apply it through the light of dispensationalism, some reject it under the notion that in the New Covenant they are just led by the Holy Spirit, and others reject the Word because their heart is full of iniquity and they hate God.

Some movements consider the Word to be archaic, others apply it through the light of dispensationalism, some reject it under the notion that in the New Covenant they are just led by the Holy Spirit, and others reject the Word because their heart is full of iniquity and they hate God. The motive really does not matter, the outcome is the same: doubt and unbelief.

Iniquity has subtly slipped into the Church by exalting Jesus' words above the Father's, as if Jesus brought a new truth. The idea that Jesus somehow did away with the commandments is in direct opposition to Jesus' own words and the teachings of the apostles. The very idea that the commandments were flawed is Luciferian propaganda. Jesus came to show us what God would look like in the flesh and how His commandments could be applied in the real world independently of legalism and religion. But the Apostle John, as well as Jesus Himself, is very clear that He is the **same word** that was with God in the beginning, not a new word, not a better word, but the Word as it was intended from the very beginning. We do have a better covenant, but the covenant does not change the Word of God.

vii *Moving Your Invisible Boundaries*

There is a pseudo-spiritual movement based on a counterfeit message of love that says God is love, I love Jesus and Jesus loves me, so we do not need the Word of God. We are free from the commandments. They are not relevant. We are led by the Spirit. All of those statements are a partial New Covenant truth, except for the idea that the commandments are not relevant and being free from the commandments is somehow synonymous with being free in the Spirit.

> There is a pseudo-spiritual movement based on a counterfeit message of love that says God is love, I love Jesus and Jesus loves me, so we do not need the Word of God.

Today I hear people saying that Jesus is grace. I assume it is their intention to exalt Jesus through their statements. There is a tendency in some of these groups to say, "since I have grace I don't need the Word. I have my own revelation from God." The problem is that there is not one Scripture that says Jesus is grace. There are Scriptures that say Jesus brought grace. There are however, Scriptures that say Jesus is the Word of God, the same Word that was with God in the beginning! This is the Word by which all things were created.[viii] It is by this living Word that all created things are upheld.[ix] It is this living Word who is the exact representation of God; there is nothing God has ever spoken that is inconsistent with Jesus' identity, life or teachings. So there is really no way to have a relationship with Jesus without having a relationship with the Word!

This move to exalt and honor Jesus apart from the Word may have good intentions, but in the end it is still iniquity. When, instead of accepting what the Scripture says about Jesus one twists the Scripture to honor Jesus, they are rejecting God's Word in favor of their own. They are doing exactly what Lucifer did when, through pride, iniquity entered his heart! It does not honor God or the Lord Jesus to reject or twist His Word, no matter the intention. It does not reveal the love of God to replace God's commandments for how to treat one another with a humanistic, philosophical version of love.

---

viii John 1:1-5, In the beginning was the Word, and the Word was with God, and the Word was God. 2 He was in the beginning with God. 3 All things were made through Him, and without Him nothing was made that was made. 4 In Him was life, and the life was the light of men. 5 And the light shines in the darkness, and the darkness did not comprehend it.

ix Hebrews 1:3, ...upholding all things by the word of His power...

Peter warns us of the tendency toward private interpretation. The whole idea behind private interpretation is related to the need to make the Word fit us, our needs, our personality and our opinions. It is exactly this type of iniquity that will disempower many Christians when faced with life-threatening situations. If we do not trust God with our doctrinal issues how will we trust Him under the threat of death? This eternal struggle began when iniquity entered Lucifer's heart. It has been, in fact, iniquity that has ushered us to the current brink of destruction. It is the mystery of iniquity (1 Thessalonians 2:7) that has been at work corrupting religion and government since the Fall of Man. The false religions of the world are all built on iniquity. The antichrist and the false prophet will deceive through iniquity. And the compromised part of the Church will be totally susceptible to deception because of iniquity.

The false religions of the world are all built on iniquity. The antichrist and the false prophet will deceive through iniquity.

We need a power greater than our own working in our hearts to overcome. Some people refer to this power as the Holy Spirit working in their life and others call it grace. The truth is they are one and the same. Grace is God's power, ability and capacity that comes by unmerited favor and works as a divine influence in our heart. It is the only thing that gives us power over sin (Romans 6:14). It is the only thing that makes us able to not simply endure but to overcome. We have access into this grace whereby we stand by faith (Romans 5:2). Faith is the immovable trust in God, not the God of our imagination, denomination, philosophy or opinion, but faith in God the Father of the Lord Jesus Christ and all He has said about Himself! The power to be all and do all the Bible promises is a work of God's empowering grace which comes by faith (Ephesians 2:8-10).

In times of tribulation and challenge we need God's grace, or you may call it the power of the Holy Spirit. It doesn't matter so much which biblical terminology you choose, what matters is this: are you experiencing supernatural power to face and conquer life's problems now? If we are alive at His coming we will need a power greater than our own. Therefore, instead of asking questions for which there are no concrete answers we should answer the question the Bible asks. **What kind of person should I be today to be ready for what I may face tomorrow?**

> *But the day of the Lord will come as a thief in the night, in which the heavens will pass away with a great noise, and the elements will melt with fervent heat; both the earth and the works that are in it will be burned up. Therefore, since all these things will be dissolved, **what manner of persons ought you to be in holy conduct and godliness,** looking for and hastening the coming of the day of God.* (2 Peter 3:10-12)

What kind of person should I be? That's the only real question I need to answer. Peter says we should live in holy conduct and godliness. This is not about earning God's protection; this is about remaining spiritually and emotionally sober so we can see clearly and so we do not become vexed and distracted with the cares of this life (Luke 21:34-35). If we become vexed, consumed or intoxicated with the things of the world, like any drunk, we become susceptible to attack. We become less vigilant.

As Peter points out, we should keep our hope alive by focusing on the promise of the coming New Heaven and New Earth. There is no power in denying what lies ahead or hoping it will not come; but there is power in the eternal promises.

> *Nevertheless we, according to His promise, look for new heavens and a new earth in which righteousness dwells. Therefore, beloved, looking forward to these things, be diligent to be found by Him in peace, without spot and blameless...*(2 Peter 3:13-16).

Keeping an eternal focus, keeping our eyes on the prize, this is exactly what Jesus did when faced with the cross.[x] The writer of Hebrews points out that hope is an anchor for the soul (6:19). If our soul is not anchored in eternal hope we will waver from position to position as the hardship of tribulation sweeps the world.

---

x Hebrews 12:2, looking unto Jesus, the author and finisher of our faith, who for the joy that was set before Him endured the cross, despising the shame, and has sat down at the right hand of the throne of God.

Peter goes on to emphasize the need to grow in grace.

> *You therefore, beloved, since you know this* ***beforehand,*** *beware lest you also fall from your own steadfastness, being led away with the error of the wicked; but grow in the grace and knowledge of our Lord and Savior Jesus Christ* (2 Peter 3:17-18).

All the early apostles faced the persecution of Jews and Romans and many were ultimately martyred for their faith. They understood as much as any who have ever faced persecution, without God's strength working in their heart they would not have survived! They knew they could only fulfil their call and live their destiny as a work of grace - God's power!

As we grow in the knowledge (experience) of the Lord we, likewise, grow in grace. It is not a state of being, it is an expression of the power of God in and through our lives.

They did not view grace as a static position; it was intimately linked with experiencing Jesus personally. As we grow in the knowledge (experience) of the Lord we, likewise, grow in grace. It is not a state of being, it is an expression of the power of God in and through our lives. It will be this grace that will empower us to the greatest ministry the world has ever seen. It will be this grace that enables us to face any situation and win!

This growth in grace is, however, something that we should experience sooner rather than later. We need to grow in our experience of the grace of God now so when we face hardship we are not standing on untested, theoretical doctrine. Instead, we are standing in the true power of God we have experienced through daily victory!

The Book of Revelation also mentions "the patience of the saints" as something that helps us endure and overcome. Patience is the ability to stand under pressure and not waver. Revelation 13:9-10 reminds us that those who violently attempt to take people captive will themselves be taken captive and die by the sword. There is hope in knowing that ultimately we not only win… they lose! They suffer the fate they attempted to bring on the world! Jesus will come and establish His Kingdom. We will rule with Him. When you know you are going to win, facing temporary hardship is not so difficult!

Then Revelation 14:12 brings an interesting but essential paradox to light. Remember, it is iniquity that brings the world to the place of total destruction; therefore, we who live by faith cannot be deceived into rejecting God's commands. *"Here is the patience of the saints; here are those who keep the commandments of God and the faith of Jesus."* We see from this Scripture that keeping God's commandments as an act of love and faith in Jesus are not mutually exclusive. We know, in fact, that if we walk in love we will fulfill the commandments and all they imply (Romans 13:9-10). We also know faith works by love (Galatians 5:6). Believers filled with grace have the power to walk in God's Word unlike the workers of iniquity who reject God's Word, these believers, through the power of God, are able to live in God's truth.

> There is hope in knowing that ultimately we not only win… they lose! They suffer the fate they attempted to bring on the world!

One destructive characteristic of the end times is that because of iniquity love will grow cold. The world will become more violent, untrusting, cynical and fatalistic. Political correctness and social justice will call evil good and good evil and the foundation of righteousness will be destroyed. But part of the magnetic draw to the Gospel of the Kingdom will be the love of the disciples in a hate-filled world. We will be the light in the darkness, the salt of the earth and the springs of living water in a thirsty world.

All outstanding attributes of an overcomer as presented throughout the Book of Revelation are based on hearing what the Spirit is saying; everything else is just information! Unless we can hear, recognize, trust and follow the direction of the Holy Spirit we will be in a tidal wave without a rudder. God alone can lead us through such perilous times. If we cannot hear and recognize the voice of God in our own heart now we cannot hear and follow Him through the *"valley of the shadow of death."*

When faced with overwhelming challenges, doctrine, philosophy and all other vain babblings and doctrinal debates are meaningless. They will not make us feel safe, nor will they be able to lead us in the pathway of life and safety.

If the Lord is our Shepherd and we know and trust Him we will experience Him as our peace!

Revelation 12:11 presents the most definitive and, no doubt, the most challenging attributes of those who overcome. It says, *"And they overcome him by: 1) the blood of the Lamb, 2) the word of their testimony 3) they love not their lives unto the death."* (numbering mine)

If the Lord is our Shepherd and we know and trust Him we will experience Him as our peace!

Revelation chapter 12 is a synopsis of world history from a spiritual perspective. It describes Satan's rebellion and his final removal from Heaven as the accuser of the brethren. Those who have overcome from that time until the end seem to share these three traits. In other words, like all truth, that which was true at any time is true at all times. This seems to be what believers have done since Jesus was raised from the dead!

Overcoming by the *"blood of the Lamb"* is an obvious reference not simply to the blood of Jesus, but to our faith in the blood. For some, the blood is nothing more than a religious incantation that is supposed to work magically under certain religious conditions. The blood, like all free gifts, was shed for all. But all do not participate and not all are cleansed by the blood, only those who believe in the death, burial and resurrection of Jesus and confess Him as Lord!

The benefit of the blood, the peace, and the close, intimate connection with God, the clear conscious, and the forgiveness of sins[xi] are all benefits that are likewise only experienced when combined with faith. While others are overwhelmed by the circumstances, the threat of death and the very real hard-

---

xi Ephesians 2:13, But now in Christ Jesus you who once were far off have been brought near by the blood of Christ.
Colossians 1:14, in whom we have redemption through His blood, the forgiveness of sins.
Colossians 1:20, and by Him to reconcile all things to Himself, by Him, whether things on earth or things in heaven, having made peace through the blood of His cross.
Hebrews 9:14, how much more shall the blood of Christ, who through the eternal Spirit offered Himself without spot to God, cleanse your conscience from dead works to serve the living God?

ships of persecution, the overcomer is experiencing these attributes. They are spiritually-minded. In other words, their attention is focused on that which is eternal. They are alive to what the Spirit of God is saying and expressing within them!

"The word of their testimony" has so many far-reaching implications. "Word" in the Greek language is *logos.* Logos is more about factors which bring about the Word than the Word itself. When God speaks the *logos* is a collection of everything He has ever spoken.[xii] His words are based on wisdom, logic and character which support His every word. His words (logos) reveal His nature and identity. The *"word of our testimony"* may be more than just the testimony of our faith in Jesus; it may be the collection of all that provides a witness to God's character. We are the light of the world and the salt of the earth. We are what the world sees which stands in contradiction to what the World's System, based on its Luciferian values, has shown the world. We are proof that God is who He says He is!

Our "testimony" is like an eyewitness in a courtroom who has firsthand knowledge and is able to validate the truth of the facts. The life of a believer is hated by the antichrist spirit. It is the proof, the testimony, the witness he seeks to remove from Planet Earth. For this reason the word "witness" took on a new meaning in the early Church. It comes from the Greek word

---

xii Logos: The great variety of meanings — word, speech, language, narrative, statement, pronouncement, question, report, account, sermon, teaching, call, sense — can be accounted for esp.: a) on philological grounds and b) on theological grounds. The root "leg" represents a comprehensive and overarching unity of meaning: gather, collect, select, report, speak. (the essential abiding law of the world, thought, and custom) (from Exegetical Dictionary of the New Testament © 1990 by William B. Eerdmans Publishing Company. All rights reserved.)
those which, having been thought i. e. gathered together in the mind, are expressed in words. Accordingly, a twofold use of the term is to be distinguished: one which relates to speaking, and one which relates to thinking.
commands, counsels, promises; a word which, uttered by the living voice, embodies a conception or idea;
(from Thayer's Greek Lexicon, Electronic Database. Copyright © 2000, 2003, 2006 by Biblesoft, Inc. All rights reserved.)
Logos: has first the sense of "collection." mathematically "proportion," "relation," then more generally "measure" or "order," and d. subjectively human reason, mind, or thought.
The stress is on the rational element in speech; rh¢¡ma carries the emotional and volitional emphasis. For Aristotle
Logos denotes the showing of something for what it is, and orientation thereto. (from Theological Dictionary of the New Testament, abridged edition, Copyright © 1985 by William B. Eerdmans Publishing Company. All rights reserved.)

"martyr." If your life gave proof of being a disciple of the Lord Jesus it meant death. As a witness you were the proof, the evidence that needed to be eradicated lest the truth be revealed.

"For everyone practicing evil hates the light and does not come to the light, lest his deeds should be exposed" (John 3:20).

In the modern world of deceit and political correctness the world and the Church were led to believe that Atheists and the many special interest groups that represent any number of expressions of iniquity really only want to peacefully coexist. But what has become painfully obvious is the fact that darkness never wants to coexist with light. Jesus says this, *"For everyone practicing evil hates the light and does not come to the light, lest his deeds should be exposed"* (John 3:20). They do not want to coexist, they want it to be against the law for us to identify as sin that which the Bible identifies a sin.

Special interest groups have never wanted co-existence. They have always wanted only one thing: the annihilation of anything or anyone who does not agree with their position. They want any harm done or any words spoken against their deeds to be considered hate crimes with special punishment. They want it to be against the law for us to pray in public or meet in our homes. Soon they will make it against the law to proclaim Jesus as the only means of salvation. Then when the antichrist is fully empowered it will be against the law to believe anything other than Islam.

Iniquity, even that which starts out as a mild compromise, is a path that always leads to hating Jesus as Lord. The idea of lordship is too restrictive. Since lordship is expressed through the written Word there must be a rejection of God's Word as absolute. It may begin with picking and choosing which parts one is willing to believe, but if this is followed it will end in the rejection of Jesus as Lord. *"...but you seek to kill Me, because My word has no place in you"* (John 8:37).

The hatred toward Jesus does not stop with Him; it is projected onto all who represent Him in a credible manner. The Lord forewarned of this scenario. *"The world cannot hate you, but it hates Me because I testify of it that its works are evil"* (John 7:7).

> *"If the world hates you, you know that it hated Me before it hated you. If you were of the world, the world would love its own. …Remember the word that I said to you, 'A servant is not greater than his master.' If they persecuted Me, they will also persecute you."* (John15:18-20)

In the former Soviet Union, China and a few other countries, for generations believers have died for their faith. This has been foreign to North Americans; we have never faced great challenges because of our faith. However, as light and darkness polarize, every person on earth will have to stand for or against God. But in these times of great darkness grace will reign. Even the most marginal believer may transform into a spiritual Samson. Ironically, we need not worry about that day; God will give us the words and strength to face whatever we must. Our only responsibility at this point is to desire such a life.

But in these times of great darkness grace will reign. Even the most marginal believer may transform into a spiritual Samson.

Ultimately, the overcomer, the one who prevails against the antichrist, has one secret weapon. This secret weapon is built on all other factors in this book that comprise Jesus' teaching about how to prepare for what is ahead, as well as what the Spirit of God revealed to John in Revelation. Being alive to God means one has already accepted the sentence of death on any aspect of life outside of Jesus. These overcomers *"love not their life to the death."*

The writer of Hebrews (2:14-15) revealed that people are held in bondage through the fear of death. When there is no fear of death the enemy has nothing with which to hold us. Freedom from this fear comes when eternity is as real as the world we now experience with our five senses. When this occurs the afterlife is no longer an uncertainty, it is a vivid, appealing reality. Jesus said, *"where your treasure is, there your heart will be also"* (Matthew 6:21). Our heart is connected and alive to that which we treasure most. As believers we must deliberately connect to eternity. The more we experience the goodness of God in real life experiences and in meditation the more our heart can connect to eternity as a reality. The more eternal life becomes real, the more we die to life in this world.

If you have lived in a free country it is not only difficult to relate to the things the Bible says about the end, it is tempting to create a fantasy doctrine filled with false hope of no suffering. No one wants to suffer; no one wants to live in persecution. But it is a realty that has been hidden from the world for generations. It is inevitable that these things will come. The irony is, if we had lived like the end was upon us, we would have probably postponed it. It may be if we live as true disciples it can still be postponed; I do not know. I simply know we should live in the paradox of plan like there is no end, but live like it is coming tomorrow! Watch and pray, minister to others, be a light in the darkness, then there will not be so much darkness!

People are held in bondage through the fear of death. When there is no fear of death the enemy has nothing with which to hold us.

So the question remains, do the overcomers live or die? When one is truly an overcomer the answer to that question does not really matter! What matters is in their heart they were never defeated, no matter what happened to their body. When Heaven becomes the treasure in one's heart, the world is of little value or consequence!

APOCALYPSE

CHAPTER 45

THE FINAL VINDICATION

We are not ready to enter into eternity until every shred of doubt and every shadow of uncertainty about God's love, wisdom and faithfulness is resolved!

RIGHT UP UNTIL THE END, LUCIFER, THE FALSE RELIGIONS AND MUCH OF MANKIND WILL CLING TO THE LIE THAT GOD IS UNJUST, CRUEL AND UNTRUSTWORTHY. Neither the world nor the angelic beings have yet truly seen the nature of God to its fullest expression. Unfortunately, many of the doctrines of the Religionists will continue to unwittingly support this Luciferian concept right until the end.

When Lucifer rebelled he was able to take one-third of the angelic population with him in his seduction of iniquity. It is hard to imagine that angels who witnessed creation and had contemplated the majesty and glory of the Godhead since before time had not realized the true nature of God, our Creator! We must, however, realize they had never seen God interact with human beings. It was not until they witnessed God's loving tenderness toward man that they began to grasp the true nature of God.

In Ephesians 3:18-11 Paul says something that I believe we are not yet capable of fully realizing.

> *To me, who am less than the least of all the saints, this grace was given, that I should preach among the Gentiles the unsearchable riches of Christ, and to make all see what is the fellowship of the mystery, which from the beginning of the ages has been hidden in God who created all things through Jesus Christ; to the intent that now the manifold wisdom of God might be made known by the church to the principalities and powers in the heavenly places, according to the eternal purpose which He accomplished in Christ Jesus our Lord.*

There has never been anything that revealed the wisdom, the love, the grace, the humility, the self-sacrifice and the kindness of God until it was seen in God's dealing with man as it is accomplished in Christ Jesus, our Lord. In eternity we will understand God's long-suffering. We will finally grasp the fullness of His plan and why this is the only way it could happen.

It has never been in the nature of God to say, "You should have known." He gave us His Word, His name and a consistent history of faithfulness as a witness to His character, nature and intention toward man. Then in every way possible He has worked in the lives of men to provide a model. But mankind, the angels and the demons have not yet had the opportunity to see the world as it could have been… as God originally intended. Remember, Lucifer brought iniquity into the world. Man corrupted his own nature and subsequently misused his authority. Man, as a result of trusting Lucifer's logic, brought sin, sickness, disease, death, religion and every evil thing into the world. Yet, God still lovingly reached out to him. But mankind and much of the body of Christ are still not convinced that God is love and everything He does is motivated by love.

Mankind, the angels and the demons have not yet had the opportunity to see the world as it could have been… as God originally intended.

We have been taught that the return of Jesus is the wrathful end of the world brought about by an angry God. All who are not saved will go to Hell at the moment of Jesus' return and everyone on earth will be serving the antichrist;

but that really is not what the Bible teaches. These are doctrines that are forced upon those who have a rigid, unscriptural interpretation of eschatology. Jesus' return is not the end of the world; it is simply the end of the World's System, but the beginning of Christ's reign on earth.

While there are things I accept and find beneficial from both the Preterists and Futurists, I do not fully embrace either doctrine as completely accurate. The Futurists who have decided upon a forced pre-tribulation rapture have to impose their ideology onto certain Scriptures. To support their belief the Bible has to say things that cannot be irrevocably proven. For example in 2 Thessalonians 2:7-8 we are told about something that is now restraining the man of lawlessness from being revealed. *"For the mystery of lawlessness is already at work; only He who now restrains will do so until He is taken out of the way. And then the lawless one will be revealed…"* From a pre-tribulation perspective I am forced to assume the Holy Spirit or the Church is that which is preventing the antichrist from emerging. This forces me to the conclusion that the Holy Spirit and/or the Church will not be present in the earth, but there is actually no scriptural proof. Or, when the angel says to John, *"Come up here, and I will show you what must take place after this"* (Revelation 4:1), the phrase *"Come up here,"* is assumed to refer to the rapture. Everything from this point is assumed to happen because the Church and/or the Holy Spirit are gone. Then, from the assumption that the events in the chapters of Revelation are in chronological order, it becomes impossible to unravel the "theological knot." In time the entire doctrine is little more than assumption and stretched Scripture that would not only cause it to lose any validity, it would become so complicated and overwhelming that few people would ever seriously read the book.

> Man, as a result of trusting Lucifer's logic, brought sin, sickness, disease, death, religion and every evil thing into the world. Yet, God still lovingly reached out to him.

The same thing happens with the Preterist view of eschatology. Scriptures have to be twisted about Titus, the coming of the Lord, the tribulation and the timing of the Church Age. Even though Jesus said that immediately after those things occurred in Jerusalem the end would come, the end didn't immediately come, unless you can redefine what it means for the end to come. Paul said after that which is restraining the antichrist would be revealed and Jesus would destroy him with the breath of His mouth. This and dozens of other Scriptures were not fulfilled after Titus destroyed the temple. Once again, there is some truth in their position, but the twisting of Scriptures to fit a predetermined idea destroys nearly all validity.

God will be vindicated in every way to all mankind and to all the angels before the end of this world. When the entire world bows before Jesus and declares Him as Lord it will be because God has finally been vindicated in every action He has ever taken and every Word He has ever spoken.

This book is about knowing what Jesus said to do to prepare for the end, which is really no different than what we need to do to live life as *more than a conqueror*. While I have discussed several eschatological possibilities, I am not concerned with concrete positions other than those that will empower us to stand strong and overcome no matter what we face.

But there is one more thing that will happen. God will be vindicated in every way to all mankind and to all the angels before the end of this world. When the entire world bows before Jesus and declares Him as Lord it will be because God has finally been vindicated in every action He has ever taken and every word He has ever spoken.

Believers will go before the Judgment Seat of Christ. Unlike the frightening words of the Religionists who said all your dirty deeds will be exposed and played in a great video before all the world, you will find that all your wicked deeds have been washed away by the blood of the Lamb. All our deeds will pass through the fire; anything that is unacceptable to our Lord will be burned. We will only stand before Him with that part of our life that brings Him glory. Only that which glorifies Him will be presented to Him, and we will receive rewards. The Judgment Seat of Christ is not a place of humiliation, it is a place glorification.[i] Everything that happens when we finally see Him as He is will lead to more trust and more adoration from those who love righteousness.

When Jesus returns to Planet Earth this will happen (not necessarily in this order):

- The Judgment Seat of Christ (believers are given rewards and responsibilities)
- The antichrist, false prophet, and his followers will be destroyed
- Satan will be bound for 1000 years
- The transformed Church will rule and reign with the Lord Jesus
- Man gets to choose what he wants without Satan there to blame
- We get to see the world ruled in absolute righteousness
- People will be born and die
- People will make decisions about God
- Some will prefer a world that fulfills their greed and lust
- There will be a final rebellion
- The Great White Throne Judgment (for those who rejected righteousness as a free gift)
- All who rejected God's gift are cast into eternal Hell
- The earth will be purged by fire
- New Jerusalem comes to Planet Earth
- The New Heavens and the New Earth
- God dwells with us eternally in New Jerusalem, here on Planet Earth

Jesus will rule on earth for one thousand years. For the first time ever man will witness what the world could have been had we trusted and applied God's

---

i 2 Corinthians 5:10, For we must all appear before the judgment seat of Christ, that each one may receive the things done in the body, according to what he has done, whether good or bad.
1 Corinthians 3:12-15, Now if anyone builds on this foundation with gold, silver, precious stones, wood, hay, straw, 13 each one's work will become clear; for the Day will declare it, because it will be revealed by fire; and the fire will test each one's work, of what sort it is. 14 If anyone's work which he has built on it endures, he will receive a reward. 15 If anyone's work is burned, he will suffer loss; but he himself will be saved, yet so as through fire. NKJV

commands as He intended, from the motive of love. If someone dies at 100 they will be considered an infant (Isaiah 65:20). God's law will be the code of justice from which He will rule. Man will be required to love one another the way God commanded, not some iniquitous, godless, humanistic imposter of love. There will be no lack. Because man is treating the earth the way God commanded we will see an overabundance of crops. This is the period of time the Bible says *"the lamb will lay with the lion."*

For the first time ever man will witness what the world could have been had we trusted and applied God's commands as He intended, from the motive of love.

Jesus, as Lord, will provide justice that could never come from any man. Listen to the description provided by the Prophet Isaiah.

> *His delight is in the fear of the Lord, And He shall not judge by the sight of His eyes, Nor decide by the hearing of His ears; But with righteousness He shall judge the poor, And decide with equity for the meek of the earth; He shall strike the earth with the rod of His mouth, And with the breath of His lips He shall slay the wicked.* (Isaiah 11:3-4)

The wealthy will not oppress the poor. The wicked will not be able to manipulate the law and beat the system. We will finally see what true justice looks like. And ironically those who held to their faith in Jesus and the integrity of His Word and died as martyrs will rule with Him. Those the world considered worthless will be the ones who rule.

We will finally see that all famines and many "natural disasters" were actually the works of evil men. We will discover that most of what we were taught about evolution, science and medicine were lies designed to alienate us from trusting God. Our eyes will be open to all that was used to deceive us. We will realize the world is full of endless resources.

At the end of the 1,000 years, Satan will be freed from his prison (Revelation 20:7-10). The word "released" does not absolutely imply that God released him. This could be another time when man uses his authority; it is somewhat ambiguous. Whatever the case may be, this is not some sick test by God.

This is man seeing righteousness for 1,000 years and those who have wicked hearts saying, "This is not what we want! We don't love God's righteousness; we want to rule the world our way."

Throughout the Book of Revelation there are people giving their lives to the antichrist, there are believers being martyred, there are people overcoming, and it seems there are those who are not committed either way. Those who are alive at His coming are not all righteous. After 1,000 years of not being able to steal, kill and take advantage of people, they will reject the righteous rule of God based on His commandments.

> Our eyes will be open to all that was used to deceive us. We will realize the world is full of endless resources.

This presents one possibility that we have not discussed. It is possible that the antichrist only has direct rule over the ten nations. These could form his base from which he would seek rule of the entire world, but not necessarily mean he has direct rule of every nation. We know the antichrist and his kingdoms destroy the Great Harlot and, thereby, destroy the economy. So, the world which was built totally on the concepts of a false economy will be in shambles. We know the Great Harlot empowers wicked men to rule who will sell out the Church for corrupt motives. These world leaders will pledge allegiance to the man of sin. We know the entire world falls under his evil. While he affects the entire world there may be "cities of refuge," places that are free from his total control. This may account for those who are alive at His coming.

In the end, God will have fully revealed His nature. There will be no room for argument or unbelief. A person who chooses rebellion at the end of the millennium will, like Lucifer, be without excuse. It is just a matter of not loving God's righteous ways. But the final rebellion after 1,000 years of righteousness, peace and abundance will finally vindicate God. No more can those created by Him call His commands unjust. They will witness His commandments being applied from love. This revelation of God will be so all-encompassing it will never grow old throughout all eternity!

During the millennium the things our humanistic, iniquity-ridden hearts cannot accept now will be seen and accepted as righteous. Our every struggle and accusation against God's commands will be understood, and love will reign in transformed hearts. Every knee will bow and not only acknowledge Jesus, they will acknowledge God as just. Our loving Father will not allow us to enter into eternity with room for doubt or any belief that would undermine our absolute trust for Him as a loving, merciful, long-suffering Father.

To the degree that we follow Jesus' teaching, learn to live by Kingdom principles, accept God's Word as true and absolute, and open our heart to the Holy Spirit, we will be able to see these characteristics of God more clearly.

To the degree that we follow Jesus' teaching, learn to live by Kingdom principles, accept God's Word as true and absolute, and open our heart to the Holy Spirit, we will be able to see these characteristics of God more clearly. This clarity will give us hope as we face the darkest days the world has ever seen. But, like Daniel, we will not stop looking and expecting until we see the Kingdom made without hands destroy all evil and establish true righteousness!

APOCALYPSE

CHAPTER 46

JESUS: THE BRIDEGROOM

We are His bride. He will protect and watch over us like a lovestruck groom!

DESPITE HOW WE HAVE RELIGIOUSLY COME TO DEFINE FAITH AT ITS CORE IS SIMPLY TRUST. As Kenneth Wuest points out, this trust is confidence in a person's character and motives.[i] In the case of God, Luciferian doctrine has so dominated Christianity that many believers are unsure of God's consistent character and unchanging motives. To ponder facing a future challenge that Jesus said was a *"tribulation such as had never been seen…"* we must be immovable in our comprehension of God's loving motives and His unblemished faithfulness. We must live and walk in true biblical faith: unwavering faith!

Faith is a matter of the heart. The heart is deeper than intellectual beliefs. It is more powerful than the fleeting, ever-changing emotions of the soul. The heart is the source of deep, subtle, inexplicable feelings that carry us through life like giant waves that roll silently across the surface of the water

---

i Word Studies in the Greek New Testament, Volume III, Kenneth S. Wuest, Wm. B. Eerdmans Publishing Company, p. 38, Grand Rapids

while moved by a massive unseen power below the surface. Our beliefs are the unseen force that moves our lives with no conscious, intentional effort or choice. It is up to us to establish our hearts in faith by renewing our minds to align with God's written Word and His law that has been written on the deep aspect of our hearts. My goal through our *Heart Physics®* programs has been to help people connect with God in their heart and sustain an immovable, ever-present sense of Christ there. My book, *Moving Your Invisible Boundaries,* lays out the scriptural model and process for learning to live from the heart.

When it comes to issues of the heart, both concepts and information are absolutely essential. However, concepts must guide the details. Consider this: all of the Old Testament commandments have been seen as negative because the interpretation of the information based on the motive of love. It is rare when people read the Old Testament as anything more than pages of commandments that were thought to earn our righteousness through obedience. Seldom does anyone read these divine prescriptions and think, "I am fully committed to walking in love and this shows me what it will look like in real life."

When it comes to issues of the heart, both concepts and information are absolutely essential. However, concepts must guide the details.

And it may be even more rare that a person reads the commandments and says, "This is not only how God wants me to treat others, this is how He treats me." If we had faith, confidence in God's character and motives, we could see that through the commandments God was telling us how to love (express value for) Him, love (express value for) one another and love (express value for) ourselves. Because we did not interpret or guide our reasoning from the motive of love, we misunderstood the purpose of the law, making it negative and restrictive. We must always be sure to read God's Word from the proper concepts or we will misinterpret the information.

As Gentiles who prefer knowledge, we have a tendency to seek information assuming should we get enough information we would come to believe. When we start with information we don't actually reach the place of faith as often as we reach the place of judgment. This is why Paul warns knowledge (information) puffs up, but love builds up. Then he tells us that faith (trust) works by love. If we begin by gathering information we simply put God on trial. If the information meets up to our intellectual standards we find Him not guilty of lying. But if the information does not meet our guidelines His Word is not trusted. If, instead of putting God on trial, we accept His Covenant and His revelation of Himself, we begin our inquiry from the place of love, our interpretation of the facts will be completely different. In other words, when we know God loves us (considers us valuable and precious) we feel safe with Him and He is easy to trust.[ii]

To properly understand the information given in the Word of God we must begin with the overriding concept that God loves us, we are precious to Him. He holds us in high regard.[iii] Before we vainly attempt to figure out all the details involved in the tribulation, the coming of Christ and what will happen to the believers, we should first revisit how God sees and relates to His Church, His family, the bride of Christ!
We should meditate and ponder these facts until they become our only view of God. Then we are ready to understand the information. Without absolute confidence (faith) in God's character and motives even if we get all the information right it will not bring peace; it will only serve to multiply our fears.

To properly understand the information given in the Word of God we must begin with the overriding concept that God loves us, we are precious to Him. He holds us in high regard.

Historically God has used terms in describing us and our relationship with Him that, when pondered, would give rise to confidence: beloved, children, household, brothers, sons, heirs, etc. Since we rarely use God's terminology and use our own we lose the value of God's descriptive language. Among the many endearing terms God uses to describe us and our relationship to Him is one in which we should direct our every interpretation of the Bible and especially our eschatology. We are the bride of Christ and He is our Bridegroom. From this terminology and the many references to this unique, spiritual relationship we can easily deduce that Jesus will treat us wonderfully, specially, gently and with all the protection of a new Groom with His new bride.

---

ii Psalms 78:37, For their heart was not steadfast with Him, Nor were they faithful in His covenant.

iii Word Studies in the Greek New Testament, Volume III, Kenneth S. Wuest, Wm. B. Eerdmans Publishing Company, p. 60, Grand Rapids

Jesus used the analogy of the bridegroom in His parables about His return. As an effective communicator He would have known all traditions of the marriage process. He used parables as a way to get people to grasp a concept that would guide their interpretation of the facts. Our ignorance of the cultural use of His terminology has limited our ability to read His words and interpret them from the intended concepts. Understanding more about the bridegroom and how he would conduct his engagement and wedding will open our eyes to the kind of treatment and protection we can expect when the world is in tribulation.

Among the many endearing terms God uses to describe us and our relationship to Him is one in which we should direct our every interpretation of the Bible and especially our eschatology. We are the bride of Christ and He is our Bridegroom.

In Ephesians chapter 5 we have this wonderful description of how a husband and wife should interact. The chauvinistic interpretation of this passage has robbed it of the beautiful picture Paul sought to paint. It doesn't take much objective consideration to realize this passage places the greater responsibility on the husband. It is the husband that initiates love. It is the husband that treats the wife like his own body. The list of attributes for the loving husband is much more than those listed for the wife. In fact, one should realize that most of the responsibilities of the wife are in response to the husband's love. The reason for this is realized in verse 32. *"This is a profound mystery—but I am talking about Christ and the church."* It seems to be quite clear that Paul is directly linking the rituals of the ancient wedding ceremony to Christ and His Church.

We see that God's teaching about marriage, while applicable to marriage, is a concept that should open our eyes to the nature and faithfulness of our Lord as our Bridegroom. Following is a general picture of engagement and marriage as the people to whom Jesus was speaking would have understood it. What I want to bring out is just a few of the parallels that apply to us.

Everything starts with the covenant.[iv] For the perspective bridegroom this is the marriage contract. The marriage contract, which the groom would present to the potential bride and her father, would spell out all that he had to offer, all of his resources and, to some degree, show his ability to provide. Everything about the marriage proposal was based on the contract.

> We see that God's teaching about marriage, while applicable to marriage, is a concept that should open our eyes to the nature and faithfulness of our Lord as our Bridegroom.

Likewise, everything we should expect from our Bridegroom is spelled out in the Covenant of Peace God made with the Lord Jesus. If we accept His proposal and become His bride we share in all He inherited.

The groom would also bring a gift to present to the bride. The value of the gift would reflect how precious the bride is to him. It was a clear indicator to the father how he could expect his daughter to be treated if this arrangement is accepted. Jesus gave His own life for us, expressing not just His value for us, but the Father's as well. In fact, the word "reconciliation" means "to exchange one thing for something else of equal value." We are as valuable as the price that was paid for our salvation. This is why John says we must look to the cross and the full price of the propitiation to grasp the extreme love He has for us.[v] Any minimizing of what Jesus did through His death, burial and resurrection minimizes His love and our faith.

According to Joe Amaral in his wonderful book, *Understanding Jesus,* if the agreement was accepted the bride, the father and the groom would drink a cup of wine, sealing the agreement. Jesus sealed His agreement with us in the cup of His blood of the New Covenant (Matthew 26:27-29)!

---

iv Many of the detail in the following segment are based on or overlap with the wonderful book, Understanding Jesus: Cultural insights into the Words and Deeds of Christ by Joe Amaral, 2011, Faith Words, New York, Boston, Nashville. Because of studying many of the some resources it is hard to separate some of his research and my own. But I feel this is such a helpful book that I must give credit and recommend it as a great resources.

v 1 John 4:10-11, In this is love, not that we loved God, but that He loved us and sent His Son to be the propitiation for our sins. 11 Beloved, if God so loved us, we also ought to love one another.

Before leaving the groom would present his gifts to the bride. In the same manner, before ascending Jesus gave gifts to the Church, His bride (Ephesians 4:7-8). We could go into many aspects of the gifts as a reminder of the groom's love and similar concepts. I would like to focus on the Holy Spirit as our guarantee (Colossians 1:13-14). The gifts given to us by our Groom serve as not only a reminder, but a guarantee that He loves us and will return for us.

When the agreement was settled and the couple was officially engaged the groom would leave to prepare a place for them to live. As Joe Amaral pointed out, this could take from one to two years. He wanted the confidence that his bride-to-be was taken care of and secure enough in the marriage contract to wait for him. This is comparable to our time on earth awaiting the return of our Bridegroom.

> *Let not your heart be troubled; you believe in God, believe also in Me. In My Father's house are many mansions; if it were not so, I would have told you. I go to prepare a place for you. And if I go and prepare a place for you, I will come again and receive you to Myself; that where I am, there you may be also. And where I go you know, and the way you know* (John 14:1-4).

The groom is now preparing the place for them to live under the father's watchful eye. Another point brought out by Amaral is the fact that the father decides when the project is satisfactory for the new bride; therefore, the son doesn't know the time of his return. This may be the parallel between the engagement process and Jesus' statement that He did not know the exact hour of His return (Matthew 24:36).

Jesus' reference to the parable of the talents could have a connection to the engagement process even though it is more obviously using the concept of a master and a worker. But consider this: the awaiting bride has what seems to be only two tasks. First and foremost, she adorns herself, which basically means to get everything in order, to make herself ready. This lends itself to the idea of taking care of business. A part of her preparation was to gather what she could to present to the groom as a gift when he returns. Likewise, at the Judgment Seat of Christ we will present the fruit of our lives to Jesus at His return.

The return of the groom is so accurately representative of Jesus' return for us. When the father gives his approval, the groom sends the groomsmen (the angels) ahead of him which usually happens at night. The groomsmen would go to the city of the bride and sound the shofar (trumpet) for her to come out and meet her husband.

One of the most important responsibilities of the bride was to be ready when the groom returned. It is interesting that the word "adorned" in the Greek New Testament comes from a word that means "to snuff the wick."[vi] This tends to bring forth pictures of a person having everything so prepared that all that left to do is snuff the wick of the candle when walking out the door. This immediately brings forth the image of the ten virgins. The five wise were ready to depart immediately when the horn sounded the coming groom.

The bride did not wait in her home for the groom; she went out to meet him, which seems to speak to us meeting Him in the air.

> *For the Lord himself will come down from heaven, with a loud command, with the voice of the archangel and with the trumpet call of God, and the dead in Christ will rise first. After that, we who are still alive and are left will be caught up together with them in the clouds to meet the Lord in the air. And so we will be with the Lord forever.* (1 Thessalonians 4:16-17)

The bride and groom would then spend seven days together in the wedding chamber. This could well be one of the sources of expecting a pre-tribulation rapture. Be sure to understand, I have no problems with when the rapture takes place; I only have a problem with a forced rapture. There will be a rapture, although I am unsure about the timing. The time is something over which I have no control, but I can control, like the waiting bride, my readiness. I can watch and pray and I can keep oil in my lamp.

There is then a celebration with the wedding party after the seven days alone in the marriage chamber. This could be a correlation to the Marriage Feast of the Lamb. With types it is sometimes difficult to make all the "dots connect," but we know there will be a marriage feast.

---

vi (kos-meh'-o); from NT:2889; to put in proper order, i.e. decorate (literally or figuratively); specially, to snuff (a wick): (Biblesoft's New Exhaustive Strong's Numbers and Concordance with Expanded Greek-Hebrew Dictionary. Copyright © 1994, 2003, 2006 Biblesoft, Inc. and International Bible Translators, Inc.)

After the feast the bride is taken to the place that has been prepared for her. This is where she will live with her groom. Revelation 21 tells us God has prepared a bride for Jesus. And when it is revealed it is New Jerusalem coming down to Planet Earth. It is here in the paradise God has prepared that the bride and Groom shall forever dwell with the Father.

Regardless of how you interpret the details, the guiding concept of interpretation should never drift away from the picture of a loving groom coming for his bride with all the passion and love of a newlywed. Just this concept gives me great hope in God's willingness and ability to guide and protect me through anything I will ever face. Prayerfully ponder and meditate on each phase of the engagement. Allow the Father to open your eyes to all the protection and provision He has for you!

Regardless of how you interpret the details, the guiding concept of interpretation should never drift away from the picture of a loving groom coming for his bride with all the passion and love of a newlywed.

APOCALYPSE

CHAPTER 47

CONCLUSION
Christ Our Deliverer

God has always delivered those who walk by faith!

GOD HAS ALWAYS BEEN OUR DELIVERER. Psalm 91 and many other passages beautifully portray us as *under the shadow of the Almighty, covered by His wings, our high tower* and many other incredibly descriptive metaphors of divine protection. Those who have embraced the extreme, unscriptural concepts of sovereignty (Fatalism) are pushed to the place of doubt and anger toward God when bad things befall them. They have been led to believe all the interactions between God and men are automatic. Therefore, if it doesn't happen the way the Bible promises, God is the one who failed. Those who embrace this Luciferian ideology will be among the ones who give up or die. They will certainly never be equipped to be overcomers!

Faith experiences grace, God's ability. When we leave the realm of grace the root of bitterness springs up defiling ourselves and others (Hebrews 12:15). Their disappointment in God to operate by their ideology makes them feel they can't trust God. This anger and distrust of God is the goal of all Luciferian doctrine. Once we begin to waver in our trust for God we stop following, we stop obeying and eventually we stop listening. Then we are limited to our own intellect and reason in a war against one who has been here since before the creation of the world, Lucifer. We, in our own strength, are the epitome of bringing a knife to a gunfight. We don't stand a chance! The weapons of our warfare are not carnal… that is, if we intend to win.

We forget that we bring one act to the table that makes all the elements of this relationship actually work: faith (trust).

We forget that we bring one act to the table that makes all the elements of this relationship actually work: faith (trust). You can't have a relationship with someone you do not trust. You can have a religious, legalistic arrangement, but that is not what God has ever sought from man. God has never wanted legalistic obedience. In fact, our obedience has always been to benefit us. It doesn't benefit God in the least! He has told how the world works. He gave us everything we need to know about how to be healthy, prosperous, live in peace… *"everything that pertains to life and godliness."* He gave us all this information because of His great love for us. He has always wanted us to have the very best. Everything He has said or done has been motivated by love. When we trust Him, His character and His motives, all obedience (following His leading) is a response of trust (faith); it is never an attempt to earn. Thus the Scripture, *"faith works by love"*!

Hebrews 11 is often called *"the roll call of faith."* It reveals a factor all forms of Religionists often overlook. All of the Old Covenant models related to God by faith; they did not trust in their works as a basis of righteousness. When we read the Old Testament we must constantly remind ourselves that everything God is doing He is doing from the motive of love. That keeps us from misinterpreting His motives even when we do not understand His actions. But we must also always remind ourselves that all those who walked with God in the Old Testament walked in faith. In both the Old and New Covenants the just (righteous) live by faith (Habakkuk 2:4; Romans 1:17). Faith comes by hearing and pondering God's Word from the perspective of the Covenant of Peace* and the Gospel of Peace (Romans 10:14-17). If it is heard from the perspective of legalism the hearer will twist it into something hard and negative. If it is heard from a heart of permissiveness it will be twisted into something that gives rise to destructive, sinful behavior. If it is heard from a heart established in the Covenant it will produce overcoming faith (Psalm 78:37). As we prepare for the days that are rapidly approaching we must establish our hearts in faith, grace, righteousness and love. This will not happen from having a positive mind-set or a humanistic philosophy. This will only come by reading and meditating on God's Word with the right frame of mind. As the world grows dark we will be filled with trust for our God and we will confidently and peacefully follow Him as our Deliverer and He will empower us as overcomers!

God has provided a record of His every significant interaction with Israel. According to the Apostle Paul and other inspired writers of the New Testament, every word God spoke, every commandment, every feast, every sacrifice and every interaction with mankind would serve as a model, example and type that would have its ultimate expression in the realities of the New Covenant. If we follow the pattern of the apostles we will learn from God's interaction with Israel, the primary difference is we will interact based on the New Covenant (of Peace) not the Old (Isaiah 54:10). However, the examples are still a witness and basis of instruction to New Covenant believers.

God's Word, when read free from legalistic judgments, reveals His loving character. It is a witness to His credibility and faithfulness. It is His testimony of Himself. As we have repeatedly established through this entire work, Religionists perverted and twisted God's Word by imposing their Luciferian doctrines onto His motives. When man took on the ability to determine good and evil for himself, he didn't realize he would use it to pass judgment on God's behavior. It is nearly impossible for a 21st century New Covenant believer to read the Old Testament without interjecting those negative character traits onto our interpretation of His Word. Only by consciously interpreting the Old Testament based on what Jesus revealed about God and His character will our eyes be opened to truth.

God's Word, which had been twisted and perverted by Religionists, was an expression of His character. Jesus came as *the Word made flesh* to show us what God's Word would have meant and looked like when it was applied from God's ultimate motive: love! The apostles then studied the (Old Testament) Scripture and by enlightenment of the Holy Spirit were able to see its expression in the New Covenant. We have the apostles' doctrine, which helps us perceive the practical application of God's Word. It is important to realize that no part of the Scripture stands alone. The apostles' doctrine and the teaching of Jesus are based on what God first revealed in the Old Testament.

The Greek translation for "word," (referring to the Word of God), is most often the word "logos." The logos (Word) of God is as much about the character, wisdom, faithfulness, logic and intent of the One who spoke the word as it is about the individual words. The spoken word is only as meaningful as the one who speaks it. God's character and motives cannot be separated from what He has said. Logos, however, goes into an even more important dimension. Logos has a collective[i] sense to its meaning. Any single word carries the meaning of every other word. As such, no Word of God is in conflict with any other Word of God. It is all spoken from the same motive with the same goal. This tells us at least three very important things.

- When we interpret any of the Word of God in a way that puts it in conflict with what God has already said we are making God a liar.
- We can learn about every promise of God based on previous things God has said and done.
- God never changes. There is no confusion, chaos or contradiction in anything He says or does.

It is important to remind ourselves that iniquity (the rejection of God's Word as the absolute standard of morals, values, integrity and love) is the single factor that will render the world uninhabitable. Lucifer's rebellion began with iniquity. Iniquity has been the cause of every woe that has befallen mankind. The antichrist is the man of iniquity, and the goal of iniquity is the eradication of the knowledge of God from Planet Earth. Believing on Jesus as Lord and applying God's Word is the key to not just enduring, but overcoming in tribulation of any kind. Legalists and Luciferians purport that the motive for God's commands were negative and tyrannical. But these kinds of accusations against God can only emerge from a) a heart that is filled with iniquity and seeks to destroy God's image or b) a religious heart that embraces a humanistic definition of love.

Everything God did was for the benefit of His children. He sought to establish them as a nation that would be a light unto the world. They were to build a house of prayer for all nations. One of the things that would draw all nations to Israel would be how fair and just their laws were. Sadly, God's justice was only seen for a short time. The religious rulers of Israel didn't apply the Word from the motive of love, but legalism. But it must be known that

---

i A collective is a group of entities that share or are motivated by at least one common issue or interest, or work together to achieve a common objective. Wikipedia.org

everything God did to deliver and protect the children of Israel was an act of love and serves as an example to us who believe His Word, His character, His motives and His promises.

With a mighty hand God delivered the Israelites from Egypt, which is a type of the world and its bondage to sin. These things were recorded for our benefit that we might have hope as God once again moves to deliver His people from the grip of the world! On the night of their deliverance the children of Israel were told to sacrifice a lamb to be eaten by each household. They were to eat it with unleavened bread and bitter herbs. They were to be fully dressed and ready for their deliverance. Most importantly, they were to take the blood of the lamb and sprinkle it on the door posts and the lintel (top) of the door frame. When the angel of death came over Egypt it would see the blood and "pass over" that household. So, wrath would only be expressed on those who did not trust the blood, subsequently refusing to follow God's directions.

We are told we can overcome (prevail) against the forces of darkness by the *blood of the lamb.* This first Passover may well be our model to ponder and find encouragement in the time of wrath to come. But it is important to note, every Israelite had to hear, trust and obey God's direction in order to be delivered. God desired to deliver all the children of Israel, but they were responsible for their own faith and obedience. We must be immovable about our deliverance from wrath based on the blood of Jesus. God's wrath was already poured out on the Lord Jesus for us. Faith in His blood is the way we apply the blood to our own heart.

We are told we can overcome (prevail) against the forces of darkness by the *blood of the lamb.*

The continued observance of Passover as a feast was a reminder of what God had done for the children of Israel in the past, but it was also a rehearsal for what God would do in the future. It is important to meditate on the blood of Jesus as our deliverance from wrath. Learn to create heart pictures* of God delivering you in the midst of world-wide tribulation. Seeing this in advance will make it familiar and believable. When the time comes you will step effortlessly into what you have seen and believed in your heart.

Throughout the wilderness journey there were many examples of God's provision, protection and leadership which we should look to for encouragement. In the wilderness they were led by the cloud by day and the fire by night. This represents God's intention to guide us through every step of the treacherous journey in a hostile world. Had they not been willing to follow God's direction they would never have been at the appointed places of provision. They ate manna, drank water from the rock and God provided them quail to eat. In fact, they could have gotten honey from the rock if they had believed God's willingness and ability to provide (Psalm 81:16).

By following the Holy Spirit's direction they secured incredible military conquests. These victories are even more impressive when we factor in all the information. They were not a militarily trained or equipped people. They had no experience at war, not to mention, they not only faced enemies of God who were experienced, vicious warriors; they were surrounded by Nephilim (giants) who existed solely to eliminate all knowledge of God from the earth. So this newly formed nation with no military training or experienced leadership won their battles against all probable odds by following, listening, trusting and obeying God. This is our model for overcoming when everyone else is giving up. It doesn't matter how powerful the forces are that rise up against us. What matters is how powerful our God is, and our willingness to hear, trust and obey!

It doesn't matter how powerful the forces are that rise up against us. What matters is how powerful our God is, and our willingness to hear, trust and obey!

It may be important, before diving into the details, to go back to their initiation into this world of protection, provision and leadership. The people trusting in the blood of the lamb, eating his flesh and metaphorically drinking his blood were delivered from wrath. They were delivered from the dominance of the most powerful nation on earth when they crossed the Red Sea. This was a type of being baptized into the body of Christ. But this was, by no means, the end of their experience or the fulfillment of necessary equipping for the journey to the place of rest. Let me remind you again, according to the New Testament all these things are examples to us.

Their next stop was Mount Sinai. This is the place where the law was given to Moses, who then presented it to the people. Moses is a type of Christ who received the New Covenant from God and delivered it to us through the person and work of the Holy Spirit. Moses received the law and the commandments from God. This law would be what would establish them as a nation. Until now they were not a nation, they were a tribe. All kingdoms consist of a king, a realm and the laws whereby the citizens can have justice, peace and security.

Mount Sinai was the first Pentecost before it was ordained as an official feast. Pentecost is a remembrance and celebration of God giving the law. It is celebrated in conjunction with the harvest. The children of Israel had to be delivered from one nation before they could become a new nation. To become this new nation they had to be willing to leave behind all the ways of the Egyptians. Their new nation would be governed by new laws and a new Lawgiver: a benevolent, loving Father who only sought the good of His children. The justice and fairness of God would bear fruit in the entire world. History reveals that nations who govern more consistently with God's command succeed, endure and have more internal peace. Those who, through iniquity, create their own codes of justice and morality can never last; they abide in constant chaos. They are always overcome by corruption.

Those who reject the law or consider it to be a horrible proposition on God's part, stumble at the idea of rejoicing and celebrating the giving of the law every year at Pentecost. Those who hate and reject the law do not understand love or righteousness. They make the mistake of looking at the law as a means of legalistic performance, totally missing and rejecting what Jesus taught and modelled concerning the law. Until Jesus, man only had man's interpretation of the law. Jesus brought grace and truth, not a new truth but a revelation of all God previously said. He revealed God's true intentions and motives for the commandments. Jesus showed what the law would look like when it is applied from the motive of love. Plus He brought grace so we would have God's power of righteousness working in us to walk in love, thereby, accomplishing the goals and intentions of the commandments.

Grace and the commandments are not mutually exclusive. Grace and legalism are, however, completely incompatible. Whether the commandments are used as God's prescription for how to walk in love (treat one another) or used for self-righteous legalism is based on what's in the heart of the believer. Two people can do the same thing for completely different reasons. But according to God's Word the law is not, nor has it ever been, evil or bad, it has been perverted by those with a crooked (iniquitous) religious heart. To call it evil is to call God evil or bad, which is the accusation of Luciferian philosophy. Luciferian philosophy always blames something external for man's problems. It opposes personal responsibility simply because personal responsibility is what God's Word requires. This is the basis for all leftist, humanistic, Progressive, World System doctrine, whether preached in the White House or the church house. The moment we blame anything outside of ourselves for our actions we are functioning in a victim's self-righteous, codependent mindset that will not follow God. The only solace for such a mindset is to blame and attack others, thereby making them responsible for our choices. Personal responsibility is one of the consistent messages in Jesus' parables of the Kingdom.

The commandments given by God at Mount Sinai were the type of the law being written in our hearts which occurs under the New Covenant. But the giving of the Law was also the prerequisite for Israel becoming a holy nation. Someone said the best way to understand the word "holy" is to look at its opposite. If something was holy it was never used for common purposes. For example, the utensils in the tabernacle were not used for daily meals; they were sanctified (set apart) for holy (uncommon) purposes. The commandments were so different from anything the world had ever seen that if applied from God's motive would have set (sanctified) Israel apart as a holy (uncommon) nation. By accepting God's commandments they were accepting God as their Lawgiver (King) and they were accepting His promise to lead them into the Promised Land and establish them as a great nation.

The commandments were divine prescriptions for how a people could function together in perfect harmony, fairness, equity and justice. None of the commandments, feasts or sacrifices were for God's benefit. In Psalm 50:10-12 God declares that if He were hungry He would kill a cow and eat it for Himself. After all, the cattle on a thousand hills belong to Him. Again in Psalm 40:6-10 He says He never desired sacrifices and offerings. If God did not desire those things why did He institute them? For our benefit! All the commandments were for the good of God's people.[ii] They had been inundated with the values and philosophies of the world. Those values and philosophies only work in the dog-eat-dog way of the World's System and all the philosophies of the World's System were derived from Luciferian philosophies.

---

ii Deuteronomy 10:13-14, ..., keep the commandments of the Lord and His statutes which I command you today for your good?

The feasts and sacrifices served as reminders that reconnected them to God's truth, and the fact that these would ultimately be fulfilled at an appointed time in the future. It was a way of influencing their hearts.

The world had never seen a fair and just judicial system that protected the poor against domination by the wealthy. They had never seen an economic system that reset itself regularly to protect the economy. They had never seen laws of any kingdom that were designed to ensure every man was treated fairly by his fellow citizen. The most astounding thing, however, was they had never seen a kingdom where the God of the kingdom initiated His love and protection rather than the people having to constantly seek to appease Him. The commandments were the laws that would govern the nation. Any individual who wanted to be a part of that nation was called upon to trust God for themselves and walk in love toward their fellowman. Based on this agreement Israel was birthed into a nation (kingdom). Israel was a type of the Kingdom of God.

The Baptism in the Holy Spirit is designed to empower the individual believer to be a witness to the resurrection of Jesus (Acts 1:8), which should result in taking the message of the Kingdom to the ends of the earth.

Mount Sinai was the forerunner of baptism in the Holy Spirit as evidenced on the day of Pentecost in the Book of Acts. This was the birth of the Church as a spiritual kingdom, just like Mount Sinai was the birth of the kingdom of Israel. Baptism in the Holy Spirit is designed to empower the individual believer to be a witness to the resurrection of Jesus (Acts 1:8), which should result in taking the message of the Kingdom to the ends of the earth. But the Religionists of the New Testament, just like those of the Old Testament, managed to somehow twist God's goals and purposes and lead the body of Christ off track.

The Church at Rome twisted theology away from the apostles' doctrine, the teaching of Christ and most vehemently against the commandments. Their doctrinal influence for so long a period has left much of the Church world with an impotent mix of occult mysticism cloaked in Christian terminology so even the Reformation and many subsequent "revivals" and "movements" have been unable to get much of the Church back on target. That's why I am so thankful for courageous visionary pastors who still believe in the gifts of the Holy Spirit, faith righteousness, unconditional love and world evangelism. No matter how bad things appear, there is always a remnant and today there are hundreds of thousands of churches and pastors that are functioning for the purpose for which God laid hold of us.[iii]

The gospel to be preached in all the earth was the Gospel of the Kingdom. We think evangelism is about making converts but, in reality, evangelism is about making disciples. Disciples are those who live for the king; their life is not their own, they know they were bought with a price. They are *in* the world but not *of* the world. They are foreigners who are just passing through. Their citizenship is in the Kingdom of God, a realm that is entered into through the heart when one trusts and applies God's truth.

The gospel to be preached in all the earth was the gospel of the Kingdom. We think evangelism is about making converts but, in reality, evangelism is about making disciples.

Just as God gave His commandments at Mount Sinai on Pentecost He poured out His Spirit and wrote His commandments on the hearts of the believers. They had the Holy Spirit in them to minister grace in their personal life and now they had the Holy Spirit upon them, flowing through them ministering to the world around them. All the commandments given at Mount Sinai were given to a nation but they had to be individually accepted by each person. Likewise, the Spirit is given to every believer without measure; however, it is the individual believer who chooses whether to yield or not to His influence and leading.

The Kingdom of God is righteousness, peace and joy in the Holy Spirit (Romans 14:17). It is not a matter of words and arguments, but of power (1 Corinthians 4:20). Those who, because they believe in God's character and motives, choose to yield to the leading and empowering of the Holy Spirit enter the Kingdom of God, a realm that is available to all, but only entered into by the kind of faith that trusts and implements the Word of God from

iii Philippians 3:12-13, I press on, that I may lay hold of that for which Christ Jesus has also laid hold of me.

God's motive. This is not to imply that it is earned by our behavior, but it is inherited in Jesus as a right that is taken hold of (received) by our faith. Not every believer is living in righteousness, peace and joy even though it has been freely given. Not every believer is experiencing power, strength and ability (grace),[iv] even though it is available. All manifestations of grace are received (taken hold of) by personal, individual faith (Ephesians 2:8). Just as it was God's intention to establish the people of Israel as a nation that would be a light in a dark world, He desires to establish us as a holy nation that will be light in the darkness, the salt of the earth and the testimony of a loving God.

After a few disasters the children of Israel launched out from Mount Sinai to journey into the unknown, but they followed the King. He was the cloud by day and the fire by night that guided them. He was the rock that followed and fed them. He was their shield and rearguard, their high tower, their strength and their banner of victory. Every act of provision, protection and leadership was for our example. When we face tribulation we will follow the Holy Spirit to every divine appointment and connection arranged for our provision and deliverance.

The second characteristic of an overcomer is, *"the word of their testimony."* The ability to express our personal testimonies is of the utmost importance. It is, without a doubt, the most powerful vehicle for introducing the love of God to others. Plus, it has a profound effect on our own hearts when we share our personal experiences. But this Scripture could be implying more than this. In the Greek this would be the "logos of our (martyrdom) testimony."

Since the "logos" is a truth that is consistent with every other truth God has ever spoken, this could be qualifying our testimony. Our testimony is the result of witnessing something. A witness has firsthand knowledge of something they have seen, heard or experienced. How much of our faith in Jesus is actually based on the scriptural account? We only experience grace based on our faith in the truth, not our version of the truth. In John 7:38 Jesus said the Holy Spirit would spring up from within us if we believe on Him…AS THE SCRIPTURE SAID! It didn't say to believe on Him as you wanted to or according to your personal experience or revelation, but *as the Scripture says.* If our testimony is the "logos" our experience must be based on everything God has said.

---

iv to be able, have power, (from Thayer's Greek Lexicon, Electronic Database. Copyright © 2000, 2003, 2006 by Biblesoft, Inc. All rights reserved.)

We must root our hope in God's protection and provision, on the promises of His Word, the examples He has provided and the Covenant He made in the Lord Jesus. In Jesus we are qualified for every promise God made to anyone (2 Corinthians 1:20, Colossians 1:12). That's why it is so important for us to know what He did for others in the past. If He did it for anyone He will do it for us.

The way of faith is to trust in God's Word because we trust in God's character and motives. Faith is what moves us from the dominion of life on this natural plane to an experience of grace that makes us superhuman. When the antichrist is waging war on the world and forcing his mark on all human beings the Bible makes an interesting statement: *"Here is the patience of the saints: here are they that keep the commandments of God, and the faith of Jesus"* (Revelation 14:12). Based on this Scripture, keeping the commandments does not negate faith in Jesus. In fact, the New Testament reveals that faith in Jesus always results in keeping the commandments.

Our legalistic interpretation of the phrase "keep the commandments" tends to result in a legalistic attempt to do everything they say. But this word seems to reflect more about an attitude than a single action. It actually means something more like "keeping them in view"[v] or "keeping an eye toward them." This brings us to the reality that while walking in faith we are ever-mindful of how God wants us to live and treat one another. Jesus made it clear that when we stop keeping or being attentive to the commands we leave the realm of His love... not His love for us, but His love expressed through us (John 15:10).

In the tribulation of the antichrist the man of iniquity clearly reveals Lucifer's true intent behind political correctness, social justice, the fairness doctrine and all the false religions. According to Daniel, he will change all (moral, spiritual, ethical and judicial) laws and even times.[vi] Why? Because he intends to force the world to not just reject God but to reject everything God has ever said and replace it with his iniquitous, pride-filled rebellion of lies. Once God's commandments are totally rejected there is no actual love on earth. *"And because lawlessness (iniquity) will abound, the love of many will grow cold"* (Matthew 24:12). When love is gone mankind will hate, abuse and murder one another with no sense of guilt.

---

v The basic meaning of this word is "to keep in view," (from Theological Dictionary of the New Testament, abridged edition, Copyright © 1985 by William B. Eerdmans Publishing Company. All rights reserved.)

vi All of this has already been done in all Muslim nations.

While he is flexing his muscle and making the world bow before his image there will be one group he cannot conquer: those who keep the commandments and the faith of Jesus! The Bible says these two attributes are the patience of the saints. Patience has many subtle meanings. In its broader sense it means "to endure hardships without giving up." But when looking at how the word is used to contrast wavering, we realize it begins to present the idea of being "able to stand under pressure without wavering." If you don't waver, you don't fall. James also says when we allow patience to have its perfect work, we will be perfect (complete), perfectly sound, lacking (needing) nothing (James 1:4-6).

Believers who fully trust God's character and motives will never blame God for the tribulation. They will always look to God for deliverance. They will have a stability that comes from trusting God's Word. Their refusal to entertain iniquity on any level reflects their confidence in God's Word, which means they will have confidence in His promises. Those who reject any part of God's Word have trouble trusting every part of God's Word. If we reject the promises it is difficult to believe them. The God that said to love your neighbor by being kind, paying him what you owe and never slander is the same God that made thousands of promises that pertain to your deliverance. When we reject any part of God's Word it is not the individual Scriptures we don't trust, it is the character and motive of God. If you don't believe the Word that tells you how to love your brother, it is self-deception to assume you will believe the promises for deliverance. Any form of iniquity causes love to grow cold… and faith works by love.

When we reject any part of God's Word it is not the individual Scriptures we don't trust, it is the character and motive of God.

The last trait of those who overcome is *"they love not their lives unto the death."* This may have some overlap with the word of their martyrdom (testimony). The word "witness" or "testimony" comes from the word "martyr." In the anti-God, anti-Jesus, Roman world being a witness to the fact that Jesus had risen from the dead was a sure and quick road to death. The idea of dying and sharing your testimony became synonymous. The one who is a personal witness to the resurrection by their experience and their belief in God's Word and who testifies to these facts has already laid down his or her life.

The truth is, if we have actually accepted Jesus as Lord and chosen to put on the new man created in true holiness, it is incumbent that we accept our death. We can't live two lives. Like Israel leaving Egypt, we can't be citizens of two kingdoms. We either live as the old man or the new man, there's not really a third option. This biblical approach to being a disciple was lost in the watered-down, socially-acceptable version of the gospel that emerged under the influence of the Religionists. We can never move from being a believer to a disciple until we are ready to accept our death with Him on the cross. This should have been our determination of faith at water baptism (Colossians 2:12). When we accept our death, the struggle to hold on to the past or to function in our old identity comes to an end. Life as a new man is easy once we accept the death of the old man. But more importantly, accepting our death in Him is the pathway to overcoming the fear of physical death, which holds people in bondage to the devil (Hebrews 2:14-15).

Many believers are looking for some doctrine that will give them the hope of never facing persecution or death for their faith. While that is certainly understandable, it is not the fruit of a person who has surrendered ALL to Jesus. It is this very attachment to the life we have in this world that could interfere with our willingness to follow God to living as overcomers and experience His supernatural deliverance! The person who has nothing else to lose cannot be controlled by fear. They have already accepted their death in this world. They can follow wherever God leads without reservation. I believe it will be this breed of disciple that will also do incredible exploits for the Kingdom.

Nearly everyone is familiar with the three Hebrews from the Book of Daniel that were thrown into the fiery furnace because they refused to worship the image set up by king Nebuchadnezzar. This is the perfect example of what many will face under the antichrist.[vii] They present what I believe to be the perfect attitude when facing death.

> *"Our God whom we serve is able to deliver us from the burning fiery furnace, and He will deliver us from your hand, O king. BUT IF NOT, let it be known to you, O king, that we do not serve your gods, nor will we worship the gold image which you have set up."* (Daniel 3 17-18).

---

vii Christians all across the Middle East are already being martyred by the thousands. Babies are being plucked from their parents arms and their heads are cut off. Other believers are being burned alive. This information iusf being withheld from the world by the Luciferian governments and their media puppets.

They knew God could deliver them, they believed He would deliver them, but even if for some reason He didn't they still had no intention of bowing. This is the attitude of a person who cannot be conquered.

One of their secrets to victory lies in the fact that they knew they were already delivered from Nebuchadnezzar even though they were unsure about being delivered from the flames. If we have been delivered from this world in our own heart, all other factors are secondary. We who have already died to this life enjoy a freedom from its allure. When facing imminent death Jesus said, *"The ruler of this world is coming and he has nothing in me."* Freedom from the man of iniquity is when we have no iniquity in us. Like Jesus, should we face death it is a matter of blinking our eyes and being in the presence of Jesus. It is time to accept what the Scripture says. Following Jesus may cost us our life. If Heaven is sure and Christ is real in your heart, you are already free from those who would seek your life. And trust this… in the time of need you will always experience the grace you need for that moment!

Following Jesus may cost us our life. If Heaven is sure and Christ is real in your heart, you are already free from those who would seek your life.

While we should all be looking for the rapture, we need not be overly concerned about when it will occur, but more concerned about our being ready for its occurrence. We should be like the bride awaiting her bridegroom, packed and ready to leave the security of her father's house to take up a new life with her groom in the place he has prepared for her. Remember, the groom did not come and remove her from her father's house; she heard the shofar and ran out to meet him. We should be like the children of Israel packed and ready to leave Egypt at the sound of the shofar! Our hearts must be free from the world. Like Paul, we must be dead to the world and the world dead to us.

I believe in the rapture. I see the plausibility of most of the doctrinal positions about the rapture. My issue is not about when the rapture will happen; it is about the idea of a "forced rapture." We have no model for God ever forcing anyone into anything. Like His examples of the bride we must have oil in our lamps, watching and praying, ready for His call. Like Enoch, we must walk by faith.

Consider this, if the rapture is our spirit and soul leaving our body this will be no different than death, other than the progression of sickness. In death we lose consciousness of the world and immediately go to be with the Lord. So other than sickness or an accident, facing the rapture could be a lot like facing death. The only difference could be the fact that we may have the choice of saying yes or no! So what is it that keeps us bound to the devil? Fear of death! So if we are not ready to face death, we might not be ready for the rapture.

What if today you had a sense that you could close your eyes and "crossover"? Would you be ready to die by faith? Revelation makes this statement: *"Blessed are those who die henceforth in the Lord"* (Revelation 14:13). Blessed means "fortunate" or "to be envied." What is so fortunate about dying? Maybe it's a reference to the honor of dying for our Lord. Or maybe it's a reference to how fortunate someone is to die and escape what is happening on Planet Earth. The Book of Enoch makes references to righteous people dying before the Flood and escaping the tragedy that had befallen the world. One can't help but wonder if they, like Enoch, crossed over by faith?

My issue is not about when the rapture will happen; it is about the idea of a "forced rapture." We have no model for God ever forcing anyone into anything.

Isaiah 57:1 tells us we fail to take to heart that when the righteous die they escape the evil to come. Should we consider that we may have the opportunity to die by faith before the world reaches a point of horror? If so, it will be just that, we will have to yield to it or choose it. As romantic a notion as this sounds, it is still dying and the question still begs to be answered, "Have I settled my fear of death?" If not, any way of escape the Lord provides may be more frightening than the tribulation of the world. I only bring up these possibilities so we can each consider how the rapture could seem like death. *Loving not our lives unto the death* is one of the key components to being an overcomer. If overcoming is in my plan I must consider these possibilities.

Even though the definite article before the word "death" is not in the original text, the context implies this is referring to the specific kind of death dealt out by the antichrist and his followers against those who hold the testimony of Jesus. Regardless of how death comes I must know that I can only be an overcomer, someone who prevails against the enemy if I am willing to die before bowing.

Every day the Israelites faced the decision of whether to follow the cloud and the fire. They had no idea where they were going next or what kind of enemy they might face. There were many who wanted to go back to the oppression of Egypt for the security of food and familiarity. Then there were the mixed multitudes who struggled with every challenge and many fell by the wayside because they would not trust and obey God. The only thing the children of Israel had to go on was they trusted in the faithfulness of God and His character.

When thinking of the rapture it is essential to consider the example of Lot's wife who looked back as they were delivered from Sodom. There are so many things that could cause one to look back. Obviously, fear and unbelief would top the list, but for those who love their family it could be concern. I would not want to hear the call of God in my heart and be hesitant or resistant because of concern about the safety or spiritual condition of a loved one. Now is the time to win our loved ones to Jesus and help them prepare. That's why I'm encouraging every family to use this book as a Bible study to prepare everyone they love for the return of Jesus. We only have two choices: prepare for the return of Jesus or prepare for the antichrist. If I'm prepared to follow and ultimately meet Jesus I need not be too concerned with the antichrist.

I would not want to hear the call of God in my heart and be hesitant or resistant because of concern about the safety or spiritual condition of a loved one. Now is the time to win our loved ones to Jesus and help them prepare.

In the days to come you will hear God's voice or sense His leading. The decisions that you make now may be crucial, preemptive preparation for the days ahead. Whether you hear it or not, recognize it or not, trust it or not… God will be attempting to prepare and lead you into the safest possibilities, the essential preparations and the needed provisions for the journey ahead of you.

Don't stress, don't try to force anything, don't try to figure it all out… rest in God. Keep your heart free from the world. Watch and pray.

> God will be attempting to prepare and lead you into the safest possibilities, the essential preparations and the needed provisions for the journey ahead of you. Don't stress, don't try to force anything, don't try to figure it all out… rest in God. Keep your heart free from the world. Watch and pray.

Between now and then Jesus gave us two primary things we should do to prepare for the end: Have a heart that is alive, attentive and obedient to God as He leads and take the gospel of the Kingdom to the world around you, and serve others by loving and leading them in their walk with Jesus.

Now you know how all this started, how we got here, how it's going to end and how to prepare. I recommend you go back and go through all the exercises suggested in all the chapters. Since this last segment was all about solutions there was no Spiritual Guide section at the end of the chapters. If you are reading this in a digital format be sure to click on all the links for other support materials. Remember, the just live by faith, so if you trust and follow Jesus you will always find your deliverance!

GLOSSARY

Words are incredibly important. Unless we are face-to-face, words are the only means of communication we have. However, what one person says and another person hears can be worlds apart. Why? Because words mean different things to different people. In writing we do not have the luxury of explaining what we mean. In order to reduce confusion I am creating a glossary of some of the words that you may not know or that I may be using in a very specific manner.

I am not saying the way I am using a word is the only way to understand it. So, I want to provide you with a general concept of what I mean when I use a certain word. In most cases I am attempting to convey a biblical concept for which we have no word. In many cases I had to either create terminologies or choose an alternate word.

Angel of light: Light represents God's truth as it has been presented in the Word of God in all its implications and intentions; therefore, and angel of light is a messenger of God that brings God's truth to mankind. Lucifer is considered by the occult to be an angel of light. Their concept of light is knowledge, specifically secret knowledge. The occult and secret societies believe that Lucifer is actually the redeemer. They believe he brought knowledge to mankind and through this knowledge man is able to advance himself and break free from the tyranny of an angry, wrathful God whose commands only serve to keep us in darkness and captivity.

Antichrist: An adversary of Christ. In a biblical sense this is used of those who present themselves as being believers but are actually opposed to the work of Christ as the only means of salvation. There have been many antichrists (1 John 2:18). The antichrist, the man of iniquity, is a copy of the real thing. He will come with lying signs and wonders and seek to deceive the world by bringing a false peace and a total rejection of God's commands as the measure for morality, morals and standards.

Apocalypse: the meaning of apocalypse has come to be very different than its original meaning. The Book of Revelation is literally the Book of Apocalypse. Most people define an apocalypse as a massive disaster of some type. But as it is used in the Bible, it is more of a disclosure of knowledge, i.e. a lifting of the veil or revelation or literally: making naked.[i] Many people feel the Book of Revelation has already come to pass. That concept is based on a confused definition of the word. This is not a revelation of the end times, but a revelation of Jesus and His solution to the tribulation that is brought on the world by the antichrist and his followers.

Appearance of Nephilim: This refers to the times throughout history that the Nephilim were prevalent in Planet Earth. This first time was before the Flood of Noah (Genesis 6:2-4). The Nephilim were most noted for being giants, but they were often considered great men with supernatural abilities. The Nephilim were the perpetrators of ancient philosophies, sciences and religions designed to undermine man's trust for God and His Word. After the Flood Nimrod, the founder of Babel, is the first Nephilim mentioned. They were later discovered in the land of Canaan. They also emerged in Phoenicia and ancient Greece. They were the first world travelers. Their remains and evidence of their godless religions (human sacrifices) and false deities have been discovered all over the globe.

Caliphate: is a form of Islamic government led by a **caliph** —a person considered a political and religious successor to the prophet Muhammad and a leader of the entire Muslim community. The Ottoman Empire was the caliphate that overthrew the Roman Empire and conquered Jerusalem. A caliphate led by the antichrist will be the religious empire of the false religion that seeks to overthrow the world and extinguish all knowledge of Jehovah as God and Jesus as Lord.

Church: The spiritual body of Christ made up of those who heard and responded to the call of God to follow Him by believing on the death, burial and resurrection of Jesus and surrendering to Him as Lord. The "called out." In the common Greek it was a body of people called out who came together

---

i from Thayer's Greek Lexicon, Electronic Database. Copyright © 2000, 2003, 2006 by Biblesoft, Inc. All rights reserved.

in an assembly. In the New Testament it more specifically refers to those who have heard and responded to the call of the Holy Spirit to the body of Christ.

Communists: are those who adhere to the political and economic doctrine that aims to replace private property and a profit-based economy with public ownership and communal control of at least the major means of production (e.g., mines, mills and factories) and the natural resources of a society. Communism is thus a form of Socialism—a higher and more advanced form, according to its advocates. Exactly how Communism differs from Socialism has long been a matter of debate, but the distinction rests largely on the Communists' adherence to the revolutionary Socialism of Karl Marx. (Britanica.com) Those who adhere to the philosophical concepts of Communism. Communists believe in absolute rule by the state. They are anti-God and anti-any religious or philosophical position that gives power to anyone other than the state.

Create heart pictures is a meditative term whereby one creates and ponders images in their own mind of themselves experiencing the promises of God.

Dualism: While there are many subtle meanings to Dualism, I am using the word to describe the faulty theology that presents God and the devil as being equal or near equal in power.

Ears to Hear: this is a term Jesus used referring to those who had the willingness and capacity to recognize the truth and application of God's Word as He presented it.

Elitist, utopian world: An elitist is someone who believes in rule by an elite group. Utopia is an imaginary, idealized society described in Thomas More's book, *Utopia*. An elitist, utopian world is the world elitists are attempting to build through a One World Government where the government controls all areas of the individual's life. This is based on the elitist concept that the unenlightened human is incapable of deciding what is best for their life; therefore, his or her decisions should be made by the state.

Enduring is more about surviving. It is one of the words used to describe believers who go through the tribulation of the antichrist.

Enlightened: Enlightenment can mean many different things, according to what group is defining the word. In general, those who consider themselves enlightened are the ones who are too advanced to believe in God, morals or any absolutes. They believe because of their enlightened state they are the ones who should make the laws whereby man should live. They seek to create a godless world where the enlightened (all those who agree with their godless philosophies) rule over the ignorant, superstitious believers in God and morality.

Enoch: Was a man who lived before Noah's Flood who, according to the Bible, walked with God. He named his son Methuselah which means "when he is gone it shall come." Methuselah lived 969 years. By his name we know that Enoch was warning the world about the coming flood. By the length of his life we see the mercy and patience of God.

Eschatology: is a part of theology concerned with the final events of history, or the ultimate destiny of humanity. (Wikipedia)

Forbidden knowledge: The Nephilim had much of the knowledge that God had used to create the world. According to the Book of Enoch they were the ones who taught mankind how to make weapons of war, astronomy, astrology and many of the sciences. They taught man geometry, which to this day is considered sacred in many secret societies. It was by this knowledge that ancient civilizations built the pyramids and other mega structures that even now cannot be built even with the use of computers and modern technology. It is this forbidden knowledge they will use to overthrow mankind in their attempt to create a world free from the influence of almighty God!

Giants: Giants are historical fact. Over 1,500 newspapers have documented the discovery of giant skeletal remains in North America alone. These remains have been discovered on nearly every continent. They are written about in Greek literature and have been thought to be mythical; yet, historical and anthropological facts prove otherwise. These skeletal remains range from 7.5 feet tall to over 30 feet tall. Most of the remains are in what have been labeled as Indian burial grounds, making them off limits for research. This proof of giants poses one of the greatest threats to the theory of evolution, the hingepin of Atheism. Giants, according to the scripture, were the offspring of relationships between women and a special class of angels called the "watchers" in ancient Hebrew literature. They are referred to as Nephilim in the Hebrew. Their presence was described in the Bible both before and after the Flood of Noah.

God's Covenant of Peace: The Covenant of Peace is the covenant that God made with Jesus as a result of His faith and obedience (Isaiah 54:10). When we are baptized into the body of Christ, by the Holy Spirit we share in His covenant.

Heart Physics is a 30-day life-transformation program, based on Jesus' teaching about the heart. It was developed by Dr. Jim Richards and designed to help the believer come into a living awareness of Christ in his or her heart.

Iniquity: In the Old Testament the word "iniquity" was sometimes associated with the idea of "twisting" or "crooked." It was used of a person who perverted or twisted God's Word. When referring to the heart it would be the idea of a crooked heart, which the Bible says is incapable of finding good. In the New Testament the word "iniquity" comes from a Greek word that means "no law." It is used of people who reject God's commands as the standard of morals, ethics, integrity and standards. In most cases people in the world who are given to iniquity reject God's Word and replace it with humanistic concepts (political correctness or social justice). In the Church people who reject God's commands tend to replace them with "personal revelations" or private interpretations.

Kingdom of God: The philosophy whereby we govern our life based on God's Word applied from faith and love.

Lucifer, the light bearer: In the World's System God is viewed as a legalistic tyrant who oppressed man with His rules and regulations. Lucifer is viewed as the one who set man free from God by giving him knowledge.

Luciferian: Lucifer is the father of all iniquity. He formed the first rebellion in Heaven against God with the intention of being god and establishing his version of truth. Through his influence Adam and Eve brought iniquity into the world when they transgressed God's warning and decided to be their own gods by claiming the right to determine good and evil apart from God.

Luciferians: Those people whether in a religious setting, a secret society, government or even Christians who knowingly or unknowingly adhere to the erroneous concepts of God introduced into this world by Lucifer and perpetuated by those who embrace such philosophies. The primary Luciferian concept is God is angry, legalistic and wrath-filled and cannot be trusted.

Mahdi: In Islamic eschatology, the Mahdi is the prophesied redeemer of Islam who will rule for seven… years. He is the one the Bible identifies as the antichrist who seeks to destroy Israel and all Christians, forcing all humans to worship Allah.

Meditation: According to Scripture, meditation is when one in their own heart and mind ponders, considers or reflects on any matter until it becomes real in their experience. In Hebrew it can mean to "frame up" or to "lay a foundation."

Mother of Heaven and the queen of Heaven are among the names and concepts given to Semiramis, the wife of Nimrod, who is also called Ishtar. When Israel went into idolatry she was one of the many false deities they worshipped. It is from the worship of Semiramis that the worship of Mary evolved as the mother. Many of the statues of Mary holding Jesus are actually replicas of Semiramis holding her son whom she claimed to have been born by the warm rays of the son god (Nimrod) flowing over her body.

Natural laws: These are the actual laws of physics whereby God created the natural world. According to the Apostle Paul, these laws that have brought all things into being reveal the true character and traits of God. Romans 1:20-21, *"For since the creation of the world His invisible attributes are clearly seen, being understood by the things that are made, even His eternal power and Godhead, so that they are without excuse."*

New World Order: The term **New World Order** or **NWO** refers to the emergence of a totalitarian world government (Wikipedia.org). While this is labeled a conspiracy theory it is a word used by President George Bush, Sr. and many government officials. It is the goal of the many secret societies, the United Nations and other international governmental agencies. Like all the other ant-God political philosophies it is totalitarian rule by the enlightened.

Occult: The word in its simplest form means "secret" or "hidden," specifically "secret knowledge." The occult and secret societies believe they have secret knowledge that gives them power over God. They believe through their secret knowledge they can control and one day rule the world.

Overcomers are believers who not only endure the tribulation of the antichrist, they actually are victorious over opposition.

Political-religious: A political-religious government requires its citizens to comply with its religious beliefs and demands, very similar to a theocracy.

Possess a human: This term refers to when a demonic spirit possesses a human being. The question is, however, what does that really mean? In the original language the concept of possession, whatever else it may imply, is rooted in the fact that a human is yielded to the influence of demonically inspired thought and behavior.

Progressives: are the adherents to Progressivism; an idea that man can progress through science and technology. It is an idea that emerged during the age of reason, which basically was a movement with the aim at eradicating faith from all social influence. It is simply another form of Communism, Socialism and the occult, which is rooted in the idea that the enlightened should rule the world.

Religionist: Religion is man's attempt to approach and/or satisfy God on his own terms. It is actually a form of Humanism. The opposite of religion is faith. When a person is in faith he or she trusts what God says and obeys. This is why the Bible refers to us as believers. Religionists are people who may be Christian or who may simply call themselves Christian. They use Christian terminology, they may employ some truly authentic biblical means, but they are more committed to their religion/culture/tradition than they are to the Word of God. They corrupt and neutralize the Word of God through their religious traditions (Mark 7:13).

Remnant: The Bible (both Old and New Testaments)always presents the idea that there is a remnant, i.e. a remaining group of believers that no matter how wicked Israel, the Church or the world has become, are pure in their love and devotion for Him.

Satanists: Satanists are people whose loyalty is pledged to Satan, his goals and objectives. They seek to live their lives independently of God and His morals and values. There are many different types of Satanists as described within this book. They range from very religious and ritualistic to those who simply live for self-gratification.

Scriptures: The Written Word of God, both the Old and New Testaments. Almost all religions have their own scriptures, which is a reference to their holy books.

Secret Societies are groups of people who have entered into a vow of secrecy. They share what they believe are the secrets whereby one can rule and control the world. They are introduced to small levels of ideology by initiation. When an initiate has proven himself or herself worthy, and when they are "brought in" to their present level of secret knowledge, they are initiated into a deeper level of knowledge. Secret societies rarely reveal their true beliefs until one is deeply indoctrinated.

Sharia law: is the Islamic legal system derived from the religious precepts of Islam (Wikipedia.org). It is the goal of Islam to force the entire world to live under the rule of Sharia law. In their current jihad they offer the option of converting to Islam and living by Sharia law or death by beheading, drowning, burning or various means of torture.

Socialists: are those who adhere to the doctrine of Socialism, a social and economic doctrine that calls for public rather than private ownership or control of property and natural resources. According to the Socialist view, individuals do not live or work in isolation but live in cooperation with one another. Furthermore, everything that people produce is in some sense a social product, and everyone who contributes to the production of a good is entitled to a share in it. Society as a whole, therefore, should own or at least control property for the benefit of all its members (Britanica.com). Socialism is little more than a modified form of Communism.

Sovereignty is the right and power to govern one's self and make laws with no outside input or interference. However, the doctrine of sovereignty as it is presented today is a false doctrine that emerged from Greek Fatalism. Fatalism presents the idea that the gods are in control and man can do nothing to alter his fate. It goes on to imply that God can do anything He wants even if it violates what He has previously stated. This doctrinal error is devastating. First, it violates the idea that man is created in the likeness and image of God therefore, he has a free will and, unlike any other created being, can change the quality of his or her life by the decisions they make. Second, it violates the faithfulness and dependability of God to His own Word. God is not a liar; He cannot and will not violate His own Word. He is bound by what He says! At its core it contradicts the clear statement that God gave authority of Planet Earth to man. The world is becoming what man chooses based on whose word he trusts. And what is so damning is the idea that God is in control of everything that happens, making Him responsible for all good and evil.

Theocrasy is the combining of all gods into one. It is a form of Universalism. It is not to be confused with a theocracy, which is a form of government ruled by clergy in behalf of their god. Islam is a theocracy.

Unseen hand is a phrase used to refer to the true power behind the governments of the world, i.e. the powers who actually influence and control the world.

World's System: There are two philosophies whereby we govern our life. One is the Kingdom of God, which is based on God's Word applied from faith and love. The other is the philosophy of the world based on iniquity and Humanism.

Zeal in modern terms is seen as fervor or passion and often has a positive connotation. However, in the New Testament it is rarely seen as a positive thing. In the Book of James zeal is connected to the root of all confusion and evil. James 3:16 says, *For where envying and strife is, there is confusion and every evil work* (KJV). The word translated as "envying" comes from the word "zeal," which in this case is "the consequence of selfish ambition."

ABOUT THE AUTHOR

In 1972, Dr. James B. Richards accepted Christ and answered the call to ministry. His dramatic conversion and passion to help hurting people launched him onto the streets of Huntsville, Alabama. Early on in his mission to reach teenagers and drug abusers, his ministry quickly grew into a home church that eventually led to the birth of Impact Ministries.

Prior to his salvation, Jim was a professional musician with all the trappings of a worldly lifestyle. More than anything, he was searching for true freedom. Sick of himself and his empty pursuits, he hated all that his life had become. He turned to drugs as a means of escape and relief. Although he was desperate to find God, his emotional outrage made people afraid to tell him about Jesus. As he searched for help, he only became more confused and hopeless than ever.

After listening to his bass player grumbling about a verse of Scripture that a Christian had shared with him, Jim had a miraculous encounter with God. From this one Scripture he was able to experience God's love! He gave his life to the Lord and was set free from his addictions. His whole life changed! Now, after years of ministry, Jim still believes there's no one that God cannot help, and there's no one God does not love. He has committed his life to helping people experience that love. If his life is a model for anything, it is that God never quits on anyone.

With doctorates in theology, human behavior and alternative medicine, and an honorary doctorate in world evangelism, Jim has received certified training as a detox specialist and drug counselor. His uncompromising, yet positive, approach to the gospel strengthens, instructs and challenges people to new levels of victory, power and service. Jim's extensive experience in working with substance abuse, codependency and other social/emotional issues has led him to pioneer effective, creative, Bible-based approaches to ministry that meet the needs of today's world.

Most importantly, Jim believes that people need to be made whole by experiencing God's unconditional love. His messages are simple, practical and powerful. His passion is to change the way the world sees God so that people can experience a relationship with Him through Jesus.

Jim and his wife, Brenda, have six daughters, 15 grandchildren, and continue to reside in Huntsville, Alabama.

For additional content and resources please visit this book's companion website: http://www.secondcomingguide.com

Made in the USA
Middletown, DE
21 July 2024